World Yearbook of Education 2022

The latest volume in the *World Yearbook of Education Series* explores the relationship between education and the globally prevalent principle of nationalism. This book identifies the diverse ways in which educational policies, discourses, curricula and pedagogy embed and promote the concept of "the nation" both historically and in the age of globalization. By challenging accounts owed to the discourse of "globalization" which conceal the presence of national epistemologies and interests in education, this book offers important insights into the role of education in making nationalism one of the most enduring and yet easily obscured forces of our time.

Organized into four sections, this book looks at the following main issues:

- **Historical (re)production of the nation** considers how countries consider and reproduce their national identity and how this is built on their history.
- **Hegemonic aspirations and interventions** examines how instruction technologies developed during the Cold War have been propagated and disseminated around the world, discusses how the development of educational policy based on the human capital theory emerged and analyzes the extent to which tech companies are intent on establishing an imperial order of learning.
- **Imperial policies and resurgences of nationalisms** explores how global or imperial policies have been indulged in different parts of the world and how new forms of nationalism have been emerging.
- **Paradoxes, inconsistencies, and a self-reflection** focuses on nations acting imperially as sites of domestic injustices, addresses unresolved paradoxes between the global and the national and includes a historically informed critical review of the *World Yearbooks of Education*.

Bringing together the voices of researchers from around the globe, *The World Yearbook of Education 2022* is ideal reading for anyone interested in learning how nationalism has affected the expansion of education systems and how its imperial aspirations are currently affecting education policy and practice.

Daniel Tröhler is Professor of Foundations of Education at the University of Vienna, Austria, and Visiting Professor at the University of Oslo, Norway.

Nelli Piattoeva is Associate Professor of Education at Tampere University, Finland.

William F. Pinar is Tetsuo Aoki Professor in Curriculum Studies at the University of British Columbia, Canada.

World Yearbook of Education Series

Series editors:
Julie Allan
University of Birmingham, UK
Antoni Verger
Universitat Autònoma de Barcelona, Spain

Examining a different topical subject each year, these fascinating books put forward a wide range of perspectives and dialogue from all over the world. With the best and most pivotal work of leading educational thinkers and writers from 1965 to the present day, these essential reference titles provide a complete history of the development of education around the globe. Available individually or in library-ready sets, this is the indispensable atlas of education, mapping ever changing aspects of theory, policy, teaching and learning.

Titles in the series:

World Yearbook of Education 2018
Uneven Space-Times of Education: Historical Sociologies of Concepts, Methods and Practices
Edited by Julie McLeod, Noah W. Sobe and Terri Seddon

World Yearbook of Education 2019
Comparative Methodology in the Era of Big Data and Global Networks
Edited by Radhika Gorur, Sam Sellar and Gita Steiner-Khamsi

World Yearbook of Education 2020
Schooling, Governance and Inequalities
Edited by Julie Allan, Valerie Harwood and Clara Rübner Jørgensen

World Yearbook of Education 2021
Accountability and Datafication in the Governance of Education
Edited by Sotiria Grek, Christian Maroy and Antoni Verger

World Yearbook of Education 2022
Education, Schooling and the Global Universalization of Nationalism
Edited by Daniel Tröhler, Nelli Piattoeva and William F. Pinar

For more information about this series, please visit: www.routledge.com/World-Yearbook-of-Education/book-series/WYBE

World Yearbook of Education 2022

Education, Schooling and the Global
Universalization of Nationalism

Edited by Daniel Tröhler, Nelli Piattoeva
and William F. Pinar

Routledge
Taylor & Francis Group

LONDON AND NEW YORK

First published 2022
by Routledge
2 Park Square, Milton Park, Abingdon, Oxon OX14 4RN

and by Routledge
605 Third Avenue, New York, NY 10158

Routledge is an imprint of the Taylor & Francis Group, an informa business

© 2022 selection and editorial matter, Daniel Tröhler, Nelli Piattoeva and William F. Pinar; individual chapters, the contributors

The right of Daniel Tröhler, Nelli Piattoeva and William F. Pinar to be identified as the authors of the editorial material, and of the authors for their individual chapters, has been asserted in accordance with sections 77 and 78 of the Copyright, Designs and Patents Act 1988.

British Library Cataloguing-in-Publication Data
A catalogue record for this book is available from the British Library

Library of Congress Cataloging-in-Publication Data
A catalog record for this book has been requested

ISBN: 978-0-367-68492-1 (hbk)
ISBN: 978-0-367-68493-8 (pbk)
ISBN: 978-1-003-13780-1 (ebk)

DOI: 10.4324/9781003137801

Typeset in Goudy
by Apex CoVantage, LLC

Contents

Contributors

Ehaab D. Abdou is Assistant Professor at the Department of Global Studies at Wilfrid Laurier University, Canada. Within the field of curriculum studies, his research aims at rendering school curricula more holistic and inclusive, especially of historically and systematically marginalized perspectives, narratives and epistemologies. Relatedly, he is interested in how the school curriculum and often-competing extracurricular narratives shape students' understanding and enactment of citizenship and civic engagement. His research mainly focuses on the Egyptian and the Canadian contexts. He has authored and co-authored academic articles published in the *Journal of Curriculum Studies*, *Theory & Research in Social Education*, *McGill Journal of Education* and *Multicultural Perspectives*. He is also co-author of the edited volume *The Struggle for Citizenship Education in Egypt* (Routledge, 2019).

Felicitas Acosta is a researcher and professor at Universidad Nacional de General Sarmiento and a professor at Universidad Nacional de La Plata. She teaches history of education, comparative education and educational foundations. Her research interests focus on the expansion of schooling from a historical and transnational perspective. She has specialized in the study of secondary education in Latin America and Europe. Her research interests also include international educational reforms and, more recently, standardized assessments and innovative finance in education. She has served as a research consultant for international organizations such as UNESCO, IIEP, UNICEF and ECLAC. In 2019 she was awarded the Margaret Sutherland Prize in Comparative Education by the Comparative Education Society in Europe (CESE) for her paper "Who is setting the agenda? OECD, PISA, and educational governance in the countries of the Southern Cone," published in European Education (2020). Her recent publications also include *The Nation-State and the Origins of Secondary Education in Argentina: The Case of the Colegio Nacional (National School)* (*Croatian Journal of Education*, 2020).

Mette Buchardt is Professor and Head of Centre for Education Policy Research, Aalborg University, Aalborg and Copenhagen, Denmark. Her research comprises the interdisciplinary field of welfare- and social-state history, church and theology history and the history of education with an emphasis on 18th to 20th century. She specializes in the relation between education and social reform in the European states, e.g. modernization and secularization, and the influence of migration on welfare state development historically and at present. Buchardt has been holding visiting professorships and scholarships at e.g. the history departments at University of Jyväskylä, Stockholm University and Umeå University, and at Nordeuropa-Institut, Humboldt University, Dept. of Curriculum & Instruction, University of Wisconsin-Madison, and Section for Church History, University of Oslo. She has published e.g. "Lutheranism and the Nordic States," U. Puschner and R. Faber (eds.), *Luther in Geschichte und Gegenwart* (Peter Lang, 2017), "Schooling the Muslim Family: The Danish School System, Foreign Workers, and Their Children from the 1970s to the Early 1990s," U. Aatsinki, J. Annola and M. Kaarninen (Eds.), *Family, Values, and the Transfer of Knowledge in Northern Societies, 1500–2000* (Routledge, 2018) and has recently contributed to the volume edited by D. Tröhler, *A cultural history of education in the age of Enlightenment* (Bloomsbury, 2020).

Euridice Charon Cardona is an honorary associate lecturer in the School of Humanities and Social Sciences (History), University of Newcastle, Australia. Her research expertise centres on historical and anthropological analysis, involving detailed archival and interview work. This has included major research projects on Cuban migration and diaspora, and more recently on Soviet women's gendered experiences in the Eastern battlefields of World War II and on the Soviet home front. That work produced significant international publications, including a co-authored monograph, *Soviet women on the front line in the Second World War* (Palgrave Macmillan 2012), which was shortlisted for the NSW Premier's History Prize in 2013, and a subsequent 2019 article in *Journal of Historical Geography*, 'The kitchen garden movement on the Soviet home front, 1941–1945'. Euridice's current work includes research centred on the Soviet Blood Donors' movement of the 1940s, Soviet women's contributions to the home-front economy and work on the history of Soviet university education aid from 1956–1991, examining its nature, reach and impacts.

Robert Cowen is an emeritus professor of education in the Institute of Education, University College, London. Most of his career has been spent in the Institute, although at various times he was a professor or visiting professor or a senior research fellow in the University of Brasilia, the Catholic University of Leuven in Belgium, the University of La Trobe in Melbourne, the University of Oxford, and SUNY, Buffalo. He has been a consultant for the World Bank and UNESCO, was a former president of the Comparative Education Society in Europe, and is now an honorary member of that Society. He serves on the editorial board of *Comparative Education*. His current academic interests include new theorizing in and about comparative education. His immediate interests are outlined in the chapter 'Educated identity, concepts, mobilities and imperium' in S. Carney and E. Klerides' (eds.) (2021) *Identities and Education: comparative perspectives in times of crisis* (Bloomsbury Academic), but the short article

'Recent developments in Comparative Education: myths, muddles, and marvels' in the *International Journal for the Historiography of Education*, 11, 11–22 (2021) was more fun to write and would probably be more fun to read.

Laura Engel is Associate Professor of International Education and International Affairs at The George Washington University. Her interests focus on global education policy trends in federal systems, including national and cross-national studies of internationalization of education. Her research, which has been funded by the American Educational Research Association, the National Geographic Society, and the Stevens Initiative, has been published in three books and over 50 articles, book chapters, and policy briefs. Her latest publications include a co-edited volume, *The Machinery of School Internationalization in Action* (Routledge, 2020), and co-authored journal articles appearing in *Educational Researcher*, *Comparative Education Review*, *British Journal of Sociology of Education*, and *Discourse: Studies in the Cultural Politics of Education*. She is currently co-editing a journal special issue titled *Global Policy Mobilities in Federal Educational Systems*. Laura serves on the board of directors of the NEA Foundation, is a Fulbright Specialist, and is joint editor of the journal *International Studies in Sociology of Education*.

Tom G. Griffiths is a professor of international education and development at Oslo Metropolitan University, Norway. Tom's research has several inter-related trajectories. First, it explores the relationships (historical, actual, potential) between systems of mass education and the socialist political projects (including cases of Cuba and Venezuela). Second, his work draws on world-systems analysis as a theoretical framework for understanding the trajectory of historical socialism within the capitalist world-economy and the modernist character of socialist education. This work, in turn, connects with critical education approaches that can respond to contemporary global crises and consciously advance efforts to prepare politically engaged students who engage with these crises. Tom's recent chapters have appeared in *The Bloomsbury Handbook of Theory in Comparative and International Education (2021)*, *Critical Reflections on the Language of Neoliberalism in Education: Dangerous Words and Discourses of Possibility (Routledge, 2021)* and *Socialist Educational Cooperation and the Global South (Peter Lang, 2020)*.

Rebekka Horlacher is Senior Researcher at the University of Zurich and a lecturer at the Zurich University of Teacher Education. Her research interests include the history of schooling and curriculum, the age of Enlightenment and historiography. She is the co-editor of the six-volume *Letters to Pestalozzi* (nzz, 2009–2015), has published a comparative cultural history on *The Educated Subject and the German concept of Bildung* (Routledge, 2016) and is a member of the editorial board of the bilingual journal *Bildungsgeschichte, International Journal for the Historiography of Education*. She is currently working on the history of school subjects and on comparative perspectives of schooling in Europe.

Moosung Lee is a centenary professor at the University of Canberra in Australia. He also holds professorship at Yonsei University in South Korea. His research areas include educational leadership and administration, social contexts of education and comparative education. He has published over 70 peer-reviewed articles in major journals such as *Educational Researcher*. He has also co-authored 30 book chapters and co-edited three volumes, including *How School Principals Use Their Time* (Routledge). He has been a Fulbright Scholar, UNESCO Fellow, Korean Foundation Fellow, Erasmus Mundus Visiting Scholar, Outstanding Visiting Scholar (at Yonsei University) and Visiting Fellow (at Seoul National University Asia Center). His work has been funded by various national and international agencies, including UNESCO, the Australian Research Council, the University Grants Council in Hong Kong, the Korea Foundation, AERA, and the IB, to name a few. He received the AERA Emerging Scholar Award (Division A) in 2015 and the University of Canberra Research Excellence Award in Social Sciences in 2018. He has served as Editor-in-Chief of *Multicultural Education Review* and Senior Associate Editor of *Journal of Educational Administration*.

Bob Lingard is a professorial fellow at the Institute for Learning Sciences and Teacher Education at Australian Catholic University. He is also an emeritus professor of education at The University of Queensland. He has authored/edited 25 books and published many articles in the leading international journals in his fields of sociology of education and policy sociology in education. His most recent books include: *Digital Disruption in Teaching and Testing* (Routledge, 2021), *Globalisation and Education* (Routledge, 2021), *Global-National Networks in Education Policy: Primary Education, Social Enterprises and 'Teach for Bangladesh'* (Bloomsbury, 2021), *Globalizing Educational Accountabilities* (Routledge, 2016), *The Global Handbook of Education Policy* (Wiley, 2016) and *Politics, Policies and Pedagogies in Education* (Routledge, 2014). With Fazal Rizvi he edits the Routledge book series, *Key Ideas in Education*, and is a former editor of the journal, *Discourse: Studies in the Cultural Politics of Education*. Bob is a fellow of the Academy of Social Sciences in Australia and also a fellow of the Academy of the Social Sciences in the UK. He is also a former president and a life member of the Australian Association for Research in Education.

Claire Maxwell is a professor of sociology, based at the University of Copenhagen, whose work focuses on social class, education, gender and mobility. In particular, her work has examined how privilege, agency and affect are mutually co-constitutive. Having initially focused her research on the English context, Maxwell now does internationally comparative work – examining how family, education systems and state policies shape the opportunities for social mobility across national contexts and how processes of internationalization and mobility are re-configuring understandings of the purpose of education and the imagined futures of young people. Maxwell has published extensively across sociological, educational and inter-disciplinary journals and has authored and edited several books on elite education, internationalization of education and most recently, written a book with Miri Yemini examining family travel practices. Maxwell co-edits the *International Studies of Sociology of Education*.

Bruce Moghtader is a doctoral candidate in the faculty of education at the University of British Columbia with a research focus on ethics. His book *Foucault and Educational Ethics* (Palgrave, 2016) explores historical identity and formation of subjectivity in an educational context. He has served as a researcher and programme-developer for Canada's public service sector and higher education institutions. His current work concerns reconceptualizing economics of education in light of globalization and digitalization.

Nelli Piattoeva is an associate professor of education at Tampere University, Finland. Her research agenda on the entanglements between education, societal context and governance is roughly split between three main domains. First, she examines school as an institution partaking in the governance of societies, for example, by zooming in on the role of formal education in nation-building. Second, she analyzes the means of governing formal education such as the introduction of performance targets and standardized numerical assessments. Third, she is interested in the politics and practices of knowledge production on education and the linkage between these practices, governance and (geo) politics, such as the protracted impact of Cold War ideologies and stereotypes on knowledge-making. Nelli's primary geographical focus of research is Russia and the post-Soviet space. Her latest publications have appeared in the *Handbook of Digital Russia* (Palgrave), *Journal of Education Policy*, *Critical Studies in Education*, *World Yearbook of Education 2019* (Routledge), *Childhood and Schooling in (Post)Socialist Societies. Memories of Everyday Life* and *Politics of Quality in Education: A Comparative Study on Brazil, China, and Russia* (Routledge). The latter volume for which Nelli co-authored three chapters won the book award of the Special Interest Group in Globalization and Education of the Comparative and International Education Society (CIES).

William F. Pinar is Tetsuo Aoki Professor in curriculum studies at the University of British Columbia, Canada. He has also served as the St. Bernard Parish Alumni Endowed Professor at Louisiana State University, the Frank Talbott Professor at the University of Virginia and the A. Lindsay O'Connor Professor of American Institutions at Colgate University. He has lectured widely, including at Harvard and the University of Chicago. Pinar was the architect of the reconceptualist movement in curriculum theory, conceived of curriculum as *currere* (www.currereexchange.com/) and founded the *Journal of Curriculum Theorizing* and its companion Bergamo Conference (www.jctonline.org/conference/), the International Association for the Advancement of Curriculum Studies (www.iaacs.ca/) and its US affiliate: the American Association for the Advancement of Curriculum Studies www.aaacs.org/). Although Pinar is known best for his publications on curriculum theory, he has also written on other topics, including cultural studies, international studies and queer studies.

Fazal Rizvi is a professor emeritus at the University of Melbourne Australia and at the University of Illinois at Urbana-Champaign. He has written extensively on issues of identity and culture in transnational contexts, globalization and education policy, higher education and Australia-Asia relations. His most recent books include a co-authored volume, *Class Choreographies: Elite Schools and Globalization* (Palgrave, 2017) and a co-edited volume, *Transnational Perspectives on Democracy, Citizenship, Human Rights and Peace Education* (Bloomsbury, 2019). Fazal is a fellow of the Australian Academy of the Social Sciences, a research fellow at the Australia India Institute, a past editor of the journal *Discourse: Studies in Cultural Politics of Education* and a past president of the *Australian Association of Research in Education*.

Edda Sant is a senior lecturer at Manchester Metropolitan University (UK). A former social studies teacher, her research interests lie in political, history and democratic education, particularly in relation to young people's political participation and the education of national identities. She has edited three books, including the *Palgrave Handbook on Global Citizenship and Education*, and published in prestigious journals (e.g. *Review of Educational Research, Theory and Research in Social Education*). Her 2016 co-authored article was recognized with a Children's Identity and Citizenship European Association Award. She is currently working on a project co-funded by the Council of Europe and the European Union and as an academic adviser for the UK's All-Party Parliamentary Group on Political Literacy. Her monograph *Political Education in Times of Populism* will be published in 2021 by Palgrave MacMillan.

Sam Sellar is Professor of Education Policy and Dean of Research in UniSA Education Futures at the University of South Australia. He was previously Reader in Education Studies in the School of Childhood, Youth and Education Studies at Manchester Metropolitan University. Sam's research is located in the sociology of education with a focus on global education policy, large-scale assessments and the digitalization and datafication of education. His recent research projects have investigated the early use of big data analytics and artificial intelligence for education policy and governance. He is currently working on a UK Economic and Social Research Council project that is investigating the use of digital platforms in higher education (led by Dr. Janja Komljenovic at Lancaster University). Sam works with teacher organizations around the world to develop professional understanding of datafication and commercialization in schooling. His latest book is the *World Yearbook of Education 2019: Comparative Methodology in the Era of Big Data and Global Networks*, co-edited with Radhika Gorur and Gita-Steiner Khamsi. Sam is also the lead editor of *Discourse: Studies in the Cultural Politics of Education*.

Hannah Spector is Associate Professor of Education at Penn State University, The Capital College. Her research interests are informed by the political theorist Hannah Arendt and involve the interplay between politics, ethics and education. She has written broadly on cosmopolitanism and totalitarianism as each pertain to education. She co-edited a special journal issue on *Maxine Greene and the Pedagogy of Social Imagination: An Intellectual Genealogy* (Review of Education, Pedagogy, and Cultural Studies, 2017), which was republished as a book with Routledge (2018). Hannah received the Early Career Scholar Award in 2019 from the American Education Research Association's special interest group: Critical Issues in Curriculum and Cultural Studies, the Dissertation Award in Canadian Curriculum Studies in 2014 and the Outstanding Publication in Canadian Curriculum Studies in 2013 for her article "Fukushima Daiichi: A never-ending story of pain or outrage?" She is currently working on a monograph that interrogates the meanings of responsibility and/in education.

Daniel Tröhler is Professor of Foundations of Education at the University of Vienna and Visiting Professor at the University of Oslo. His research interests include the international and transnational developments of the last 250 years and relating the history of modern ideas to the history of institutions in the context of a broader cultural history by focusing on political and educational ideas and their materialization in school laws, curricula and textbooks, comparing different national and regional developments and investigating their possible mutual influences. He received the American Education Research Association's Outstanding Book of the Year Award in 2012 for *Languages of Education: Protestant Legacies, National Identities, and Global Aspirations* (Routledge, 2011). His recent publications include being volume editor of *A Cultural History of Education in the Age of Enlightenment* (Bloomsbury, 2020) and guest-editor of the special issue *Education, "Doing Nation," Nation Building and the Development of National Literacies* (Croatian Journal of Education, 2020). He is currently working on the development of an ERC project proposal titled *Nation-State, Curriculum and the Fabrication of National-Minded Citizens*.

Nadezhda Vasileva is a doctoral researcher at the Faculty of Social Sciences, Tampere University, Finland. Vasileva specializes in youth research. She started her research career at the Center for Youth Studies at National Research University Higher School of Economics in St. Petersburg. Her research interests lie at the intersection of young people's political and civic participation, life course theory, critical urban theory, nationalism and digitalization. Vasileva's ongoing doctoral study examines how young people participate in authoritarian and neoliberal society by engaging in leisure activity that reshapes the city space.

Edward Vickers is Professor of Comparative Education at Kyushu University, Japan, where he also holds the UNESCO Chair in Education for Peace, Social Justice and Global Citizenship. He is the author or editor of numerous books on the history and politics of education in contemporary East Asia, including (with Zeng Xiaodong) Education and Society in Post-Mao China (2017); (with Krishna Kumar) *Constructing Modern Asian Citizenship* (2015); (with Alisa Jones) *History Education and National Identity in East Asia* (2005); and the sole-authored monograph *In Search of an Identity: the Politics of History as a School Subject in Hong Kong, 1960s–2002* (2003). He is also co-author, with Krishna Kumar and Yoko Mochizuki, of the UNESCO report, *Rethinking Schooling for the 21st Century* (2017). Besides education, he also researches the politics of heritage across East Asia and is co-editor (with Mark Frost and

Daniel Schumacher) of *Remembering Asia's World War Two* (2019). He is Director of Kyushu University's interdisciplinary Taiwan Studies Program, Secretary-General of the Comparative Education Society of Asia and co-editor of *The East Asian Journal of Popular Culture*.

Christian Ydesen is a professor (WSR) at the Department of Culture and Learning, Aalborg University, Denmark. He is the PI of the project 'The Global History of the OECD in education' funded by the Aalborg University talent programme and the project 'Education Access under the Reign of Testing and Inclusion' funded by the Independent Research Fund Denmark. He has been a visiting scholar at Edinburg University (2008–2009, 2016), Birmingham University (2013), Oxford University (2019) and Milan University (2021) and published several chapters and articles on topics such as educational testing, international organizations, accountability, educational psychology and diversity in education from historical and international perspectives. He currently serves as an executive editor of the *European Educational Research Journal*.

Miri Yemini is an associate professor of comparative education, tenured at Tel Aviv University, with interests in internationalization of education in schools and higher education, global citizenship education and education in conflict-ridden societies. She has also developed a strong research contribution around the involvement of external actors in schools. In addition, Prof. Yemini is an active member of CIES, CESE and BAICE and she is a president elect for the Israeli Comparative Education Society. Prof. Yemini has published extensively, among others in: *Educational Administration Quarterly*, *Educational Management Administration & Leadership*, *Comparative Education Review*, *Teaching and Teachers Education*, *Compare*, *Discourse: Studies in the Cultural Politics of Education*, *Journal of Studies in International Education*, *Globalisation, Societies and Education*, *Urban Education*, *Educational Review*.

Theodore G. Zervas is Professor of Education at North Park University in Chicago, USA, and distinguished visiting professor at the American University in Cairo. His research interest includes national state building and education, national identity formation, modern Greek educational history, teacher training/preparation and curriculum and textbook development. He has published three books and over 25 articles. His recent publications include *Educating Greek Americans: Historical and Contemporary Pathways* (Palgrave), co-edited with Fevronia Soumakis, and *Formal and Informal Education During the Rise of Greek Nationalism: Learning to be Greek* (Palgrave). He is working on an edited volume with Ehaab D. Abdou, *Reconciling with Ancient and Indigenous Belief Systems: Textbooks and Curricula in Contention* (University of Toronto Press).

Education, nationalism and the ordering construction of the world (Introduction to the WYBE 2022)

This volume addresses a core, globally effective element of political-cultural order and reality. It is about the conceptually complex phenomena of nation, nationalism and nation-state and their intertwinement with education, school policy, schooling and curriculum; it is about collective identities, loyalties and cultural distinctions and, at the same time, about imperial aspirations, whose effects are frequently understood as globalization. Given their actual impact and effectiveness in our daily lives, the phenomena – and this is the main motive of this volume – have not received the research attention they have actually deserved for at least a third of a century.[1]

For a quarter of a millennium, the development of modern education in its institutionalized forms has been closely linked to the cultural imaginaries related to the concept of the "nation." Modern education has benefited massively from the fact that the "nation" entered into an entangled relationship with the "state" in the long 19th century. Yet, even with this lengthy history, hasty interpretations of the geopolitical situation around 1989 – the fall of the Iron Curtain and the end of the Cold War – have led some scholars to focus on "globalization," viewing the nation-state as a compliant agent in the more-or-less voluntary implementation of global policies.

Some scholars did not turn their interest away from the nation-state out of enthusiasm for globalization – they have actually frequently argued critically when examining its manifestations and effects – but they did so due to a certain unease about phenomena associated with concepts such as the nation, nationalism and the nation-state. Indeed, there are perfectly good reasons for this kind of distrust, especially if one interprets the history of the first half of the 20th century as an expression of brutally excessive and imperialistic nationalism. However, turning away from a problem by reducing it to its extremely blatant expressions does not help in really understanding it. Beyond what can be called aggressive nationalism, there is one that can be called everyday or "banal" nationalism (Billig, 1995). This version of nationalism is the focus of this volume.

We have now lived through more than two decades in the 21st century, and we are faced with a world in which nationalism can simply not be ignored or regarded as eclipsed by globalization. Today, crude nationalists have taken over

DOI: 10.4324/9781003137801-1

political power in many places on Earth – including through democratic elections by nationally – nationally-minded electorates. From what do they derive the legitimacy of their decisions? Reality has taught us that we cannot make nationalism disappear just by condemning it. Understanding and explaining this reality is, however, the obligation of the academic world. Silencing what is underway worldwide by condemning it as an undesirable is not.

The silencing of analyses of the nation and its close relationship to the state means that conceptual, definitional work has been largely left undone, leaving us with a jumble of terms that does not favor lucid conceptualization. Outside the field of nationalism studies, there is too little understanding of the role of nationalism in shaping people's lives. It was not that it simply led to two terrible world wars that brutally exposed its malignancy in the first half of the 20th century nor that its rise had been a response to two pressing problems in the 18th century. These, in their turn, had been discussed within the framework of what is called the "Enlightenment," an era that embodied many of the ideals to which most scholars still subscribe today (Tröhler, 2020a). On the one hand, there was the question of how the peaceful and solidary coexistence of people could be guaranteed despite discussions about natural law, social contracts, a natural estate and inalienable human rights, which imaginarily freed people from their social obligations or let them be interpreted as the result of a contract they had entered into as completely free and unbound. On the other hand, there was the question of how a political order could be shaped after it had overcome absolute monarchy, itself derived from God. It was at precisely this time that recourse was made to the old but insufficiently discussed concept of the "nation." It was also at this time that the fundamental meaning of a political constitution and the promises of a republic were debated and implemented. What followed was the establishment of constitutional nation-states in the long 19th century.

The prerequisite for their establishment was the idea of a modern, that is constitutional, state as well as the idea of a nation that claimed a cultural communality beyond natural rights and that was "politicized" to the extent that it could enter into an alliance with the modern state for mutual advantage. Nationalism was the result of this targeted, politically relevant intellectual engagement with the old, hardly politically meaningful concept of the nation. Thus, the meaning of "nation" also changed, so that even today not a few equate nation and state, such as the example of the United Nations Organization, which does not gather the nations of the world, but rather states, only some of which are indeed nation-states.

There are impressive studies that show how schooling was a central (but not the only) part of nation-building, such as Eugene Weber's *Peasants into Frenchmen* (Weber, 1976) or – with regard to the disputed borderlands of Alsace and Lorraine – Stephen Harp's *Learning to be Loyal* (1998). More recently, Machteld Venken published a comparative study on *Borderland Schooling in Interwar Europe* (Venken, 2021), reconstructing national idiosyncrasies in state schools from the perspective of children's experiences. Modern school systems vividly illustrate how state institutions promote national identities and form loyal national citizens, and at the same time, they reflect the ordering ideas of inclusion and selection, ideas which are different everywhere.

All these striking publications and many more, though far from enough, point to how the modern school, as developed during the 19th century, aimed at developing a national literacy in children as future citizens (Tröhler, 2020b) that enabled them to become part of a larger whole, the nation institutionalized in a state. It was a way of "doing nation" (Tröhler, 2020c) and about state-organized learning opportunities intended to develop a particular kind of identity in the younger generation, an identity that was – and still is – simultaneously collective and individual (Millei, 2019; Millei & Lappalainen, 2020).

Despite all the present unease about the nation, one must first bear in mind that the nation institutionalized in the state has made and continues to make much possible. It united people against absolute rulers, such as when, in the first French constitution of 1791, the French king was proclaimed king of the French or of the French nation, thus constitutionally implementing *national* equality for everyone. The idea of the nation was also able to provide the idea of communality and feelings of sameness to people even in conditions of social inequality, and it created the legal subject of the citizen as the beneficiary and bearer of the modern constitutional state (Piattoeva, 2016). The citizen, in turn, had to be made loyal via multiple institutionalized processes and practices, foremost of which were modern schooling and its curriculum.

Yet it is also true that nation-states create, even magnify, problems and injustices, some of which are very serious. Beyond the foreign policy aspects of these problems, which are all too obvious – espionage, election interference, embargoes, fomenting revolutions in third-world countries, waging wars of conquest – there are also domestic ones. Precisely because the "nation" is not a state but a most effective cultural thesis about who one "is" or has to be, there are people within the sovereign territory of a nation-state who have the power to define the "nation" and to suppress or discriminate alternative and more inclusive visions about commonality. This problem has a state-legal side, which, today, has been largely adjusted without really preventing injustice. After all, cultural and social practices of exclusion and discrimination have not dramatically ceased with the formal-legal desegregation and equalization within the respective countries, and this national demarcation often begins with admixtures of skin color, ethnic origin, language, religion and sexual preference (Pinar, 2001).

In many of the dominant countries in the world today, it is still an advantage to be white (or at least whiter than others) because this seems to be an important part of the dominant ideas of respective nations as a cultural thesis of who we are or should be; these express visions of commonality (and exclusion) institutionalized in the respective states. This, of course, still applies to democracies, including the United States, South Africa, Australia, India and also Israel, which is struggling to recognize black-skinned Ethiopian Jews with their own Jewish tradition as "real" Jews and which – despite the famous Law of Return that unconditionally guarantees every Jew to gain Israeli citizenship – sends them to re-education programs before they are eligible for Israeli citizenship (Marom, 2020).

*

Neither the nation nor nationalism is innocent, but they are effective global realities, and they are closely linked to modern education systems. This volume examines these realities, their genesis, impacts, problems and inconsistencies. The introductory essay (Daniel Tröhler) analyzes how the nation has been marginalized or even silenced under the spell of globalization; it argues for the need to address the nation, nationalism and the nation-state and their interconnections with education and schooling then, now and presumably in the future. This is followed by case studies grouped into four categories.

The first section deals with the *Historical (Re)Production of the Nation* beyond the classic works focusing so often on France or Germany. It includes an analysis of how Spanish South America, which had belonged relatively uniformly to the Spanish Crown, slowly saw the emergence of competing nation-states over the course of the long 19th century (Felicitas Acosta). It also includes a historical reconstruction of how China managed to spread the idea of a nation in the 20th century, calling for loyalty in a vast territorial state (Edward Vickers). Next is a comparison of two modern nation-states, Egypt and Greece, tracing how national identity can be created today in history classes through the construction of a history that relates today's forms of national life and dignity back to ancient civilizations (Theodore G. Zervas and Ehaab D. Abdou).

The second section, *Hegemonic Aspirations and Interventions*, starts with an examination of how certain forms of instruction developed during the Cold War and were then propagated and disseminated around the world, including through programmed instruction, learning machines and New Math (Rebekka Horlacher). The economic-theoretical side of these hegemonic aspirations is illuminated with a reconstruction of the development of human capital theory and its dissemination through the OECD (Bruce Moghtader), and the following chapter shows how national policies became instruments of imperial aspirations within the framework of the OECD (Christian Ydesen). The fourth paper in this section examines the extent to which tech companies today are intent on establishing an imperial order of learning and thus of people's thinking (William F. Pinar).

The third section addresses *Imperial Policies and Resurgences of Nationalisms* and examines how global or imperial policies are indulged in different parts of the world and how, despite and perhaps due to this, new forms of nationalism have been emerging that were not present, for example, in the 19th century. One case study compares how two federal states like Australia and Canada have constituted quite distinctive national reactions to the normative assessment tool developed by PISA (Sam Sellar, Bob Lingard and Edda Sant); a second case study detects how the construction and expansion of a state-wide large-scale assessment through digital and bureaucratic infrastructures has enabled and enforced Russia's exercise of power over a vast territory and the lives of its population to craft a nation and mark its territory (Nelli Piattoeva and Nadezhda Vasileva). Another focuses on an almost equally large territory with many more inhabitants, India, and investigates how nationalist narratives are currently used in the service of right-wing populist politics to promote a particular understanding of national belonging and to privilege the political claims of a particular group of people and exclude others (Fazal Rizvi). The last examines Cuba, showing how national identity, Cubanness, was specifically promoted through an economic and social order that aimed at a global uniform order in which national differences were to remain marginal (Tom G. Griffiths and Euridice Charon Cardona).

The last of the four sections of the volume, *Paradoxes, Inconsistencies and a Self-Reflection*, focuses on imperially acting and exposed nations, and it includes a historically informed critical review of the World Yearbooks of Education. One case study examines how – under the catchword of cosmopolitan nationalism – global citizenship rhetoric has aligned with the curricular-designed fabrication of future loyal citizens in South Korea, Israel and the United States (Miri Yemini, Laura Engel, Moosung Lee and Claire Maxwell). Another case study focuses exclusively on the United States and its human rights education efforts, which conspicuously seek atrocities from afar while remaining silent about its own humanitarian disasters (Hannah Spector). The following chapter focuses on the issues of internationality and nationality using the example of migration and schooling, highlighting the construction of the migrant child in the welfare state of Denmark (Mette Buchardt). Both the fourth section and the volume itself are concluded by a historically informed review of how – within the framework of the World Yearbooks – comparative education has been guided by interest in its own nation, without being aware of it, and the more so with time (Robert Cowen).

Based not least on the analysis in the last chapter, the editors of the volume are well aware of breaking new ground, especially in the context of the *World Yearbook of Education*. In doing so, contributors specifically address a formative force in the shaping of identities and ways of life that is not so easily explained by referring to "globalization," but which is understood here more as imperialisms – the globalized expression of nationalism(s). In this respect, the series editors are to be thanked for allowing a perhaps somewhat unusual, but certainly legitimate and necessary, look at the educational reality of our planet.

Note

1 We acknowledge the publication of the WYBE 2005, which was devoted to the topic of *Globalization and Nationalism in Education* (Coulby & Zambeta, 2005). In contrast to that volume, this WYBE 2022 can benefit from numerous definitions that have become clearer in the meantime, such as the distinctions between nation and nationalism, nation and society, nation and state, and the special significance of the combination nation-state. Moreover, rather than emphasizing a binary world order between globalization and nationalism, this volume explores the diverse, often subtle workings of the national at different times and in different spaces beyond interpretations committed to the concept of globalization. Evidently, then, this volume emphasizes not the aggressive forms of nationalism, but the "banal" forms (Billig, 1995). In other words, this volume focuses on the everyday discursive practices that are found in ordinary educational settings and that give us a collective identity of which we are often not even aware or want to be aware.

References

Billig, M. (1995). *Banal nationalism*. Sage.

Coulby, D., & Zambeta, E. (Eds.). (2005). *Globalization and nationalism in education* [WYBE 2005]. Routledge Falmer.

Harp, S. L. (1998). *Learning to be loyal: Primary schooling as nation building in Alsace and Lorraine, 1850–1940*. Northern Illinois University Press.

Marom, M. (2020). A second exodus: Ethiopian Jews in Israel between religion, nation and state. In D. Tröhler (Guest-Ed.), Education, "doing nation," nation building and the development of national literacies. *Croatian Journal of Education, 22*(Special. Ed. 2), 171–190. https://doi.org/10.15516/cje.v22i0.4127

Millei, Z. (2019). Pedagogy of nation: A concept and method to research nationalism in young children's institutional lives. *Childhood, 26*(1), 83–97. https://doi.org/10.1177/0907568218810078

Millei, Z., & Lappalainen, S. (2020). Learning nation in early childhood education: Multisited comparison between pedagogies of nation in Australia and Hungary. *European Education, 52*(1), 33–47. https://doi.org/10.1080/10564934.2019.1691015

Piattoeva, N. (2016). Citizenship and nationality. In J. Stone, R. M. Dennis, P. S. Rizova, A. D. Smith, & X. Hou (Eds.), *The Wiley Blackwell encyclopedia of race, ethnicity, and nationalism*. Wiley Online Library. https://doi.org/10.1002/9781118663202.wberen560

Pinar, W. F. (2001). *The gender of racial politics and violence in America: Lynching, prison rape, and the crisis of masculinity*. Peter Lang.

Tröhler, D. (2020a). Learning, progress, and the taming of change: The educational aspirations of the age of Enlightenment. In D. Tröhler (Ed.), *A cultural history of education in the age of Enlightenment* (pp. 1–23). Bloomsbury Academic. https://doi.org/10.5040/9781350035164.ch-001

Tröhler, D. (2020b). National literacies, or modern education and the art of fabricating national minds. *Journal of Curriculum Studies, 52*(5), 620–635. https://doi.org/10.1080/00220272.2020.1786727

Tröhler, D. (2020c). Nation-state, education and the fabrication of national-minded citizens. In D. Tröhler (Guest-Ed.), Education, "Doing Nation," nation building and the development of national literacies. *Croatian Journal of Education, 22*(Special. Ed. 2), 11–27. https://doi.org/10.15516/cje.v22i0.4129

Venken, M. (2021). *Peripheries at the centre. Borderland schooling in Interwar Europe*. Berghahn Books.

Weber, E. (1976). *Peasants into Frenchmen. The modernization of rural France, 1870–1914*. Stanford University Press.

1 Magical enchantments and the nation's silencing

Educational research agendas under the spell of globalization

Daniel Tröhler

The end of the Cold War in 1989 triggered many fantasies about the present and future. Some of these fantasies were owed to an epistemological spell that channelled the view of the world as developing in a one-sided way. This epistemology was part of a discourse that configured itself around the word *globalization*, which at the same time meant the decline if not the end of the importance of the nation-state and even of democracy (Guéhenno, 1993). According to this discourse, the world seemed to be moving towards a global unity in which cultural and national differences were deemed as not really essential anymore. The task left was of how to recognize, explain or interpret this development and its consequences properly.

Obviously, *globalization* refers to a connection between singular phenomena and universal globality and vice versa, and in this way it marginalizes the relevance of any kind of meso levels: here, concretely the ordering and regulating power of the nation-state. In the beginning, frequently under the keyword *de-nationalization*, globalization primarily meant the privatization of the economy, which was, not coincidentally, often exemplified by the example of France, which has the most state-run economy in the West (Schmidt, 1996; Daley, 1996). The economy should therefore be privately financed. The vision was that henceforth there should be no more state-owned enterprises, and nation-states should restrain themselves from regulating and taxing companies so that they could successfully compete in the global market.

These economic visions and legitimations of a free global market economy subsequently prompted comprehensive reinterpretations of human life, which was, again, understood as moving toward greater social and cultural unity across the globe. As early as in 1990, globalization was defined as "all those processes by which the peoples of the world are incorporated into a single world society, global society" (Albrow & King, 1990, p. 9) or as "the intensification of worldwide social relations which link distant localities in such a way that local happenings are shaped by events occurring many miles away and vice versa" (Giddens, 1990, p. 64). The epistemological presuppositions that were part of these definitions and their associated research programs became clear when Robertson emphasized – in addition to his metaphoric definition of globalization as the "compression of the world" – a simultaneous "intensification of the consciousness of the world as a whole" (Robertson, 1992, p. 8). Epistemologically, this is revealing because it

DOI: 10.4324/9781003137801-2

obviously says that the historical development of the globe can be correctly rec-ognized only when an awareness of this development has been generated. Under this intended epistemological shift of emphasis – the spell of globalization – certain topics in the research agendas have been overemphasized and others marginalized.

Accordingly, since about 1990 we have seen the proliferation of writings describing, asserting and explaining this global movement towards "the world-system" (Wallerstein, 1986) or "a single world society" (Archer, 1990, p. I). It is noticeable that these explanations do not actually critically question the thesis of globalization but look for evidence that makes the presupposed thesis plausible in some way or another (Steger, 2004, pp. 1–12). In addition, it is remarkable that although the phenomenon described or explained by globalization is actually a fundamental historical matter, most authors are not historians but sociologists. While acknowledging that the term *globalization* is new, they claim that the thing it describes is much older. Robertson (1992, p. 8) makes this assumption in the same way as James and Steger (2014), who assert that "globalization began centu-ries before it was named as such" (James & Steger, 2014, p. 431): one has simply only now realized where the historical journey came from and where it is going to. Perhaps the most famous construction of these "great histories" assumes a 500-year world development starting from an initially homogenous world "around 1500" (Meyer et al., 1987, p. 23) that has been governed by "cultural principles exogenous to any specific nation-state and its historical legacy" (Meyer & Ram-irez, 2000, p. 115), laying the foundation of the emerging "world society" (Meyer et al., 1997).

The striking attention that renowned sociologists pay to centuries-old develop-ments towards a predictable future – this is the general thesis put forward here – has to do with the fact that sociology is not simply an academic discipline that investigates social facts and relations, but it has emerged as a particular discourse that constructs its own object of research. Dependent in one way or another on the previously mentioned epistemological "intensification of consciousness of the world as a whole" (Robertson, 1992, p. 8), it relies on a particularized depth of field for its research lenses, which leads to an increased awareness and certainty of grand world historical developments. At the same time, however, it tends to over-look the effectual mechanisms of the everyday reproduction of national identities, particularly in education (Tröhler, 2020a). The situation is somewhat reminiscent of a fair in which the spectators watch spellbound as a magician, whose art lies essentially in distracting the attention of the spectators, performs a hiding trick, which then amazes the enchanted spectators. Instead of looking more closely at the magician's unobtrusive hand movements, the spectators are fascinated by the glamor, the illusion and the amazement. For indications of nationalism, now ram-pant for at least two decades across the globe, there was little research sensitivity left in this deluded attraction to globalization.

In itself, one could or even should have been sensitized in 2001, after the 9/11 attacks – at least 12 years after the Cold War. From this time on, "international terrorism" was reacted to with drastic measures to ensure "national security," even if that also often affected, sometimes severely, the global liberty rights of humans.

Freed from the enchantment connected to globalization, it has become more than evident that it was precisely during this period of the last 20 years that all the bold and crude nationalists we know today came to power, supported by the electorate, in Hungary, Turkey, Poland, England, the United States, Israel, Brazil, India, Australia and China, to name a few, and they came close to power in Italy, France, the Netherlands, Belgium and Austria. Hardly anyone has asked what had actually framed the nationalist minds of the people to vote for the Orbans, Erdogans, Trumps, Modis, Morrisons or Johnsons. And if that wasn't enough, the undoubtedly global Coronavirus pandemic of 2020–2021 has brought to light numerous nationalisms across the globe, and not just by childishly calling the virus the "China virus." China boasted that it could fight the pandemic more efficiently than the rest of the world; Russia made international propaganda that it was the first country in the world to vaccinate its people (and actually named its vaccine "Sputnik" as a reminder of the technological ignominy the USSR had inflicted on the United States in 1957).[1] A little later, the United Kingdom came along and boasted that it was the *first Western* country to vaccinate its population, and Switzerland followed by emphasizing that it was the first country that had approved vaccination in an orderly (and not accelerated) way; shortly after, Israel proclaimed it wanted to be the "world champion" in the vaccination of its national people. The internationally operating pharmaceutical companies profited massively from the national race for the vaccines, when competition drove up prices and alleged or actual supply shortages for at least some countries soon led to accusations of "vaccine nationalism." But research, still fascinated by the supposed cultural and social globality of our existence and foremost morally indignant about the Coronavirus in schools, has remained remarkably silent: the nation(-state) had been removed from the research agenda, and where nationalism was addressed at all, it was treated as a moral problem that had to be countered with morals and human rights, which had to be taught not least through education for tolerance and intercultural education.

This volume aims at a disenchantment of education research under the spell of globalization. Unlike the melancholic motifs expressed by Max Weber in his observation of a "disenchantment of the world" (Weber, 2008), this motif promises illuminating clarifications through a conscious questioning of the epistemological delusion which has had two related consequences. On the one hand, it led to the educational research agendas under the spell of globalization, and at the same time it largely left out the question of national identity (re-)production. The result has been that neither the globality nor the paradox of the imperialist character of nationalism have received sufficient attention.

This research intention underlying this volume is made plausible here in four steps. First, it analyzes how sociology, by virtue of its own conditions of emergence, can function as a particular epistemology that suggests globalization. In a second step, it is first shown how a certain form of educational research – here labeled as "large-scale test psychology" – owes itself to globalized, i.e., largely imperial, world views, whereupon reference is subsequently made to how it is foremost sociologically inspired educational research that takes these global enactments for granted and undertakes endeavors to describe, criticize or explain them. In a third step, it is indicated by way of example that, at least in the field of education and schooling, there can be little talk of global isomorphism if one actually looks historically and reveals the essential differences which indicate that school systems in general and curricula in particular have been attuned to the great cultural theses of respective nation, institutionalized in the modern state and its organizations, such as schools. The fourth part formulates research desiderata at the intersection of education and nationalism. Their implementation promises to provide a better theoretical understanding of nation, nationalism and nation-state, as well as to expose the educational imperialism of a few nation-state agents. Above all, one can expect that the educational mechanisms reproducing national identity, which are still very effective in nation-states, will be recognized more adequately. After all, this reproduction affects not only the school but also the epistemologies in academic research.

1 Who speaks "globalism"?

The "rhetorical package," or discourse, in which the concept of globalization has been relevantly configured in the past 30 years can be labeled as "globalism" (Steger, 2004, pp. 4–5). This would be equivalent to how "nationalism" is now understood as a discourse, i.e., as "a particular way of seeing and interpreting the world, a frame of reference that helps us make sense of and structure the reality that surrounds us" (Özkirimli, 2010, p. 206). In the latter case, the spatial claim associated with this discourse (p. 208) is a limited, at best internationally recognized, state territory; in the former case, it is the entire world, the globe.

A rough look at the question of who speaks the language of globalism gives a relatively clear answer. The average spokesman of this language is firstly a sociologist and secondly an Anglo-Saxon, i.e., more precisely, British or U.S.-American. While today the first feature – sociology as epistemology – almost necessarily takes the whole world for spatial reference, the second feature, the particular national provenance of the speakers, tempts them to imperialize their own national idiosyncrasies.

It is quite noticeable that it is mainly sociologists who deal with globalization theses. This is no coincidence insofar as this has to do with (conditions of) the very origin of sociology as an academic research and teaching subject. Sociology, like history and education or psychology, is a "child of the 19th century." Unlike history and education, however, sociology (like psychology) has an imaginary research object: society. Society, like the soul, is a (quite useful and effective) imagined construction that is assumed to exist as a "unit of analysis" in order to be explored. No one has ever seen a society, just as no one has seen the soul, which in the course of the 19th century was nobly called "psyche" to cover up its theological origins. Yet over the last 150 years, both have become extremely powerful interpretation systems in our making sense of the world.

The very premise of sociology, the assumption of an existing society, has its pitfalls. These are not without irony since the modern concept of "society," as it was conceptualized in the course of the 19th century, was closely related to the nation-state and its particular imaginary. With the French Revolution, an important and extremely sustainable synthesis of two different ideas and principles had occurred, those being the idea of the "nation" as a cultural thesis of commonality, collective being and belonging on the one side and the idea of the "state" as an organizing principle of power distribution on the other. This synthesis was the "birth" of the nation-state. Both ideas benefit(ed) from this fusion, with the state profiting from loyal citizens and the nation from state institutions that perpetuate the idea of the nation. As a sceptical voice from Germany noted as early as 1850, where the loose community (*Gemeinschaft*) of the medieval estates was still being held onto as an ideal for a very long time, it was precisely in this amalgam of nation-states that the modern idea of "society" grew (Stein, 1850).

Since then, the concept of society, if it has not addressed a business corporation or the rich "high society" in large cities, has always been nationally framed: there is a German society, not a Hessian one; there is an American society, not a Pennsylvanian one; there is an Australian society, not a Queensland one. There were quite good reasons for this kind of configuration of society within the framework of the nation-state. Since the nation-state builds its power on the identification of the citizens with the idea of the nation perpetuated by the state institutions (not least the school), there was the danger – at least in the eyes of the hitherto privileged or ambitious citizens – of leveling differences. This was precisely the decisive power behind the idea of society. While "nation" meant the cultural unity that holds people together, "society" aimed at social distinctions within that unity. The modern concept of society, of course, has a prehistory where it was primarily related to an urban milieu – in religious circles even to humanity. But with the French Revolution, it was extrapolated from the cities to the whole nation-state, just like the concept of citizen, which had previously meant a municipal legal status (Prak, 2018). This legally defined modern citizen – the object of modern schooling – is thus always both nationally united *and* socially distinguished.

Society, from which modern sociology developed in the 19th century, thus largely presupposes the idea of the nation as institutionalized and perpetuated in the modern constitutional state. This constellation, which tied society to the nation-state, was broken in 1989 with the end of the Cold War, which certainly did not suggest a return to the strong nation-state, but rather to a global alignment with Western political orders and styles of life. Under the conditions of a globally oriented economy, then, the next, larger unit of analysis – after the society of the apparently obsolete nation-state – was obviously the society of the world, the world society. Accordingly, some sociologists reacted by extending their traditional unit of analysis from the nation-state to the whole world and advocated "Sociology's Great Leap Forward" (Tiryakian, 1986). This program was labeled as "Internationalising Sociology" and envisaged as a "universal social science" (Albrow & King, 1990), and it was supported by the foundation of the journal *International Sociology* in 1986: "A simple awareness of sociological diversity worldwide will not do, the task is the integration of diversity" from a global point of view (Archer, 1990, p. I). One then recognized "globality" because one had to believe in it and recognize it for reasons of the academic discipline, whose traditional object – "society" within the nation-state – seemed to have become irrelevant. Henceforth, attention was focused on the global, which was conspicuously often explored in terms of nationally or regionally connoted concepts such as culture, society and citizenship, as well as curriculum, and many competing theories (and concerns) vied for the audience's attention, thus helping to stage the performance of enchantment that largely ignored the post-millennial resurgence of nationalism.

Yet, globalism is not simply a language spoken primarily by an academic discipline. There is a second specification which refers to the national origin or affiliation of the spokesman and speakers because they actually seem to come from countries that were or still are themselves extremely strong nation-states in the last 200 years and thereby have behaved or still behave imperially: Great Britain and the United States.[2] The imperial nationalism behind these interpretations was straightforward. Francis Fukuyama, an American famous for his thesis about the end of history after 1989, which was published in the American bimonthly conservative magazine *The National Interest* (!) (Fukuyama, 1989), had himself stated that globalization was in fact a euphemism for the "irreversible Americanization of the world," even if he himself did not see it as only positive (Fukuyama, 2003). In this way, Fukuyama received a great deal of attention in the global enthusiasm that gripped parts of the world after 1989. Of course, his theses were vulnerable to attack, as scholars in the first decade of the 21st century were to prove (Steger, 2004, p. 9) especially after 9/11, when market globalization was blended with "national security" against "international terrorism." The result of this has been that the vision of the "global empire . . . is more imperialistic and militaristic than its economistic predecessor" in the 1990s (Steger, 2004, p. 10): "economic globalism" has transformed into "imperial globalism" (Steger, 2005).

As a consequence, research agendas became more critical and more complex, and de-nationalization was distinguished from globalization (Sassen, 2003). Yet, the epistemological spell could, apparently, not really be avoided: one looked now for *diverse* evidence of globalization beyond the economic and military realms, especially at the level of the nation-state. "One central task we face" in researching globalization, Sassen argued, is "to decode particular aspects of what is still represented or experienced as 'national,' which may in fact have shifted away from what had historically been considered or constituted as national" (Sassen, 2003, p. 3). Following an idea developed in gender studies, this can be understood as an epistemological "doing global": issues that were previously considered national should henceforth be better understood as particularly subtle performances of the "global." One wonders, some 18 years after this argument was made, how this agenda would explain Donald Trump's 2020 election result with over 74,000,000 votes or the election victory of Joe Biden, who essentially argued in his campaign for what he called the "battle for the soul of the nation" (Cummings, 2020)[3] and who, in his presidential inauguration address on January 20, 2021 (Thrush, 2021), invoked again and again the unity not so much of the United States but – as also became very clear on January 6, 2021 – of the American nation.[4] Amanda Gorman, who gave a poem recital on this occasion, also praised this American unity with its oldest (Protestant) national metaphor: the hill. And one wonders,

18 years after Sassen's argument, how this agenda from 2003 would explain Brexit, which was enforced in 2020, and the Scottish national independence movement, which was fuelled by Brexit. There is a remarkable silence on this side of explaining the world.

One way to understand these movements and events is to understand nationalism as a global principle of the political, social and cultural world order: nothing is as international or global as nationalism, the discourse that attracts political power and that governs nation-states and the identities of their inhabitants (Thiesse, 1999, p. 11). An important question concerns, therefore, where these inhabitants as citizens and electorates get their national identities from, a question which evidently puts schools and curricula in the center of interest. This question poses the opposite of that raised by Sassen (2003, see earlier in the text): namely, not what is actually global in the national but how global performances are reinterpreted nationally and how they are (ab)used in order to strengthen national political agendas, especially at a time when mass immigration is challenging the emphasis and institutionalization of the dominant cultural theses of the particular nations.

2 Education research under the spell of "globalization"

In many respects, education was always and still is a servant of more powerful masters, such as philosophy, theology, military, state, economy or even nation, or it has also been, then, a problem-solver of developments that went wrong in exactly these fields. This later phenomenon was subsumed under the catch-word *educationalization*, not only reactively but prospectively with regard to the whole world (Tröhler, 2017). Accordingly, there was an immediate response to the imaginary of the one "world society" and its cosmopolitan or global citizens and their alleged challenges or demands for education (Demaine, 2002; Brodie, 2004; Davies et al., 2005; Blee et al., 2008; Bates, 2011). Yet, promptly after a good decade of euphoria related to global citizenship education came the warning voices, which articulated the dangers of the imperial ideologies of this educationalized global citizenship construction (de Oliveira Andreotti & de Souza, 2012; Pais & Costa, 2020). It seems that in the meantime, and perhaps due to this postcolonial criticism, the interest in global citizenship education has somewhat evaporated.

In contrast, a global dimension of education is still intensely discussed, albeit in a different context: one related to the governance of large-scale assessments coupled with the desire for what is called evidence-based policy in education. This type of school policy and the associated contract research, which appeared after the end of the Cold War and was consolidated after 2000, is known to have sometimes been met with harsh criticism, but it has also been defended. Arguably, nowhere has the clash of these two ideological groups been as intense as in Germany (Tröhler, 2011), and the defense strategy of the profiteers of this governance, usually test psychologists, made quite blunt use of the idea of a "world culture" or of "world society" models propagated by neo-institutionalist sociology (Baumert et al., 2001, p. 21): a remarkable ecumenism of two academic disciplines that each owe their existence to cultural constructions, society and soul, and which otherwise hardly trust each other in their exclusive claims to explain the world to its inhabitants.

These large-scale assessments, which are intended to provide data for decision making in educational policy, started to be organized internationally at the time when the end of the Cold War was becoming foreseeable and the first theories of globalization were emerging, i.e., in the second half of the 1980s. In this case, "international" meant that the national systems or their performances are assessed comparatively, and the educational policy goals following these comparative assessments are then (re-)defined to achieve better results in a subsequent international comparison, i.e., to be better ranked. Obviously, the motivation is nationalism, i.e., the will of the respective nations to be better than their neighbors or, even more exciting, than any other country in the world. But the nationalist motivation to be better than others is misguided in that the epistemological model associated with the assessments and rankings does not represent the respective strength of each participating nation-state but, as a long-standing World Bank staff member and comparative educationalist said in a blunt – and nationally proud – keynote speech to the Comparative and International Education Society (CIES) in 2002 (Heyneman, 2003), uses an imperialized yardstick largely defined by one single nation: the United States.[5] Hence, the model of this type of educational policy agenda is in itself not global, but national-imperial. It was institutionalized in the United States after *Sputnik* in 1957 and later spread globally through international organizations (Tröhler, 2013). The educationalization of the Cold War was a means of imperial political power that had to be implemented in the individual autonomous countries, and statistically based rankings comparing outputs would prove to be the most efficient means in this respect.

The model, however, was, in 1957, anything but new. It dates back to the turn of the century, when concerned Presbyterians in particular made the national fate of the United States, which was facing numerous challenges, accordingly dependent on a fundamental change in educational policy and school instruction, thus propagating an alternative to Congregationalist pragmatism. It was about nothing less than the question of what the United States is as a nation (beyond the state): organized locally or controlled by central, but not state, institutions like foundations. Hidden in this model was an inherent sciento-social epistemology – sustainable until today – which combined test psychology, hierarchic expertocracy (rather than democracy) and a world mission, and the religious zeal behind this model reinforced the faith in data which we are witnessing today across the globe (Tröhler & Maricic, 2021).

Source-supported historic reconstructions of the origins, emergence and development of this model are the exception (see Tröhler, 2010, 2013; Bürgi, 2017; Bürgi & Tröhler, 2018; Ydesen, 2019), although they can help to expose the overzealousness and intellectual naivety of the global educational elite and thus to disenchant the magic to which much of the research dealing with globalization has succumbed. Imposing a Western-style global world order had become a national Cold War-confession with global salvation aspirations which, not coincidentally, prevailed after 1989, and many researchers have taken it upon themselves to examine the effective consequences of this policy, the beginnings of which have been dated back to 1990 and for which actual evidence is anything but overwhelming. Of course, not all research has to go straight to 16th-century Scotland in order to detect the origins of the sciento-social epistemology which has considerably helped shape the OECD's education policies (see Tröhler & Maricic, 2021). But it is quite astonishing how much attention global, large-scale assessments have been able to attract and that outstanding researchers in education have been induced to write their fingers to the bone in dealing almost exclusively with this global theater; hardly a day goes by without a new contribution to understanding what is supposedly going on with these assessments being published somewhere in this world. There are certainly more publications on global test culture and its consequences than there are tests.

Sometimes these publications are critical and offer warnings, such as the writings of Joel Spring (e.g., 2004, 2008) or the most current book by Ian Hardy (2021), while others are much more affirmative and descriptive and based on great narratives (e.g., Baker, 2014). Many of them are sceptical in their basic attitude but hermeneutic in their intention, i.e., (world-)explanatory. Most authors of this latter genre are not surprisingly sociologists or sociologically inspired comparativists, thus following the sociological extrapolation of the unit of analysis from the nation-state to the globe and thereby devoted to identifying how the global affects the national (Parcerisa et al., 2020). In these reports explaining the effects of PISA, for instance, the nation-states appear to be confused and disoriented essentially because of the PISA data, and they are, therefore, receptive and willing to implement reform recipes.[6]

By introducing new labels into the discussion that were supposed to help solve the self-imposed hermeneutical task, such as "accountability" or "datafication" (Grek et al., 2020), the effectiveness of the epistemological spell that came with globalization after 1990, largely ignoring national effects of education, was reinforced. Too much (intellectual) credit has been given in recent years to the protagonists of global, evidence-based policy performance and test-psychological expertocrats,[7] and this credit has taken away much of the sensitivity and energy for researching the effectiveness of school and curriculum.

3 Nation, nation-state and the organization of school education

Citizenship, nationality and education have been interrelated since the beginning of the time labeled as the "long nineteenth century" (Hobsbawm, 1987, p. 8), and this interrelation works to a greater extent today than in the past, not least because the modern constitutional nation-state and its powerful institutions have skillfully orchestrated these three elements. Today's dominant theories on nationalism refer repeatedly to the importance of education in the perpetuation of nationality, but they do so in a very generic way. As a rule, they use simple, generally shared convictions of the importance of education – an exemplary expression of the aforementioned educationalization as a cultural disposition for interpreting the world – to support their own theory models of explaining nationalism without going deeper into the varieties of school mechanisms, such as how curricula transmit national identities (Tröhler & Maricic, forthcoming).

This would actually be the field of education research. But instead of asking how it was and is possible that national reproduction could become a global phenomenon, not least through education, under the spell of globalization, the question suddenly became how globality affects the nation. With the unit of analysis extrapolated from the nation-state to the entire world in the discourse of globalism, globalization and globality were suddenly taken for granted and the effective sites of identity reproduction, the nation or the nation-state, were largely ignored – or silenced. For many scholars in the field of education, globalization is not necessarily a phenomenon with which they sympathize, but a dazzling white swan, a fascinating opportunity to perform on the academic stage, while the nation has become an ugly duckling, something one prefers not to have too much to do with, especially not with regard to how it influences one's own thinking. As Billig has observed, nationalism is something that we have located to the "periphery," it is seen "as the property of others, not of 'us,'" while we would consider us – if at all – as patriotic (Billig, 1995, pp. 5, 15–17).

Part of the debt of these preferences has to do with conceptual ambiguities, which in turn are the result of under-research. The first and perhaps greatest problem is that, in the linguistic usage of at least the English-speaking world, the concept of "nation" is hardly distinguished from that of "state," so that the meaning of the word combination of "nation-state" is rarely fully explored. Certainly, what *nation* means is controversial in research, but what in the cultural dimension of human existence is not? Nevertheless, one may assume that the majority conceptualizes nation as something like a cultural thesis about "what we are," and by that who "we" are to be and "others" not. Nationalism is then a particular discourse or a cultural preconception of identity that includes certain people and excludes others (Özkirimli, 2010, p. 206). Nationalism, nationalization and nation are thus discursively related in a similar way to globalism, globalization and the globe, except that the first discourse has the "advantage" of having a powerful partner in the state and its institutions which the second discourse – apart from governmental and non-governmental organizations and a globally aspired economy – can do comparatively little to oppose.

The United Nations Organization has less influence in relation to the world than a state has on its territory, if only because there are members, super strong nation-states, which have the power of veto – China, France, Russia, the United Kingdom and the United States – and can thus put their national interests before the interests of the world community; this is quite apart from the fact that the term itself, *United Nations*, is a misconception. That which is called the *United Nations Organization* is precisely not the organizational union of nations, because otherwise the Scots, the Sami, the Kurds or the Rohingyas and others would be represented (as they certainly are nations), but not Bosnia and Herzegovina, Belgium and, for other reasons, Monaco or Singapore, which indeed are states but certainly not "nation-states," for they do not contain any culturally distinguishing feature that can be called a "nation" which is organized and sustained in a state and its organization of power.[8] Accordingly, one should not speak of "de-nationalization" in the context of the economic movements since 1989, because economic globalization is less directed against a discourse of nationalism than against state claims to ownership or regulation. The contrast to private enterprise is not the nation, but the state.

Most of the Western states are or consider themselves to be nation-states, i.e., an extremely powerful and effective amalgam of a dominating cultural theory about national identity and a state as a system of power distribution and participation. These two elements are linked by their respective constitutions which define the dominant national visions of social order, citizenship and political and economic latitude of these citizens. This is exactly what, since the French Revolution, has made "citizenship" related to the nation organized in the state. It contains a legal dimension of rights and duties within the state, and it contains a normative dimension that is linked to expectations regarding behavior towards the state, the economy and fellow human beings or co-citizens. This double dimension is quite evident in school acts (Westberg et al., 2019) and the respective curricula. While curriculum studies have more or less agreed that curricula in their respective totalities can be understood as having been designed to educate loyal citizens of and for the respective individual nation-states, that is, the cultural-normative aspect, political education as the curricular area labeled as "civics" usually focuses on the formal and legal aspects of citizenship in the respective nation-states (Horlacher, 2020). It is no coincidence that almost every time in the turbulent history of Europe that a state adopted a new constitution – thus institutionalizing a different concept of what national culture meant – a new school law and thus a new curriculum were immediately adopted in order to fabricate the desired citizen (Tröhler, 2016).

How educationalized these complexes of nation, state and society, not least with regard to citizenship, are becomes evident in the organization of the school, for no state institution has corresponded to this dual frame of reference – national unity and social distinction – more than the modern school, which has been divided into the elementary school and the tracked secondary school. While the elementary level aimed for unity, the tracked secondary school prepared or reinforced social stratification. However, the differences between the individual national configurations remained very considerable. England, because of its weak state in terms of social balance, invested little in the broad education of its people, which led to an exclusive private education system that is still effective today (besides the often poorly financed state schools). Prussia, on the other hand, which received wide admiration for its educational system,[9] made admission to the *Gymnasium* – the gateway for careers in the state and for social improvement – dependent on a knowledge of Latin, which was, however, not taught in the free elementary school but in paid preschools (*Vorschulen*) that only parents of rich families could afford. And France, the most *étatist* state in the Western world, built up a competition with the traditional universities at the tertiary level: the national *Grandes écoles*, whose admission is not guaranteed by the *baccalauréat*, as it is in the case of the universities, but by extremely competitive entrance examinations, which are promising only after one or two years of intense additional studies after the successful completion of the *lycée* (Bourdieu, 1996).

Many of these historically developed school systems, which are intertwined with the nation's cultural self-image of who they are, have remained largely effective to this day. The German-speaking countries, for example, have developed a dual construction of vocational training after compulsory schooling, which provides for close consultation and cooperation between business and the state; while in France, the state has almost completely overtaken vocational training in its *lycée technique*; and in the Anglo-Saxon countries, almost no efforts can be seen in terms of solidly organized vocational training. In most continental European countries, a high school diploma guarantees access to universities without major hurdles – except for study restrictions due to excessive demand for places – whereas in the United States, a high school diploma is anything but a guaranteed gateway to institutions such as Harvard, Yale or Stanford.

Behind these various institutionalized educational regimes of social stratification are the dominant visions of organizing the nation as a cultural idea about collective being, belonging and acting, that is, of social order and loyal citizenship, and these have not changed at all in the last 30 years since globalization became almost a fetish in social research related to education. The highly ranked universities in the United States still, and unaltered, provide immense professional and social benefits without this being severely questioned (Labaree, 2017), and there is no change detectable in Italy or Austria, either, where school children are selected after only four years of schooling – at the age of 10 – into one of the different tracks of secondary schooling that highly affect their professional and social chances. There is no adaptation to other countries, no isomorphism. In Luxembourg, for instance, with its global banking industry, the trilingual school system favors those who receive French lessons during elementary school in a kind of private, shadow education system, which then facilitates the transition to the more prestigious track of the secondary school, the *lycée classique*, where they are taught in French (in contrast to the less prestigious track, the *lycée technique*, where they are taught in German), allowing them to later become civil servants and enter the higher administrative professions, where the official language is French.

Of course, things have changed, but these changes have not had much substance with regard to the national reproduction of identities. Curricula have been reformulated to focus on so-called "competencies" without ever providing a halfway valid definition of competencies but with the main purpose of making it easier to test the school in comparative assessments. The associated hope was that improved comparable testability would provide more evidence for improved policy, but to date there is no evidence to support that the desired effects of evidence-based policy have ever taken place. Above all, however, this somewhat exalted test culture has – and this is exactly the effect of the essence of the magic trick, to draw away the attention of the audience – changed neither the different stratification mechanisms within nation-states nor the basic principle that schools and their curricula teach essentially national literacies. Against this background, it is difficult to understand why so much research energy is devoted to investigating what kind of effects globalization has on individual school systems instead of asking how it is that citizens accept the prevailing social stratification regimes.

4 The world of nations and educational research desiderata

The most compelling thesis for why people accept highly stratifying educational regimes is still that they feel – beyond all social differences – nationally united with their peers. They were brought up to be loyal citizens of their respective nation institutionalized and organized in a state, and they have learned to accept the idiosyncratic system of social selection and stratification, the configuration of society in which the educational system is largely involved and which it expresses. This also applies to so-called immigration societies (which have long since ceased to be so, at least not without sharp selection): it is difficult to assess the challenges this national system of identity and social ordering poses for people who have been socialized (or nationalized) elsewhere and have had to migrate to other countries, for example as refugees. It can hardly be assumed that they are understood to act as agents of globalization of the target country, and it is much more the case that they are blamed if a country performs worse than its neighbors in comparative, large-scale studies. Accordingly, many of the comments about Finland's very good performance in the first PISA study in 2001 pointed out that Finland had just a small percentage of foreigners, thus embodying a more homogeneous nation than other nation-states. There is obviously no getting around the nation-state, even with supposedly global test instruments.

Yet the question of nation, nationalism and nation-state, at least as far as education and school are concerned, has not yet been sufficiently clarified. But to place them at the center means to escape the spell of what is meant by globalization, which greatly underestimates the effective power of the national at, epistemologically, both the state and global-imperial levels. This is probably not very popular because acknowledging the nation somehow contradicts the self-image of the humanities and social and cultural studies scholars. According to this, they are secular and rational, that is, "liberated" from church and religion; they are open-minded and unprejudiced and not subject to racism; and they are gender-neutral and have emancipated themselves from patriarchal thought patterns. Part of this self-image is, too, that one would of course never define oneself as national or even nationalist, although knowledge production and science communication are still just as nationalist as education policy (Tröhler, 2020b).

There are two "good" reasons for not escaping the epistemological spell associated with globalization, and they are the same reasons for not wanting to see through a magic trick. On the one hand, to see through a magic trick means to be deprived of the thrill and amazement of the trick and – ultimately – to be disappointed with the magician. On the other hand, if you then explain to the audience the trick as it was really performed, you are quickly seen as a spoilsport because you have disillusioned them too. But disenchantment presupposes deception, and if there is indeed a difference between the purpose of sacred rites and scientific research, it is that of facing one's own deceptiveness, which is closely related to the epistemological preferences one shares.

One does not understand the immense and sometimes ruthless efficacy of the nation as a state-supported cultural thesis on being and conferring identity, its inclination towards self-aggrandizement and its latent tendency towards imperialism – in the guise of what is called globalization – if one ignores it. But at least since the resurgence of nationalism – which has spread globally under the radar of scholarly attention since 2000 – it seems imperative to ask how national reproduction functions in institutional arrangements and the micro-practices of everyday life in general and of education in particular. Certainly, compulsory schooling is by no means the only state institution that generates national uniformity and identity, but it is particularly effective in this regard. This applies to the whole arrangement of the individual parts and links of the system as well as to the school subjects, and here it applies not only to subjects like history or geography (Gotling, 2020; Maricic, 2020) but also to subjects like mathematics (Boser, 2020) or extracurricular school practices (Hofmann, 2020). Today, and probably to a much greater extent than 200 years ago, what was said in the past is true: "The primary schools are the cradle of the citizen. Therefore, the youth has to be trained in the practice of all the civic, moral, and religious virtues that a true citizen has to be accustomed to" (Witry, 1900, p. 34). Those citizens who are educated to be loyal also accept stratification, especially if both are produced in the same (school) system.

It is difficult to understand how it can be assumed today that international testing regimes, which are supposedly global but in fact imperial, can change schools so easily. Historians of education have pointed out many times how reforms have repeatedly failed or have had unintended effects. One of the reasons for the persistence of the school is certainly, to speak of early neo-institutionalism, its "institutionalization," i.e., its deep entanglement with what have been called "taken for granted assumptions" that appear to be lawful (Meyer et al., 1987, p. 10): that is, with the nation as a shared cultural thesis about commonality and identity that is perpetuated by the state. Information about this is provided by the various national or regional traditions of schooling, that is, of curriculum in a broad sense, encompassing school content, textbooks, school subjects, school levels and transition regimes. An impressive 34-country overview is provided by the *International Handbook of Curriculum Research* (Pinar, 2014) in which the editor deliberately emphasized the distinction between "internationalization" as an "ethical engagement with difference" and "globalization" as "neo-imperialism enforced through economic and educational standardization" (Pinar, 2015, p. 36).

This opens up a – thoroughly global – field of research in which, for example, it is examined how nation as a cultural thesis of commonality, collective being and belonging was and is able to assert itself in each case already within a state and through its institutions, not least its schools, against other domestic cultural theses. One could, relatively easily, show this with the example of the Bretons in

France or the Welsh in Great Britain, where one can already speak of "internal colonialism" (Hechter, 1975). There are related questions about, for example, how schools, as the backbone of organized, national reproduction, react to massive immigration, through which other value systems are brought into a country, challenging the dominant one. Another topic is the paradoxical property of nation-states to become imperial and to use various strategies for this purpose, especially transnational organizations. And last but not least, it must be examined how – and this has become clear especially in the last 10 or 15 years – the identity reservoir in the context of so-called banal nationalism (Billig, 1995) can suddenly explode to aggressive nationalism in times of crisis perception.

Notes

1 In contrast, for the occasion of the *Perseverance*'s landing on Mars on February 18, 2021, U.S. President Joe Biden commented on Twitter about the newest achievement of NASA – founded in 1958 as one of the two reactions to the Soviet *Sputnik* (the other one was the National Defense Education Act) – in the following way: "Today proved once again that with the power of science and American ingenuity, nothing is beyond the realm of possibility" (Biden, 2021).

2 Both the United States and Britain are characterized by strong imperial nationalism, weak states in terms of social redistribution (and thus with comparatively little interest in a high level of public education) and strong states in terms of protecting their globally operating national companies, for instance, by virtue of their secret services.

3 This is reminiscent of arguably the most substantive definition of *nation* in the 19th century, when the French intellectual Ernest Renan rejected all essentialist definitions and insisted that the nation was a soul or spiritual principle that had to be affirmed daily in silent plebiscites (Renan, 1882, pp. 26–27).

4 In what the media have called his "insurrection speech" on January 6, 2021, President-elect Joe Biden proclaimed to the American people how America as a nation expresses a cultural thesis about who they are – and, in this case, who they are *not*: "Let me be very clear. The scenes of chaos at the Capitol DO NOT reflect a true America – do not represent who we ARE" (Jazzaintmusic, 2021).

5 An impressive example to show how much internationality or globality is extrapolated from the academic tradition of one nation-state can be illustrated by the fact that, of the 61 presidents of the CIES to date, 50 have come from the United States, 10 from Canada and one from Hong Kong (www.cies.us/page/CIESPresidents). One can see why there are wicked tongues that claim that the "I" in CIES does not stand for "international" but for "imperial."

6 The fact that they can also engage in this "imitation" for very strategic national(istic) reasons, that is, in order to assert national ideals all the more strongly, was recently suggested by a group of international researchers (Piattoeva et al., 2019).

7 Some 15 years ago, it was discovered that this type of research based on a medicalized epistemology (see Tröhler, 2015) does not meet its own requirements as about half of the studies in the human sciences, cognitive neuroscience and psychology could not be reproduced. Against the background of this "replication crisis," one wonders what kind of evidence is meant when "evidence" changes with each study on the same issue (see Ioannidis, 2005; Szucs & Ioannidis, 2017).

8 Not too many countries on the African continent can be interpreted as nation-states, if only because most of their ethnic groups were never granted nation status by the colonial powers and because they were never able to claim their own autonomous state territory. The matter becomes even more complicated when looking at indigenous people in the

former colonies after the British Empire: Aborigines in Australia, Native Americans in the United States and First Nations in Canada. None of those, of course, is represented in the United Nations. For example, the Bedouins in Lebanon, which was founded by the French as a Middle Eastern nation-state, have no citizenship rights and thus no voting rights because, first, they are Muslim and, second, they are not sedentary and were therefore simply ignored in censuses (Chatty, 2013).

9 This did not mean, however, that the model was simply imported and applied in other countries.

References

Albrow, M., & King, E. (Eds.). (1990). *Globalization, knowledge and society. Readings from International Sociology*. Sage.

Archer, M. S. (1990). Foreword. In M. Albrow & E. King (Eds.), *Globalization, knowledge and society. Readings from International Sociology* (pp. 1–2). Sage.

Baker, D. P. (2014). *The schooled society. The educational transformation of global culture*. Stanford University Press.

Bates, R. (Ed.). (2011). *Schooling internationally: Globalisation, internationalisation and the future for international schools*. Routledge.

Baumert, J., Stranat, P., & Demmrich, A. (2001). PISA 2000: Untersuchungsgegenstand. Theoretische Grundlagen und Durchführung der Studie. In J. Baumert (Ed.), *PISA 2000. Basiskompetenzen von Schülerinnen und Schülern im internationalen Vergleich* (pp. 15–68). VS Verlag für Sozialwissenschaften.

Biden, J. [@POTUS]. (2021, February 18). Congratulations to NASA and everyone whose hard work made Perseverance's historic landing possible. Today proved once again that with the power of science and American ingenuity, nothing is beyond the realm of possibility [Tweet]. Retrieved February 19, 2021, from https://twitter.com/POTUS/status/1362536116197470210

Billig, M. (1995). *Banal nationalism*. Sage.

Blee, H., Britton, A., & Peters, M. A. (Eds.). (2008). *Global citizenship education. Philosophy, theory and pedagogy*. Sense Publishers.

Boser, L. (2020). Nations and numbers: Elementary mathematics education as a nationalizing tool. *Croatian Journal of Education, 22*(Sp.Ed.2), 47–63. https://doi.org/10.15516/cje.v22i0.4128

Bourdieu, P. (1996). *The state nobility: Elite schools in the field of power*. Stanford University Press.

Brodie, J. (2004). Introduction: Globalization and citizenship beyond the national state. *Citizenship Studies, 8*(4), 323–332. https://doi.org/10.1080/1362102052000316945

Bürgi, R. (2017). *Die OECD und die Bildungsplanung der freien Welt: Denkstile und Netzwerke einer internationalen Bildungsexpertise*. Barbara Budrich. https://doi.org/10.2307/j.ctvddzx13

Bürgi, R., & Tröhler, D. (2018). Producing the "right kind of people": The OECD education indicators in the 1960s. In S. Lindblad, D. Pettersson, & T. S. Popkewitz (Eds.), *Education by the numbers and the making of society: The expertise of international assessments* (pp. 75–91). Routledge.

Chatty, D. (2013). *From camel to truck: The Bedouin in the modern world*. White Horse Press.

Cummings, W. (2020, August 13). "Battle for the soul of the nation": Before they were running mates, Joe Biden and Kamala Harris both used slogan. *USA Today*. Retrieved from https://www.usatoday.com/story/news/politics/elections/2020/08/13/biden-and-harris-both-see-election-fight-soul-nation/3355971001/

Daley, A. (1996). *Steel, state, and labor: Mobilization and adjustment in France*. University of Pittsburgh Press.

Davies, L., Harber, C., & Yamashita, H. (2005). *Global citizenship education: The needs of teachers and learners*. Centre for International Education and Research CIER, University of Birmingham.

Demaine, J. (2002). Globalisation and citizenship education. *International Studies in Sociology of Education, 12*(2), 117–128. https://doi.org/10.1080/09620210200200086

de Oliveira Andreotti, V., & de Souza, L. M. (2012). *Decolonizing global citizenship education, or postcolonial perspectives on global citizenship education*. Routledge.

Fukuyama, F. (1989). The end of history? *The National Interest*, 3–18. https://www.jstor.org/stable/24027184

Fukuyama, F. (2003). *Economic globalization and culture. A discussion with Dr. Francis Fukuyama*. Retrieved December 3, 2020, from http://pratclif.com/fukuyama/fukuyama.htm

Giddens, A. (1990). *The consequences of modernity*. Polity Press.

Gotling, N. (2020). National textbook narratives and historiography: Presenting a same that is never the same. *Croatian Journal of Education, 22*(Sp.Ed.2), 65–82. https://doi.org/10.15516/cje.v22i0.4124

Grek, S., Maroy, C., & Verger, A. (Eds.). (2020). *World Yearbook of Education 2021: Accountability and datafication in the governance of education*. Routledge. https://doi.org/10.4324/9781003014164

Guéhenno, J.-M. (1993). *La fin de la démocratie*. Flammarion.

Hardy, I. (2021). *School reform in an era of standardization. Authentic accountabilities*. Routledge.

Hechter, M. (1975). *Internal colonialism: The Celtic fringe in British national development, 1536–1966*. Routledge & Kegan Paul.

Heyneman, S. P. (2003). Quantity, quality, and source. *Comparative Education Review, 37*(4), 372–388.

Hobsbawm, E. (1987). *The age of empire, 1875–1914*. Pantheon Books.

Hofmann, M. (2020). Swiss Alpine milk, education, and the fabrication of the ideal Swiss citizen. *Croatian Journal of Education, 22*(Sp.Ed.2), 101–114. https://doi.org/10.15516/cje.v22i0.4118

Horlacher, R. (2020). Civics in the curricular construction of the loyal national citizen: A comparative view of Switzerland. *Croatian Journal of Education, 22*(Sp.Ed.2), 83–99. https://doi.org/10.15516/cje.v22i0.4121

Ioannidis, J. P. A. (2005). Why most published research findings are false. *PLOS Medicine, 2*(8). https://doi.org/10.1371/journal.pmed.0020124

James, P., & Steger, M. B. (2014). A genealogy of "globalization": The career of a concept. *Globalizations, 11*(4), 417–434. https://doi.org/10.1080/14747731.2014.951186

Jazzaintmusic. (2021, January 6). *Joe Biden. "We The People".. Full Insurrection speech.. Jan 6th 2021* [Video file]. Retrieved February 15, 2021, from www.youtube.com/watch?v=wON7_nAcbjg

Labaree, D. F. (2017). *A perfect mess: The unlikely ascendancy of American higher education*. University of Chicago Press.

Maricic, V. (2020). National identity textbooks: Teaching Scottishness in the wake of the Union of Parliaments. *Croatian Journal of Education, 22*(Sp.Ed.2), 29–46. https://doi.org/10.15516/cje.v22i0.4125

Meyer, J. W., Boli, J., & Thomas, G. W. (1987). Ontology and rationalization in the Western cultural account. In W. R. Scott & J. W. Meyer (Eds.), *Institutional environments and organizations: Structural complexity and individualism* (pp. 9–27). Sage. (Original work published 1994)

Meyer, J. W., Boli, J., Thomas, G. M., & Ramirez, F. O. (1997). World society and the nation-state. *American Journal of Sociology, 103*(1), 144–181.

Meyer, J. W., & Ramirez, F. O. (2000). The world institutionalization of education. In J. Schriewer (Ed.), *Discourse formation in comparative education* (pp. 111–132). Lang.

Özkirimli, U. (2010). *Theories of nationalism: A critical introduction* (2nd ed.). Palgrave Macmillan.

Pais, A., & Costa, M. (2020). An ideology critique of global citizenship. *Critical Studies in Education*, 61(1), 1–16. https://doi.org/10.1080/17508487.2017.1318772

Parcerisa, L., Fontdevila, C., & Verger, A. (2020). Understanding the PISA influence on national education policies: A focus on policy transfer mechanisms. In S. Jornitz & A. Wilmers (Eds.), *International perspectives on school settings, education policy and digital strategies. A Transatlantic discourse in education research* (pp. 185–198). Barbara Budrich Verlag.

Piattoeva, N., Tröhler, D., Cowen, R., Acosta, F., Valero, P., Zhao, W., . . . Grek, S. (2019). Debatte – Discussion: The nationalism-trap in education research: Shared pathos, practiced ideals, and spectra of banal nationalism. *Bildungsgeschichte. International Journal for the Historiography of Education*, 9(2), 244–278.

Pinar, W. F. (Ed.). (2014). *International handbook of curriculum research* (2nd ed.). Routledge.

Pinar, W. F. (2015). Internationalization. In W. F. Pinar (Ed.), *Educational experience as lived: Knowledge, history, alterity. The selected works of William F. Pinar* (pp. 36–46). Routledge.

Prak, M. (2018). *Citizens without nations: Urban citizenship in Europe and the world, c. 1000–1789*. Cambridge University Press. https://doi.org/10.1017/9781316219027

Renan, E. (1882). *Qu'est-ce qu'une nation?* Calmann Lévy.

Robertson, R. (1992). *Globalization: Social theory and global culture*. Sage.

Sassen, S. (2003). Globalization or denationalization? *Review of International Political Economy*, 10(1), 1–22. https://www.jstor.org/stable/4177449

Schmidt, V. A. (1996). *From state to market? The transformation of French business and government*. Cambridge University Press. https://doi.org/10.1017/9781316219027

Spring, J. (2004). *How educational ideologies are shaping global society: Intergovernmental organizations, NGOs, and the decline of the nation-state*. Routledge.

Spring, J. (2008). *Globalization of education: An introduction*. Routledge.

Steger, M. B. (2005). From market globalism to imperial globalism: Ideology and American power after 9/11. *Globalizations*, 2(1), 31–46. https://doi.org/10.1080/14747730500085049

Steger, M. F. (2004). *Rethinking globalism*. Rowman & Littlefield.

Stein, L. v. (1850). *Der Begriff der Gesellschaft und die sociale Geschichte der französischen Revolution bis zum Jahre 1830* [first volume of the three volume set *Geschichte der socialen Bewegung in Frankreich von 1789 bis auf unsere Tage*]. Wigand.

Szucs, D., & Ioannidis, J. P. A. (2017). Empirical assessment of published effect sizes and power in the recent cognitive neuroscience and psychology literature. *PLOS Biology*, 15(3). https://doi.org/10.1371/journal.pbio.2000797

Thiesse, A.-M. (1999). *La création des identités nationales: Europe XVIIIe-XXe siècle*. Editions du Seuil.

Thrush, G. (2021, January 20). President Biden's full inauguration speech, annotated. *The New York Times*. Retrieved March 9, 2021, from www.nytimes.com/2021/01/20/us/politics/biden-inauguration-speech-transcript.html

Tiryakian, E. A. (1986). Sociology's great leap forward: The challenge of internationalisation. *International Sociology*, 1(2), 155–171.

Tröhler, D. (2010). Harmonizing the educational globe. World polity, cultural features, and the challenges to educational research. *Studies in Philosophy and Education*, 29(1), 5–17. https://doi.org/10.1007/s11217-009-9155-1

Tröhler, D. (2011). Concepts, cultures and comparisons. PISA and the double German discontentment. In M. A. Pereyra, H.-G. Kotthoff, & R. Cowen (Eds.), *PISA under examination: Changing knowledge, changing tests and changing schools* (pp. 245–257). Sense Publishers.

Tröhler, D. (2013). The OECD and Cold War culture: Thinking historically about PISA. In H.-D. Meyer & A. Benavot (Eds.), *PISA, power, and policy. The emergence of global educational governance* (pp. 141–161). Symposium Books.

Tröhler, D. (2015). The medicalization of current educational research and its effects on education policy and school reforms. *Discourse: Studies in the Cultural Politics of Education, 36*(5), 749–764. https://doi.org/10.1080/01596306.2014.942957

Tröhler, D. (2016). Curriculum history or the educational construction of Europe in the long nineteenth century. *European Educational Research Journal, 15*(3), 279–297. https://doi.org/10.1177/1474904116645111

Tröhler, D. (2017). Educationalization of social problems and the educationalization of the modern world. In M. Peters (Ed.), *Encyclopedia of educational philosophy and theory* (pp. 698–703). Springer. https://doi.org/10.1007/978-981-287-532-7_8-1

Tröhler, D. (2020a). National literacies, or modern education and the art of fabricating national minds. *Journal of Curriculum Studies, 52*(5), 620–635. https://doi.org/10.1080/00220272.2020.1786727

Tröhler, D. (2020b). Knowledge, media and communication. In J. Harford & T. O'Donoghue (Eds.), *A cultural history of education in the Modern Age* (pp. 35–56). Bloomsbury.

Tröhler, D., & Maricic, V. (2021). Data, trust and faith: The unheeded religious roots of modern education policy. *Globalisation, Societies and Education, 19*(2). https://doi.org/10.1080/14767724.2021.1872371

Tröhler, D., & Maricic, V. (forthcoming). Education and the nation: Educational knowledge in the dominant theories of nationalism. In D. Tröhler (Ed.), *Education, curriculum and nation-building. Contributions of comparative education to the understanding of nations and nationalism*. Routledge.

Wallerstein, I. (1986). Societal development, or development of the world-system? *International Sociology, 1*(1), 3–17. https://doi.org/10.1177/026858098600100102

Weber, M. (2008). Science as vocation. In J. Dreijmanis (Ed.), *Max Weber's complete writings on academic and political vocations* (pp. 25–52). Algora Publishing. (Original work published 1917)

Westberg, J., Boser, L., & Brühwiler, I. (Eds.). (2019). *School acts and the rise of mass schooling. Education policy in the long nineteenth century*. Palgrave Macmillan. https://doi.org/10.1007/978-3-030-13570-6

Witry, T. (1900). *Statistique historique du Grand-Duché de Luxembourg: La situation de l'enseignement primaire dans le Grand-Duché de Luxembourg pendant la période de 1815 à 1900*. V. Buck.

Ydesen, C. (Ed.). (2019). *The OECD's historical rise in education: The formation of a global governing complex*. Palgrave Macmillan. https://doi.org/10.1007/978-3-030-33799-5

Part I

Historical (re)production of the nation

2 Nation-states, nation-building and schooling

The case of Spanish America in the long 19th century

Felicitas Acosta

In *The making of citizens. A study in comparative education*, British comparativist Robert Edward Hughes states:

> The nineteenth century will certainly be remarkable for the growth of the National School, and may with some reason be characterised as the Century of Education, the period in which the necessity for a training of all citizens of the State was first recognised and provided for. Wherever we look, whether in Europe or America, we see the movement for national training taking place.
>
> (1907, p. 2)

According to this, the 19th century witnessed not only the expansion of schooling in Western countries but also the circulation of a three-component travelling policy: schooling, State and the national. "The fact is, the school is a political institution maintained by the State for the cultivation and propagation of national ideals" (Hughes, 1907, p. 4). At least, in the author's view, "in the four principal countries of the world, England, France, Germany, and the United States" (p. 3).

This chapter presents the circulation of this travelling policy from Western Europe and its encounter with emerging socio-political configurations after the post-independence wars in Hispanic America. This process involved the articulation of different elements, from political-organizational structures to the construction of new identities. In the case of Spanish America, breaking with the Spanish crown in 1810 and onwards implied a change of identity. The legacy of the empire was no less, since for Spain the conquest was guided by the principle of building a new society: a Spanish, European and Catholic America, but above all, a colonial empire.[1]

Both the circulation of Enlightenment thinking and the 1776 and 1789 revolutions provided the background to the pro-independence movements in the region triggered by the political crisis caused by Napoleonic expansion into Spain in 1808. Following the revolutions, civil wars broke out between those who wanted to remain under the Monarch's rule and those who supported independence. Final liberation was achieved through a costly armed struggle against the metropolis, especially in South America.

DOI: 10.4324/9781003137801-4

An increased awareness of the peculiarities of the former colonies emerged in this context: they were actual, established societies composed of a diverse population, different from the metropolis and different among themselves. At first, the search for a new identity relied on a late 18th-century idea: *our* America as opposed to Spain's America. Independence leader Simón Bolívar insisted on this idea as early as in 1818: "May Heaven answer our plea, the Americas thus united shall be called the kingdom of nations and the mother of republics" (as quoted in Filipi, 2017, p. 44). Thus, the first years after independence witnessed several attempts to consolidate great state unities although none of them succeeded.

Between 1820 and 1830, the independence victories resulted in the disintegration of the territories, which became separate states. Despite Bolívar's unifying efforts at the Congress of Panama in 1826, the former overseas Spanish empire was divided into several republics that held no ties among them.[2] One of the peculiarities of nation-building in the region was the adoption of the modern one-state, one-nation formula at the same time states were being built based on republican arrangements as a rule (Sabato, 2006).

In this sense, the building of new nation-states went hand in hand with the construction of political citizenship on basically liberal normative bases. The political organization scheme defined and presupposed an ideal citizen, with political rights that transformed him into a member of a national community, which, paradoxically, tended to erase and/or marginalize pre-established population groups (Centeno & Ferraro, 2013; Puiggrós, 1994). As in other latitudes, the nation-state's social invention leaned on the development of the state infrastructure power (Mann, 2006), with schooling being a central part of it (for specific data see Paglayan, 2020).

In the following, I aim to show how during the 19th century the three-component travelling policy switched in Spanish America: from schooling, State and the national to schooling, nation-state and the national. Also, I argue that the predominant combination was that of schooling and republics, where nation-states played a defining role in materializing the former but not the latter. Of course, different assemblages emerged during this period but withheld two main features: the idea of future as a link between identity-building, nation and education and the need for the state's organizational capacity to guarantee schooling.

Thus the chapter is organized in two sections. The first one offers a conceptual framework regarding the historical connection between nation-building, nation-states and schooling. It also elaborates on the conceptual construction underlying this connection in the case of Spanish America. The second section deals with the actual process of nation-building and schooling expansion through the State infrastructure. This section is itself divided in two parts: the first analyzes the relation between republics, nation-building and education; the second considers the role of the State through the growing centralization, passing of laws and school finance by the end of the 19th century and the beginning of the 20th century. Finally, the conclusions present a summary of the ways this travelling policy deployed in the region together with their possible connections to the forms that schooling and nationalism would later take towards the 20th century.

The chapter uses primary sources as school acts and secondary sources linked to the state cultural machinery reared towards nation-building such as schooling enrolment and expenditures. Taking into account the vastness and diversity of Hispanic America, the analysis is based on the identification of general trends with reference to particular cases when needed.

1 Nation-building, nation-states and schooling: A three-component travelling policy in the case of Spanish America

The study of the relation between nation- and state-building and schooling is still a work in progress. As Trohler and Maricic (forthcoming) point out, although education or schooling – most often undifferentiated – are included in the theories about nation and nationalism, their use is rather ordinary, unspecified and unsupported by research (p. 46). At the same time, Tröhler (2020) warns about the limits posed by equating "nation" with "State" to understand the role of schooling, regardless of the compulsory education laws enacted by the State, when nations and nation-states were formed.

Our starting point to go over the long 19th century is the three-component travelling policy already referred to: schooling, State and the national. However, in the case of Spanish America, we will depart from the nation-state building process, which presupposed the coordination between the construction of new territory-based political communities after independence and the development of a state apparatus that would provide those communities with their actors, i.e., citizens. The deployment of mass schooling as designed in Western Europe during the 18th century embodied the state apparatus while providing identity-related content to the construction of a national imagery.

In this regard, Tröhler (2020) offers a fertile conceptual framework to clarify different notions at stake. On the one hand, he picks up on the necessary differentiation between the concepts of nation, state and nation-state: nation as a cultural thesis of belonging and identity, and the state as an apparatus of power (distribution), participation and administration. Of interest to Spanish America is his idea of the nation-state as a *constitutionally rooted* constellation in which both the dominant vision of the nation and the stability of the state benefit each other mutually.

The enactment of the first constitutions in the region and the necessary formation of the state have shown this (Centeno & Ferraro, 2013). Constitutions play a key role in marking off nations because "nations as limited communities experience the ongoing construction of internal and external boundaries and are therefore based on a constant tension between inclusion and exclusion" (Itzighon & Vom Hau, 2006, p. 196). The definition of the scope of civil or political citizenship as provided for by constitutions is an example of such tension.

Indeed, between 1813 and 1830 alone there were more than 50 constitutional projects (Demélas, 2010), while Ossenbach (2010) speaks of an avalanche of constitutions seeking a post-independence balance. But nation-states are related to the nation-building process as well, which "also involves political measures ranging from immigration policies to education and infrastructure projects aimed at the consolidation of state power among the resident population" (Itzighon & Vom Hau, 2006, p. 197).

This goes hand in hand with Tröhler's (2020) dynamic perspective when differentiating not only concepts but also processes located in precise historical times: there is education and nation-building, and education and state-building before the French Revolution, but only education and nation-state-building afterward. In this line of studies, several authors acknowledge the increasing global visibility of public education as a state's tool during the 19th century (Green, 1990; Meyer & Ramirez, 2002) related to the idea of schooling as a travelling policy as mentioned earlier.

The triumph of the modern school as the hegemonic educational form was only possible with the State's intervention. The organization of schooling by the State is connected to what Mann (2006) has called the infrastructural power of the state: its institutional capability to exercise control and implement policy choices within the territory it claims to govern (see Centeno & Ferraro, 2013; Soifer & Vom Hau, 2008 for a critical use of the concept).

On how that process ensued in the West and the place the State occupied in it, Green (1990) underscores the differences in both the timeframes and modalities adopted by each country when implementing a widespread model of schooling. He distinguishes different arrangements within a global model embraced by Western nations, a model characterized by a publicly funded system with an administrative bureaucracy for the regulation of schools and by increasingly structured educational institutions and agents. Regardless of differences in timeframe, the expansion of schooling, in all cases, depended on assigning the State a key role in the process of systematization or what could be called State systematization (Acosta, 2019). Indeed, By the end of the 19th century, in Spanish America the state defined itself as the educating state (Ossenbach, 2010).

From our perspective, the issue is also about considering these processes in their transnational dimension. Several authors point out that internationalization processes intensified since the end of the 18th century and throughout the 19th century (see Schriewer, 2010; Tröhler, Popkewitz, & Labaree, 2011). The neo-institutionalist school, for instance, has tried to demonstrate the worldwide expansion of certain ideas typical of modernity with no direct relation to the appropriation context. Regardless of the criticism this school received (see Schriewer, 2013; Tröhler & Lenz, 2015, among others), Roldán Vera and Caruso (2007) agree that the development of the mass education ideal or the adoption of schooling was related to a concrete economic need or to a local political demand only in a few cases.

This may be the case of the post-revolutionary Spanish Americas. Following Konig (2003), the question that arises is which factors served as the core of or the basis for the nation-state-building process after independence since there were no culturally or ethnically determined nationalities as the foundations of the new states (see also Chiaramonte, 1997), and the conditions for a new state apparatus to develop – for instance, the provision of schools – were limited (Centeno &

Ferraro, 2013). In this context and under such conditions, how did schooling relate to identity-building nation-states in Spanish America?

An answer may lie in the situation after the rupture with Spain and the need to establish a new sovereign: the nation-state-building process in Spanish America started with the concept of civic nation or a citizens' nation. The legacy of the circulation of the Enlightenment thinking among the Creole elites and the emerging liberalism at the beginning of the 19th century provided that idea with content: the states associated with such values as equality, political engagement, freedom and economic progress meant a new promise (Konig, 2003). Following Sabato (2009), we argue that they pursued this idea in the form of a republican political agreement and equality under the law, although this did not translate into the formation of nations of citizens. In any case, there were different ways to get this new promise – chiefly among them was education.

In this regard, Konig (2003) maintains that it was necessary to develop the national component that would enable the population's cultural integration in order to promote a new form of collective identity across scattered and heterogeneous populations, strained by local or provincial loyalties. To do so, the elites resorted not only to physical symbols such as flags but also to the education structure.

In general terms we agree with such perspective, though it poses several problems to our attempt to look into the complementary nature of the nation-building, nation-state-creation and schooling processes – i.e. the three-component travelling idea. On the one hand, it seems to be a top-down form wherein the elites receiving transnational ideas promoted change processes, a perspective already overcome by studies in nationalism (Miller, 2006). On the other hand, schooling appears as an epiphenomenon of other variables, in this case political ones – an idea that has been well-discussed since the last third of the 20th century (Archer, 1979).

In the last decade, relevant literature has identified a concurrence of bottom-up practices in the construction of nation-states, including schooling (Roldán Vera & Caruso, 2007). We should also consider the interaction with longer historical experiences, such as educational practices and discourse that inherited the 18th-century ideals, Simón Rodríguez's project, or even post-revolution ideas, such as the introduction of the Lancasterian method in several states that were being formed during the first part of the 19th century.

Thus, in the following section we will analyze the nation-state formation in dialogue with the nation-building and schooling processes considering the convergence of a republican envisioned future as a leitmotif for the newly created nations and the need for a state infrastructure that could materialize this promise via schooling.

2 Nation-building, nation-states, schooling and future imagineries

In the previous section we stated that our starting point to go over the long 19th century in Spanish America is the nation-state building process, triggered by the revolutions and the following independence wars. We focus on the deployment of a three-component travelling policy: schooling as a way to embody what we call State systematization, including the state apparatus, while providing identity-related content to the construction of a national imagery.

Following Miller (2006), the issue is not so much whether state came before nation in Spanish America, but the extent to which state-building and nation-creation were related processes, sometimes reinforcing each other but sometimes undermining each other. In this section we argue that the deployment of this three-component travelling policy in the Spanish America withheld two major features: an envisioned republican future provided by education and the resort to the State infrastructure to materialize it.

The idea of future: Republics and education

According to Chiaramonte (1997), before 1810 Ibero-American elites ignored the concept of nationality and used "nation" and "State" interchangeably. After independence, to construct a nation was to organize a State through a process of political negotiations to conciliate parties' interests according to *jus gentium*. Thus, the emergence of different nationalities had its roots in political agreements supported by the construction of state apparatus, which created such a legal fiction as the idea of nation to provide them with sovereignty. It was not until 1830 that state organization projects emerged based on the principle of nationality (Chiaramonte, 2004).

In connection with our focus on the construction of the state apparatus in the emerging nation-states, López-Alves (2011) highlights the confluence of different players, from government elites to subordinate populations, grassroots organizations, Creole interest groups and, later on, migrants. All of them contributed to the conceptualization and imagining of the nation as well as its gradual construction. Yet there is consensus the State was the most important nation-builder (Paglayan, 2020). Social and ethnic stratification in Hispanic colonies was one of the main reasons why the Creole ruling class sought to prevent state power from remaining without direction for a long time (Lynch, 1985).

However, it is a well-known fact that somehow all states invent traditions or favour a particular kind of *imagining* of the nation (Hobsbawn, 1995; Anderson, 1990), promoting conceptualizations about it. As we saw, in Spanish America, after independence and the frustrated attempts at integration between the territories of the viceroyalties, a variety of desired and current "nations" emerged. What distinguished the region was that, in most cases, the process of constructing the nation and imposing some conceptualization of it on the popular imaginary included ideas about *the future of the nation* (López-Alves, 2011).

This future was condensed in the form of republics guided by ideals of progress and justice, for which the Creole elites had to bestow the emerging states with a new legitimation basis (the sovereignty of the people) and secure the rules of that new order through mechanisms such as those of liberal democracies, unknown to them and in experimentation in Europe (Waldmann, 2001).

Indeed, republicanism was an element that was constituted as a desirable stage for enlightened thought in the Río de la Plata even before independence. As Sabato maintains (2009), throughout Latin America, with the exception of Brazil, the republican option entailed a decisive change in the basics of political power. Naturally the option of republican forms of government implied an idea of nation: "the liberal notion of the nation as an abstract entity of sole and indivisible sovereignty integrated by free and equal individuals – the citizens – circulated from early on; . . . popular sovereignty, representation and nation were connected concepts that also referred to closely related realities" (p. 25).

Notice that the author mentions another key feature: a liberal notion of the nation based on citizen's sovereignty. The author stresses the direct relation between political institutions of the state apparatus; we add citizenry and nation (Sabato, 2006). Roldán Vera and Caruso (2007) agree on this point when they emphasize that liberalism and its basic concerns for state's legitimacy and authority-creation became both the founding myth of the new states and a key player in their constitution as nations. Furthermore, the authors indicate the conjunction of liberalism and republicanism as the framework where the post-colonial horizons of expectations were formed within a context of uncertainty and of a legitimacy crisis.

A place of condensation of this future imaginary on the emerging nations was their constitutions, a key reference for the understanding of nation-states as noted in the previous section. Along with Demélas (2010), we have already highlighted the proliferation of texts of this kind since the first revolutions in 1810. For the author, the central concern was the legitimacy for the existence of the new states and new powers, for which rights had to be enforced and new forms of sovereignty reaffirmed. Less attention was paid to the forms of exercising power. Waldmann (2001) agrees on this point when he emphasizes that most of the Latin American constitutions drafted during the 19th century were inspired by liberal and republican ideas, a fact that contrasted with the concrete forms of exercising power.

The author cites the example of Juan Bautista Alberdi, ideologist of the Argentine constitution of 1853 (see also Dussel, 2011). Among the functions of the constitution were: to promote the country's development, especially through directed immigration; to *educate* the sovereign, that is, the people, so that they adopted a republican attitude; to *educate* those who would have the state power in their hands, that is, accustom them to the use of law through the granting of generous powers before turning the laws into instruments that would later control these very same representatives. Alberdi warned that citizens were not yet well prepared to live in a republic and that they should be educated in this regard (Waldmann, 2001, p. 83).

This register can be perceived both in the ideas of independentists and in the first few constitutions. In 1826, Simón Bolivar's draft for the Constitution of the Republic of Bolivia stated: "Article 13. To be a citizen it is necessary: 1) To be Bolivian. 2) Be married, or older than twenty-one years. 3) Know how to read and write. 4) Have a job or industry; or profess any science or art, without subjection to another as a domestic servant" (as quoted in Guánchez de Méndez, 2005, p. 81). The 1812 Constitution of Cádiz, with jurisdiction in Spanish America, imposed literacy; same as the Peruvian Constitution of 1826. In Mexico, each state got to decide the date for the enforceability of the restriction on illiterate citizenry – generally, between 1836 and 1850.

For this reason, the necessity of schooling was established in the first few constitutions, such as the Constitution of Guatemala in 1825 and the congress of Gran Colombia in 1821, or when the Government *Junta* of Chile mandated the creation of schools, which were to fit the number of inhabitants and to be financed by the locals. Also, in Bolivia, the Education Statute of 1827 called on every town with more than 200 inhabitants to open a school. As Newland (1992) wisely points out, this was more a case of political/educational optimism than a reality.

However, three elements stand out from the Hispanic American constitutions per se as the ideology for a collective identity under construction via education. First of all, the notion of educability, a clearly Rousseaunian heritage: men keep in themselves the possibility of being educated. Secondly, trust in the value of culture and proper education to achieve the citizen of the republic. Thirdly, the constitution is taken as a sign of state respectability before others. It was not so much about ensuring the mechanisms to warrant the effective realization of constitutional precepts, but rather to have a teleological instrument – a new political and social order for which men can and should be educated.

Constitutions appear as an expression of the process of educationalization of social problems (Tröhler, 2019), but they also reflect a regional uniqueness: "a continual return, despite all the obstacles, to the cause of making knowledge and culture more accessible" (Miller, 2020, p. 6). As a result, from the first phase of the formation of the Spanish American nation-states, intellectual elites showed an interest in the extension of education, an interest that political elites will increasingly assume in the progressive construction of a state schooling apparatus.

Of course, as in the case of political rights, the inclusion of the population as a whole had varying temporalities, consolidating in some countries as late as the 20th century. In any case, I want to highlight here the place that education took in the joint process of conceptualization, planning and definition of the nation as an instrument but also as an intrinsic component of the imagined future. And, as López-Alves (2011) emphasizes when referring to nationalism in the region, this is part of the reason why nation-states rather than national states emerged in Spanish America.

Schooling and nation-states: Materializing future imaginaries

The articulation between nation-states and schooling can be described through four milestones in the transition from post-colonialism to nation-building: 1) circulation of Enlightenment ideas; 2) introduction of the Lancaster method; 3) reorganization of universities and preparatory schools; and 4) implementation of compulsory elementary education. The relevant literature points to a certain continuity from the point of view of institutions; however, as early as in the post-revolutionary period, some innovations were introduced.

Circulation of Enlightenment ideas. The first milestone is the continuity of the renovating influence exerted by the circulation of the Enlightenment ideas. Although these ideas did not bring about major institutional changes, they did play a role in anchoring the importance of education. There were innovative experiences such as *Las escuelas de la Patria* by independence leader José Gervasio Artigas (in current Uruguay) in 1815; the expansion of schooling, such as the founding of schools across provinces led by Argentine independence leader Manuel Belgrano, and the sustainment and reorganization of the existing offer through the schools run by the town council in many cities. In most cases, these were short-lived experiences, even in terms of curricula: in 1811, revolutionary leader Mariano Moreno, secretary of the first national government in Buenos Aires, made the reading of Rousseau's *The Social Contract* mandatory in the city's public schools, a regulation that was withdrawn the following month (Espinoza, 2019).

A decentralized educational offer – through private and municipal institutions – took a prominent role for a long part of the century and was, in this regard, a continuation of the colonial model. In Mexico, Bolivia, Cuba and Uruguay, municipal schools played an important role. According to Newland (1991), between 25% and 40% of Spanish American schools were municipal at mid-century; they were attended by 40%–60% of the total student population; the rest attended private – secular or religious – schools (the author estimates that up until 1870, depending on the country, between 30% and 100% of primary enrolments corresponded to the private sector).

Regardless of the weight of the municipal – not yet national – offer, it is interesting to highlight the growth in the state's assumption of the educational offer, albeit at the local level. There was even advancement over the religious offer. In the 1830s in Mexico, the laws called on convents to open schools. Likewise, in 1812 in Chile, women's convents were obliged to open schools for girls, and in 1830, when seized temporalities were returned to convents, they were all urged to open schools. The order was given again in 1832, indicating that if they did not set up schools, municipalities would do so, but convents would have to finance them. The mandate imposing convents to open schools was endorsed in the Chilean education law of 1860 as well as in Gran Colombia in 1821.

Yet slowly and increasingly, in the second half of the century, the national state – or provincial governments – started to intervene in municipal education and tended to offer it directly. This happened despite the fact that in some countries, such as Bolivia, Mexico and Uruguay, municipalities put up some resistance to change, as they sensed this meant losing grasp of one of their roles (Espinoza, 2019; Ossenbach, 2010).

Introduction of the Lancaster method. A salient, second, milestone is the introduction of the Lancasterian method from 1822 onwards in cities and states such as Montevideo, Buenos Aires, Lima, Chile, Mexico, Venezuela and Colombia (Weinberg, 1995). Although in most cases these schools lasted approximately five years, in other cases, such as Mexico, they lasted until 1890. Even more: in 1842 the Lancasterian Company was set up as the Directorate-General for Primary Instruction all over the Mexican nation (García Benavente, 2015).

According to Newland, the Lancasterian method caused a sensation due to its utility, inexpensiveness and discipline. In the recitals of a decree establishing the creation of a teacher training Lancasterian school in Peru in 1822, the same sentiment was shared: "it is still impossible to imagine the revolution that mutual instruction will spark around the world when it finally becomes widespread across civilized peoples; the kingdom of ignorance will be absolutely finished" (as quoted in Newland, 1991, p. 343).

Regardless of their duration, it is noteworthy that for the new territories, Lancasterian schools meant a choice of institutional systematization that expressed the will to organize some kind of school offer. Their success or failure was linked to several variables – among them, the financing difficulties of the public purse and the opposition of the most conservative Catholic sectors. They impacted on the configuration of new political sociabilities because they entailed the creation of civil societies focused on education development (Roldán Vera, 2011) and they influenced the future schooling systems, especially in certain states such as Mexico.

Reorganization of universities and preparatory schools. Thirdly, an interest in organizing the post-revolutionary educational offer is expressed in future secondary education and universities. The new governments reviewed the statutes of colonial universities, with presence in the region since mid-16th century through Dominic and, above all, Jesuit orders, and they created new offer. It was the most active areas that drove the independence process: they had been more distanced from the core of the Empire's traditional power in Hispanic America. Thus, state universities were created in Buenos Aires (1821), Bogota (1826), Santiago de Chile (1842) and Montevideo (1849; HEAL, 2020). These institutions began to play an increasingly important role in the formation of the new political elites that would shape the state apparatus.

Secondary education was subjected to intervention by the new states even before primary education with the aim of instructing the elites. During the course of the century, existing Latin schools together with new institutions evolved into self-contained secondary schooling. In Chile in 1843 the national government introduced a secondary curriculum that placed emphasis on Latin language and literature. The official goal was molding a virtuous political elite. In New Granada (modern Colombia), the private *Colegio del Espíritu Santo*, founded in 1846, combined preparatory and university-level courses and required the study of Latin as well as modern languages (Espinoza, 2019).

In Argentina by the mid 1850s, two schools were created by provincial states and not by religious orders for the first time in the history of the Provinces of the Río de la Plata: the Colegio del Uruguay, in the province of Entre Ríos, and the Colegio de San Miguel, in the province of Tucumán. As from 1863, the national state created a national school in each province with a gradual incorporation of national content, albeit one still in debate with the cultural-generalist model. An exclusive identification of the national language, without indigenous components, and a history of the homeland from the first year of school appeared to be the basis of the individual to be promoted (Acosta, 2020).

Implementation of compulsory elementary education. The fourth milestone concerns the gradual increase of elementary education. Legislation on educational matters was very abundant and intense throughout the 19th century, and the principle of the *educating state* was gradually introduced in the new political constitutions and laws. Nevertheless, and despite the will of intellectual elites referred to earlier, the secondary role that elementary education held during much of the 19th century in the vision of the ruling sectors was correlated with the public funds that were allocated to it.

In Colombia, for example, in 1847 the investment made in secondary education was 22 times higher than that made in primary education, while the investment in university education was 34 times higher; a similar situation in Chile still in 1875 (Donoso Romo, 2010). In 1856 in Bolivia, the budget for primary education was less than half the budget for secondary and university education. Hence the constant complaints of Argentine educationist Sarmiento about the unfairness of public spending on education: more money was spent on mid-level and higher education, for the wealthy classes, than on elementary education for the masses which meant starting "from the head down to the feet" (as quoted in Newland, 1991, p. 356).

Priority factors, chief among them the economic situation, delayed until the last quarter of the 19th century the development of the educational systems already foreseen in the first Spanish America constitutions. Although it is well known that the explosive increase in educational coverage in Latin America only occurred towards the middle of the 20th century, it is interesting to note that it is in this period that a sustained increase in elementary education began.

As a result, while in the mid-19th century around 85% of the population was illiterate, in 1900 this percentage dropped to 72%; in 1925 it was close to 50%. Among the countries that achieved greater coverage in these years were Argentina, Chile, Costa Rica, Cuba, Uruguay and Mexico (Donoso Romo, 2010). Similarly, Frankema (2009) provides information about primary school enrolment rates between 1870 and 2000 showing a similar trend: in the last three decades of the 19th century the expansion of primary schooling is most notable in Argentina, Chile, Costa Rica and Uruguay as shown in Table 2.1.

Table 2.1 Gross enrolment rates in elementary schools; selected countries 1870–1920.

Period Country	1880	1890	1900	1910	1920
Argentina	20.4	38	46.3	58.4	78.3
Chile	18.5	32.0	40.8	71.8	70.3
Costa Rica	-	23.7	43.2	51.0	54.8
Mexico	31.2	30.2	30.8	31.0	38.8*
Peru	-	-	19.2	23.8	28.8**
Uruguay	-	-	34.5	48.7	53.8

*1930: 71.2
**1930: 45.4

Note: Based on Frankema (2009); enrolment rates 1870–1920 obtained from Lindert (2004, pp. 91–93 cited in Frankema, 2009) and Mitchell (2007, cited in Frankema, 2009); enrolment rates 1930–1955 obtained from UNESCO, World Survey of Education (Frankema, 2009).

The growth in the enrolment rate in elementary schools went hand in hand with increased national spending on education. In 1884 in Argentina, the country spent nearly 3.8% of its budget on elementary education (with a large part going to subsidies for the provinces); the overall public spending earmarked for primary education amounted to 4.9% at the national and provincial levels. In the 1880s in Uruguay, the approximate number was 4%. In 1856 in Bolivia, 2.4% of the budget went to primary education, yet by 1868, the number rose to 4.2%. In Chile, between 3.4% and 5% of the national budget was spent on education before 1850, and this went up to 5.7%–8.2% in the 1870s.

The laws passed from 1860 onwards also showed that the new nation-states were increasingly interested not only in organizing elementary education but also in regulating their orientation regarding instruction on the national content. National Act 1420 of Argentina (Ley, 1420, 1884) established in Section 6 that the minimum compulsory instruction encompassed "the Republic's specific geography and a basic knowledge of universal geography, the Republic's specific history and a basic knowledge of general history, the national language; morality and civility; a basic knowledge of hygiene; . . . a knowledge of the National Constitution."

The General Primary Education Law of Chile (Ley Jeneral, 1860) established "at least reading and writing the national language, Christian doctrine and morality, concepts of practical arithmetic and the legal system of weights and measures [in higher schools], more prominence shall be given to religious instruction, linear drawing, geography, the History of Chile and political Constitution of the State compendium" (Section 3). At the same time, the Organic Act of Public Instruction in the Federal District, Mexico, (Ley Orgánica, 1867) stated: "In primary education schools attended by children from the District and paid for with public funds, the subjects taught shall be [among others] morality, civility and a basic knowledge of constitutional law and rudiments of history and geography, especially of Mexico."

Similarly, Section 2 of the Decree of Public Instruction in Venezuela (Decreto 1723, 1870) established that "the compulsory instruction is one that the law requires of all Venezuelans of both sexes and that the public powers are in the duty of giving free and preferentially . . . it includes the general principles of morality, the reading and writing of the homeland language, practical arithmetic, the metric system and the compendium of the Federal Constitution." While in Uruguay Act 1350 of Common Education (Ley 1350, 1877) included the teaching of "lessons on objects, reading, writing and drawing, arithmetic, composition, grammar and rhetoric, geography, with notions of history, bookkeeping and mercantile calculation, rights and duties of the citizen, history of the Republic, morals and religion, notions of algebra and geometry, physiology and hygiene, physics and natural history" (Section 16).

The route taken has made it possible to show the interconnection between travelling ideas related to the role of education, state-building and nation-creation. In the case of Spanish America, the search for identity-building experienced two moments. One involved a symbolic materialization, expressed in the Constitutions, under the idea of a future scenario: the educated republic. The other entailed a concrete materialization and took the form of schooling extension. The latter moment was gradual, and its pace varied greatly from country to country. However, it was possible to identify milestones that reflect the increasing interest of – first – intellectual elites and – later – political elites in shaping the nation-state through a school system. The gradual inclusion of national content in school curriculum accompanied this process.

3 Conclusions

The construction of nation-states during the long 19th century encompassed almost the entire western world. It was a process with different temporalities, although triggered by the dynamics of the revolution. Three moments took place in Spanish America: the rupture with the Spanish crown through revolutions at the beginning of the century; the internal wars after independence until, depending on the case, half of that century; and the consolidation of the nation project between the end of the 19th century and the beginning of the 20th century.

This chapter considered the transnational circulation of what we call a three-component traveling policy: schooling, State and the national. The development of this policy in Spanish America showed a change in the articulation of these components given the central place that the configuration of the nation-state occupied in the region. As shown earlier, different assemblages, anchored in diverse rhythms, emerged during the long 19th century. Our focus were some common trends: the idea of future as a link between identity-building, nation, and education and the need for the state's organizational capacity to guarantee schooling.

In this sense, it is important to consider that the post-revolutionary process became consolidated through the disintegration of the Empire's administrative units. The aspiration of certain independence leaders regarding a unified political/territorial reconfiguration failed to materialize for different reasons. In any case, such diversity is a sign of the symbolic construction of the national identity-building processes. In a context of clashing interests and impoverishment as a result of independence wars, the new governments expressed their interest in education and schooling as part of the future republic. This interest did not extend much to the population, at least until the 1880s, but it accounts for the relevance assigned to education in the construction of a future scenario. This idea is also close to the social function that education, through the expansion of schooling, acquired in the Western world from the late 18th century onwards.

The resulting nation-states show at least two major characteristics. On the one hand, a strongly state-centred form. The existence of a world market enabled the generalization of a nation-state form that established itself before the local bourgeoisie were formed nationally, a process opposite to that of Europe, where the development of the local bourgeoisie preceded the nation-state (Ossenbach, 2010). In the context of the late capitalism that unfolded in Spanish America, cohesion seemed possible only if coming from the state sphere. For the national states to be consolidated it was necessary that extensive forward-looking interest groups were formed and became stronger and that they could serve as unifying factors. That means that from the end of the 19th century onwards, the State was the only player capable of mobilizing resources and creating the necessary conditions to overcome divisions.

Still by the end of the 19th century, these new nations presented a dichotomy: many symbols of modernity and of diverse successes in the field of public policy and infrastructure, such as schooling in some of them, together with weak public institutions at the fiscal level, unsolved internal conflicts in areas far from the national capitals, and single commodity-based economies exposed to global market fluctuations (Centeno & Ferraro, 2013). In this sense, Paglayan (2021) indicates that even until the beginning of the 20th century most of the Spanish American nation-states were still non-democratic, even those who had increased schooling such as Argentina, Chile and Uruguay. Interestingly enough, the author shows a similar trend in some European countries who were, at the least, in transition to democracy.

In any case, to the same equality principle established during the decades of the republican initiatives, the 20th century would add actual equality through the introduction of democratic forms of organization and government. But, as indicated by several studies on this topic (see Vom Hau, 2009), the transition into democratic republics was accompanied by a new turn in our travelling policy.

During the first half of the 20th century, and even up until the Second World War, some countries such as Mexico, Peru and Argentina, among others, underwent a reconstruction of the national component through the recreation of national history in some cases and through the building of a new nationalism focused on the search for identity roots from the native peoples in other cases. But in all of them schooling played a key role by means of the curriculum, the celebration of national holidays at schools, the control over textbooks and a certain degree of militarization of teaching practices. Nation-states, based on their infrastructural capacity, were the support for this new interaction among schooling, State and the national.

Notes

1 By 1810 Spanish America was composed of four large viceroyalties: New Spain (currently Mexico, among other territories), Peru (currently Peru and Colombia), Río de la Plata (now Argentina, Bolivia, Paraguay and Uruguay) and New Granada (currently Ecuador and part of Colombia). Each of them depended on the Spanish Crown, was locally administered and had few ties with the rest. Also, several captaincies were established, such as those of Venezuela, Guatemala, Chile and Cuba, whose governments were independent from the viceroyalties although they were supervised by some of them.
2 The Congress of Panama (also called the Amphictyonic Congress) was a failed attempt promoted by Simón Bolívar to create a league of American republics, with a joint military, a mutual defense pact and a supranational parliamentary assembly. Chiaramonte (2004) identifies some of the causes underlying the territorial disintegration that followed independence: mainly the vastness of the territory, the irregularity of demographics and the state of communications.

References

Acosta, F. (2019). Educationalization, schooling, and the right to education. In R. Bruno Jofré (Ed.), *Educationalization and Its complexities: Religion, politics, and technology* (pp. 299–331). Toronto: University of Toronto Press.

Acosta, F. (2020). The nation-state and the origins of secondary education in Argentina: The case of the Colegio Nacional (National School). *Croatian Journal of Education*, 22(2), 115–132.

Anderson, B. (1990). *Imagined communities*. London: Verso.

Archer, M. (1979). *Social origins of educational systems*. London: Sage.

Centeno, M., & Ferraro, A. (2013). Republics of the possible: State building in Latin America and Spain. In M. Centeno & A. Ferrero (Eds.), *State and nation making in Latin America and Spain republics of the possible* (pp. 3–24). Cambridge, USA: Cambridge University Press.

Chiaramonte, J. C. (1997). La formación de los estados nacionales en Iberoamérica. *Boletín del Instituto de de Hiistoria Argentina y Americana Dr. Emilio Ravignani*, 3(15), 143–165.

Chiaramonte, J. C. (2004). *Nación y Estado en Iberoamérica*. Buenos Aires: Sudamericana.

Decreto 1723. Instrucción pública, gratuita y obligatoria. 27 de junio de 1870. Retrieved from www.anhvenezuela.org/pdf/textos%20historicos/010044.pdf

Demélas, M. M. (2010). Las primeras constituciones de la América española (c. 1810–1830). *Revista de Historia Americana y Argentina*, 45, 47–70.

Donoso Romo, A. (2010). La nación como protagonista de la educación en América Latina1870–1930. *Revista de Historia de la educación latinoamericana*, 14, 239–266.

Dussel, I. (2011). Republicanism "out of place". Readings on the circulation of republicanism in education in 19th-century Argentina. In D. Tröhler, Th. Popkewitz, & D. Labaree (Eds.), *Schooling and the making of citizens in the long nineteenth century. Comparative visions* (pp. 131–152). New York, NY: Routledge.

Espinoza, G. A. (2019). National Education Systems: Latin America. In J. L. Rury & E. H. Tamura (Eds.), *The Oxford handbook of the history of education*. Oxford: Oxford University Press.

Filipi, A. (2017). Utopía y necesidad histórica de la la patria grande. Los retos de la cultura jurídica de la emancipación nuestroamericana. In *Atlas histórico de América Latina y el Caribe* (pp. 44–61). Argentina: Universidad Nacional de Lanús.

Frankema, E. (2009). The expansion of mass education in twentieth century Latin America: A global comparative perspective. *Journal of Iberian and Latin American*, XXVII(3), 359–395.

García Benavente, J. (2015). La escuela Lancasteriana en México y en América Latina como solución del estado liberal ante el vacío dejado por la Iglesia. *Boletín Virtual*, 4(7), 48–66.

Green, A. (1990). *Education and state formation. The rise of education systems in England, France and USA*. London: The Macmillan Press.

Guánchez de Méndez, Z. (2005). Simón Rodríguez, la Constitución de 1826 y el proyecto de educación popular. *Revista de Pedagogía*, XXVI(75), 63–103.

HEAL Historia de la educación argentina y latinoamericana. (2020). *Sistemas educativos y estados nacionales en América Latina*. Ficha de cátedra. Universidad Nacional de La Plata.

Hobsbawn, E. (1995). *Naciones y nacionalismos desde 1870*. [Nations and Nationalisms since 1870]. Barcelona: Crítica.

Hughes, R. E. (1907). *The making of citizens. A study in comparative education*. London: Walter Scott Publishing.

Itzighon, J., & Vom Hau, M. (2006). Unfinished imagined communities: States, social movements, and nationalism in Latin America. *Theory of Sociology*, 35, 193–212.

Konig, J. (2003). Discursos de identidad, Estado-nación y ciudadanía en America Latina: Viejos problemas – nuevos enfoques y dimensiones. *Historia y Sociedad*, 11, 9–31.

Ley 1350. Instruccion pública. Enseñanza primaria. 24 de agosto de 1877. Retrieved from www.impo.com.uy/bases/leyes/1350-1877

Ley 1420. Ley reglamentando la Educación Común. 8 de julio de 1884. Retrieved from www.bnm.me.gov.ar/giga1/normas/5421.pdf

Ley Jeneral. Lei jeneral de instrucción primaria. 24 de noviembre de 1860. Retrieved from www.memoriachilena.gob.cl/archivos2/pdfs/MC0018152.pdf

Ley Orgánica. Ley orgánica de la instrucción pública en el Distrito Federal. 2 de diciembre de 1867. Retrieved from www.sep.gob.mx/work/models/sep1/Resource/3f9a47cc-efd9-4724-83e4-0bb4884af388/ley_02121867.pdf

López-Alves, F. (2011). Nation-states and national states: Latin America in comparative perspective. In M. Hanagan & C. Tilly (Eds.), *Contention and trust in cities and states* (pp. 113–128). Dordrecht: Springer.

Lynch, J. (1985). *América Latina entre colonia y nación*. Barcelona: Crítica.

Mann, M. (2006). El poder autónomo del Estado: sus orígenes, mecanismos y resultados. *Revista Académica de Relaciones Internacionales, 5*, 1–43.

Meyer, J., & Ramirez, F. (2002). La institucionalización mundial de la educación. In J. Schriewer (Ed.), *Formación del discurso en la educación comparada* [Discourse formation in comparative education] (pp. 91–110). Barcelona: Ediciones Pomares.

Miller, N. (2006). The historiography of nationalism and national identity in Latin America. *Nations and Nationalism, 12*(2), 201–221.

Miller, N. (2020). *Republics of knowledge. Nations of the future in Latin America.* Princeton, NJ: Princeton University Press.

Newland, C. (1991). La educación elemental en Hispanoamérica: desde la independencia hasta la centralización de los sistemas educativos nacionales. *Hispanic American Historical Review, 71*(2), 335–364.

Newland, C. (1992). *Buenos Aires No es pampa: La educación elemental porteña 1820–1860.* Buenos Aires: Grupo Editor Latinoamericano.

Ossenbach, G. (2010). Las relaciones entre el Estado y la educación en América Latina durante los siglos XIX y XX. *Docencia, 15*(40), 23–31.

Paglayan, A. (2020). *Civil conflict, state consolidation, and the spread of mass education.* Working paper. Retrieved from https://e50c00f1-c826-48c4-98ce-bef51415dedc.filesusr.com/ugd/a763a0_3c0969e92a88497199045762a0e14df1.pdf

Paglayan, A. (2021). The non-democratic roots of mass education: Evidence from 200 years. *American Political Science Review, 115*(1), 179–198.

Puiggrós, A. (1994). *Imaginación y crisis en la educación latinoamericana.* Buenos Aires: Aique.

Roldán Vera, E. (2011). Internacionalización pedagógica y comunicación en perspectiva histórica: la introducción del método de enseñaza mutua en Hispanoamérica independiente. In M. Caruso & H. Tenorth (Comps.), *Internacionalización. Políticas educativas y reflexión pedagógica en un medio global* (pp. 297–344). Buenos Aires: Granica.

Roldán Vera, E., & Caruso, M. (2007). Introduction: Avoiding the National, Assessing the Modern. In E. Vera Roldán & M. Caruso (Eds.), *Imported modernity in post-colonial state formation. The appropriation of political, educational, and cultural models in nineteenth-century Latin America* (pp. 7–30). Frankfurt: Peter Lang.

Sabato, H. (2006). La reacción de América: la construcción de las repúblicas en el siglo XIX. In R. Chartier & A. Feros (Comps.), *Europa, América y el mundo: tiempos históricos* (pp. 263–279). Madrid: Marcial Pons.

Sabato, H. (2009). Soberanía popular, ciudadanía y nación en Hispanoamérica: la experiencia republicana del siglo XIX. *Almanack braziliense, 9*, 23–40.

Schriewer, J. (2010). Comparación y explicación entre causalidad y complejidad. In J. Schriewer & H. Kaelbe (Comps.), *La comparación en las ciencias sociales e históricas. Un debate interdisciplinar* (pp. 17–62). Barcelona: Octaedro/ICE-UB.

Schriewer, J. (2013). Cultura mundial y mundos de significado culturalmente específicos. *Educar em Revista, 49*, 275–297.

Soifer, H., & Vom Hau, M. (2008). Unpacking the strength of the state: The utility of state infrastructural power. *Studies in Comparative International Development, 43*(3), 219–230.

Tröhler, D. (2019). The dignity of the Protestant souls: Protestant trajectories in the Educationalization of the World. In R. Bruno Jofré (Ed.), *Educationalization and its complexities: Religion, politics, and technology* (pp. 27–49). Toronto: University of Toronto Press.

Tröhler, D. (2020). Nation-state, education and the fabrication of national-minded citizens (Introduction). *Croatian Journal of Education, 22*(2), 11–27.

Tröhler, D., & Lenz, Th. (2015). Trayectoria del desarrollo de la escuela moderna. Entre lo nacional y lo global: Introducción. In D. Tröhler & Th. Lenz (Comps.), *Trayectorias del desarrollo de los sistemas educativos modernos. Entre lo nacional y lo global* [Trajectories of development of modern schooling. Between the national and the global] (pp. 11–19). Barcelona: Octaedro.

Trohler, D., & Maricic, V. (forthcoming). Education and the nation: Educational knowledge in the dominant theories of nationalism.

Tröhler, D., Popkewitz, Th., & Labaree, D. (Eds.). (2011). *Schooling and the making of citizens in the long nineteenth century. Comparative visions.* New York, NY: Routledge.

Vom Hau, M. (2009). Analizando la escuela: nacionalismo y educación en México, la Argentina y Perú. Papeles de trabajo. *Revista electrónica del Instituto de Altos Estudios Sociales de la Universidad Nacional de General San Martín, 2*(5). Retrieved from file:///Users/acostafelicitas/Downloads/Dialnet-AnalizandoLaEscuela7463988%20(1).pdf

Waldmann, P. (2001). La relevancia de la constitución durante la fase de la creación de los Estados Unidos y de los Estados latinoamericanos. *Iberoamericana, I*(4), 69–89.

Weinberg, G. (1995). *Modelos educativos en América Latina.* Buenos Aires: Kapelusz.

3 Towards national socialism with Chinese characteristics?

Schooling and nationalism in contemporary China

Edward Vickers

1 Anything but "banal" – nationalism, the state and Chinese citizenship

Banal nationalism, a concept central to the framing of this Yearbook, has been characterized as "a pervasively unnoticed facet of everyday life in the West" (Goode, 2020, p. 974). To what extent, though, is East Asian nationalism banal? Much about the institutional structure of the nation-state and education in this region seems familiar to the Western eye: written constitutions construct citizens by elaborating their rights and duties; schooling underpins common values by projecting a shared identity; citizenship is defined in language implying general equality before the law. In the People's Republic of China (PRC), Soviet-inspired formulae originally defined the state as a radically egalitarian alliance of productive "classes." But following a dilution of revolutionary rhetoric from the early 1980s, the construction of nationhood might now appear, superficially at least, to replicate more closely still the familiar Western pattern.

However, interpreting Chinese nationalism in a Western frame can prove highly misleading. Predominant notions of nationhood, and the role assigned to schooling in constructing citizenship, diverge significantly from conventional Western models. This difference does not stem from any ineffable, ageless cultural "essence" conferring immunity to alien influence. In fact, China has been profoundly transformed by its encounter with the modern West and Japan, in ways especially pertinent to a discussion of nationhood, citizenship and schooling (Harrison, 2001). But rather than prompting convergence, this encounter has both shaped and been shaped by intense and ongoing struggles over the meaning of modern 'Chineseness.'

These struggles derive largely from China's status as an empire masquerading as a nation-state. The objective distinction between empire and nation is admittedly murky, given the difficulty of defining either political form, and the "multiethnic populations of most contemporary states" (Esherick, Kayali, & Van Young, 2006, p. 3). Crudely put, however, nations are based on the principle that "the political and national unit should be congruent" (Gellner, 1983, p. 1), while an empire is "a large, composite, multiethnic polity formed by conquest by a strong centre . . ., and characterized by some form of indirect rule of the subordinate parts" (Esherick

DOI: 10.4324/9781003137801-5

et al., 2006, p. 5). As in Russia and India, nationalism in China has reimagined a large, highly diverse and explicitly imperial polity as a single national community, attempting to bind its subordinate parts more closely to the centre, while redefining imperial subjects as national citizens.

Key among the resultant contradictions are parallel and incompatible definitions of Chineseness: one premised on shared ancestry and Han culture (though "Hanness" itself is vastly diverse; Joniak-Luthi, 2015); the other invoking inter-ethnic brotherhood between Han and various minority ethnicities. These contradictory definitions are manifested in the different narratives deployed to legitimate Chinese claims to Hong Kong and Taiwan on the one hand, and Tibet, Xinjiang and Inner Mongolia on the other: the former deemed Chinese by virtue of primordial Hanness; the latter through inter-ethnic unity in a shared multicultural destiny. Vestiges of a class-based, more ethnically neutral narrative have persisted more strongly in relation to minorities. But today, these conflicting visions – ethnically essentialist and multiculturally inclusive – are increasingly subsumed in exhortations to share in a "Chinese Dream" of reassuming China's rightful place in the world.

Meanwhile, banal, everyday reality for PRC residents is marked by segregation, competition and insecurity. Access to schooling, healthcare, pensions and other benefits is radically differentiated by residency status, with stratification increasingly justified through assessments of "merit" (Wan & Vickers, 2021). During the Cultural Revolution, radical Maoism inverted the long-established principle of merit-based hierarchy, but Mao's death prompted a drastic swing back towards unapologetic meritocracy (Vickers & Zeng, 2017). Today, notions of "just hierarchy" underpin the state's legitimating ideology and governmental practice (Bell & Wang, 2020).

The strain of holding together a society shot through with profound divisions of class, residency, culture and ethnicity falls largely upon schooling and propaganda, backed up by repressive violence. Far from taking shared identity for granted, schools incessantly preach the imperative of absolute loyalty to the Communist Party (CCP) regime as the sole legitimate representative of the Chinese nation. This imperative is reinforced by a victimhood narrative designed to impress upon every citizen the grave peril of disunity and weakness, and the consequent necessity to subordinate individual aspiration to national demands.

Following a brief review of the place of education in previous analyses of Chinese nationalism, this chapter begins with a concise historical overview of debate over identity and nationhood up to the end of the Mao era in the 1970s. The main focus then falls upon the post-Mao period. After considering major trends in policy and curriculum development, I home in on three contemporary challenges to national unity and stability – social inequality; inter-ethnic strife; and the Hong Kong and Taiwan "questions" – examining the role of education in the state's response to each. The chapter concludes by discussing the prospects for success, on its own terms, of China's vastly ambitious nation-building project, and its domestic and global implications.

2 Education in the study of Chinese nationalism

Despite the considerable literature in English on the history and politics of Chinese nationalism, sustained analysis of the role of schooling is remarkably rare. Historians have examined the early-20th-century advent of modern schooling and its contribution to reframing political identity, highlighting the influence of Japan (Moloughney & Zarrow, 2011; Harrison, 2001; Dikötter, 1991; Leibold, 2007). Political scientists have integrated analysis of school curricula into their analyses of nationalism (Hughes, 2006; Wang, 2012). However, it is telling that Wang still considers it a revelatory insight that "to understand a country, one should visit the country's primary schools and high schools and read their history textbooks" (7). Meanwhile, the historian Rana Mitter's analysis of "circuits of memory" underpinning "China's new nationalism" entirely omits schooling (Mitter, 2020).

The thinness of much educational scholarship is partly to blame here. Most research on China's education system tends to be presentist, apolitical and 'practice-oriented,' focusing on questions of access, quality, finance and governance, without seeking to prise open the black box of curriculum, analysis of which is often rather descriptive and uncritical (on citizenship, see Law 2011; for more critical treatment, see Chen, 2020). Perry's observation that a "mutually advantageous state-scholar nexus" fosters "educated acquiescence" to Chinese authoritarianism applies especially to scholarship on education (Perry, 2020, p. 1).

Scholarly neglect of sensitive curricular fields, including history, is undoubtedly exacerbated by Chinese politics. But pathological incuriosity concerning the *content* of schooling extends to influential multinational bodies such as the OECD. For many observers, curriculum consists simply of knowledge and skills geared to maximising human capital. But China reminds us forcefully that the agenda of national education systems is always profoundly political, for better or worse.

3 Historical overview – the meaning of "Chineseness"

The official narrative of Chinese state formation is a teleology of ever-closer unification, culminating in the vastness of the contemporary PRC. In essence, Communist orthodoxy today, shorn of enthusiasm for class-based revolution, is similar to that of the Nationalist Kuomintang regime overthrown by the CCP in 1949. The Nationalist vision was still promulgated until the 1990s in the "Republic of China" on Taiwan, where history textbooks itemized four "special characteristics of our country's [China's] history" (quoted in Liu, Hung, & Vickers, 2005, p. 121):

1　Length: celebrating "traditions . . . passed down in an unbroken line from generation to generation" (over more than 3,000 years).
2　Assimilation of different ethnic groups (*minzu ronghe*) through "a long process of contact, intermingling and cultural exchange."
3　An emphasis on propriety, stemming from what the PRC regime today terms "our country's outstanding traditional culture" (*woguo de youxiu chuantong wenhua*).

4   A love of peace: "the Chinese are a peace-loving, warm-hearted people, . . . who have very seldom mounted armed invasions [of other countries]."

In fact, rather than smooth progress towards ever-greater unity, what we today call China has witnessed alternation between unified rule and division. While the Han, broadly speaking, trace their ancestry to the subjects of the Ming Dynasty (1368–1644), more than half of PRC territory was incorporated into the Manchu Qing Empire only during the 17th and 18th centuries, following often bloody military campaigns.

Chinese nationalism originated in the late Qing as both a Han revolt against alien Manchu overlordship and a self-strengthening drive for modernization. Han identity took a self-consciously "nationalist" form from the 1890s, as students travelled to Japan to study Asia's first successful experiment in Western-inspired modernization. There, many drank deeply at the well of Social Darwinism (Price, 2004). Spencerian evolutionary theory taught that relations between races and racialized nations were governed ultimately by the law of survival of the fittest. Progress implied the domination of superior races over "lesser breeds," with colonial empires both symbols of national virility and props for survival in a world of inveterate competition.

The influence of Social Darwinism helps explain why a Chinese nation whose shared identity is infused with memory of colonial victimhood has itself remained a determined exponent of colonialism. As the Qing Empire was succeeded by the Republic of China (ROC), anti-Manchu Han nationalists sought to cling on to the empire in its entirety. Donning the mantle of multi-ethnic pluralism, they promoted a vision of a "Five-Nation Republic" (Leibold, 2007). A Han "ethnie," rooted in the mythology and symbolism of shared ancestry (Smith, 2000), supplied the basis of national consciousness, but nationalists now sought to encompass the various ethnicities of the Qing beneath a republican carapace. Multi-ethnic statehood was acceptable, it transpired, so long as proper inter-ethnic hierarchy could be restored, with the Han on top.

In this respect, China's revolutionaries blazed a trail followed also by Russia's Bolsheviks. Soviet proclamations of "liberation" similarly served to legitimate enduring domination by the core (Russian) ethnicity over peripheral nationalities (Slezkine, 2000). The similarities became still more apparent when Soviet precedent influenced PRC minorities policy in the 1950s. Whereas the Nationalists envisioned inter-ethnic relations in blatantly hierarchical terms, the Communists proclaimed inter-ethnic equality. In practice, however, the new regime established unprecedented central control over the non-Han periphery. CCP officials meanwhile adapted the Stalinist model, envisaging an even more active, interventionist role for the state in redefining and reshaping ethnic identity (Mullaney, 2011).

Here it is pertinent to note one striking difference between China and *all* other vast, post-imperial states: both the ROC and PRC have been unitary rather than federal polities. The option of federalism was floated early in the Republican period, only to be emphatically rejected by both Nationalists and Communists (Duara, 1995). Federalist ideas were rejected precisely at a time – the early 1920s – when China was divided into sparring statelets ruled by rival warlords.

Rather than recommending federalism, this fragmentation was widely blamed for chronic vulnerability to foreign, especially Japanese, predation. Obsession with national unity and strength was further intensified by the subsequent long struggle against Japanese aggression (1931–1945).

That preoccupation in turn shaped official framing of the national past. A vulnerable China needed non-Han regions not least as buffers against malevolent imperialists. But vulnerability shaped national consciousness in more profound ways, too. Wang writes aptly of a "chosenness-myths-trauma complex" constructed around a narrative of "national humiliation" from the Opium War to the Japanese invasion (2012). The acute sense of humiliation stems ultimately from a vision – manifested in the discourse of "special national characteristics" – of China as predestined to play a special role in world history. How, then, could *this* happen to *us*?

China's Communists differentiated themselves from the Kuomintang less through consistent socialist internationalism than through a claim to be more effective champions of the national cause. Portraying old elites as locked in "semi-feudal, semi-colonial" subordination to foreign imperialists, the CCP hailed the downtrodden "productive classes" as the nation's beating heart. But in education, this rhetoric masked ongoing tension between radical egalitarianism and a pragmatic focus on fostering talent (Pepper, 1996). The Communists established "key-point high schools," restored the imperial practice of annual examinations for recruitment into the state elite, and segregated rural and urban households, with peasants tasked with securing an agricultural surplus to fund industrialization.

The Cultural Revolution (1966–1976) temporarily inverted the urban-rural hierarchy – to the enduring outrage of educated urbanites. However, in their conception of nationhood, Maoists were far less radical. With blanket rejection of "tradition" came intense xenophobia and mistrust of China's own minorities, tainted by Lamaist or Islamic feudalism. Han youth rampaged across Tibet and Xinjiang, destroying monasteries and mosques and struggling against all vestiges of reactionary thought. But even while cultural diversity was abjured and most museums closed, official support was channelled to the "Peking Man" site at Zhoukoudian, near Beijing, where hominid fossil finds buttressed claims that human life had evolved separately in China. Despite its voluble advocacy of proletarian brotherhood and global revolution, even Maoism espoused a totalizing vision of Chinese nationhood, based on blood (Schmalzer, 2009).

The homogenizing national imaginary of both Nationalists and Communists nonetheless has not gone uncontested. Especially in Taiwan and Hong Kong, new conceptions of identity, citizenship and the state itself have been invoked to challenge visions of Chineseness premised on uniform and primordial Hanness. Despite the curricular dominance of authoritarian state agendas, alternative notions of what it means to be modern and Chinese have sometimes been forcefully articulated.

Post-Mao reforms – recalibrating education for political socialization

The Maoist critique of meritocratic stratification was rapidly jettisoned after 1976, when rusticated urbanites returned to power determined to expunge leftist extremism. Nationwide college entrance examinations were reinstated, selective key-point schools re-established and "talent" prioritized. Industrial and technological modernization now overrode any commitment to egalitarianism.

The embrace of marketization and meritocracy implied recasting the Party's legitimating narrative. Sweeping denunciations of "feudal" elites became more muted in post-Mao textbooks. Signalling a less class-based, more inclusive vision of nationhood, elite figures, such as 19th-century "self-strengthening" reformers who had resisted Western imperialism, were designated national heroes (Jones, 2005). Efforts to heal the scars of Mao's mass campaigns also extended to minorities, who were permitted some recovery of their distinctive cultural life. Minorities were still treated as deficient, vis-à-vis a normative image of urban, Han and male citizenship. Nonetheless, the 1980s witnessed exceptional openness, with China, prior to Soviet *glasnost*, seeming to point the way to a milder form of Communism. As Hong Kong began its transition towards Chinese rule from 1984, many saw it as a model for the mainland's further liberalization.

But the upheaval of 1989 hardened official insistence on the imperative of control and heightened xenophobia (Fewsmith, 2012). Both the tumult of China's own Student Movement and the subsequent collapse of European Communism profoundly shocked the CCP leadership. One eventual outcome was a decision to shore up performance legitimacy through renewed commitment to market-driven economic growth. But Western sermonizing over human rights, and the disastrous spectacle of World Bank-sponsored "shock therapy" in Eastern Europe, reinforced paranoia concerning "imperialist" malevolence. Social Darwinist anxieties, never far below the surface, forcefully reasserted themselves.

Inveterate Western hostility became a major theme of the Patriotic Education Campaign, launched in the aftermath of the 1989 crackdown. Hong Kong's 1997 retrocession occasioned a flurry of anti-imperialist triumphalism. On Tiananmen Square, a countdown clock in front of the Museum of Revolutionary History measured the seconds until the territory's return to the "motherland." That museum itself recounted foreign efforts to divide, weaken and humiliate China, epitomized by the loss of Hong Kong and Taiwan. National honour and security demanded full recovery of sovereignty over both lost territories (Denton, 2014; Vickers, 2013).

Xenophobic nationalism, always present in Communist ideology, assumed centre stage as class struggle and revolution lost significance. Amidst rising social inequality, appeals to nationalism assumed heightened importance for regime legitimation. A discourse of the national situation (*guojia qingkuang*) was elaborated, emphasizing the complex and unique challenges posed by China's modernization and the need for firm and far-sighted CCP leadership and unwavering loyalty from all citizens (Jones, 2005; Vickers, 2009). No matter if some got rich more quickly; in the end, all would benefit from China's inexorable rise.

As an object lesson in the imperative of patriotism and unity, the story of the War of Resistance Against Japanese Aggression (AJW) assumed greater prominence in public culture. During the Mao era, festering tensions with the Nationalists, now confined to Taiwan, remained important. However, thawing relations with America, PRC admission to the United Nations, and erosion of National-ist dominance on Taiwan all contributed to a change of tack. Memories of the national struggle against Japan were now celebrated, both to facilitate cross-Strait reconciliation and supply a parable of patriotic unity against foreign aggression. The fundamental basis for unity was now simply shared consciousness of nation-hood itself, conceived in starkly ethnocultural terms.

So much for the ideological message, but what of its curricular delivery? The post-Mao return to the pre-Cultural Revolutionary status quo saw the re-establishment of the People's Education Press (PEP) and its monopoly of textbook publication. However, the elitist focus on "talent" generation implied a widening educational divide. Standardization and control pulled in one direction, but marketization and competition in another, especially following a late-1990s move towards fee-funded mass higher education. While the CCP preached collectivism under the banner of state-centred patriotism, the ultra-competitive logic of the education system was profoundly individuating (Woronov, 2015).

These countervailing impulses yielded parallel but seemingly contradictory poli-cies. Alongside the Patriotic Education Campaign there arose, in the 1990s, calls for enhancement of educational quality (*suzhi*). Ranging from eugenicist fretting over "population quality" to anxiety about subway etiquette, *suzhi* discourse was profoundly intertwined with the Darwinian obsessions of Chinese nationalism (Kipnis, 2006). To achieve the competitiveness on which national prosperity – even survival – depended, proponents of *suzhi* argued for curricular diversification and flexibility to encourage the most talented to reach their full potential.

The drive for quality education (*suzhi jiaoyu*) culminated in a 2001 curriculum reform that abolished PEP's monopoly under the slogan of "One syllabus, many textbooks." Shanghai had earlier experimented with locally produced school text-books; now other provinces and municipalities were granted similar autonomy. However, the sacrifice of state control was more apparent than real. Textbook vet-ting procedures became outwardly similar to those elsewhere in East Asia, but in China all competing textbook publishers remained state-owned. The reform was nonetheless cautiously welcomed by liberal-minded educators as an incremental shift away from the stultifying pedagogical emphasis on conformity and "correct thinking" (Li, 2011).

But while some invested hope in the rhetoric of pluralism and critical think-ing, more conservative elements were focused on maximizing human capital. This instrumentalist vision, rather than any humanist epiphany, gave the reforms trac-tion with senior Communist leaders. And while reformers lamented the deadening effects of examination-oriented cramming, curricular change brought no overhaul of the national testing regime. Licensed to race ahead of their peers, schools in China's most prosperous cities excelled at producing test-taking aces. Between the 2008 Beijing Olympics and the 2010 Shanghai World Expo, Shanghai's pupils notched up another competitive milestone, topping the 2009 PISA rankings.

But Shanghai also witnessed early inklings of a push-back against the 2001 reforms. In 2006, local schools began using history textbooks that embraced a cosmopolitan "global" approach somewhat distinct from the conventional nation-centred narrative. Enthusiastic endorsement from the *New York Times*, noting the absence of references to Chairman Mao, attracted adverse notice in Beijing, and the new texts were swiftly withdrawn. A conservative backlash was building, prompted partly by fears of ideological laxity and partly by misgivings amongst teachers, still overwhelmingly focused on examination preparation. Replacement textbooks for Shanghai reverted to an uplifting national narrative, adorned with plentiful images of Mao and other bygone heroes (Vickers & Yang, 2013).

Global and domestic shifts reinforced this backlash. In 2001, a triumphant post-Cold War West still seemingly offered a template for economic and technological success. Transferring Western pedagogical practice was seen as important for innovation, despite anxiety about the risks of undermining conformity. But the 2008 financial crisis and its handling by many Western liberal democracies; political unrest across the Arab World and the former Soviet sphere; and revolt in Tibet, Xinjiang and Hong Kong all strengthened the hand of CCP conservatives. So too did China's relatively successful response both to the 2008 financial crisis and the Coronavirus pandemic of 2020–2021.

Under Xi Jinping (president from 2012), the focus thus shifted from selective emulation of the West to celebration of distinctively Chinese models. This was accompanied by renewed stress on a patriotism associated with traditional Chinese values. Propagandistic use of the AJW persisted, but with enhanced emphasis on China's "victorious" contribution to the global anti-fascist struggle (Frost, Vickers, Schumacher, 2019; Mitter, 2020). Meanwhile, attempts to shape foreign views of China intensified, with concerted efforts to influence curricula and media overseas (Hamilton & Ohlberg, 2020).

All of this aligns with a new rhetorical emphasis on national self-confidence. As the latest high school *Thought and Politics* textbook puts it,

> If we ask which political party, which country, which nation can be self-confident in facing today's world, then the Chinese Communist Party, the People's Republic of China, and the Chinese nation have the greatest cause for self-confidence.
>
> (PEP, 2019a, 40)

But the very intensity of attempts to assert authoritarian political control betrays profound insecurity. Anxious concerning both popular loyalty at home and China's reception overseas, the CCP under Xi Jinping is using education to appeal to, and disseminate, a more strident and intolerant brand of nationalism that sees enemies everywhere.

4 Threats to national "stability" in the early 21st century, and the educational response

The prioritization of control permeates not just the content but also the organization of education. In what follows, I therefore discuss the "hidden curriculum" of schooling – communicated through its structures – as well as more explicit ideological messages. Justifying a profoundly unequal distribution of educational opportunity remains a central challenge for China's authorities, and their response reflects the pervasive discourse of quality (*suzhi*) alluded to earlier. Habits of differentiation by quality are relevant also to the educational treatment of minorities, repression of whom has intensified under Xi Jinping. Meanwhile, with respect to Han-dominated Hong Kong and Taiwan as well as minority regions, a narrative of foreign-inspired subversion both explains resistance to central authority and "underlines the urgency of quashing it."

Inequality, meritocracy and 'just hierarchy' – the hidden curriculum of social control

Like other industrialising societies, only faster than most, China has urbanized: over 80% rural in the 1980s, the majority of the population is now city-dwelling. Vital for propelling economic growth, mass migration to the cities has unsettled both established urbanites and a regime fixated on stability. The official response has reflected profoundly hierarchical, segregated notions of national citizenship.

Besides employment, the allure of city life lies largely in the superior quality of urban public services. Ever since the 1950s, a household registration or *hukou* system has sorted all citizens at birth into urban and rural residents. Full access to local public services is typically available only to local hukou-holders. This system bestows vast privileges on formal residents of megacities like Beijing and Shanghai. With elite schools concentrated in the largest cities, educational advantages pertaining to urban hukou are the object of particular envy.

In confining migrant workers to second-class urban citizenship on the basis of birth, the *hukou* system has proven increasingly hard to defend. But rather than tackling the thorny problem of stratified entitlements head-on, the regime has sought a new basis for legitimating them. New "transparent" application procedures for urban residence and school places entrench segregation on grounds of merit-based "quality." The outcome has been characterized as "meritocratic apartheid" (Wan & Vickers, 2021).

The mechanism for this meritocratic segregation is ostensibly similar to points-based immigration systems in use around the world, but applied in this instance to the ranking and sorting of fellow-nationals. The result has been "new forms of educational and social stratification, aimed at increasing control over migrant selectivity" (Dong & Goodburn, 2020, p. 1). This is one aspect of a much larger project of governance by assessment and monitoring, extending to a new system of 'social credit' designed to 'score' citizens' behaviour for the application of rewards or sanctions. A state-mandated programme of 'genomic surveillance' (first piloted in Tibet and Xinjiang) is meanwhile harvesting the DNA of all male citizens (Dirks & Leibold, 2020).

Points systems determine not only access but also the type or level of school migrant children can attend. They remain largely segregated from local hukou-holders in separate public schools or school branches. At high school level, those permitted to continue their education locally are mostly channelled into the low-status vocational track, otherwise shunned by urban residents (Woronov, 2015).

Informing governance by assessment are beliefs concerning suzhi or "quality" also reflected in curricular content, which establishes an urban, Han and male benchmark of "advanced," "scientific" culture. Inspection of the most recent (2017–2019) crop of textbooks indicates that, if anything, this bias has strengthened: minorities are largely invisible; women invariably subordinate; and peasants backward and dependent on guidance from the party-state. Meanwhile, since the 1990s, a policy of concentrating rural schooling in county towns, particularly at secondary level, has facilitated dissemination of urban norms, causing many peasants to internalize a vision of themselves as deficient in suzhi. The aim is to "turn peasants into modern Chinese citizens" who know their place in a hierarchically ordered society geared towards state-determined goals (Murphy, 2004).

The success of this strategy relies upon both persuasion and intimidation. Technologically assisted surveillance and stringent sanctions supply the latter. But alongside fear, propaganda also inspires hope in a vision of an ever-stronger and more prosperous nation. As the latest high school text for Thought and Politics puts it, "For a country to be strong, the economic system must also be strong" (PEP, 2019b: 38). Economic strength in turn depends on the "unwavering consolidation and development of a state-managed economy" (8). A strong and efficient state ruled by law and unswervingly loyal to the CCP is required to counter the twin menaces of subversion and corruption (PEP, 2019c: Chapter 9). The welfare of all Chinese thus flows ultimately from the party-state, which ensures just and adequate provision of public goods (PEP, 2019b, 44–56). But citizens should avoid emulating profligate Europeans, who burden their states with unsustainable expectations of "high welfare" (PEP, 2019b, 55). Patriotic Chinese are animated less by self-centred talk of personal "rights" than by consciousness of their "duties" (PEP, 2017a, pp. 31–58).

Renewed emphasis on the imperative of a strong state is reflected also in the textbook production apparatus. The 2001 move towards qualified textbook pluralism was substantially reversed in 2017, with all texts for Chinese language, history, "Morals and Rule by Law" (at junior high) and "Thought and Politics" (at senior high) now once again published by PEP in Beijing.

Accompanying this reassertion of central curricular control is enhanced emphasis on the virtues of concentrated state power, manifested most obviously in a Xi Jinping leadership cult. A high school text on "Socialism with Chinese Characteristics" concludes by detailing the "new era" of Xi Jinping, whose thinking must guide China's fate over the long term (PEP, 2019a: 55–61). Xi's signature slogan, "The Chinese Dream of the Great Revival of the Chinese Nation" (Figure 3.1) is portrayed as the culmination of an epochal struggle to "save" China, dating back to the Opium War. But while the text avers that "only socialism can save China" (20), the emphasis on "revival" is grounded in the vision of a proud and ancient civilization brought low: "The culture of socialism with Chinese characteristics originates in the superior Chinese traditional culture nurtured during the more than five-thousand-year history of the Chinese nation" (39). Socialism in today's China is associated not with egalitarianism, but with hierarchical ordering of a citizenry exhorted to conflate their interests with those of the nation, as defined and embodied by the Communist leadership.

Figure 3.1 Propaganda poster promoting the 'Chinese Dream' (Shanghai, 2017). The slogan reads: "Country as Family; A spirit of happiness; diligence as the core; frugality nurturing virtue; sincere behaviour; lawful conduct; prioritising filial piety; treasuring harmony."

Inter-ethnic strife and the educational response

The identification of socialist nationhood with five millennia of implicitly Han culture poses awkward questions for the status of non-Han minorities. A chapter on "Civilization and Home" in the 2017 *Morals and Rule by Law* Year 9 text depicts four children in ethnic costumes describing different ethnic festivals (PEP, 2017b, p. 58). But the text then emphasizes Chinese uniqueness and ethical superiority in homogenous and totalizing terms: "China's unique cultural tradition, unique historical destiny and unique basic national conditions determine our adherence to values rooted in the fertile soil of Chinese culture, and to the values of Socialism with Chinese Characteristics" (70). Patriotism is represented diagrammatically as the ethical core (67), and the importance of "cultural self-confidence" is relentlessly emphasized. Adopting a strikingly biological metaphor, China's "superior traditional culture" is portrayed as a "gene" (*jiyin*) "rooted in the heart of the Chinese people, subtly influencing their thought and behaviour" (70; see also Yan, 2020).

The condescension and suspicion nowadays directed at minorities contrast with trends in the early post-Mao years, when a more mutually respectful vision of Han-minority relations was articulated (Yan & Vickers, 2019). Informed by new developments in archaeology, the narrative of China's origins officially promoted during the 1980s and 1990s emphasized plurality and diversity, albeit within a teleology of ever-greater unity. Non-Han regimes were included in the dynastic register, and their cultural attainments acknowledged. In particular, the Mongol and Manchu "conquest dynasties" were portrayed more sympathetically and non-Han figures, including Genghis Khan, celebrated as national heroes. The narrative remained highly selective, mostly ignoring or glossing over periods when the ties of peripheral regions to the Chinese state were weak or non-existent. But while the ultimate objective remained legitimation of Communist rule, non-Han cultures were accorded greater respect than hitherto.

Signs of resurgent Han chauvinism followed the reforms of 2001 (Yan & Vickers, 2019). Official nervousness over any hint of minority subversion had been reinforced by Soviet and Yugoslav fragmentation, as well as by continued rumblings of discontent among Tibetans and Uyghurs. Meanwhile, rapid economic growth and patriotic boosterism both fuelled Han pride and alienated minorities, whose sense of economic as well as cultural marginalization intensified.

Despite the post-Mao abandonment of egalitarianism, the influence of Marxian historical materialism endured. CCP elites, apparently believing their own propaganda, assumed that once the benefits of "advanced" civilization had percolated to peripheral regions, inter-ethnic tensions would dissipate. A "Great Western Development Strategy," launched in 1999, promised to accelerate this process. Meanwhile, expanded boarding programmes for Tibetan and Uyghur youth in inland (*neidi*) high schools sought to hasten assimilation, although minority students, like many rural migrants, were typically confined to segregated campuses (Leibold & Chen, 2014).

However, discontent in Tibet and Xinjiang was exacerbated rather than quelled by a development strategy widely perceived as benefiting ethnic Han settlers and entrepreneurs. Violent unrest in Tibet in 2008 was followed, in 2009, by conflict in Xinjiang, sparked by attacks on migrant Uyghur workers in prosperous Guangdong Province (another instance of the overlap between migrant and minority categories

Figure 3.2 Benevolent Uncle Xi and grateful ethnic minorities, Minorities Culture Palace, Beijing, 2019.

on the margins of Chinese society). In response, the regime intensified propaganda hailing the developmental achievements of Communist rule. In mid-2008, Beijing's Minorities Culture Palace mounted an exhibition celebrating Tibet's liberation from lamaist medievalism and the manifold benefits of CCP rule – from roads and railways to schools and hospitals. Such messages are directed at the Han majority at least as much as at minorities themselves, with official praise for "outstanding traditional Chinese culture," both reinforcing and responding to rising Han chauvinism in popular culture (Carrico, 2017) (see Figure 3.2).

Widespread belief in the innate backwardness of minorities has fuelled growing Han resentment at their ingratitude for the redemptive efforts of the party-state (Leibold, 2014). Harsh repression of Tibetans and Uyghurs, when discussed at all within China, appears widely endorsed. Following the unrest of 2008–2009, and a spate of attacks in the early 2010s linked to Uyghur separatists, China's restive western regions witnessed severe crackdowns. In Xinjiang, a vast network of concentration camps was established, with the declared aim of "re-educating" Muslims of supposedly suspect loyalty.

Meanwhile, longstanding guarantees of cultural and educational distinctiveness have been rescinded or drastically curtailed. Inmates of Xinjiang's camps are forced to speak Mandarin and forbidden religious observance – a prohibition increasingly applied beyond the camp gates (Elborzi, 2020). Provision of bilingual instruction in Mandarin and minority languages during the compulsory phase of schooling has been significantly eroded, even for communities long reconciled to Chinese rule. In 2020, parents and students in parts of Inner Mongolia mounted a short-lived school boycott after textbooks for literature, previously taught in Mongolian, were replaced with PEP texts in Mandarin. History, morals and politics texts were scheduled to follow suit (Wu, 2020).

What survives of multiculturalism is an increasingly hollow shell. In 2015, PEP published a six-volume set of supplementary textbooks on *China's Outstanding Traditional Culture* for junior high schools. This feature isolated units dealing selectively with non-Han "ethnic customs" (*minzu fengqing*). The section on the Uyghurs, for instance, highlights their love of singing and dancing, traditional clothing and culinary specialities. While failing to mention Islam, the text hails Uyghur contributions to "opposing imperialist invasion" and "preserving the unity of the motherland" (Ye, 2015: 34), suggesting that the dominant aim is to admonish rather than inform.

The unfinished business of national unification: Hong Kong and Taiwan

For decades after 1949, the championing of China's "outstanding traditional culture" was in fact the preserve of the CCP's opponents. Confronting socialist barbarism or the indignity of colonial subjugation, both Taiwan's Nationalists and exiled traditionalists in Hong Kong saw themselves as keepers of the sacred flame of Chineseness (Kan, Vickers, & Morris, 2007). School curricula in these societies propagated a chauvinist vision divorced both from the local context and the contemporary mainland. Hong Kong's curricular bastions of Chineseness – the Chinese history and literature subjects – were hotly defended by critics of the colonial authorities. Most Hongkongers, like Taiwan's "mainlander" elites, claimed a more authentic Chineseness than that of the Communists.

But from the 1980s, this Chinese identity "in the abstract" steadily wilted on exposure to mainland reality, prompting frustration and incomprehension in Beijing. Ironically, it was precisely the experience (for Hong Kong) or threat (for Taiwan) of reunification that fuelled growing alienation from China. A pivotal moment came in 1989, when violent repression of China's Student Movement coincided with a largely peaceful transition to democracy in Taiwan. As the CCP claimed custodianship of "outstanding traditional culture" – invading ideological territory previously occupied by its opponents – young Hongkongers and Taiwanese increasingly rejected the equation of Chinese culture or ethnicity with nationality.

In Hong Kong, pro-Beijing elements insisted that the deracinating influence of colonialism be purged by a hefty dose of national education. Following a decade of gradually intensifying patriotic indoctrination after 1997, mainland officials voiced impatience at the lack of progress in transforming local consciousness. In 2012, the authorities sought to introduce a new compulsory school subject, moral and national education (MNE), only to back down following widespread public uproar spearheaded by secondary students themselves (Morris & Vickers, 2015).

The history of KMT rule in Taiwan had already demonstrated the power of lived experience to undermine even the most forceful campaign of nationalist indoctrination. There, four decades of martial law were followed by the rapid unravelling of nationalist orthodoxy, as native Taiwanese, long marginalized by mainlander elites, sought to articulate a multicultural identity distinct from China. Early 21st-century Hong Kong witnessed a similarly visceral rejection of a homogenizing vision of Chineseness. That this sentiment was strongest among youngsters with no memory of colonial rule was due in part to their declining economic prospects. Whereas Hongkongers formerly disdained their rustic, mainland country cousins, the young now found themselves disadvantaged in competition for credentials and employment with well-heeled immigrants from across the border.

But unlike the Nationalists in 1980s Taiwan, Communists in Hong Kong today do not rely on the consent of the governed. Confined to its island redoubt, the Kuomintang was ultimately forced to adapt its nationalist fantasies to Taiwanese reality. By contrast, its decreasing economic and strategic importance to Beijing gives Hong Kong little prospect of similarly transforming its rulers. And whether or not Communist efforts at thought reform are effective within Hong Kong itself, CCP policy is dictated above all by fear that unsuppressed dissent there may infect the mainland. Moreover, Beijing's control of immigration into the region, along with a likely exodus of many local-born residents, means that demographic change may gradually accomplish the aim of "dissolving the people" and remaking Hong Kong in the mainland's image (Turner, 1995).

The 2020 National Security Law imposed on Hong Kong by Beijing mandates "national security education." Determined to erase the humiliation of the 2012 MNE fiasco, the government swiftly signalled its intent to instil "a sense of identity, belonging and responsibility towards the nation, the Chinese race, and our society" (Kwan, 2020). Measures announced in the November 2020 Policy Address included an enhanced programme of tours to the mainland for primary and secondary students, which by promoting understanding of "the essence of Chinese culture" would nurture "moral character and cultural identity." Teachers' quality would meanwhile be enhanced through stronger training in ethics, character and conduct. A liberal studies subject compulsory at secondary level since 2009, which aimed to encourage critical discussion of current affairs, was renamed Citizenship and Social Development and reoriented towards instruction in patriotism, national development and lawfulness (Chan & Magramo, 2021).

Invoking loyalty to "the nation, the Chinese race, and our society" is a long-established trope of national education rhetoric (Vickers, 2011). The official lexicon defines Hong Kong as a mere society; identity derives from nationhood, imagined as a blood-bond. Identical tropes are deployed by the CCP in relation to Taiwan (Vickers, 2021). Moreover, the logic of this vision of nationality implies profound ambivalence regarding the status of ethnic Chinese citizens of other states. A 2019 exhibition at the National Museum of China, commemorating the 70th anniversary of the PRC's establishment, celebrated the contribution to the Communist Revolution of overseas Chinese in Southeast Asia, deploying imagery of roots to imply that their primary loyalty was to the ancestral motherland rather than to the societies of which they are citizens. For China's 21st century Communist ideologues, blood is destiny.

5 Conclusion

This emphasis on ancestry conforms to central themes of the national narrative as conveyed through the latest PRC history textbooks. Like previous editions, these commence with discussion of Peking Man and the legendary Yan and Yellow Emperors (Yandi and Huangdi), even while highlighting the distinction between "myth" and historical "fact" (PEP, 2016, pp. 12–16). The terminology "descendants of Yan and Huang [emperors]" (*Yan Huang zisun*) is used to denote the "Chinese race-nation" (*zhonghua minzu/huaren*), depicted as deriving from an ancient fusion of various tribes. Although the text refrains from explicitly claiming Peking Man as the ancestor of modern Chinese, an ancestral link is implied, as the primordial origins of an ethnically cohesive China are asserted.

Meanwhile, plural, multi-ethnic conceptions of Chinese nationhood, always somewhat marginal, have become increasingly so in the early 21st century. The CCP today is more determined than ever to invoke nationalism to legitimate its absolute authority. The orthodox national narrative blends paranoia over malign foreign imperialism with triumphalism over China's "outstanding traditional culture" and the achievements of the contemporary People's Republic. The people who form the narrative subject are defined no longer in terms of class, but of shared ancestry and culture. Nationhood is available to the residents of Hong Kong and Taiwan, and to the mainland's ethnic minorities, only as citizens of the PRC.

If for Hongkongers and Taiwanese this means accepting ancestrally bestowed destiny, recalcitrant ethnic minorities increasingly face a choice between assimilation and eradication. Alongside forcible re-education, restriction of religious observance and destruction of heritage, the Xinjiang authorities have reportedly conducted forced sterilizations of Uyghur women (Zenz, 2020). This is an extreme manifestation of a broader drive to marginalize minority languages and cultures, with the aim of accelerating assimilation to a monolithic Han cultural template.

Chinese nationalism thus remains far from banal, as the CCP intensifies the internal colonization not only of minority regions, Hong Kong and Taiwan, but also of the peasantry and the migrant underclass in the cities. Meritocracy, hierarchy and regimentation are crucial ingredients of the ideological mix. Just as minorities must conform to the "advanced" model of urban Han modernity, so the Han themselves are increasingly assessed and ranked for various purposes, marking them for rewards or sanctions dispensed by the state. Meritocracy justifies a hierarchical ordering of the national body, subordinated ultimately to the party-state. Repression, surveillance and constant assessment may perhaps become banal once embedded in Orwellian routine, but state violence implies that identification with the CCP definition of nationhood is far from taken for granted.

Moreover, as Carrico argues in his study of popular Han nationalist activism, nationalism derives much of its force and appeal not from banal structures or habits, but from fantasy, passion and spectacle. Xi Jinping's "Chinese Dream" is the latest in a long series of campaigns to dramatize the national story and foment patriotic enthusiasm (Carrico, 2017, p. 23). Besides schooling, the state deploys monumental public museums, pageants (such as the 2008 Olympic opening ceremony), festivals, parades and the full range of modern media to render Chineseness exciting and glamorous.

Elements of the vision thus articulated have strong appeal for many at the top of the national pecking order: educated, urban Han Chinese. This is enhanced by the sense that, under Xi Jinping, a rejuvenated China is at last resuming its proper place in the global hierarchy of nations. But an educational approach that seeks to flatten China's vast diversity – through intensifying regimentation, strengthening autocracy and demands for absolute obedience to a leadership embodying a racialized nation – threatens to exacerbate domestic and international tensions. In 2016, the political scientist Stein Ringen suggested evolution into "the perfect fascist state" as one of five possible scenarios for China's medium-term future (Ringen, 2016, p. 174). That scenario looks increasingly close to realization.

References

Bell, D., & Wang, P. (2020). *Just hierarchy*. Princeton, NJ: Princeton University Press.

Carrico, K. (2017). *The Great Han*. Oakland: University of California Press.

Chan, H., & Magramo, K. (2021, March 31). Hong Kong's liberal studies to be renamed "citizenship and social development" as part of massive overhaul. *South China Morning Post*.

Chen, S. (2020). Rethinking citizenship and citizenship education in contemporary China: Discourses and politics. *Chinese Education and Society, 53*(1–2), 3–13.

Denton, K. (2014). *Exhibiting the past*. Honolulu: Hawaii University Press.

Dikotter, F. (1991). The discourse of race in modern China. London: Hurst.

Dirks, E., & Leibold, J. (2020). *Genomic surveillance: Inside China's DNA dragnet*. Canberra: Australian Strategic Policy Institute.

Dong, Y., & Goodburn, C. (2020). Residence permits and points systems: New forms of educational and social stratification in urban China. *Journal of Contemporary China, 29*(125), 647–666.

Duara, P. (1995). *Rescuing history from the nation*. Chicago, IL: Chicago University Press.

Elborzi, A. (2020, March 2). Surveillance, repression and reeducation in China's Xinjiang Uyghur Autonomous Region. *SOAS Blog*. Retrieved March 10, 2021, from https://

study.soas.ac.uk/surveillance-repression-and-re-education-in-chinas-xinjiang-uyghur-autonomous-region/.

Esherick, J., Kayali, H., & Van Young, E. (2006). *Empire to nation*. Lanham: Rowman and Littlefield.

Fewsmith, J. (2012). *China since Tiananmen*. Cambridge: Cambridge University Press.

Frost, M., Vickers, E., & Schumacher, D. (2019). Introduction: Locating Asia's war memory boom. In M. Frost, E. Vickers, & D. Schumacher (Eds.), *Remembering Asia's world war two* (pp. 1–24). London and New York: Routledge.

Gellner, E. (1983). *Nations and nationalism*. Ithaca, NY: Cornell University Press.

Goode, P. (2020). Guest editor's introduction: "Everyday nationalism in world politics: Agents, contexts and scale. *Nationalism Papers*, 48(6), 974–982.

Hamilton, C., & Ohlberg, M. (2020). *Hidden hand: Exposing how the Chinese Communist Party is reshaping the world*. London: Oneworld.

Harrison, H. (2001). *Inventing the nation: China*. London: Arnold.

Hughes, C. (2006). *Chinese nationalism in the global era*. London and New York: Routledge.

Jones, A. (2005). Changing the past to serve the present: History education in Mainland China. In E. Vickers & A. Jones (Eds.), *History education and national identity in East Asia* (pp. 65–100). New York, NY and London: Routledge.

Joniak-Lüthi, A. (2015). *The Han: China's diverse majority*. Seattle, WA: University of Washington Press.

Kan, F., Vickers, E., & Morris, P. (2007). Keepers of the sacred flame: Patriotism, politics and the Chinese history subject community in Hong Kong. *Cambridge Journal of Education*, 37(2), 229–247.

Kipnis, A. (2006). Suzhi: A keyword approach. *The China Quarterly*, No. 186, 295–313.

Kwan, R. (2020, November 26). Policy address 2020: Hong Kong education to instil Chinese belonging and identity; quality of teachers to be "enhanced". *Hong Kong Free Press*. Retrieved January 10, 2020, from www.hongkongfp.com.

Leibold, J. (2007). *Reconfiguring Chinese nationalism*. New York, NY: Palgrave Macmillan.

Leibold, J. (2014). Han Chinese reactions to preferential minority education in the PRC. In J. Leibold & Y. B. Chen (Eds.), *Minority education in China* (pp. 299–319). Hong Kong: Hong Kong University Press.

Leibold, J., & Chen, Y. (Eds.). (2014). *Minority education in China*. Hong Kong: Hong Kong University Press.

Li, F. (2011). New curriculum reform and history textbook compilation in contemporary China. In G. Muller (Ed.), *Designing history in East Asian textbooks* (pp. 137–146). London and New York, NY: Routledge.

Liu, M., Hung, L., & Vickers, E. (2005). Identity issues in Taiwan's history curriculum. In E. Vickers & A. Jones (Eds.), *History education and national identity in East Asia* (pp. 101–132). London and New York, NY: Routledge.

Mitter, R. (2020). *China's good war*. Cambridge, MA: Harvard University Press.

Moloughney, B., & Zarrow, P. (2011). *Transforming history: The making of a modern academic discipline in twentieth-century China*. Hong Kong: Chinese University of Hong Kong Press.

Morris, P., & Vickers, E. (2015). Schooling, politics and the construction of identity in Hong Kong: The 2012 "Moral and National Education" crisis in historical context. *Comparative Education*, 51(3), 305–326.

Mullaney, T. (2011). *Coming to terms with the nation*. Berkeley: University of California Press.

Murphy, R. (2004). Turning peasants into modern Chinese citizens. *The China Quarterly*, 177, 1–20.

PEP. (2016). *Zhongguo Lishi (Chinese history)*, Year 7, Vol. 1. Beijing: People's Education Press.

PEP. (2017a). *Daode yu fazhi (Morals and rule by law)*, Year 8, Vol. 2. Beijing: People's Education Press.

PEP. (2017b). *Daode yu fazhi (Morals and rule by law)*, Year 9, Vol. 1. Beijing: People's Education Press.

PEP. (2019a). *Sixiang Zhengzhi: Bixiu 1 – Zhongguo tese shehuizhuyi (Thought and politics: Compulsory course vol. 1 – socialism with Chinese characteristics)*. Beijing: People's Education Press.

PEP. (2019b). *Sixiang Zhengzhi: Bixiu 2 – Jingji yu Shehui (Thought and politics: Compulsory course vol. 2 – economy and society)*. Beijing: People's Education Press.

PEP. (2019c). *Sixiang Zhengzhi: Bixiu 3 – Zhengzhi yu Fazhi (Thought and politics: Compulsory course vol. 3 – politics and rule by law)*. Beijing: People's Education Press.

Pepper, S. (1996). *Radicalism and education reform in twentieth-century China*. Cambridge: Cambridge University Press.

Perry, E. (2020). Educated acquiescence: How academia sustains authoritarianism in China. *Theory and Society, 49*, 1–22.

Price, D. (2004). From might to right: Liang Qichao and the comforts of darwinism in late-Meiji Japan. In J. A. Fogel (Ed.), *The role of Japan in Liang Qichao's introduction of modern western civilization to China* (pp. 68–102). Berkeley: University of California Institute of East Asian Studies.

Ringen, S. (2016). *The perfect dictatorship*. Hong Kong: Hong Kong University Press.

Schmalzer, S. (2009). *The people's Peking man: Popular science and human identity in 20th-century China*. Chicago, IL: Chicago University Press.

Slezkine, Y. (2000). The USSR as a communal apartment. In S. Fitzpatrick (Ed.), *Stalinism: New directions* (pp. 313–347). New York, NY and London: Routledge.

Smith, A. D. (2000). *The nation in history*. Cambridge: Polity Press.

Turner, M. (1995). 60s/90s: Dissolving the people. In *Hong Kong's cultural identity* (pp. 13–36). Hong Kong: Hong Kong Arts Centre.

Vickers, E. (2009). Selling socialism with Chinese characteristics: 'Thought and Politics' and the legitimisation of China's developmental strategy. *International Journal of Educational Development, 29*(5), 523–531.

Vickers, E. (2011). Learning to love the motherland. In G. Muller (Ed.), *Designing history in East Asian textbooks* (pp. 85–116). London and New York, NY: Routledge.

Vickers, E. (2013). Transcending victimhood: Japan in the public historical museums of Taiwan and the People's Republic of China., *China Perspectives, 2013*(4), 17–28.

Vickers, E. (2021). Three faces of an Asian hero: Commemorating Koxinga in contemporary China, Taiwan and Japan. In C. Shei (Ed.), *Taiwan: Manipulation of ideology and struggle for identity*. London and New York, NY: Routledge.

Vickers, E., & Yang, B. (2013). Shanghai's history curriculum reforms and shifting textbook portrayals of Japan. *China Perspectives*, (2013/4), 29. doi:https://doi.org/10.4000/chinaperspectives.6317

Vickers, E., & Zeng, X. (2017). *Education and society in post-Mao China*. New York, NY and London: Routledge.

Wan, Y., & Vickers, E. (2021). Towards meritocratic apartheid? Points systems and migrant access to urban Chinese public schools. *The China Quarterly* (forthcoming).

Wang, Z. (2012). *Never forget national humiliation*. New York, NY: Columbia University Press.

Woronov, T. (2015). *Class work*. Stanford University Press.

Wu, H. (2020, September 2). Students in inner Mongolia protest Chinese language policy. *The Diplomat*. Retrieved January 7, 2021, from www.thediplomat.com.

Yan, F. (2020). Competition or cooperation: Configuring "International" in Chinese school textbooks. In UNESCO-APCEIU, *International understanding and cooperation in education in the post-Corona world* (pp. 87–116). Seoul: UNESCO-APCEIU.

Yan, F., & Vickers, E. (2019). Portraying "minorities" in Chinese history textbooks of the 1990s and 2000s: The advance and retreat of ethnocultural inclusivity. *Asia-Pacific Journal of Education, 39*(2), 190–208.

Ye, L. (2015). Zhonghua Youxiu Chuantong Wenhua (Chinese superior traditional culture). Year 9, Volume 1. Beijing: PEP.

Zenz, A. (2020). Sterilizations, IUDs and mandatory birth control: The CCP's campaign to suppress uyghur birthrates in Xinjiang. Washington, DC: The Jamestown Foundation.

4 Modern education and national identity in Greece and Egypt

(Re)producing the ancient in the school textbook

Theodore G. Zervas and Ehaab D. Abdou

In this chapter we attempt to compare and contrast major educational developments, especially as manifested in curricular and textbook content, in Greece and Egypt to demonstrate how national identities are shaped in schools, especially through the teaching of ancient history.

Ancient history is a historiographical construct. Thus, we focus especially on how these two Mediterranean nation-states narrate and label their respective histories as "ancient" in an attempt to transfer and reinforce national identity and loyalty via the celebration of ancient exceptionalism. Given that we are guided by Billig's constructivist approach, which holds narrative as central to the process of national identity formation, we find it appropriate to analyze history textbook content in these two contexts to unpack the narratives constructed to narrate those countries' ancient histories. Further, we attempt to analyze the dynamics shaping continuities and changes, and what interests and visions they might have served.

In both cases we analyzed textbooks from 1952 to the present, as for both countries the mid-20th century marked a significant turning point. For Greece it was the end of the Greek Civil War, in which the conservative Greek government army, supported by the United Kingdom and the United States, defeated the Democratic Army of Greece (DSE), the military branch of the Communist Party of Greece (KKE). For Egypt, it was the rise of Gamal Abdel Nasser, the leader of the popular *coup d'état* to overthrow the Muhammad Ali Royal Dynasty along with King Farouk, president of Egypt from 1954 until his death in 1970. By the 1960s both countries struggled socially and politically. A *coup d'état* in Greece in 1967 led to a military dictatorship by a group of army colonels, while Egypt witnessed a revival of pan-Arabism and a war with Israel. The 1970s and 1980s marked the end of the military dictatorship and a reinstatement of a parliamentary democracy in Greece. This same period marked the rise of Anwar Sadat and a peace deal with Israel in Egypt. By the 1990s and the first two decades of the 21st century, social and political unrest in Greece (fuelled by global debt-crises) and two major political revolutions in Egypt led both countries to reconsider the essence of their "nation" in general and how their national histories were to be taught in their schools, sometimes in subtle ways and sometimes in more explicit ways.

DOI: 10.4324/9781003137801-6

This chapter is divided into several sections. The first two sections are a discussion on historical consciousness, how the nation is imagined and reimagined and the role that nation-states play in individual and collective identity formation. Following these sections, we look at how Greece and Egypt considered their ancient pasts when constructing their own national histories, especially in their curricula and textbooks. Thus, the chapter provides an extensive discussion of the teaching of history in both countries. Several textbooks are analyzed to show how ancient histories are represented in each of these countries. Given that there have been only a few studies that examine how nations construct and (re)present ancient histories, this chapter aims to make a contribution to this generally understudied question.

1 Theoretical perspectives

History education and historical consciousness

National identities essentially act as appeals for legitimacy, and it is not least through the medium of the school that nation-states reinforce national identities. Thereby, as Eric Hobsbawm and Terrence Ranger (1993) demonstrate, nation-states sometimes invent traditions or twist the truth about their history to secure their place in the world. They also argue that nation-creation is an ongoing project in which both recent and aged nation-states continually construct ties between the past and the present in order to justify their respective existences and unite their populations. The constructivist theory of nationalism pursued by scholars such as Billig and Özkırımlı challenges the notion that there is a pre-existing characteristic that brings people together to define a nation (Billig, 1995; Özkırımlı, 2017). Rather, it is the recognition of a common bond, relying heavily on national symbols and signs, that legitimizes the nation.

Historical consciousness has an especially important role to play in nation and state formation. It helps shape "historical identity," formed through the cumulative "representation of historical events" including events that hold a "positive founding or constituting function" or "chains of events" transmitted through the generations (Rüsen, 2005, p. 193). The concept of 'identity' as Billig reminds us, is reinforced through representations of national symbols, which build a sense of belonging for those who feel that they are part of a nation (Billig, 1995, p. 40). However, there have been some useful formulations of historical and narrative identities. French philosopher Paul Ricoeur argues that narratives are an integral part of shaping identity. He introduced the concept of 'narrative identity,' stressing how it "allows various, different, partly contradictory circumstances and experiences to be integrated into a coherent temporal structure, thus making it possible to sketch a person's identity" (cited in Wodak, de Cillia, Reisigl, Rodger, & Liebhart, 2009, p. 14).

Recent literature focusing on the nation has found that while nationalism may be politically motivated, the state is not necessary for nation creation. Veronica Maricic's recent textbook study on Scotland found that Scotland as a nation without a state did not need to be a state in order for a Scottish national identity to take shape in the wake of the Union of Parliaments in 1707 (Maricic, 2020). We see similar phenomena in various other contexts whereby such national identity sentiments fuel calls for separation and self-determination, such as in the case of Quebec in Canada and with the Catalan and Basque peoples in Spain. On the other hand, Nicole Gotling's (2020) study on the treatment of the Prussian Wars (1864–1871) in history and geography textbooks in Austria, Denmark, France and Germany showed how each of these nations, states or nation-states treated the same set of historical events differently and how they "developed their own historiographies and narratives for textbooks and other teaching materials (such as maps) . . . in ways which remained relevant to the developing nation-state's trajectory" (p. 67). Similarly, Kevser Muratović and Florian Gimpl's study found that two new nation-states (Austria and Turkey), both emerging from the First World War out of multi-ethnic empires, understood the modern concepts of nation and nationalism very differently from one another (Muratović & Gimpl, 2020).

An excellent contemporary example was Greece's insistence that the former Yugoslav Republic of Macedonia (FYROM) change its official constitutional name, "The Republic of Macedonia," to one that ensured a rupture with an Ancient Macedonian past. The "Macedonian Issue" (*To Makedoniko*) was seen by many Greeks as threatening Greece's territorial sovereignty and national identity, thus creating political tensions between Greece and the Republic of Macedonia.

In discussing the discursive construction of national identity in Austria, Wodak et al. (2009) stress the significance of such argument in establishing that identities are dynamic and variable as well as easily manipulated by manipulating historical narratives. Rüsen (2005) captures a similar concept of how historical narratives shape subjectivities. Through the uniquely human ability of temporal connection of the past, present and future, Rüsen (2005) argues that humans gain a "historical identity," allowing individuals to identify themselves as "part of a temporal whole larger than that of his/her personal life" (p. 25). In his model, historical identity of individuals evolves from the traditional type where a self-understanding "is imprinted by tradition" and progresses into an identity shaped by "fragile balance engendered by multidimensional, multiperspectival genetic forms" (p. 36). Like Wodak et al. (2009), he elaborates on the connection between this historical identity and national identity. In an argument reminiscent of Anderson's (2006) and Hobsbawm's and Rangers' (1993) arguments of how nations and national identification are built on visions of the past, oftentimes infused with strong mythical elements, Rüsen (2005) argues that "a more familiar example of such 'temporal immortality' (as historical identity can be characterized) is national identity. Nations often locate their wellsprings in a hoary and ancient past, and project an unlimited future perspective embodying national self-assertion and development" (p. 26).

Constructing historical narratives of ancient histories

Several scholars have shown how historical narratives have long been constructed – or manipulated – to control populations in different ways. For instance, informed by his constructivist approach, Billig emphasizes the key role that narratives play in forming and shaping national identities. According to Billig, "[If] national uniformity removed, a variety of national forces is released. Within the national territory, multiple narratives and new identities are emerging" (Billig, 1995, p. 133). Thus, these multiple narratives make it even more difficult to control populations or unite them around a common history.

Although adopting more of a modernist understanding of nations and national identities, in his seminal book *Imagined Communities*, Benedict Anderson (2006) shed light on how historical narratives, including their constructions of ancient civilizations, have been a tool that was manipulated by modern colonizing forces in their efforts to distance locals from a sense of greatness or self-confidence. For both Billig and Anderson, nonetheless, contemporary nation-states and their ruling elites construct and re-construct their histories to fulfil particular interests and purposes through essentializing particular cultural identities as well as normalizing economic and political structures and social constructs.

In the last few decades, the world has arguably become more isolationist, and the policies of governments in many nation-states have become more nationalist. As noted earlier, Benedict Anderson's (2006) arguments ring true today as they help explain how nation-sates around the world continue to revise their national curricula and national histories to help unite their people around a common national identity. This is true in India, where some textbooks and curricula have been revised to promote a Hindu history, slowly remaking India into an essentially Hindu nation (Traub, 2018).

Ernest Gellner helped formulate the idea that the nation was an artificially constructed or fabricated concept, and that nations and nationalism were often shaped by historical events (Gellner, 2009). Similar to Gellner, Thongchai Winichakul argued that there was nothing inherent or pre-existing about the nation (Winichakul, 1997). He agreed with both Anderson and Gellner that the nation was an imagined community. Furthermore, Winichakul finds that nationalism is dependent on its physical geography, demarcated by its borders. According to Thongchai, borders and territory help define the nation and set the limits to national identity (Winichakul, 1997). Billig and Özkırımlı, who pursue constructivism, find that the nation is not pre-existing, and that any ethnic, racial or ideological commonality that exists within a group of people is artificially constructed (Billig, 1995; Özkırımlı, 2017). Eric Hobsbawm (2012), a proponent of this idea, argued that national identity is constructed and transmitted to people through sources such as government-regulated institutions like public schools. Through the school, people are taught about their national past and their national identity. They learn to feel that they are part of a broader community that shares a supposedly unique character and common heritage, distinguishing between those who are part of their nation and those who are not.

Drawing especially on the constructivist theorizations about the nation (e.g., Billig, 1995), we turn to the contexts of Greece and Egypt. Similar to other contexts, a national history is extremely important to constructing national identities in both Greece and Egypt. As we demonstrate in this chapter, these two contexts clearly share commonalities with and differences from other contexts in the ways they construct and imagine their ancient histories. We liken both their nationalisms – shaped by various institutions and ideological movements – to the symbolism found in Egyptian-born Greek poet Constantine Cavafy's poem "An Old Man:" nostalgic yet hopeful, deceptive yet honest (Cavafy, 1976).

In the two contexts, the constructions of this kind of national identity-creating history argued for a continuous and unbroken history from ancient past to present. For Greece, after independence from the Ottoman Empire in 1821, Greek historians worked steadfastly to cultivate this history and argued that there was in fact no difference between the ancient Greeks and the Greeks of today (Zervas, 2012). Drawing on the concept of historicism and promoting what Rüsen (2005) would describe as an uncritical 'traditional-type' historical consciousness, the past and present were intimately intertwined and helped explain how one's own national identity and consciousness was connected to the past. One could use the past to understand the present, and the past became related to one's national consciousness.

In our textual analyses, we attempted to analyze history textbooks in the two contexts, especially those from the early 1950s until the present. The Greek textbooks were all accessed through archives available online, while the Egyptian textbooks were accessed through the textbook archives located at the Ministry of Education in Cairo. The textbook analyses entailed reading the ancient history sections of all grade levels, especially from the 1950s onwards, multiple times. In addition, some earlier textbooks were consulted to compare and contrast. In all these analyses, we were guided by the key questions of how the people as well as key historic events and figures were constructed. Informed by a grounded theory approach in our coding and thematic analyses (Glaser & Strauss, 1967), we paid particular attention to shifts in the historical narrative and representations that might have been introduced during key political and ideological turning points in the context being studied. It is worth noting that the authors conducted their own translations as the first author is proficient in Greek, while the second author is proficient in Arabic. Further, as is clear throughout this chapter, we also draw on some of our earlier peer-reviewed and published textual analyses.

Competing Imaginings of the Nation in Greece and Egypt

The constructed modern Greek national identity was predominately aligned with European notions of a Greek identity and mostly ignored Greece's Ottoman past (Gourgouris, 1996). It rested on a highly "imaginative" or even "imaginary" Greece that dated back to antiquity. It assumed a synthesis of the transcendent ideals of *Hellas* and modern Greece, and the existence of ancient Greece within the cultural and historic *milieu* of the modern Greek state (Zervas, 2017). At the same time, this identity was heavily linked to ancient Greek history and Greek Orthodox Christianity. These key pillars were arguably imported into Greece in the late 18th and early 19th centuries by western European and diasporic Greek intellectuals, who advocated the creation of Greek statehood and the revival of ancient Greece in the form of Modern Greece (Zervas, 2017). This timeless historical framework from past to present, first envisioned by the Greek historian Constantine Paparrigopoulos (1886) in *History of the Greek Nation (Ιστορία του Ελληνικού Εθνους)* published in the mid-19th century, continued well into the present in the writing of history curriculum and textbooks.

Despite some movements envisioning Egypt as essentially being part of the Ottoman Empire or perhaps the larger Muslim *umma*, several ideological movements in Egypt – including the nationalist territorial 'Egyptianst' movement or the Pan-Arabist movements – had a nationalist "problem" with the Ottoman Empire's past, similar to the one the Greeks had. Here, the Ottoman colonial rule ended in 1882 to be replaced by the British mandate over Egypt, which lasted until 1954. As noted earlier, in 1952, a *coup d'état* led by Nasser ushered in an era that exhibited a strong anti-colonial sentiment whether against the colonial British mandate over Egypt or other western imperial and colonial powers, while largely adopting and propagating Pan-Arabism and a socialist agenda.

Afterwards, Sadat (1970–1981) adopted a largely pro-western approach and a strong free-market economy, reversing much of Nasser's socialist policies. Assassinated at the hands of Islamist extremists, Sadat was followed by Mubarak (1981–2011). After mass demonstrations led to the ousting of Mubarak in 2011, the Muslim Brotherhood's Mohamed Morsi came to power in 2012. Just a year later Morsi was overthrown, putting in place the current president of Egypt, Abdel-Fattah El-Sisi. Significantly, Nasser, Sadat, Mubarak and El-Sisi all hail from the Egyptian military establishment.

There have been various political and cultural ideologies that have been in competition for control over interpretations of Egypt's history and its cultural identity. The period from the late 1800s up until the middle of the 1900s especially witnessed the emergence of various political ideologies, each with a different understanding of the nation's history. With clear parallels to Greece's ruling elite's efforts to develop a unique national identity that connected the country to its ancient past and to Christian Orthodox identity, while distancing itself from Ottoman Turkish cultural influences (Paparrigopoulos), in the case of Egypt, the Egyptianist (or territorial nationalist) ideology played a key role. It constructed the country's history in ways that largely distanced modern Egyptians from Ottoman and Arab cultural influences, positing those largely as invaders. Egyptianism, thus, emphasized that modern-day Egyptians were the inheritors of ancient Egypt, with a strong emphasis on a cultural continuity that informs the commonalities and unity of modern Egyptians across religious or other divides, especially against their colonial enemies (Colla, 2007; Haikal, 2003; Gershoni & Jankowski, 1986). It is important to note that some of these competing ideologies were not necessarily mutually exclusive. For instance, Mustafa Kamil – one of Egypt's leading intellectuals and political leaders against the British colonization in the early 1900s – advocated for Egypt as essentially belonging to the larger Ottoman Empire. However, his writings and political speeches reveal that he did not see this as mutually exclusive with having some Egyptianist tendencies, still seeing Egypt's Muslims and Copts as "one *umma* [nation]" (Gershoni & Jankowski, 1986, p. 8). Further, he was a strong advocate of constructing the nation's ancient history in ways that empha-sized "historical continuity" whereby modern Egyptians are represented as one homogenous group of people who share the same ancient Egyptian heritage and ancestry (Gershoni & Jankowski, 1986, p. 12).

The key elements of this dominant historical narrative include characteriz-ing Egyptians as descendants of a great, ancient, settled and agrarian civilization (Makar & Abdou, 2021). It also subtly constructs Egyptians as having always been largely "pacifist reactive citizens who obey authority and rarely challenge it" except mostly against foreign intervention (Abdou, 2017, p. 91). It also pre-sents ancient Egyptians as religious by nature (Abdou, 2017; Makar & Abdou, 2021), whereby history textbooks continue to cite ancient Greek historian Hero-dotus's reference to ancient Egyptians as the 'most pious people' (Abdou, 2018b, para. 15). This narrative also posits the ancient Egypt civilization as having dis-proportionately – and often unilaterally – contributed to other ancient civiliza-tions (e.g., Abdou, 2018b). This ancient history is also constructed in ways that present Abrahamic monotheism as supreme to other faith systems, emphasizing how ancient Egyptians yearned for and were always inclined towards monotheism, despite the power-hungry and corrupt ancient religious clergy who might have sought to divert them from the righteous monotheistic path for their own purposes (Abdou, 2018b).

The early 1920s and 1930s also witnessed the emergence of the competing ide-ology of political Islam (or Islamism), as embodied in the Muslim Brotherhood movement, which saw Egypt as one part – although central and significant – within the larger Muslim *umma* (nation) (Starrett, 1998). And with the mid 1950s emerged a consolidation of a Pan-Arabist vision seeing Egypt as a central part and a leader within a larger 'Arab Nation.' Clearly, all these various ideologies organ-ized in interest groups aimed to influence Egypt's educational system and its cur-ricular content with varying degrees of success. However, as would be expected, it was perhaps the ideologies of those in control of the government and the ruling elites that were most successful in introducing and securing their desired changes in the curricula.

Similar to the case of Greece, despite the various competing ideologies since the late 1800s in Egypt, there has been a clear and resilient nationalist narrative that in a primordial attitude essentializes the nature of the Egyptian nation-state and its people. These nationalist interpretations that have dominated the modern Egyp-tian national historiographies have been challenged by some of Egypt's modern historians (e.g., Fahmy, 1997), who critiqued some underlying assumptions that:

> "Egypt" has always had a unified, self-contained, clearly recognizable identity, and that its inhabitants have always realized – through their strong attach-ment to its soil, and through their conscious links to its history – that they are, and have always been, clearly and exclusively "Egyptians." . . . that Egypt is an undivided subject and that the Egyptian nation is a primordial, eternal entity.
>
> (Fahmy, 1997, pp. 312–313)

The next three sections outline the key findings of our textual analyses. We start by presenting some of the key defining elements of the constructions of ancient histories in the two contexts. In the following section we engage with the key turning point of military rule, while the third section is dedicated to current curricula and engages with some key continuities and changes.

2 Key features defining the teaching of (Ancient) history in Greece and Egypt

Greece

In Greece, today's pupils at an early age become inundated with images of the Greek nation as well as the nation's place in history. As mentioned earlier, Greek history since the 19th century has been presented in Greek school textbooks as one continuous unbroken historical thread from the heroic ancient past to the present (Avdela, 2000). This successful narration constructing this line of identity-building was inaugurated after the Greek Revolution (1832) – Greek's independence from the Ottoman Empire – when state authorities were allowed to build their own historical narrative in curricula and textbooks. Students learned that they were part of a broader national community that was linked by a shared national past and common blood. Through the teaching of a common Greek history, Greek language and the virtues of Greek Orthodox Christianity, students also learned to develop an emotional connection to the nation (Zambeta, 2000).

After the publication of Constantine Paparrigopoulos's *History of the Greek Nation*, links to the ancient Greeks became ever more important in school textbooks (Zervas, 2012). Greece was also looking to expand its territory in the Balkans. Often called the *Megali Idea* ("Great" or "Grand Idea"), this iridescent policy sought to claim or (re)claim lands that were deemed to be Greek. From a geopolitical standpoint, ancient Greece was far smaller in size and much farther south than the geographically expansive Byzantine lands had been. This posed a serious problem for the devisers of the Megali Idea (1844–1922), who envisioned a large and powerful Greek state that stretched from Romania to the southern tip of the Greek peninsula.

This nationalist agenda dominated Greek foreign policy for much of the 19th and early 20th centuries. The Megali Idea proposed that the Greek state should be extended to include all Greeks, not just the minority who lived in the area congruent with ancient Greece – they wanted a Greek state that would dominate most of the Balkan region.

After the Greek Revolution, the adolescent Greek state lobbied internationally for the reunification, incorporation, annexation or return of unredeemed Greek lands. Its claims were based on modern Greece's historic and cultural links to the ancient Greek and Byzantine world. In order to legitimate such claims, Greek history needed to be presented as one continuous and unbroken thread from ancient to Byzantine to Modern Greece. By the late 19th and early 20th centuries, international support favoured Greece's modern territorial claims.

In line with this direction, Greek textbooks after World War II continued to foster notions of citizenship, and loyalty to the nation and state. An elementary textbook on ancient history from 1947 emphasizes the inevitable ancient unification of Greeks under one nation. It begins by telling students, "Our nation in ancient times was not always united. It was divided in many small kingdoms. . . . The people from these kingdoms however shared the same language, worshiped the same gods and celebrated the same holidays" (Douka et al., 1947, p. 3). The textbook goes on to show how the Greek nation was finally united under Phillip II and Alexander the Great in the 4th century BCE and how this led to the rise of Hellenism (Douka et al., 1947, pp. 4–5).

Similarly, another textbook used in the Greek elementary schools between the 1950s and 1970s states that, "Our first ancestors, the ancient Greeks, originally lived in the northern parts of Central Europe with other nations that were similar to them. Over time however they migrated southwards and settled in our nation, which since then has been called Greece" (Douka et al., 1947, p 6). The textbook goes on to suggest that the ancient Greeks were creative and ahead of their time and that all Greeks today share many attributes with ancient Greeks.

These examples illustrate how textbooks from the last century adopted a narrative that emphasized the continuum from ancient to modern Greece.

Egypt

In the case of Egypt, although elements of both Egyptianist and Pan-Arabist ideologies seem to clearly co-exist throughout, as will become apparent from the analyses presented here, there was a clear shift from an Egyptianist influence on the textbooks' narration of ancient Egyptian history prior to the 1950s to a more Arabist influence throughout the 1950s and 1960s.

For instance, when narrating Egypt's ancient history, the textbooks of the late 1800s and early 1900s provided some detailed accounts of the origins of ancient Egyptians, often attempting to offer scientific and genetic explanations, outlining how they intermarried with Semitic groups that immigrated and settled in Egypt. The Semitic peoples are said to have had significant influences on the Egyptian language (e.g., SN268 (1912); SN483 (1929)).[1] Importantly, and in sharp contrast to later Pan-Arabist textbooks, an 1893 textbook makes a clear distinction between Egyptians and other Arabic-speaking peoples. In discussing the Asiatic Hyksos tribes' occupation of ancient Egypt, the textbook reminds students that the Hyksos were from the same ethnic and racial backgrounds as the peoples of Arabia and the Levant (Shaam), explaining why they favoured their people over the Egyptians (SN3, 1893, p. 33).

Pan-Arabist influences: With the Nasser regime's strong turn to Pan-Arabism, post-1952 textbooks mark a sharp shift around the origin of Egyptians, emphasizing the common origin which unifies Egyptians with all Arabs. Some of these textbooks included phrases reminding students that they are first and foremost Arabs, such as "You are an Arab citizen" (e.g., SN79, 1960, p. 11) or "You are an Arab" (1971, p. 12) (see also, Makar & Abdou, 2021). Some 1960s textbooks went as far as using this claim of ancient Arab cultural and linguistic ties to reinforce the narrative that countries such as Egypt fully embraced, and in fact welcomed, the conquest by Arab and Muslim armies in 641 CE (e.g., Abdou, 2018a).

To establish its legitimacy and emphasize the centrality of the Arab cultural identity among Egyptians since ancient times, the Pan-Arabist perspective needed to construct the commonalities that united all ancient 'Arab' peoples. Building on this construction of an ancient cultural commonality, to serve its purposes, the narrative of the textbooks normalized a political and economic unity among those peoples under one modern Arab nation as an inevitable and teleological destiny. In doing that this narrative also clearly underplayed, if not altogether omitted, the region's ancient rich cultural, linguistic and ethnic diversity and plurality which would be clearly documented in numerous historical sources. Thus, starting in the 1950s and through the early 1970s, the peoples of Egypt, Palestine, Syria, Iraq were all represented as predominantly originating from the Arabian Peninsula, claiming that this naturally led these ancient peoples to create civilizations that were nearly identical in their essence, which is presented as testimony that unity of the Arab nation goes back to the earliest of times (SN144, 1960, pp. 14–15). Further, linguistically, the textbooks of this era mostly used "country" (*balad*) or "countries" (*buldan*) when referring to individual nations or states, while exclusively reserving the term "nation" (*ummah*) to refer to the 'Arab' nation, under which all these countries or entities were arguably destined to unite culturally, politically and economically.

Starting in the early 1980s onwards, Egyptian textbooks generally steer away from providing details about the racial or ethnic origins of modern Egyptians. Some actually clearly point to the difficulty of pinning down the exact racial and ethnic origin of ancient Egyptians (e.g., SN320, 1987, p. 25). While such a strong explicit reference to the Arab ethnic and racial origin of Egyptians is less evident in more recent textbooks, there are still some subtle messages that imply that ancient Egyptians might have originally been 'Arab,' even before the Arab Muslim conquest, foreclosing the question of how cultural identities might have shifted with that conquest. For instance, a 2013 textbook describes how the "Roman Empire was colonized and abused several *Arab* [emphasis added] states such as Egypt and the Levant" (Abdou, 2016, p. 239).

While perhaps there is a stronger emphasis and space dedicated to ancient Egyptian history in textbooks that emerged in the late 1960s and early 1970s until the present, the Arab Muslim identity remains subtly and explicitly normalized as a key defining pillar of the cultural identity of Egyptians. One other area of clear continuity since the late 1890s onwards, and which merits more in-depth study as it could point to the ebbs and flows of Islamist ideological influences, is the textbooks' representations of ancient Egyptian religions and clergy. Egyptian textbooks consistently vilify ancient Egyptian clergy and narrate ancient Egyptian events and religious beliefs using a clearly Abrahamic (Judeo-Christian-Islamic) monotheistic tradition's lens, more specifically Islamic. This becomes apparent in representing monotheism as a superior belief system (e.g., Abdou, 2016, 2018b) and in how Abrahamic religious terminology is employed to narrate or explain ancient Egyptian events (e.g., Botros, 2012). While textbooks from the 1920s to the 1940s similarly maintained that overarching Abrahamic narrative approach, adopting an Egyptianist approach propelled them to insert references that clearly aimed for students to appreciate the cultural continuity and some key similarities between ancient Egyptians' religious beliefs and practices and those of modern-day Egyptian Muslims and Christians (Copts) (Abdou, 2018a).

Another key continuity relates to presenting the Egyptian people as a primordial and homogenous historical bloc since ancient times. While recent textbooks steer away from making definitive arguments about the origins of Egyptians, they continue to essentialize Egyptians as a continued and non-changing racially and culturally homogenous group of people, which is among the key elements that Fahmy (1997) and other scholars have problematized.

3 (Re)Producing the ancient during military rule

Greece

In 1967 a group of Army Colonels in Greece who would later be called the Junta overthrew the Greek king and Greek government. After the Junta took power, they took steps to revise school textbooks and the way history was being taught in schools. The first page of all textbooks included the Junta's revolutionary emblem, the mythical ancient Greek Phoenix rising from the flames. The image reflected the Junta's belief that their revolution saved the nation from falling into the hands of Communism and that there would be a new beginning in Greece.

In clear parallel to the textbook revisions introduced into how ancient Egyptian history was narrated after the military takeover in the 1950s, in Greece, during the Junta's reign, some key revisions were made to several textbooks that were already being used in schools (Zervas, 2016). A comparison between the 1955 and the 1973 versions of G. Kalamatianou et al.'s school reader reveal some of these changes made after the Junta took power. The first part of the 1973 edition begins with an image of Jesus Christ followed by two short poems titled "Christmas" and "The Miracle," both of which do not appear in the 1955 edition (Kalamatianou, 1973). The 1955 edition includes instead three short stories: "December for the Orphans," "The Eternal Mystery" and "The Sacrifice of Iphigenia." Later in the 1955 edition, there is a short story titled "One Nation and One King" (Kalamatianou, 1955). The 1973 edition on the other hand is purged of any stories about the Greek monarchy. Included instead are short biographies of individuals who extolled traditional values. One such example is a biography of Albert Schweitzer (1875–1965), the German/French polymath who believed that western civilization was in a cultural decline because of the spread of socialism and communism. Another story from the 1955 edition, "H Arapitsa," which deals with a child's visit to a factory, does not appear in the 1973 edition. Overall, the changes made between the two texts are few and minor. However, after an analysis of both textbooks it is clear that after the Junta took power, more stories with ancient and national themes appeared in the textbooks (Zervas, 2016).

Egypt

After the abolishment of the Egyptian kingdom in 1954, textbooks in Egypt started to represent ancient Egyptian events and institutions in ways that legitimize the modern military-backed rule. Given the centrality of the Egyptian military in politics ever since then, post-1954 textbooks emphasized the army's ancient origins and key role throughout the Egyptian nation-state's history. Textbooks since then have focused on how the army consistently took good care of its people and how Egyptians passionately joined it, regardless of their social classes and backgrounds (e.g., SN67, 1953, pp. 60–61; SN159, 1971, pp. 110–118). Recent textbooks describe the ancient and continued necessity to establish a national army, explaining in detail these ancient armies' structures and battlefield strategies (e.g., Abdou, 2018b). Further, among the textbooks' stated objectives of narrating ancient history is for students to "appreciate and be proud of the role that the military and the police institutions play in maintaining peace and stability, and protecting the country's borders" (Grade 10, 2019, p. 34). This very positive portrayal is in clear contrast to some pre-1952 textbooks that sometimes were critical of the military. For instance, a 1911 textbook lumps corrupt religious leaders and the military together, critiquing how ancient Egyptians sometimes blindly and uncritically followed those two institutions in what might even be considered "enslavement" (SN10, 1911, p. 13). Such references which might cast any doubt even remotely on the military have altogether disappeared in post-1954 textbooks.

4 Current representations of ancient histories: continuities and changes

Greece

After the collapse of the Greek economy in 2008, many Greeks became disillusioned with the country's major ruling parties. Other fringe parties like SYRIZA and Golden Dawn (Chrisy Avgi) found support, and by 2015, SYRIZA (Greece's radical left party) took the majority of seats in Greek Parliament. While SYRIZA revised the curriculum based on the recommendations made by the previous government, one major change was a revision to a sixth-grade textbook. The new textbook written by Koliopoulos et al. (2012), which included a student workbook and a teacher's manual, was introduced in Greek schools during the 2012–2013 academic year (Zachos & Michailidou, 2014). The textbook was seen as being less Greek-centric and more global and multicultural in perspective. The text itself stressed the need to respect people of different backgrounds and to find similarities rather than differences between the diverse peoples in Europe. Critics in Greece found the textbook to undermine the accomplishments of Greece and celebrate more those of Europe.

In 2017, the Institute of Educational Policy (IEP) commissioned a team to revise the history curriculum in Greece. Rather than focusing mostly on ancient Greek history, the revised history curriculum was

> an attempt to strike a balance between local history, national history and global connections through the use of prehistory. . . . Prehistory is pushed to the foreground compared with previous curricula, enabling students to gain a better understanding not only of the common origin and evolution of the human species, but also to provide them with the knowledge to counter the many existing stereotypical public perceptions of the period.
>
> (Kasvikis & Kouseri, 2019, p. 187)

Unlike SYRIZA, Golden Dawn (Greece's far-right party, which also rose to prominence after the 2008 crisis) pushed for changes in the Greek curriculum and Greek history textbooks. Sofia Vasilopoulou and Daphne Halikiopoulou (2015) examined some of Golden Dawn's educational initiatives. They found that the party was looking to revise Greek textbooks to highlight even more of modern Greece's "ties with ancient Greece, past wars, imperial experience during the Ottoman years, and the invasion in the 1940s" (p. 64). The authors state:

> Historical figures, whether heroes of ancient Greece, Byzantium, the Greek War of Independence, the Second World War, or Cyprus, are glorified for their heroism, bravery, and sacrifice. By referring to a very large array of officially recognized historical events, personalities, and national identity traits, and placing them within the ethnic election framework, Golden Dawn successfully integrates them into its ultra-nationalist palingeneric ideology.
>
> (Vasilopoulou & Halikiopoulou, 2015, p. 64)

While never implemented, SYRIZA had proposed a broader history of Europe where Greek history would still be presented separate but involved in the history of Europe and the world. Ultimately, more on European and global narratives were introduced in the history curriculum (Traianou, 2019).

In Greece, ultra-nationalist groups like Golden Dawn retained traditional notions of what defined a Greek but adopted symbols and practices from Nazi Germany while ignoring Nazi atrocities on the Greek people during the Second World War (Zervas, 2017). To Golden Dawn whether these traditions, customs, practices, symbols and historical figures were part of nation's past was not important; what mattered was that they were imbedded within the memory of the people (Zervas, 2017).

Egypt

Except for the explicit Pan-Arabist revisionist and propaganda-style approach to textbooks in the 1950s and 1960s, the dominant representations and constructions of the nation's ancient history – the key elements of which have been outlined– seem to have been resilient with no urgent need for drastic changes by the successive military-backed regimes. In terms of cultural identity, it seems the 1950s and 1960s pointed to the most drastic shift in the cultural ideology, with the demonstrated shift from the Egyptianist paradigm to more of a Pan-Arabist perspective. As demonstrated, both ideologies continue to influence current textbooks, whether explicitly or implicitly, however perhaps arguably with more prominence of the Egyptianist approach. The lack of need to introduce any drastic changes since the late 1960s could be explained by the fact that the textbooks' portrayals of Egypt's ancient history essentialize visions that conveniently serve the hegemony and normalization of the successive ruling elites' ideologies and approaches.

A clear testimony to the lack of need to revise the textbook content is that since the early 2000s – despite the two massive and historic revolts of January 2011 and June 2013 and their aftermaths – there have only been very few or no changes to the curricular content. The few exceptions include the textbooks' acknowledgment of these massive revolts, lumping them together as testimonies of the resilience of Egyptian people. For instance, in its section entitled "Political and Administrative Life," a 2019 textbook states that it aims for students to be able to compare and contrast 'social revolutions in ancient Egypt' and the 2011 and 2013 revolutions (Grade 10, 2019, p. 34).

Recently, the Egyptian Ministry of Education's Curriculum and Instructional Materials Development Center introduced a "General Framework for the General and Technical Education Curricula 2018–2030" (Egyptian Ministry of Education, 2019, p. 11). Currently implemented within Kindergarten II through Grade 3 classes, similar curricular and teaching guidelines are expected to be prepared and rolled out for higher grades over the coming years (personal communication, 2020).[2] If fully implemented, such reformed curricular and pedagogical frameworks would eventually allow Egyptian teachers and students to develop more critical approaches and skills. Those would hopefully include conducting more independent historical research into constructions of the country's historical narratives.

5 Discussion: similarities and differences between the two cases

As we hope has become apparent from the analyses presented, there are a few points of convergence and divergence between the two cases of Egypt and Greece. In both cases, as Billig (1995) would argue, the educational system constructs a primordial nation and attempts to essentialize a connection between this primordial nation and its people. In doing so, the two nations construct ancient histories in ways that legitimate their modern national identities while underplaying their populations' potential heterogeneity and diversity. Those curricular narratives clearly also downplay and often altogether omit any indepth discussion or critical engagement with continuities and changes in historiographical or curricular representations of these nations' cultural identities and these ancient histories.

To foster the historical consciousness of their students and ensure their sense of belonging to the 'nation,' these two nations' textbooks constructed and clearly revised the narration of ancient history to legitimize modern nations, their key institutions and structures, political and economic ideologies, and cultural identities. In their representations, the textbooks of Greece and Egypt seem to propagate what Rüsen (2005) would characterize as a 'traditional' approach as opposed to a more desired "multidimensional, multiperspectival genetic" approach that would encourage a critical engagement with these constructions and the interests they serve (p. 36). Building on Rüsen's theorization and most studies focusing on textbook analyses, our analyses point to the importance of not only focusing on constructions of modern events in curricula, but the need to analyze references to, and representations of, ancient histories which could fundamentally shape students' outlooks, approaches and understanding of various other historical narratives they would subsequently be exposed to.

Further, building on constructivist theorists' contributions such as Billig and Özkırımlı, our analyses point to the importance of paying closer attention to the dynamics and nuances at play, and changes informed by shifting ideologies and ruling elites. Engaging with these dynamics can offer some helpful keys into analyzing how historical narratives in general are constructed and reconstructed to serve particular purposes and interests. Additionally, such analyses point to the importance of theorizing further about the elements in these historical narratives that might be propagated and accepted by various of these often-competing ideological movements, which makes them more resilient and foundational. Given the wider acceptance they gain, these elements have become more deeply entrenched, thus making them even more difficult to challenge and unsettle.

In contrast to most national narratives, (whose national identities consider mostly contemporary indigenous models) Greece looked to its ancient past when constructing its national identity (Zervas, 2012). Similarly, Egypt continued to look to its ancient Egyptian past, but with various lenses and optics clearly influenced by the dominant ideological perspectives of the time. Regardless of dominant or competing ideologies, both Greece and Egypt invested heavily in archaeology and antiquities to help showcase and even prove their historic and cultural connections to their ancient past. Yannis Hamilakis (2007) best illustrates this when he says, "The material manifestations of antiquity, the ancient ruins and artefacts have been central to the production and continuous reproduction of national imagination, from the nineteenth century to the present. . . . They became the most important symbolic resource for the modern Greek state" (p. 290–291).

In this chapter we attempted to present some key milestones and turning points in the modern histories of Egypt and Greece, and to show how their successive ruling elites have reconstructed their ancient histories to normalize and legitimize particular worldviews, political ideologies and discourses. Our aim is to not only shed light on these two important contexts, but to also point to the need for more scholars to attempt to study and elucidate this important yet generally understudied question. While many studies have critically analyzed constructions of modern history, very few studies have analyzed constructions of ancient histories in textbooks. Given that most nations, if not all, draw legitimacy from an origination and foundation myth of some sort, we believe that any analyses of how nations construct a national identity need in fact start with analyzing how the country constructs its ancient history in its national textbooks and curricula.

Notes

1 To facilitate future references, SN refers to the serial number of the textbook being referred to in the Egyptian textbooks' archives located at the Egyptian Ministry of Education in Cairo.
2 This is based on a personal interview conducted with one of the key advisors to the Minister of Education, who shared these insights. Further details about this framework and some of the recent reform efforts could be found on the Ministry of Education's website: http://portal.moe.gov.eg/eng/Pages/default.aspx

References

Abdou, E. D. (2016). Confused by multiple deities, ancient Egyptians embraced monotheism': Analysing historical thinking in Egyptian history textbooks. *Journal of Curriculum Studies*, 47(6), 1–26.

Abdou, E. D. (2017). Construction(s) of the nation in Egyptian textbooks: Towards an understanding of societal Conflict. In M. Bellino & J. Williams (Eds.), *(Re)constructing memory: Education, identity and conflict* (pp. 75–98). Rotterdam, The Netherlands: Sense Publishers.

Abdou, E. D. (2018a). Copts in Egyptian history textbooks: Towards an integrated framework for analyzing minority representations. *Journal of Curriculum Studies*, 50(4), 476–507.

Abdou, E. D. (2018b, December 21). Reconciling Egyptians with their ancient past? Analyzing students' perspectives and curriculum representations of ancient Egyptian history. In *Mada Masr Online Portal*. Cairo, Egypt: Mada Masr.

Anderson, B. (2006). *Imagined communities: Reflections on the origin and spread of nationalism.* New York, NY: Verso Publishing.

Avdela, E. (2000). The teaching of history in Greece. *Journal of Modern Greek Studies*, 18(2), 239–253.

Billig, M. (1995). *Banal nationalism.* Thousand Oaks, CA. Sage.

Botros, A. (2012). Reconficguring the past: History, memory and ideology in Egyptian history textbooks between 1932 and 2009. In S. Alayan, A. Rohde, & S. Dhouib (Eds.), *The politics of education reform in the Middle East; self and other in textbooks and curricula* (pp. 112–130). New York, NY: Berghahn Books.

Cavafy, C. P. (1976). *Complete poems of Cavafy.* London: SPCK Publishing.

Colla, E. (2007). *Conflicted antiquities: Egyptology, Egyptomania, Egyptian modernity.* Durham, NC: Duke University Press.

Fahmy, K. (1997). *All the Pasha's men.* Cairo: The American University in Cairo.

Gellner, E. (2009). *Nations and nationalism.* Ithaca, NY. Cornell University Press.

Gershoni, I., & Jankowski, J. (1986). *Egypt, Islam and the Arabs: The search for Egyptian nationhood, 1900–1930.* New York, NY: Cambridge University Press.

Glaser, B. G., & Strauss, A. (1967). *The discovery of grounded theory.* London: Weidenfeld and Nicholson.

Gotling, N. (2020). National textbook narratives and historiography: Presenting a same that is never the same. *Croatian Journal of Education*, 22(2), 65–82.

Gourgouris, S. (1996). *Dream nation: Enlightenment, colonization, and the institution of modern Greece*. Palo, Alto: Stanford University Press.

Haikal, F. (2003). Egypt's past regenerated by its own people. In S. MacDonald & M. Rice (Eds.), *Consuming Ancient Egypt* (pp. 123–138). Walnut Creek, CA: Left Coast Press.

Hamilakis, Y. (2007). *The nation and its ruins: Antiquity, archaeology, and national imagination in Greece*. Oxford, UK: Oxford University Press.

Hobsbawm, E. (2012). *Nation and nationalism since 1780: Programme, myth, reality*. Cambridge, UK: Cambridge University Press.

Hobsbawm, E., & Ranger, T. (Eds.). (1993). *The invention of tradition*. Bristol, UK: Cato Press.

Kasvikis, K., & Kouseri, G. (2019). Antiquity revisited: Challenges and opportunities in the creation of the new Greek history curriculum. *History Education Research Journal*, *16*(2), 182–194.

Makar, F., & Abdou, E. D. (2021). Egyptian textbooks in times of change: 1952–1980. *Arab Studies Journal*, *29*(1), 8–37.

Maricic, V. (2020). National identity textbooks: Teaching Scottishness in the wake of the union of parliaments. *Croatian Journal of Education*, *22*(2), 29–46.

Muratović, K., & Gimpl, F. (2020). Doing nation in empires: The emergence of Turkey and Austria. *Croatian Journal of Education*, *22*(2), 151–169.

Özkırımlı, U. (2017). *Theories on nationalism: A critical introduction*. New York, NY and London: Red Globe Press.

Paparrigopoulos, C. (1886). *History of the Greek nation* (Ιστορία του Ελληνικού Έθνους). Athens, Greece: Anestis Konstantinidis.

Rickford, R. (2016). *We are an African people: Independent education, Black power, and the radical imagination*. Oxford, UK: Oxford University Press.

Rüsen, J. (2005). *History: Narration, interpretation, orientation*. New York, NY: Berghahn Books.

Sauquet, M. (2014). *Propaganda art in Nazi Germany: The revival of classicism*. Hartford, CT: Trinity College Digital Repository.

Starrett, G. (1998). *Putting Islam to work: Education, politics, and the transformation of faith*. Berkeley, CA: University of California Press.

Traianou, A. (2019). "Greece: Towards Europeanization?" In A. Traianou & K. Jones (Eds.), *Austerity and the remaking of European education* (pp. 147–176). London and New York. Bloomsbury Academic Press.

Traub, A. (2018). India's dangerous new curriculum. *The New York Review*. Retrieved from www.nybooks.com/articles/2018/12/06/indias-dangerous-new-curriculum/

Vasilopoulou, S., & Halikiopoulou, D. (2015). *The Golden Dawn's nationalist solution: Explaining the rise of the far right in Greece*. New York, NY: Palgrave Macmillan.

Winichakul, T. (1997). *Siam mapped. A history of the geo body of the nation*. Manoa, HI. University of Hawaii Press.

Wodak, R., de Cillia, R., Reisigl, M., Rodger, R., & Liebhart, K. (2009). *The discursive construction of national Identity*. Edinburg, UK: Edinburg University Press.

Zachos, D., & Michailidou, A. (2014). "Others" in textbooks: The case of Greek sixth grade's history textbook. *Theory in Action*, *7*(3), 1–25.

Zambeta, E. (2000). Religion and national identity in Greek education. *Intercultural Education*, *11*(2), 146–156.

Zervas, T. G. (2012). *The making of a modern Greek identity: Education, nationalism and the teaching of a Greek national past*. New York, NY: Columbia University Press.

Zervas, T. G. (2016). Greek school textbooks at a political crossroads: (Re)defining the Greek citizen in the Greek school during the reign of colonels (1967–1974). *American Educational History Journal*, *43*(2), 117–127.

Zervas, T. G. (2017). *Formal and informal education during the rise of Greek nationalism*. New York, NY: Palgrave Macmillan.

Textbooks and Teacher Guides Analyzed

Douka, D. et al. (1947). *Αρχαία Ελλάδα Ιστορία Για την Δ Τάξη του Δημοτικού Σχολιέου* (Ancient Greek history for the fourth year of elementary school. Athens, Greece). Τυπογραφείο Α Σιδέρη.

Egyptian Ministry of Education. (2019). *Kindergarden II. Discover teacher's guide 2019/2020 term 1*. Cairo: Egyptian Ministry of Education.

Grade 10 (2019–2020). Shalabi, M., Nosseir, A., Abdul-Wahab, A., Abdul-Aziz, A., Salama, H., Shalabi, M., & Ismail, H. *Misr al-Hadarah: Jawla fi-Hadarat Misr wa Hadaaraat al-'Alam al-Qadim* (Egypt's civilization: A tour of Egypt's and the ancient world's civilizations). Cairo: Wizarat al-Tarbiya wa-l-Ta'lim.

Kalamatianou, G. et al. (1955 and 1973). *Αναγνωστικών Ε. Δημοτικού*. Elementary Reader Third Year. Athens, Greece: Οργανισμός Εκδόσεως Διδακτικών Βιβλίων.

Koliopoulos, G. et al. (2012). *Ιστορία Στ' Δημοτικού, Ιστορία του Νεότερου και Σύγχρονου Κόσμου-- Τετραδίου*. Sixth Grade History, History of the Modern World – Workbook. Athens, Greece: Διόφαντος.

SN3 (1893): Azmi, S. (1893). *Tarikh al-Masalik al-Ibtida'iyah fi-Tarikh al-Umam al-Sharqiyah* (Basic historical understanding of the history of Eastern nations). Cairo: Al-Matabi'al-Amiriya.

SN10 (1911): Azmi, S. (1911). *Kitaab ithaaf abnaa' al-'asr bi-thikr qudamaa' muluk Misr* (10th ed.) (Inspiring today's generation by narrating the stories of Egypt's ancient kings). Cairo: Al-Matabi'al-Amiriya.

SN268 (1912): Hussein, M. (1912). *Al-Modhakirat al-Tarikhiyah li-l-Madaris al-Thanawiyah* (Historical notes for secondary schools). Cairo: Al-Matba'ah Al-Jamaliyya bi-Misr.

SN483 (1929): Henry Prested, J. (Dr. Hassan Kamal, Trans.). *Kitaab Tarikh Misr Min Aqdamm Al-'usur ila al-'asr al-farisi* (History of Egypt since ancient times until the Persian conquest). Cairo: Al-Matabi'al-Amiriya. *[Note: the book seems to have been originally written in 1905. Also, it clearly indicates that this is targeted for pre-service teachers]*

SN67 (1953): Uthman, A., 'Ali, Z., Hashim, A., Ziyada, M., Khalil, A., & 'Issa, S. *Tarikh Misr al-Qadim wa-l-Islami* (Egypt's ancient and Islamic history). Cairo: Al-Matabi'al-Amiriya.

SN79 (1960): al-Rifa'i, A., & 'Arif, A. *Suwar min al-Tarikh al-Qadim li – l-Jumhuriyya al-'Arabiyya al-Mutahidah wa-l – Tarikh al-'Arabi l-il-Saf al-Khamis al-'Ibtida'I* (Images from the ancient history of the United Arab Republic – Grade 5). Cairo: Wizarat al-Tarbiya Wa-l – Ta'lim – al-Iqlim al-Janubi.

SN144 (1960): Sayfuldin, I., Hums, M., Al-Shihabi, M., Al-Gindi, M., & Al-Sayhi, M. *Tarikh al-Watan al-'Arabi fil-'Usur al-Qadima lil Saff al-Awwal al-I'dadi* (Ancient history of the Arab Nation – Grade 7). Cairo: Wizarat al-Tarbiya wa-l-Ta'lim – al-Iqlim al-Janubi.

SN159 (1971): Mukhtar, M. *Al-Tarikh al-Qadim li-l- Watan al 'Arabi* (The ancient history of the Arab Nation). Cairo: Wizarat al-Tarbiya wa-l-Ta'lim.

SN320 (1987). Ibrahim, S. A., Salamah, M., Shehata, M. H., Hassanein, I., & Al-Hakim, R. *Tarikh misr wa-l-'alam al-qadim lil-saff al-awwal al-thanawi* (History of Egypt and the ancient World – Grade 10). Cairo: Al-Matabi'al-Amiriya.

Part II

Hegemonic aspirations and interventions

5 Bringing pedagogy in line

Globalizing nationally programmed instruction, new math, film and media education

Rebekka Horlacher

The first decades after World War II were characterized by an earnest optimism about planning progress and by a fundamental belief in the potential for social and cultural improvement through technical innovation in general and education in particular (see e.g. Vogt, 1967a, p. 70). This conviction became manifest in the development of tremendous energy sources (e.g. nuclear power) serving both large industries and the armed forces, in numerous technical aids to facilitate daily (house) work, in automation processes of industrial activities and in family planning devices such as the contraceptive pill. This attitude did not stop at education; quite the contrary (Rudolph, 2002; Tröhler, 2013a; Rohstock, 2014). One example was the field of learning technologies, which – along the lines of technical innovations and the associated rationalization processes – claimed to make the transfer of knowledge easier and faster and – above all – more efficient and secure.[1] In the field of pedagogy, it is undoubtedly programmed instruction which represents the model of this ideology of development (Horlacher, 2015), and which is connected with teaching and learning machines (Hof, 2018; Deplazes, 2020) and the language laboratory (Bosche & Geiss, 2011). In addition, the introduction of new math (Phillips, 2015), the fundamental discussion about the use of educational technologies and the media in schools and their effects on pedagogy, educational sciences and research are to be located in this context (Nicholson, 2007; Kurig, 2015; García del Dujo & Martín-Lucas, 2020; Hof, 2020).

Spurred in no small part by the hope of keeping the costs of education under control, as they had risen steadily due to increasing numbers of students (Vogt, 1967a, p. 155), all these innovations were not limited to a specific, nationally framed context, but understood themselves explicitly as global phenomena. Some, like especially programmed instruction, had been developed initially in or advocated by Cold War-US and discussed, exchanged and implemented across national borders and even across the Iron Curtain (Boretska, 2019). This worldwide discussion, however, was not an expression of a dogma like the Habermasian "domination-free discourse," but must be seen in its geopolitical entanglements. This is all the more true for the politically heated climate of the 1960s, when development and progress were always a question of the respective political power constellations, although not all curriculum and school reforms undertaken in the 1960s and 1970s can be subscribed to this particular discourse (Openshaw &

DOI: 10.4324/9781003137801-8

Walshaw, 2019, p. 6). Thus, this chapter deals with the "national dimensions" of the various learning technologies and pedagogical innovations which were designed to be globally valid and independent of culture, as they were based on psychological and thus "natural" principles (Skinner, 1961), on the logic of mathematics (Bourbaki, 1939–1968) or on the spatial independence of broadcasting. It illustrates that – and in which ways – this claim to universality was expressed and how the implementation of pedagogical innovations had to be adapted to national frameworks and cultural characteristics. Consequently, the question is addressed as to whether the national characteristics of pedagogy are more than just coincidental manifestations of a "uniform idea" or whether they are culturally determined adaptations of general principles that are adaptations to the circumstances of the individual, nationally shaped schools.

The first part of this chapter deals with programmed instruction, a teaching method which was overwhelmed with extensive expectations, but very soon also aroused great fears. The second part discusses the implementation of new math, which claimed a gain of substantial quality of "thinking" instead of "dumbing down through calculation." The third part deals with film education, which soon developed into media education and tried to position itself as an up-do-date education science and a theoretical guideline for contemporary education and curriculum. The fourth and concluding part focuses on the pedagogical discussions accompanying these new subjects and pedagogies and asks whether and to what extent the national characteristics of pedagogy must be seen as a result of independent national logics.

1 The introduction of programmed instruction

Programmed instruction roots in behaviourist psychology and is mainly associated with the American psychologist Burrhus F. Skinner, who, since the early 1950s, had made some very effective criticisms of traditional teaching methods (Skinner, 1965). Skinner emphasized a strict stimulus-response pattern of learning and propagated organizing teaching along this logic. Since at least the 1960s, programmed instruction had become a worldwide phenomenon, which is documented in a two-volume bibliography holding over 1,000 entries of publications from Canada, the United States, Great Britain, France, East and West Germany, and other countries in Western and Eastern Europe, including the USSR (IPN, 1966). In this context, an international conference on programmed instruction and teaching machines was held in Berlin in 1963. It was organized by the *Pädagogische Arbeitsstelle Berlin*[2] and by the World Confederation of the Organizations of the Teaching Profession. Moreover, it was supported by several public bodies and private foundations from the US, Germany, Great Britain and France. It was by no means coincidental that Berlin had been chosen as the host city, as the schools senator for Berlin, Carl-Heinz Evers, stressed that this conference was also about showing that "by being cosmopolitan and open to innovations, free Berlin is striving to make the advantages of the democratic way of life visible." The conference on programmed instruction was thus part of the political competition between systems, even if all the participants were "inspired by the idea that the great task of our time to provide more and more people an ever better education" could only be fulfilled if "the latest findings in science and technology could be used to serve the learning process" (Evers, 1964, VII.). However, the reports of the individual workgroups[3] illustrate that the countries implemented this claim quite differently and thus adapted it to the different national circumstances.

The workgroup which dealt with programmed instruction in industrialized countries stated that the development there was still in its infancy and that the organizations which were in charge of it differed widely (Schultze, 1964, p. 1). In Sweden and Great Britain, for instance, the promotion of programmed instruction was in the hands of a Royal Commission, whereas teachers' associations were dealing with the issue on a rather experimental level. France on the other hand was not only discussing programmed instruction, but also questions of cybernetics, adapting both concrete programmes from the US and developing its own, new ones. Regardless of their respective thematic priorities and their supporting organizations for the promotion of programmed instruction, all the participating countries shared the conviction that "programmed instruction can help to solve certain problems which we encounter in industrialized countries" (ibid., p. 2), first and foremost in adult education and professional training, and as a supplement to or preparation for "traditional" tuition. Moreover, programmed instruction was deemed to hold some potential for improving access to education in rural areas, as it could be very useful with "home-work" (ibid.).

Apart from stressing the advantages, this workgroup also discussed the problems and open issues connected with programmed instruction. One open question was whether the currently great motivation to work with the programmes would last once the novelty was worn off. Another question was whether the knowledge acquired through the programmes was applicable. It was also stated that the main objective of schools, namely "to educate the student to become as independent as possible in acquiring the necessary knowledge" (ibid., p. 3), could not be attained solely by programmed instruction, especially in subjects like biology, art or citizenship education. The workgroup maintained that "programmed instruction is a method of rationalization," and that it is neither possible to rationalize all educational goals of schools nor is it the intention or aim of schools to do so. "Not everything that *could* be learned by programmed instruction *should* be learned by programmed instruction. A careful evaluation of the whole curriculum seems to be necessary" (ibid.). Thus – and to eliminate pre-existing misunderstandings – it was necessary to introduce programmed instruction carefully and to inform teachers about the advantages and disadvantages of the new teaching method. Moreover, considering the scepticism among teachers, one had to be careful not to "advertise" programmed instruction too strongly with the method's underlying behaviourism. "In some European countries at least this would upset psychologists and teachers from the very beginning" (ibid., p. 5). Teachers' (pedagogical) practices, which had been acquired based on other psychological theories, had to be considered when introducing programmed instruction.

The discussions in the workgroup dealing with programmed instruction and teaching machines in the schools of the developing countries took a slightly different course. Here, it was stressed that it was primarily the supervisory school authorities which had to be persuaded of the meaning and necessity of programmed instruction, an interest which was taken for granted in the industrialized countries. "Pilot projects, and model school situations" (Farrag, 1964, p. 7) were the main means to reach this goal. The aim was to make the advantages and chances of programmed instruction visible by concrete examples. The obstacles to block the introduction of programmed instruction were limited financial resources and deficits in teacher training, as well as the lack of specified targets in education and schools. In principle, efficiency was to be raised in all areas of school and tuition. Whereas the first workgroup had discussed the possibilities of rationalization as a potential problem, this group saw them as an opportunity or gain.

While the industrialized countries conveyed an image of cultural unity – or at least did not identify existing differences as problematic – cultural differences did arise as a subject of discussion in the workgroup of the developing countries. Not only did its members demand that the teaching materials yet to be developed should "meet the needs of the children," but they should also consider "cultural differences" (ibid.). This is why there could be, for example, no common teaching materials. The different languages also had to be considered, a claim which additionally accentuated the meaning of "effective techniques for teaching reading of local language and for teaching common language of the country or the region" (ibid., p. 8). Moreover, the "problem of resistance to social change" was mentioned, i.e. the concrete question of "how to encourage the teacher to use new techniques, and how to convince the parents to accept those techniques" (ibid.).

Thus, the proposals for overcoming these challenges differed substantially from the considerations of the industrialized countries. However, both workgroups were consistent when it came to the fundamental limitations of the usage of programmed instruction. It was stated that programmed instruction and teaching machines could not fully convey skills like "problem solving, creativity or application of facts to life situations" (ibid.). The developing countries attached great importance to the dissemination and publication of these new pedagogical possibilities. They maintained that in order to gain broad acceptance of the innovations, it was necessary not only to inform teachers, but also to win over the public, by using the media or film. This workgroup also discussed the desire to include international organizations like UNESCO in the respective campaigns (ibid., p. 9). Compared to the industrialized countries, experts were ascribed a much greater role, as professionals and international organizations had to bring the new knowledge to the individual countries "from the outside" and distribute it to the various stakeholders and interest groups.

Using Egypt as an example, the workgroup proposed a concrete plan for the implementation of programmed instruction. It illustrates that programmed instruction was not associated primarily with educational goals, but was seen as an opportunity to adjust schools to changing circumstances – a motive which would also emerge with new math and film education. It was said that there was an "increased interest in education and a demand for the expansion of educational facilities and the application of new theories and the utilization of new educational methods and techniques." Supposedly, this interest had become apparent because of generally tight finances, changing economic requirements and an increased awareness of pupils' individual needs and characteristics. Therefore, there was an urgent need for the introduction of programmed instruction, especially in those areas in which teachers were less effective, concretely in the field of "conveying information, routine instruction, symbol manipulation, and the like" (ibid., p. 11). When implementing this programme, which was described in detail and in the sense of a concrete instruction, one would have to not only create an understanding for the necessity of programmed instruction, but also to install a responsible commission which – consisting of the minister for education, representatives of the university and professionals – would organize the necessary steps for the implementation.

There was also mention of the benefits of programmed instruction for the former colonies, e.g. in a report from Central Africa (Malawi, Zimbabwe, Zambia), although the question was raised about whether – considering the low quotas of school attendance – it was sensible to introduce a relatively expensive technical method like programmed instruction (Hawkridge, 1966a). At the same time, it was stressed that programmed instruction was a good means to eradicate existing (knowledge) deficits in the training of pupils and teachers, as the use of teaching programs could boost self-instruction (Hawkridge, 1966b). Besides, programmed instruction was also said to be helpful in vocational training, which was explicitly welcomed with regard to the promotion of the domestic workforce, i.e. the "nationalization" of leading positions in politics and the economy (Hawkridge, 1966a).

To sum up, one may say that the debates and problems certainly differed, depending on the economic and political contexts in which programmed instruction was discussed. The different authors agreed both on the potentials and on the limitations of programmed instruction. The more "developed" a country was, the more pedagogical freedom it granted to individual teachers and the less importance it saw in the gain in efficiency and rationalization associated with programmed instruction. Programmed instruction was either considered a possible threat to pedagogical routines (industrialized nations) or as a gain in the quality of education (developing nations) or even as an opportunity to qualify domestic workers for leading positions and thus to support the administrative detachment of the colonies from their motherlands (Central Africa).

2 The aspirations of new math

Apart from programmed instruction, the 1960s also saw the discussion of new math,[4] a curricular innovation which was – as opposed to programmed instruction – not motivated by considerations of learning psychology and was not a genuinely pedagogic reform. In fact, new math was based on fundamental discussions of mathematics, the consequences of which were to be incorporated in the curriculum (Moon, 1986, p. 5–6; Phillips, 2015, pp. 13–21). This claim was, however, heavily criticized by some representatives of pedagogy (e.g. Karaschewski, 1966, pp. 18–23). The fundamental discussions of mathematics had been essentially initiated by a group of French mathematicians named Nicolas Bourbaki. On the basis of an axiomatic representation of set theory based on David Hilbert, these mathematicians wanted to bring the existing mathematical knowledge into a stringent context (see Aubin, 1997). All mathematical assertions were to follow a strict logic and had to be deduced from superordinate assertions. As a consequence, *Éléments de mathématique* (published by the group) included no references outside the group's own publications (Dieudonné, 1970, p. 138) and thus also stood for a context-free, "pure" representation of the fundamental mathematical principles, independent of space and time.

The tuition of math was to be reformed along these principles. It was not to focus solely on the acquisition of calculating skills, but to promote an understanding for abstract structures with the help of the axiomatic set theory. In doing so – according to the propagandists of new math – "the stultification by calculating" could be countered, and finally "rational thinking" would be taught (Wolfer, 1972, p. 682; Phillips, 2015, p. 13). Thus, new math, following the principles of the Bourbaki group, was not an "American" project located within the context of the Cold War and the question of the predominance of political systems, but first of all a project to present the "true" mathematics. In terms of the national location, it was a European/French project, which had its roots in the interwar period and which was picked up, discussed and propagated in the Cold War years by the OEEC (later OECD) and UNESCO as a global endeavour.

In 1959, on the initiative of the OEEC, an international conference on new math was held in Royaumont, a town north of Paris. The objective of the convening educationalists, mathematicians and education policy makers of the OEEC's member states (De Bock & Vanpaemel, 2019, p. 74) was to document the status quo of math tuition, clarify the purpose of it, pin down the necessary reforms and develop a schedule for its implementation (OECD, 1961, p. 12) – a programme which one of the protagonists of the Bourbaki group, Jean Dieudonné, summarized with the slogan "Euclid must go!" (ibid., p. 35). Two years later, the scholars gathered for another conference in Dubrovnik, and another two years later in Athens, in order to discuss "new methods for teaching the modern mathematics" (Fehr, 1964, p. 4). The main issue at the conference in Dubrovnik, which was in fact a four-week workshop in Yugoslavia (OEEC, 1961, p. 3), was to phrase a "synopsis, describing several possible ways of modernization" (OECD, 1961, p. 123), on the basis of which new teaching materials were to be developed. The central issue was a curricular reform on secondary school level, i.e. in gymnasiums, lycées and high schools, rather than a reform in elementary math tuition. It became equally clear that the programmes which had been developed within the framework of this conference had "to be adapted to the traditions and the needs of the different countries in which the modernization of mathematics curricula is undertaken" (OEEC, 1961, p. 5). New math was decidedly not considered a reform programme to be integrated in different school contexts, but a foundation for the reform of math tuition.

As in the case of programmed instruction, the Royaumont conference's suggestions for reform and the resolve for reforming math tuition along the principles of new math stated there initially fell on sympathetic ears with stakeholders of education policy both in Europe and in the US, although interest slackened again in the 1970s. In the US, the introduction of new math was not only one of the few national curricula reforms (Phillips, 2015, p. 96) but also an expression of a fundamental hope for reforms in the context of the Cold War. This hope was neither restricted to math tuition nor did it merely aim at improving the quality of tuition or increasing learning success, but it held the promise of "a new form of mental discipline" which "was required for US citizens facing an assortment of political, social, technical and moral quandaries in the 1960s" (ibid., p. 97). Thus, this curriculum reform became a clearly non-pedagogical one, but it was justified with the general educational mandate of schools, which were said to be more successful in reaching their goals by using new math, as it went beyond mere math tuition.

In the Netherlands, a country with equally decentralized organization, the reform of the mathematics curriculum was also initiated by the ministry of education. In 1961, it installed the *Commissie Modernizering Leerplan Wiskunde*, a commission for the modernization of mathematics education (Moon, 1986, p. 72) which based its objectives on the action programme of the Royaumont conference. Similar developments appeared in France (ibid., p. 102), although – unlike the Netherlands and the US – France has a centralist system, also in matters of school and education.

Information on the implementation of new math in various countries is also provided by the reports of a commission appointed by the International Commission on Mathematical Instruction (ICMI)[5] to advise UNESCO on mathematics education, which were published in two issues of *Educational Studies in Mathematics* in 1978.[6] The responding countries had to comment on the changes in "subject matter, teaching method, attitude towards mathematics" and "relations between mathematics and other subjects." Meanwhile, the person responsible for this survey, Hans Freudenthal – a critic of new math (Wardekker, Volman, & Terwel, 2014, p. 347) – stated that, on the basis of the received answers, "if there is one common lesson learned by all concerned in the process of innovations, then it is: better understanding of the part played by the teacher in the course of change" (Freudenthal, 1978, p. 145).

Mathematics professor Larry Blakers, for example, pointed to the fact that the reforms in Australia were "overseas-inspired, but not blindly copied" and that "the process of adaptation" differed from state to state (Blakers, 1978, p. 152). The various reforms, which were supported by the conviction of being part of a "historically significant educational process" (ibid., p. 153), had been prompted by individuals and then adopted by the different authorities. The reforms in Great Britain had avoided "the 'New math' excesses of overabstraction to be observed in the United States and on the continent," as they had been built upon the English tradition of applied mathematics (Howson, 1978, p. 188). Of the numerous reform projects which were documented in the report from Great Britain, only the Swansea scheme – the point of which was "that pupils can be given a better understanding of the nature of mathematics than has hitherto been possible" – was associated with being an actual new math reform project (ibid.). However, this reform project supposedly did not last long, because the text book, i.e. its content, was rather addressed to a university audience and had thus aimed beyond targeted secondary level.

In contrast, the report from Bangladesh describes the reform of math tuition predominantly as an expansion of mathematics education and a standardization, which guaranteed a certain quality level. In Bangladesh, the support of the "average pupil" and the association of math tuition to "everyday life" were considered central (Sharfuddin, 1978, p. 163). The author of the country's report, also a mathematics professor, went on to stress the limitations of the reform: "The development of an integrated syllabus on modern lines was not undertaken by the committee because such a syllabus could only be interpreted by teachers trained in such methods and we did not have such teachers in the required numbers" (ibid.). He mentioned that nevertheless, the perception of school, including math education, had changed since Bangladesh had become independent (1971): "For the first time, men from outside the education system have seen it as a form of national investment and as related closely to the economic and political growth of the country" (ibid., p. 167). To this, Sharfuddin attached the hope of a general improvement of the quality of schools and tuition. It can be said that for Bangladesh, new math was not only a curricular reform project, but it coincided with an increased visibility and importance of schools. In fact, new math was being used to carry out school reforms.

This illustrates that the global debates on new math triggered some of the curriculum reform processes in the 1960s and 1970s. These reforms were, however, not only about replacing traditional math education by new math. In fact, their goal was to supplement math education or to adapt it to changed circumstances. Each country defined this in its own way, and the developing countries attached different goals to it than countries in the Global North. The debates on new math were therefore primarily an impulse to implement existing or new reform ideas which concentrated not only on the inner logic of mathematics, but they also included educational and structural aspects – questions which went far beyond the "actual" concern of new math.

3 The case of film and media education

Developments similar to those in the cases of programmed instruction and new math took place in the handling of film and television at school. In fact, the use of films and television had been a postulation of the Royaumont-conference for improving math instruction (OECD, 1961, pp. 27–28). The starting point of schools cooperating with film and television can be located in the America of the 1920s (Orgeron, Orgeron, & Streible, 2012). A major reason for the successful introduction of the new medium into schools was the possibility to at least partially compensate for a lack of teachers and bring "the world" into the classroom (Cuban, 1986, pp. 9–26; Smoodin, 2011, p. 21). Educational television could ensure instruction even in remote regions – an argument which had also been important in the context of programmed instruction, and a possibility which was used especially in Australia and Japan (Beneke, Wagner, & Wieczerkowski, 1981, p. 25; Meyer, 1994, p. 357). After World War II, educational television spread to large parts of the world. In Italy, for example, the *telescuola* was established in 1958 to redress the high number of illiterates, especially in the south of the country (Hollmann, 1996, p. 11). However, it also offered secondary school degrees. Educational television also established itself in the USSR and Eastern Europe, in France, Great Britain, Germany and Switzerland. Last but not least, worldwide conferences made the new medium better known to the various countries and offered opportunities to exchange experiences (ibid., p. 12).

Once more, Berlin and its *Pädagogisches Zentrum* turned out to be an active intermediary, organizing an international congress on educational television in September 1966. Whereas the conference on programmed instruction had in fact been an international convention, in which not only the welcoming speech had stressed the international relevance and emanation of Berlin as its venue, but which had also mirrored this internationality in the constitution of the participants, the conference on educational television was a predominantly "German" gathering with international participation, as the distribution of the contributions illustrates. Of a total of 23 contributions only three dealt with the situation of educational television outside Germany, namely in France, Great Britain and the USSR.[7]

The contribution from France was basically a sort of account on French educational radio and television between 1963 and 1967, as well as an outlook on the planned activities until 1970 on primary and secondary level and in the field of extracurricular activities. Primarily, the latter dealt with supporting and consolidating the transfer of school knowledge (e.g. during school holidays), but it also included questions of transferring knowledge on the professional world and issues of adult education (Brunswic, 1967, pp. 274–275). The contribution from Great Britain presented a more fundamental discussion of the subject of educational television on the background of a largely decentralized organization of schools and broadcasting organizations. Its first part featured the situation and financing of the Independent Television System (the alternative to the BBC) and pointed to the fact that although the statutory basis included a mandate for "information, education and entertainment," there was no mandate for "educational programmes" (Weltman, 1967, p. 280). The second part discussed the purpose and mandate of educational programmes. Here, the question was raised as to whether educational broadcasting was "merely" yet another medium in the sense of a "completely neutral instrument of communication, a servant and a reflection of the educational system as it is" or "a novel and independent educational institution with a unique contribution of its own to make" (ibid., p. 284). Not only was it the financial difficulties of British schools in connection with increasing demands and numbers of pupils which brought forward the report's argument in favour of educational television as a new player in the educational system; it was also claimed that television was to bring about a fundamental change with regard to the contents and methods of education, and that it could introduce the world into schools, thus contributing to make "education . . . relevant" (ibid., p. 285).

The report on the USSR, authored by Marburg-based Hartmut Vogt, pointed out that in comparison to Western Europe or the US, the meaning of "educational television" in the USSR was different, because the medium of television in itself was intended to be more educational than entertaining (Vogt, 1967b, p. 296). But even there, one could distinguish between "general educational television" and "specific educational and instructional television" (ibid., p. 297). However, in contrast to the remarks from Great Britain, educational television in the USSR was certainly "only" one of many teaching aids, a supplement to existent tuition and established pedagogical tools, and it was seen rather as a sort of second or additional teacher who was to be embedded into "normal" teaching by the actual teacher (ibid., p. 305).

Even more pointedly than in the debates about new math, the discussions on film and television in school education showed that they did not simply deal with the use of a new medium in class, but that this new medium also included the expectancy of possibilities to reform school education fundamentally and, most of all, to adapt it to the requirements of the present day or even to prepare it for the future, i.e. to make schools and tuition "relevant" – as the British contribution had phrased it – or to democratize it (Chresta, 1963, p. 13). This claim soon turned educational television into media education, a development which shall be illustrated more concisely using the example of Switzerland.

In 1968, the Swiss 'national' broadcasting company aired its first programmes of educational television, and shortly thereafter, it was stressed that "film education is an urgent necessity" (Frehner, 1968, p. 1). The focus of such education was not placed on the technical aspects of films, but rather on the pedagogical treatment of the new medium, whereby the term 'film education' subsumed all aspects dealing with "moving pictures." It was mentioned that film had become an "environmental factor to be interpreted" instead of being neglected in school, because "a large number of boys and girls have access to films via television and forbidden cinema" (ibid., p. 2). Therefore, guidance by teachers was all the more necessary. The aim of such educational activities was not so much to avoid contact with "bad films," but rather to awaken an understanding of "film as a work of art" and to confront the children "with its message" (ibid., p. 3). In addition, "in the conscious confrontation with films" pupils were to learn that a film is "a means, a possibility to represent things of life or life itself in one way or another" (ibid.). Therefore, films had to be made "comprehensible as an experience" and were seen as a possibility "to bring up a certain problem and to process it in conversation" (ibid., p. 2). Thus, film education meant primarily transferring knowledge about the production of films, which was in turn important to counter the seductive power of moving pictures. This also points to the fact that the use of film and television in the classroom very soon developed from a pedagogical tool to a fundamental pedagogical issue, a fact which was expressed when the term *film education* turned into *media education*.

The educational demands associated with media education became clear at a conference in 1978. At this conference, a variety of projects were presented, including an empirical study on the impact of the mass media on the lives of school children (Saxer, Bonfadelli, & Hättenschwiler, 1979), an explanation on the basic features of "action-oriented media education" (Baacke, 1978, p. 14) and a report by representatives of the Catholic film office, the Protestant film service and the trade unions which pointed out in what ways these organizations were specifically involved in media education. The Swiss Youth and Mass Media Working Group suggested the establishment of a "general, supra-regional and supra-confessional coordination office for documentation and information" (Meier, 1978, p. 3). A lecturer working at the local teachers' college made a case for media education as being practical communication training. His argument in favour of media education almost took on world-saving traits, as it was claimed to help "reduce alienated learning and stress at school," grasp the "student in his or her entirety" and make "lively learning" possible "by causing personal dismay and leaving the constitution of meaning to the learner" by conveying "insights into social, political and economic contexts" and by initiating "the development of individual and collective strategies for coping with the damaged life in a damaged world" (Ramseier, 1978, pp. 9–10). Thus, this conference assembled very different ideas on the content and the function of the media, some of which also contradicted each other. It also became clear that media education and its starting point, film education, was in fact a teaching or even a life principle almost paradigmatically promising to redeem the contemporary pedagogical demand for a curriculum oriented to the world in which we live.

This comprehensive claim also explains why – not only in Switzerland (Brown, 1991, pp. 224–272) – discussions on film and television education so quickly turned into the much broader issue of media education. If film education was to be part of the orientation of the curriculum towards the surrounding, modern world, it also had to turn to other media, whereby the practical implementation did not question the instructional dimension and thus the normative side. Although, at its beginning, the aim of film education in Switzerland had been to understand the history of the production and the staging of a film, this enlightening intention was soon associated with a normative dimension, since the aim was to learn to distinguish reality from fiction, to read medial staging and acquire additional knowledge in order to protect oneself from the danger of indoctrination. Especially in film education, normative convictions could be supported by aesthetic arguments which could easily give the impression of being "non-normative" – a conviction readily embraced by media education.

4 Global or national pedagogy?

These insights into various curriculum reform debates and school reform projects illustrate that despite all the common interests, the headwords of programmed instruction, new math and film education embraced quite a number of different concerns and reform projects. The reason for this was that debates with global perspectives had to be implemented into national settings, a process in which adaptations were imperative. However, these examples also show that they are to be understood as part of a globally shared conviction to make teaching more effective and better through a new or at least improved pedagogy and at the same time to bring it "closer to life." Thus, pedagogy holds the promise to provide answers to societal, social or economic problems, however these problems were formulated nationally. These three examples are therefore not to be understood as three independent reform projects having emerged more or less simultaneously. They are, in fact, three different expressions of the same idea, i.e. the belief in social and cultural improvement through education, which had become globally predominant in the 1950s and 1960s.

It has also become clear that the various reform debates quickly started to focus on pedagogical questions and questions of teaching practice, for example in Czechoslovakia, where discussions led from behaviourism as "a base too narrow for programmed instruction" on Jean Piaget and Gestalt psychology to Jerome Bruner's *Process of Education* (Lindner, 1966, p. 19). The publication which was both a summary of and an elaboration on the discussions from a conference in Woods Hole (USA)[8] dealt with the questions of "What shall be taught, when, and how? What kinds of research and inquiry might further the growing effort in the design of curricula?" (Bruner, 1960, pp. 2–3).[9] The attendees of the conference had discussed the new technical possibilities of film and television, of learning machines and of further pedagogical tools, without reaching a "consensus on the subject" (ibid., p. 15). The only issue which the attendees agreed upon was the assessment that "not teaching devices but teachers were the principal agents of instruction" (ibid.), although the question of how to support teachers best and most effectively remained unanswered.

Thus, the conference attendees had discussed the same pedagogical question which also crystallized in the aforementioned case examples as the question to be answered when the first euphoria about pedagogical innovations has evaporated and possible structural obstacles have been removed. This question can only ever be answered on a national level, because not only schools but also teacher training are organized nationally and because schools as places of "educating the future citizen" are always related to a national context into which and for which education and training are provided. Therefore, pedagogical reform movements may well enter the stage with a global perspective and expand to different national contexts. But the concrete implementations are always moulded by the individual countries and must therefore be discussed and reconstructed on a national level, without, however, turning a blind eye to the global interlacement of national developments.

Notes

1 This hope has accompanied pedagogy since its beginnings and intensified around 1800 in the context of the "educationalization of social problems" and the promises of concepts like "method," developed and propagated by Johann Heinrich Pestalozzi (1746–1827) (Tröhler, 2013b).

2 The *Pädagogische Arbeitsstelle*, which was superseded by the *Pädagogische Zentrum*, was a model institution for interlinking theory and practice in education and school. In 1994, it was superseded by the *Berliner Institut für Lehrerfort- und -weiterbildung und Schulentwicklung BIL* (Berlin institute for continued teacher training and school development) (Furck, 2003, p. 269).
3 The conference proceedings include the speeches held in Berlin and the protocols of a total of five workgroups and two commissions. The workgroups dealt with programmed instruction and teaching machines in schools in industrial and developing countries (groups 1and 2), questions of the psychology of learning and pedagogy (groups 3 and 4) as well as with programmed instruction in industrial training courses (group 5). The two commissions developed a plan of action and addressed the terminology of programmed instruction.
4 In this chapter the keyword *new math* refers solely to the reform projects of math tuition which can be traced back directly to the debates of the Bourbaki group. The curriculum reform debates in the US with regard to the STEM fields since the 1950s, which first of all advocated for a "scientific" curriculum and a general rejection of the life-adjustment movement, will not be considered here (see Phillips, 2015, chapter 2).
5 The ICMI was founded in 1908 by a group of mathematicians. It promotes international programmes with activities and publications which improve the collaboration, exchange and dissemination of ideas and information on the theory and practice of contemporary mathematical education (see Lehto, 1998).
6 There was a total of 16 published national reports (Australia, Bangladesh, France, Great Britain, Hungary, India, Iran, the Netherlands, Nigeria, Poland, Sierra Leone, Sri Lanka, Sudan, Thailand, U.S.A., West Indies). It is not clear whether all of the submitted contributions were published, as it was stated that "a large number of countries" had answered the call (Freudenthal, 1978, p. 145).
7 This imbalance in contributions might be related to the fact that the respective national broadcasting organizations played an important role as providers of teaching materials for educational television and that – for financial and regulatory reasons – these broadcasting organizations focused on national audiences.
8 The conference in September 1959 was conducted by Bruner. It included 34 American and European scholars and was one of the educational answers to the competition between systems during the Cold War (see Tröhler, 2014, p. 751; Pinar, Reynolds, Slattery, & Taubman, 1995).
9 This publication is therefore considered to be the "fundamental text" on curriculum studies.

Unpublished sources

Forschungsbibliothek Pestalozzianum, Zurich

Baacke, D. (1978). Pädagogische Aspekte der Medienerziehung, Vortragstyposkript für die Informationstagung SGKM "Medienpädagogik in der Schweiz", 2./3. Juni. Pestalozzianum, Archiv Wymann 122/91.
Frehner, P. (1968). Zusammenfassender Bericht der Kommission zum Studium des Ausbaus der Filmerziehung im Kanton Zürich, 5. November. Pestalozzianum, Archiv Wymann 120/2.
Meier, P. (1978). Das medienpädagogische Konzept der ajm, 29. Mai. Pestalozzianum, Archiv Wymann 122/91.
Ramseier, E. (1978). Medienpädagogik in der Lehrerbildung. Pestalozzianum, Archiv Wymann 122/91.

Sources

Aubin, D. (1997). The Withering Immortality of Nicolas Bourbaki: A Cultural Connector at the Confluence of Mathematics, Structuralism and the Oulipo in France. *Science in Context, 10*(2), 297–342.

Blakers, A. L. (1978). Change in mathematics education since the late 1950's – Ideas and realisation Australia. *Educational Studies in Mathematics, 9*, 147–158.

Bourbaki, N. (1939–1968). *Eléments de mathématique, 10 volumes*: Paris: Hermann.

Bruner, J. (1960). *The Process of Education*. Cambridge: Harvard University Press.

Brunswic, E. (1967). Etat Actuel et Perspectives de la Radio-Télévision Educative en France. In G. Müller (Ed.), *Schul- und Studienfernsehen 1966* (pp. 268–276). Weinheim: Beltz.

Chresta, H. (1963). *Filmerziehung in Schule und Jugendgruppe*. Solothurn: Schweizer Jugend-Verlag.

Dieudonné, J. A. (1970). The Work of Nicholas Bourbaki. *The American Mathematical Monthly, 77*, 134–145.

Evers, C.-H. (1964). Vorwort. In Pädagogische Arbeitsstelle & Sekretariat Pädagogisches Zentrum (Eds.), *Internationale Konferenz. Programmierter Unterricht und Lehrmaschinen, 9.-15. Juli 1962* (pp. VII–VIII). Berlin & Bielefeld: Franz Cornelsen.

Farrag, O. L. (1964). Final Reports, Group 2. In Pädagogische Arbeitsstelle & Sekretariat Pädagogisches Zentrum (Eds.), *Internationale Konferenz. Programmierter Unterricht und Lehrmaschinen, 9.-15. Juli 1962* (6–15). Berlin & Bielefeld: Franz Cornelsen.

Fehr, H. (1964). Preface. In OECD (Eds.), *Mathematics to-day. A guide for teachers* (3–4). Paris: OECD.

Freudenthal, H. (1978). Change in mathematics Education since the late 1950's – Ideas and realisation. *Educational Studies in Mathematics, 9*, 143–145.

Hawkridge, D. G. (1966a). Programmierter Unterricht in Zentralafrika. *Programmiertes Lernen und programmierter Unterricht, 3*, 62–63.

Hawkridge, D. G. (1966b). First Results of Programmed Learning Research in Central Africa. *Programmed Learning, 3*(1), 17–29.

Howson, A. G. (1978). Change in mathematics education since the late 1950's – Ideas and realisation Great Britain. *Educational Studies in Mathematics, 9*, 183–223.

IPN=Institut pédagogique national (France) (1966). *Bibliographie sur l'enseignement programme et les machines à enseigner*. Paris: IPN.

Karaschewski, H. (1966). *Wesen und Weg des ganzheitlichen Rechenunterrichts*. Stuttgart: Ernst Klett.

Lindner, H. (1966). Der programmierte Unterricht in der Tschechoslowakei. *Programmiertes Lernen und programmierter Unterricht, 3*, 19–20.

OECD. (1961). *New Thinking in School Mathematics*. Paris: OEEC.

OEEC. (1961). *Synopses for modern secondary school mathematics*. [Paris]: OEEC.

Schultze, W. (1964). Final Reports, Group 1. In Pädagogische Arbeitsstelle & Sekretariat Pädagogisches Zentrum (Eds.), *Internationale Konferenz. Programmierter Unterricht und Lehrmaschinen, 9.-15. Juli 1962* (pp. 1–5). Berlin & Bielefeld: Franz Cornelsen.

Sharfuddin, S. M. (1978). Change in mathematics education since the late 1950's – Ideas and realisation Bangladesh. *Educational Studies in Mathematics, 9*, 159–170.

Skinner, B. F. (1961). Why We Need Teaching Machines. *Harvard Educational Review, 31*, 377–398.

Skinner, B. F. (1965). The technology of teaching. *Proceedings of the Royal Society B, 162*, 427–443.

Vogt, H. (1967a). *Bildungsprobleme der Industriegesellschaft in West und Ost*. Braunschweig: Westermann.

Vogt, H. (1967b). Aufgaben und Formen des Bildungsfernsehens in der UdSSR. In G. Müller (Ed.), *Schul- und Studienfernsehen 1966* (pp. 296–306). Weinheim: Beltz.

Weltman, J. (1967). The Schools Service of British Independent Television. In G. Müller (Ed.), *Schul- und Studienfernsehen 1966* (pp. 277–293). Weinheim: Beltz.

Wolfer, P. (1972). Modeartikel "Neue Mathematik". *Schweizer Schule*, 59(17), 682–684.

References

Beneke, K.-M., Wagner, H., & Wieczerkowski, W. (1981). *Schulfernsehen in Theorie und Praxis*. Wiesbaden: Springer.

Boretska, V. (2019). Johnny and Ivan learning in a programmed way: The reinvention of one American technology. *Bildungsgeschichte. International Journal for the Historiography of Education*, 9(1), 29–46.

Bosche, A., & Geiss, M. (2011). Das Sprachlabor: Steuerung und Sabotage eines Unterrichtsmittels im Kanton Zürich, 1963–1976. *Jahrbuch für Historische Bildungsforschung*, 17, 119–139.

Brown, J. A. (1991). *Television "critical viewing skills" education*. Hillsdale: Lawrence Erlbaum.

Cuban, L. (1986). *Teachers and machines. The classroom use of technology Since 1920*. New York, NY and London: Teachers College.

De Bock, D., & Vanpaemel, G. (2019). *Rods, sets and arrows. The rise and fall of modern mathematics in Belgium*. Cham: Springer Nature.

Deplazes, D. (2020). "Die Lernmaschinen waren … ein Zückerchen": das Gelfinger Schulexperiment von 1968 bis 1972. *Paedagogica Historica*. doi:10.1080/00309230.2020.1838575.

Furck, C.-L. (2003). Das Pädagogische Zentrum in Berlin – eine Verbindung von Wissenschaft und Praxis. *Jahrbuch für Historische Bildungsforschung*, 9, 269–282.

García del Dujo, A., & Martín-Lucas, J. (2020). Towards "Onlife" education. How technology is forcing us to rethink pedagogy. In A. V. Martín-García (Ed.), *Blended learning: Convergence between technology and pedagogy* (pp. 1–19). Cham: Springer Nature.

Hof, B. (2018). From Harvard via Moscow to West Berlin: Educational technology, programmed instruction, and the commercialization of learning after 1957. *History of Education*, 47(4), 445–465.

Hof, B. (2020). The turtle and the mouse: How constructivist learning theory shaped artificial intelligence and educational technology in the 1960s. *History of Education*. doi:10.1080/0046760X.2020.1826053.

Hollmann, C. (1996). *Fernsehmachen für die Schule. Konzeption und Filmpsychologie des Schulfernsehens am Beispiel des Faches Geschichte*. Wörth: Andreas Diecke.

Horlacher, R. (2015). The implementation of programmed learning in Switzerland. In D. Tröhler & T. Lenz (Eds.), *Trajectories in the development of modern school systems. Between the national and the global* (pp. 113–127). New York, NY: Routledge.

Kurig, J. (2015). *Bildung für die technische Moderne. Pädagogische Technikdiskurse zwischen den 1920er und den 1950er Jahren in Deutschland*. Würzburg: Königshausen & Neumann.

Lehto, O. (1998). *Mathematics without borders: A history of the international mathematical union*. New York, NY: Springer.

Meyer, M. (Ed.). (1994). *Kultur- und Bildungsprogramme im Fernsehen – Defizite, Unterstützung, Chancen. Beiträge zu einem internationalen Symposium*. München: K.G. Saur.

Moon, B. (1986). *The 'new maths' curriculum controversy. An international story*. London: The Falmer Press.

Nicholson, P. (2007). A history of e-learning. In B. Fernández-Manjón, J. M. Sánchez-Pérez, J. A. Gómez-Pulido, M. A. Vega-Rodríguez, & J. Bravo-Rodríguez (Eds.), *Computers and education: E-learning, from theory to practice* (pp. 1–19). Dordrecht: Springer.

Openshaw, R., & Walshaw, M. (2019). *Transnational synergies in school mathematics and science debates*. Cham: Palgrave Macmillan by Springer.

Orgeron, D., Orgeron, M., & Streible, D. (Eds.). (2012). *Learning with the lights off. Educational film in the United States*. New York, NY: Oxford University Press.

Phillips, C. J. (2015). *The new math. A political history*. Chicago, IL and London: The University of Chicago Press.

Pinar, W. F., Reynolds, W. M., Slattery, P., & Taubman, P. M. (1995). *Understanding curriculum*. New York, NY: Peter Lang.

Rohstock, A. (2014). Antikörper zur Atombombe. Verwissenschaftlichung und Programmierung des Klassenzimmers im Kalten Krieg. In P. Bernhard & H. Nehring (Eds.), *Den Kalten Krieg neu entdecken. Beiträge zur sozialen Ideengeschichte* (pp. 259–284). Essen: Klartext.

Rudolph, J. (2002). *Scientists in the classroom: The cold war reconstruction of American science education*. New York, NY: Palgrave Macmillan.

Saxer, U., Bonfadelli, H., & Hättenschwiler, W. (1979). Die Massenmedien im Leben der Schüler. Ergebnisse einer Untersuchung im Kanton Zürich. In Audiovisuelle Zentralstelle am Pestalozzianum (Ed.), *Grundlagen einer Medienpädagogik* (pp. 61–102). Zug: Klett & Balmer.

Smoodin, E. (2011). "What a power for education!" The cinema and sites of learning in the 1930s. In Ch. R. Acland & H. Wasson (Eds.), *Useful cinema* (pp. 17–33). Durham and London: Duke University Press.

Tröhler, D. (2013a). The technocratic momentum after 1945. The development of teaching machines, and sobering results. *Journal of Educational Media, Memory, and Society*, 5(2), 1–19.

Tröhler, D. (2013b). *Pestalozzi and the educationalization of the world*. New York, NY: Palgrave Macmillan.

Tröhler, D. (2014). The medicalization of current educational research and its effects on education policy and school reforms. *Discourse: Studies in the Cultural Politics of Education*, 36(5), 749–764.

Wardekker, W., Volman, M., & Terwel, J. (2014). Curriculum research in the Netherlands. In W. F. Pinar (Ed.), *International handbook of curriculum research* (pp. 340–350). New York, NY: Routledge.

6 Schooling humans as a form of capital

The national and imperial context

Bruce Moghtader

Isn't it dictatorial or obtuse to apply a single set of norms to all the world's peoples? Doesn't this way of proceeding smack of imperialism?

(Nussbaum, 2011, p. 101)

Martha C. Nussbaum (2011) reminds us that the "rules of global competition are in many ways advantageous to the richer nations, as are the policies of the World Bank and the International Monetary Fund" (p. 116). Imperialism often proceeds from policies that sustain domestic economic and military advantages of some nation-states and direct social organizations of others. Among these policies are those that are derived from human capital theory and that are designed to impact educational institutions. From its very beginning, human capital theory postulated two fundamental assumptions: 1) humans are a form of capital (Schultz, 1959; 1963); and 2) knowledge is a form of capital (Becker, 1964, 1994; Schultz, 1993). The first assumption attempts to normalize the treatment of humanity as a means to achieve political and economic goals. The second assumption channels the personal, ethical and social aspects of knowledge to economics.

In its history, *capital* includes slaves, machines, animals and property. This leads to the question of how is it that in forward-looking democratic societies – capitalists and socialists alike – parents encourage their children to become a form of capital? Although there is a history of human capital, before the 20th century, there was no comprehensive *theory* of human capital; it was not developed until the Cold War. In this chapter, I focus on formation, expansion and contribution of human capital theory first in its national and then in its imperial aspirations. After reviewing the conceptual framework that produced the theory, I contextualize its global expansion and impact. Human capital theory continues to be instrumental in local, global and glocal economic policies that targets identity formation through schooling. The American neo-liberals' defence of human capital theory conjured up political force through international organizations and led the campaign of commodifying human development and corroborating a global hegemony over digitalization of education.

DOI: 10.4324/9781003137801-9

1 Why human capital theory?

Since the 18th century, *educationalization*, assigning education institutions the task of combating imagined and real social problems, has contributed to the modern narrative of progress in the West (Tröhler, 2017). Educationalization has attributed to the alignment of citizens to the ideals of the nation-state (Tröhler, 2020). It often proceeds from conceptualizing a problem (e.g. criminality, sexuality, economy) by expert knowledges to creating a regime of truth which individuals and groups then apply to themselves. The role of policy is pivotal in directing educationalization. For example, the industrial model of school materialized as the 19th century elites relied on "propaganda" to institute taxation for public education in the "interests of both public and private welfare" (Cubberley, 1922, p. 347). If the 19th century schooling of the poor population and indigenous people of the colonies was to align them with religious and industrial learning, the second half of the 20th century began to demand that schools train human capital. The persuasiveness of arguments for training human capital grew from the United States in light of the national crisis after the launch of *Sputnik* by the Soviet Union in 1957 (Pinar, 2004, p. 65; Tröhler, 2017). "The scientific and military failure was recoded as the failure of public education" (Pinar, 2019a, p. 120). In this context, traditional liberal ideals were adjusted to "a constant adaptation of the legal order to scientific discoveries" and "to the progress in economic organization" by neoliberals, Milton Friedman, Theodore Schultz, Gary S. Becker, the primary proponents of human capital theory (Foucault, 2008, p. 160).

Becker's (1960) statement that the "panic in the United States engendered by the more spectacular Soviet accomplishments has in turn spawned a re-examination of American policies and procedures relating to economic growth and military technology" (p. 346) underlined a "national urgency" to fundamentally reconstruct education institutions to aid (domestic) "economic and military development" (p. 352). In suggesting that individuals and society benefit from investment in education, Becker (1960) admitted it is "difficult to calculate the economic returns," particularly "for children from lower strata families since they are more ignorant of the returns to college education" (p. 353). However, he stressed that "a policy designed to spread information, especially among the low-income families" will support national economic development (p. 354). The search for an economic answer to domestic military and political issues proceeded by manufacturing information and distracted attention from social inequalities and the civil rights movement. By the end of 1950s, Jacob Mincer (1958) acknowledged that "the emphasis of contemporary research has been almost completely shifted from the study of the causes of inequality to the study of the facts and of their consequences for various aspects of economic activity, particularly consumer behaviour" (p. 281). The attention to "behaviour" of so-called consumers grew from deductive approaches to national statistics that allowed for: 1) capitalizing associations between education and income; and 2) producing policies that indicated education is both an investment and a consumption.

Not only did the new approach to economics neglect the causes of inequality, but it also diverged from previous conceptualizations of humans as contributors to national wealth. Before reliance on statistical techniques, William Petty (1623–1687) and Adam Smith (1723–1790) had argued for the inclusion of people as part of the national wealth and had outlined the importance of schools to improve the dexterity of the workers. For example, Petty (1666/1862) in his conceptualization of the industrial schools, stressed that the training of the working class can best be governed by those who employed them. And, although Adam Smith (1789/1904) defended liberty, he too opted for utilitarian valuations of schooling:

> A man educated at the expense of much labour and time to any of those employments which required extraordinary dexterity and skill, may be compared to one of those expensive machines. The work which he learns to perform, it must be expected, over and above the usual wages of common labour, will replace to him the whole expense of his education, with at least the ordinary profits of an equally valuable capital. It must do this too in a reasonable time, . . . in the same manner as to the more certain duration.
>
> (p. 103)

However, Smith (1789/1904) distinguished among "education, study or apprenticeship" and acknowledged that as processes they required time and labour. He added that the "improved dexterity in the workman can be considered in the same light as a machine or instrument" (p, 265). In contrast to Adam Smith, Milton Friedman (1962) proposed that "investment in human capital is precisely analogous to investment in machinery, building on other forms of non-human capital" (p. 100). Unlike Smith's advocacy for the role of impartial legislators, Friedman (1955) advocated for privatization of education and elimination of the state's role in education. Friedman's approach to education assumed that private business' propensity for profit increases efficiency in producing economic outcomes and offers parents and children from low socio-economic status with choices and contributes to competitive markets.

The process of aligning individuals with businesses required normalization of the economic approach to education. In this context, both Theodore Schultz and Gary Becker extended the role of economics in public schooling. Schultz (1963), for example, acknowledged the growing intrusion of "efficiency experts" into education institutions had undermined the "human factor" (p. 12). However, he explained the role of economics in education seeks to calculate the "value of schooling," "economize the time of students," manage the "incentives" of the "earnings that students forgo," and by "adopting new techniques" and "new kinds of inputs" increase economic outputs (Schultz, 1963, p. 13). Thus, the "human factor" was undermined by the primacy given to the economic calculations. Schultz (1963) returned to the economic thesis and explained that if people are "an important part of the wealth of nations" then their education is "a special priority" (p. 109). Education was also a special priority in the context of offshoring labour for lower costs of production, dismantling union movements and replacing human labour by automation to maximize profit. Conceiving education as a consumable directed the workers to training, but it also articulated that the boom and bust in employment is an individual and national problem – and has little to do with social responsibility of the elites to the public.

The conception of education as training had a wider significance: The aims of raising healthy and civil children were enveloped in an emphasis on *learning*, improved by further adaptation to business efficiency models in schools. By equating "learning and training," to education, Becker (1964) thought that "a school can be defined as an institution specializing in the production of training," and he continued: "School and firms are often substitute sources of particular skills" (p. 29). This is alarming because on various occasions, Becker (1964) stressed that "employees pay for general on-the-job training by receiving wages below what they could receive elsewhere" (p. 13) and firms "shift training costs to [the] trainee and have an incentive to do so when faced with competition for their services" (p. 22). By the analogy of school to business, children bear the cost of schooling while they are trained to be more productive and profitable employees. Families conduct themselves as investment firms, calculating returns on the education of their children. According to Becker (1964), "People choose learning only if it is a sufficiently good investment" (p. 46). Furnishing moral sentiments with economic prospects, Becker advocates for negligence when learning is not a sufficiently good investment. According to Folbre (2009), "The increasing importance of human capital dramatizes the realm of family life. Much as we like to think of ourselves as producers, we are, ourselves, produced" (p. 301). By stressing the utility of children, human capital theory misconceived education as training "*homo economicus*," who exchange ethical and political rights to self-maximize and in so doing become integrated into the market (Foucault, 2008).

Human capital theory underscores a shift from liberal possessive individualism (Macpherson, 1962) to neoliberal competitive individualism in a national context that, perhaps with the exception of the New Deal, traditionally pursued extremely liberal economic policies or even saw the promotion of economic and trade freedom as their essential national goal. This shift was made possible by reliance on utilitarian cost-benefit analysis and the prospect of economic incentives. For example, Becker (1964) thought that "young people have a greater incentive to invest [in education] because they can collect the return over more years" (p. 50). The same logic applied to education of women. According to Becker (1964), women "spend less time in the labour force than men and therefore, have less incentive to invest in market skills" (p. 51). The incentives were far from guaranteed. They were probable as education became subject to supply and demand of the labour market. Individuals were not altogether enterprises to themselves, but the bearer of the risks. Friedman (1953) had articulated that risk, choice and chance (leaving out affordability of an education) have to be calculated in order to explain individual income differences. And Becker (1994) admitted: "While business investments are often said to pay off within five or ten years, the payoff from college takes much longer" (p. 204). Instead of adding clarity, Becker (1994) continued: "A long payoff period increases risk along with low correlations between returns by reducing the value of information available when investing" (p. 204). Becker (1976/2013) assumed humans possess "stable preferences" and "accumulate . . . information and other inputs" from the "markets" to "maximize" their utility (p. 14). Information plays a double role in human capital theory. First, information directs personal decisions, evaluations and judgments. In this sense, it has a diminishing value for those it targets. Second, information directs public opinion and, in this sense, information has an increasing value for those who produce and distribute it.

2 Global uniformity and conformity

Becker confessed that he "hesitated a while before deciding to call" his 1964 book *Human Capital*: "In the early days, many people were criticizing this term and the underlying analysis because they believed it treated people like slaves or machines" (Becker, 1994, p. 16). However, by the time of the third publication of *Human Capital*, the term was circulating beyond economists to school principals, academics, journalists and policy makers. Human capital had become a "good rationale for obtaining public monies;" according to Becker (2009), "this partly explains its success" (p. 261). The reward of obtaining public money explains the change in behaviour as politicians, policymakers and administrators began to accept the term and its implications. Human capital theory harmonized public and private economic interests. For the neoliberal proponents of human capital theory, economic growth served to increase national productivity, combat international adversaries and project American values outwards. The prospect of monetary incentives, Becker mentioned, also became a "good rationale" for the adoption of human capital theory outside of the United States.

In pretence defence of liberalism, the neoliberals sought to safeguard capitalism at the scale of the entire world. The emphasis on the role of global market facilitated the creation of multitiered government and the world order in which "the financial services sector would play a key role in directing investment" requiring the Global South to adhere "to the rules that would secure predictability for investors" (Slobodian, 2018, p. 249). The formation of the World Bank and Organization for Economic Cooperation and Development (OECD) facilitated a global move to marketize education across national borders. While human capital theory trained policymakers in incentivizing public education for economic outputs, the model of competitive individualism explained by the American neoliberals was customized to meet the dominant ideologies of the socialist and communist countries. In suggesting universal validity of his theory, Becker (1994) claimed that human capital theory was "extensively used in the Soviet Union, Eastern Europe, and China" (p. 16) even prior to its popularization in the United States. The theory provided a rubric that supported treating education of citizens as a means to economic production. And since education is treated as an augmentation to labour power, education could only be improved by incorporation of technology.

Initially, the investment on human capital was advanced for the sake of improving technological progress during the Cold War. The lessons of industrial revolution had demonstrated that the disruption of knowledge passed on from parents to children was made possible by public schools (Schultz, 1953, p. 125). And Becker (1993) admitted: "Compelling evidence of the link between human capital and technology comes from agriculture" and added that "[e]ducation and training is also helpful in coping with changing technologies" (p. 25). The model of training pushed certain populations to simply *cope* with technological change. "In a dynamic technological environment, economic agents must adjust to disequilibria created by the introduction of innovative inputs" (Wozniak, 1987, p. 101). Economists are often complicit to note that the innovative inputs come with agents who profit from disequilibria they introduce. Since technology is governed by logics of efficiency and lowering costs, it works towards devaluation of human labour and learning. In a world dominated by information production, technological progress is both the cause and condition of remodelling other societies.

Information technology acts as an extension of the nervous system, supplementing physical and social power (McLuhan, 2005). And human capital theory was part of an information campaign that surpassed its national aims. For example, Schultz (1959) suggested that investment in education had a power to remedy the problems of the "poor countries" if they accepted the "decentralized character" of the American economy governed by market rationality (p. 113). The new economic imperialism asked for compliance to market mechanism by misconstruing that both markets and technological progress are autonomous processes unto themselves. Sen (2002) corrects the misconception about the markets: "The market mechanism has a role in protecting 'autonomy of decisions' as well as immunity from encroachment'" as long as "the levers of decision and control are in the hands of the respective individuals" (p. 512). The market mechanism can *promote* freedom, but by itself it is inadequate to serve as a *platform* for equity and distribution of wealth. Neoliberals' misrepresentation of the market mechanism facilitated a continuous expansion of policies that deterred teachers' agency in an international scale by the doctrine of economic progress that conceived students as commodities (Grimmett, 2009). By the first decade of the 21st century, the economic approach to education had scholars from Canada, Columbia, Mexico and Portugal lamenting the cumbersome effects of human capital theory in their local schools (Smith, 2013; Diaz Barriga, 2013; Montoya-Vargas, 2013; Pacheco & Seabra, 2013). Through the Organization for Economic Cooperation and Development (OECD) and the World Bank policies, the theory asserted that people irrespective of their locality are to be schooled by the model of human capital theory. The theory's influence was felt at both international level, within OECD and the EU, and within national education systems impacting countries such as "Scotland, England, Wales, Norther Ireland, Eire, Norway, Sweden, Denmark, Finland, Germany, Austria, Slovakia and Czech Republic" (Gillies, 2011, p. 228; Gillies, 2015). The new imperialism proceeded from knowledge production to shift policies across nation-states by targeting learning and consequently labour. For this a system of standards and accountabilities would further reduce education to the business of training workers and consumers.

The process of aligning schools with business had begun since the Industrial Revolution. However, during the Cold War, the educational reforms in the United States sped up the process by the discourse of standardization. Teachers were made "accountable for students' learning" (Pinar, 2019a, p. 121), and standardized measures, as Taubman (2009) points out, subjected teachers to rational uniformity of an audit culture and misplaced politicians' responsibility for the nation's economic well-being. One impact of the over-emphasis on standards in education was accommodation of technological metaphors of machine and property advanced by human capital theory. As learning became reduced to "accessing information" and thinking to "problem solving," teachers became classroom managers (Taubman, 2009, p. 169). It became easier to neglect that human development and cognition are socially situated. The standardized measures reduced teacher agency but also fertilized the ground for further corporatization of schooling within the United Sates and beyond (Spring, 2019).

At public costs, the mass production and distribution of standardized products moved forward. According to Saltman (2016), the media and technology corporations hired lobbyists who influenced politicians to pass legislations that supported homogenization and automation of pedagogy. The standardized products sold to administrators furthered the idea of data collection and categorization of the human capital and advanced future consumption and dependence on technologies. Such a political strategy became part of the prevailing discourse of public and private partnership and prompted the so-called consumers to personalize learning tools. Every learning is personalized learning, however, the learning that relied on information technology was praised for its efficiency, convenience and flexibility as well as for its power to reform learning, misconstrued as education. "Advocates for personalized learning technology suggest that if digital platforms such Google, Netflix, Amazon, and Facebook have transformed the way we conduct business, work, shop, communication, travel, organize, and entertain" so they should reinvent education (Roberts-Mahoney, Means, & Garrison, 2016, p. 406). The digital platforms mentioned are imploring techniques to further secure profit for their shareholders. As enterprises they are invested to expand their role in public domain and, by means of connectivity, change *engagement* and *participation* in schools.

Standard measures also proliferated globally in defence of economic individualism exemplified by the United States. Through the OECD's Programme for International Student Assessment' (PISA) a model of standardization is universalized by testing students' knowledge and skills, devoid of history and place. Context diminishes if it is possible to produce reports that homogenize *quality education* across nations. Through PISA, it is possible to miss the fact that an Afghan child does not share the same life as a Canadian child. PISA also signifies the creeping Western power-knowledge axioms on every culture and living being on Earth (often blurring the distinction between war, business and education in renewal effort of colonization). PISA ranks nations vertically based on students' performances and thus certain values are inherent in the process. The nations internalize competitive market ideologies as they compare their year-over-year rankings. The arbitrary rankings ignite national educational reforms and inform uncritical acceptance of the discourse of globalization (Takayama, 2008). Questions on soundness of cross-national convergence of PISA is absorbed into scripting a discourse of quality that standardizes human capital production for a global knowledge economy (Robertson, 2005). The OECD and the World Bank policies have altered political constitutions and informed the modality of globalization by decentralizing government programmes across nation-states and subjecting local value systems to new media and mediums of communication (Spring, 2015; 2019). The British historian of nationalism, Anthony D. Smith explains:

> The threat to independence in the late twentieth century from the new electronics could be greater than was colonialism itself. We are beginning to learn that de-colonization and the growth of supra-nationalism were not the termination of imperial relationship but merely the extending of a geo-political web which has been spinning since the Renaissance. The new media have the power to penetrate more deeply into a 'receiving' culture than any previous manifestation of Western technology.
>
> (Anthony Smith quoted in Said, 1993, p. 292)

According to Edward Said (1993), the "unopposed expansion of various forms of cultural control that emanated from the United States has created a new mechanism of incorporation and dependence" by which a "handful of American transnational corporations" reign the world (p. 292). Human capital policies "resulted in a scenario of the Bank loaning money to developing countries that, in turn, use the money to buy educational technology from global firms" (Spring, 2015, p. 120).

Information technology and human capital theory had a dialectical relationship on establishing a truth about globalization (Smith, 2006). The story of treating humans as a form of capital accompanied aspirations for rationalized infrastructure platforms, both describing a predestined economic growth. Rabid consumerism and technological utopianism, conjured forth that the new technologies will promote democracy, equality and liberty. However, Mosco (2004) emphasized that "equality," "liberty" and "democracy are seriously jeopardized, by a world in which key economic, political, social and cultural dimensions are set by a global network of firms" (p. 60). Free competition, free markets and rights to privacy – once promoted by the United States – are subject to the growth of transnational corporations housed in Silicon Valley. "Big tech considers the concentration of power" an "urgent social good" (Foer, 2017, p. 12). Foer (2017) explains that the transnational tech companies "aspire to escape competition, to exist on their own plane, so they can fulfil their transcendent potential" (p. 12). Their transcendent potential feeds from human consumption of their technology, builds dependence to their virtual ecosystem and exerts resources (time, labour and minerals) from the biosphere. Silicon Valley's venture philanthropists also offer an "attractive technocratic alternatives to bureaucratic state governance" but also "represent the displacement of power from the institutions of public education" and toward "high-tech corporatized schooling" (Williamson, 2018, p. 234). Philanthropy is an investment, in their eyes, to experiment with public education and in return gain entry to act on schools of tomorrow. They also gain redemption by wanting to make the management of human capital *efficient* while selling their technical solutions for statecraft.

Technological capabilities offer richer nation-states prospects of absorbing human capital. In the late 20th century nation-states softened their "strict discriminations between the citizens and foreigners" in "favor of the pursuit of human capital" (Ong, 2006, p. 499). Market freedom enabled categorizing humans as skilled immigrants, foreign workers, international students, entrepreneurs and investors. Technology promoted creation of digital citizens who self-identified with these categories. The Internet afforded certain groups access to travel and migration. It made acquiring human and non-human assets more seamless for the economically advanced nations and private entities. The time-space compression (Harvey, 1990) of the Internet aided the market for human capital. The new mediums detached persons from "'traditional' morality and politics" and "simultaneously" universalized and homogenized "cultural and political institutions" (Pinar, 2019b, p. 106). As human capital schematically outlined the course for an economic approach to humanity, the Internet transformed the quality of citizenship.

"The Internet, presents new opportunities for imperialism" (Pinar, 2015, p. 67). The collection and distribution of information plays a more important role in this model of imperialism. According to Koopman (2019), "the value of information conditioned the acceptance of information theory, and not the other way around" (p. 17). The value of information, as communicated bits, is generated by its supply and its use. Evidently, schools habituate the future generations to the informational world. The platforms in which the learning depends on unfolds in a perpetual supply and demand condition for mediums and media dominated by few for-profit companies. By modelling what it means to school a population the economically advanced nations set directions for other countries. In this context, the national education reforms are central to the legitimacy of discourses and practices of global schooling.

3 From national investment on learning to global extraction

Implicit to the call for improvement of learning and access to knowledge is a global upgrade to the notion of human capital as decontextualized economic entity, data. As the technologization of education proceeds, "[h]uman capital theory remains a powerful political influence" in creation of "'flexible specialists' who can adapt to fluctuations and changes in market demands" (Williamson, 2013, pp. 48–49). Today's markets no longer defend liberty but obstruct freedom and make *demands* (Brown, 2016). The rise of technocrats from market ideology presents the possibility of dispossessing teachers from their ethical conduct and eliminating the role of the state as "the central source of authority" in education (Williamson, 2013, p. 122). Williamson (2013) observed that the "two groups" that are "controlling the agenda for the curriculum of the future" are "psychologists and computer scientists" (p. 65). Leaving teachers out signifies an escalation of impersonal control that increases efficiency in government of the human capital as flexible specialists. In this, transnational corporations see opportunities for ongoing profit from educational institutions across nations. Based on human capital theory, schools are simply institutions where investment on learning occurs. Becker (1964) had arrived at "the conclusion that learning is a way to invest in human capital that is formally no different from education, on-the-job training, or other recognized investment" (p. 46). It is not the case that capital is invested in humans. The focus of investment is in making people learn themselves as certain beings. Human capital theory erodes the distinction between education and other conventional investment. It also allows for inclusion of "the physical and psychological factors associated with learning theory" (Becker, 1964, p. 47) and the technologies that can facilitate commercialization of human beings. Private technological corporation set networks across the globe during the 1990s, at the time markets' self-regulating powers were defended. At the turn of the 21st century, the neoliberal defence of "market globalism morphed into imperial globalism," initiated by the United States' War on Terror (Steger, 2006, p. 41). The myths of progress and liberty embedded in globalization normalized imperialism and control.

"Empires can succeed only if they foster quasi-autonomous local administration that are run by the peoples themselves" (Hacking, 2007, p. 289). Hacking (2007) suggests that throughout history imperial bureaucracies contrive their organizational power from social and physical sciences. Derived from a social science, human capital theory presents the case in which local educational institutions are targeted for remodelling societies and technology serves as an enabler for this remodelling (by transforming human life to data). Today's technological corporations support research and knowledge production in learning sciences. They deploy cognitive-behavioural and social and emotional learning theories to inform the development and expansion of their technologies. For example, most recently the "OECD's turn to Socio-Emotional Learning" advances measurement technologies that "are based on standardized models and instrument for precisely recording, measuring and classifying human affects and traits from autonomic biological processes in ways that may be presented as quantifiably objective, unambiguous and precise" (Williamson, 2021, p. 361). According to Williamson (2021), the quantification of biological and mental processes is explained as justifiable for having "policy relevance" and determining "priorities for interventions" (p. 362). And trans-national technological corporations have a stake in collection, exploration, distribution and possession of these data. Meanwhile, data is treated as a form of capital often harvested without consent for *improvement* purposes (Sadowski, 2019). When consent is obtained the quantification schemes, often automated, leave individual actors with little choice on how their data will be used.

Algorithms and machine-learning are becoming ever more involved in the design and administration of public and private policies. O'Neil (2017) observed that mathematical models of algorithms are micromanaging the economy, from prisons to schools. Their "value-added" logics of optimization "have different pay-offs. For the school district, the payoff is a kind of political currency, a sense that problems are being fixed. But for businesses it's just the standard currency: Money" (O'Neil, 2017, p. 12). The "problems" are not being fixed for schools. According to O'Neil (2017), the "trouble is that profits end up serving as a stand-in, or proxy, for truth" (p. 12). A truth-teller, O'Neil erased ambiguities that privacy, liberty and health are becoming "a luxury that only the wealthy can afford" (p. 170). As public schools are being subject to vague and unsubstantiated claims about efficacy of technology, Benjamin (2019) reported, "[m]any tech insiders choose a more judicious approach to tech" and "send their children to schools in which devices are banned or introduced slowly, in favour of pencil, paper, blackboard and craft material" (p. 15). While corporate elites "sell educators, the latest products couched in a concern that all students deserve access – the more privileged *refuse it*" (Benjamin, 2019, p. 16). Those who can "afford the luxury of opting out" are concerned with "tech addiction" and worry about the lack of "data privacy" (Benjamin, 2019, p. 16). Benjamin's (2019) observation suggests that financial capital plays an ever more determining role in production of the regime of truth about production of human capital assembled by information. Meanwhile, data accumulation in surveillance commerce proceeds from connectivity to abstraction of real-world experiences.

According to Zuboff (2019), surveillance capitalism is moving from extraction-and-execution to behavioural and biological manipulation and modification. The aims are not to impose behavioural norms of conformity or obedience, but rather to produce behaviours that reliably and definitively leads to desired commercial results (Zuboff, 2019). Behind the data-driven order are "the worlds' two most powerful states (the United States and China), who are competing for leadership of the social quantification sector" and appropriation of human capital (Couldry & Mejias, 2019, pp. 168–169). In the new management scheme, machine-to-machine connections significantly deepen the new web of knowledge production by the privately owned control systems. Since machines can communicate with each other instantly and continuously, they further the time-space compression that brought the previous models of colonization. Humans are both the raw materials and products of the new digital economy. Couldry and Mejias (2019) documented:

> [I]f you are one of the two billion Android users in the world (Android being a 'free' operating system), you represent a $363 value to Google. Each Facebook user (using the 'free' website) is worth $233 to the company. To parent company Tencent, based in China, each user of the 'free' app WeChat represents a $539 value. Even when we pay for a service, the data obtained from us has considerable worth. A mobile phone company might record a user's location about three hundred times a day. That company can then turn around and sell the data as part of an industry that generates $24 billion a year.
>
> (p. 37)

This paragraph indicates the global users of operating system are connected to companies in particular countries. Moving away from earlier forms of imperialism based on state's territorial control, new technologies – advanced through economism – enable global powers to target and profit from human life irrespective of place. While a global movement has taken place in producing information targeting local schools for being inefficient and in need of technological upgrade, it is important to follow the money and examine how social values that direct human habits perpetuate unequal freedom, nationally and internationally. In this context, assessment of education policies will benefit from: 1) re-evaluation of the ontological and epistemological assumptions manufactured by the Western power-knowledge axioms (Webb & Gulson, 2015); 2) attention to supranational economic policies and sanctions that hinder national sovereignty and facilitate crises of pedagogy (Hwami, 2020); 3) excavation of what knowledge economy does to human ethics (Moghtader, 2018).

Conclusion

The proponents of human capital theory provided indicators for their aims. First, Becker (1992) noted "that the process of investing or disinvesting in human capital often alters the very nature of a person" (p. 392). Second, Schultz (1993) found knowledge production as an important part of the internalization of economic tools to educate humans to be entrepreneurs who "cannot escape" their dynamic economies (p. 3). Third, after four decades, Friedman (1997) observed that the "the quality of schooling is far worse today than it was in 1955" (p. 342), the year he coined the term *human capital*. He continued to note that "technological and political revolutions" promise a major increase in economic output but also "threaten advanced countries with serious social conflict arising from a widening gap" in income (p. 341). He thought the adaptation of a voucher system can help private enterprise to fence off the thread of social conflict. For Friedman (1997), "[i]t is essential that no conditions be attached to the acceptance of vouchers that interfere with the freedom of private enterprises to experiment, to explore and to innovate," for it has potential implications for American businesses to expand "around the world" (p. 344). The increased use of technology in education offers suggestive signals of how the freedom of private enterprises to experiment with personal and social life can endanger the moral and political implications of education. According to Piketty (2014), since the 1970s the "income inequality has increased significantly in the rich countries, especially [in] the United States" (p. 15). While the "net private wealth" in Europe and the United States has increased, "there is no evidence that education has really increased intergeneration mobility" (Piketty, 2014, p. 420). Piketty suggested that, the technological rationality will not automatically lead to valuing human life over financial capital.

Human capital theory mainstreams technological rationality in educational institutions. The theory also offers one avenue to better understand American exceptionalism – that the United States is different from other nations and at once serves as a model for other nations in national policy-making (Lipset, 1996; Alasuutari & Qadir, 2013). Extolled as an instrument of economic liberalism, human capital policies formalized an administrative apparatus for nation-building by decentralized markets that use humans as resources for generating economic outputs. Advanced through supranational agencies (the World Bank and the OECD) and domesticated by local actors, human capital theories enable both state and non-state actors to cooperate in order to profit from public education. Today, "some of the most radical changes to the globalizing world are being written, not in the language of law and diplomacy," Easterling (2014) notes, but "in infrastructural technologies" – "often because market promotions or prevailing political ideologies lubricate their movement through the world" (p. 15). As the world is persuaded by information production of the richer nations, investments in educational institutions are directed towards personalized learning technologies that treat humans as depersonalized data. Roberts-Mahoney and colleagues (2016) show that there is "zero scientific evidence that personalized learning systems enhance education efficacy" (p. 417). Personalized learning technologies advance the role of trans-national corporations in reforming public education; as they advertise their platforms by the discourse of access and efficiency, they misconstrue continuous and seamless surveillance as social good. The deployment of information technologies supplements commodification and marketization of education while utilizing investment and return rubric of human capital theory to alter personal, social and cultural values of education across nation-states.

Acknowledgement

I would like to thank the editors for their constructive feedback.

References

Alasuutari, P., & Qadir, A. (Eds.). (2013). *National policy-making: Domestication of global trends*. Routledge. doi:10.4324/9780203082157

Barriga, F. D. (2013). Curriculum research in Mexico. In W. F. Pinar (Ed.), *International handbook of curriculum research* (pp. 29–339). New York, NY: Routledge.

Becker, G. S. (1960). Underinvestment in college education? *The American Economic Review*, 50(20), 346–354. Retrieved from www.jstor.org/stable/1815038

Becker, G. S. (1964). *Human capital: A theoretical and empirical analysis, with special reference to education*. New York, NY: Columbia University Press.

Becker, G. S. (1976 [2013]). *An economic approach to human behaviour*. Chicago, IL: University of Chicago Press.

Becker, G. S. (1993). Nobel lecture: The economic way of looking at behavior. *Journal of Political Economy*, 101(3), 385–409. Retrieved from https://EconPapers.repec.org/RePEc:ris:nobelp:1992_001

Becker, G. S. (1994). *Human capital: A theoretical and empirical analysis, with special reference to education* (3rd ed.). Chicago, IL: University of Chicago Press.

Becker, G. S. (2009). Gary Becker. In W. Breit & B. T. Hirsch (Eds.), *Lives of the laureates: Twenty-three novel economists* (5th ed., pp. 251–272). Cambridge, MA: MIT Press.

Benjamin, R. (2019). *Race after technology: Abolitionist tools for the new Jim Code*. Cambridge, MA: Polity Press.

Brown, W. (2016). Sacrificial citizenship: Neoliberalism, human capital, and austerity politics, *Constellations*, 23(1), 3–14. doi:10.1111/1467-8675.12166

Couldry, N., & Mejias, U. A (2019). *The costs of connection: How data is colonizing human life and appropriating it for capitalism*. Stanford, CA: Stanford University Press.

Cubberley, E. P. (1922). *A brief history of education*. New York, NY: Houghton Mifflin.

Easterling, K. (2014). *Extrastatecraft: The power of infrastructure space*. London: Verso.

Foer, F. (2017). *World without mind: The existential threat of big tech*. New York, NY: Random House.

Folbre, N. (2009). *Greed, lust & gender: A history of economic ideas*. New York, NY: Oxford University Press.

Foucault, M. (2008). *The birth of biopolitics: Lectures at the Collège de France 1978–79*. London: Palgrave Macmillan.

Friedman, M. (1953). Choice, chance, and the personal distribution of income. *Journal of Political Economy, 61*(4), 277–290. Retrieved from www.jstor.org/stable/1826880.

Friedman, M. (1955). The role of government in education. In R. A. Solo (Ed.), *Economics and the public interest* (pp. 123–144). New Brunswick, NJ: Rutgers University Press.

Friedman, M. (1962). *Capitalism and freedom*. Chicago, IL: University of Chicago Press.

Friedman, M. (1997). Public schools: Make them private. *Education Economics, 5*(3), 341–344. doi:10.1080/09645299700000026.

Gillies, D. (2011). State education as high-yield investment: Human capital theory in European policy discourse. *Journal of Pedagogy, 2*(2), 224–245. doi:10.2478/v10159-011-0011-3

Gillies, D. (2015). Human capital theory in education. In M. Peters (Ed.), *Encyclopedia of educational philosophy and theory* (pp. 107–123). Springer. doi:10.1007/978-981-287-532-7_254-1

Grimmett, P. P. (2009). International teacher education: Liberal cosmopolitanism revisited or post-modern trans-nationalism, *Teacher Education Quarterly, 36*(4), 7–25. Retrieved from www.jstor.org/stable/23479281

Hacking, I. (2007). Kinds of people: Moving targets. *Proceedings of the British Academy, 151*, 285–318. Retrieved from www.thebritishacademy.ac.uk/documents/2043/pba151p285.pdf

Harvey, D. (1990). *The condition of postmodernity: An enquiry into the origins of cultural change*. Cambridge, MA: Blackwell.

Hwami, M. (2020). Education under siege: Exploring how international economic sanctions create crises of pedagogy. *ECNU Review of Education*, 1–20. doi:10.1177/2096531120950330

Koopman, C. (2019). *How we became our data: A genealogy of the informational person*. Chicago, IL: University of Chicago Press.

Lipset, S. M. (1996). *American exceptionalism: A double-edged sword*. New York, NY: W. W Norton.

Macpherson, C. B. (1962). *The political theory of possessive individualism: From Hobbes to Locke*. Oxford, UK: Clarendon Press.

McLuhan, M. (2005). *Understanding me: Lectures and interviews*. Toronto, ON: McClelland & Stewart.

Mincer, J. (1958). Investment in human capital and personal income distribution. *Journal of Political Economy, 66*(4), 281–302. Retrieved from www.jstor.org/stable/1827422

Moghtader, B. (2018). Pastorate power, market liberalism and a knowing without knowing. *Knowledge Cultures, 6*(1), 18–35. doi:10.22381/KC6120183

Montoya-Vargas, J. (2013). Curriculum studies in Colombia. In W. F. Pinar (Ed.), *International handbook of curriculum research* (pp. 134–150). New York, NY: Routledge.

Mosco, V. (2004). *The digital sublime: Myth, power and cyberspace*. Cambridge, MA: MIT Press.

Nussbaum, M. C. (2011). *Creating capabilities: The human development approach.* Cambridge, MA: Harvard University Press.

O'Neil, C. (2017). *Weapons of math destruction: How big data increases inequality and threatens democracy.* New York, NY: Broadway Books.

Ong, A. (2006). Mutations in citizenship. *Theory, Culture and Society, 23*(2), 499–531. doi: 10.1177%2F0263276406064831

Pacheco Jose, A., & Seabra, F. (2013). Curriculum research in Portugal: Emergence, research and Europeanisation. In W. F. Pinar (Ed.), *International handbook of curriculum research* (pp. 397–410). New York, NY: Routledge.

Petty, W. S. (1862). Plan of an industrial school. In *Education, the school and the teacher in English literature: Republished from Barnards American Journal of Education* (pp. 188–208). Retrieved from https://archive.org/details/educationschoolt00barnuoft/page/n9/mode/2up.

Piketty, T. (2014). *Capital in the twenty-first century.* Cambridge, MA: Harvard University Press.

Pinar, W. F. (2004). *What is curriculum theory?* (1st ed.). New York, NY: Routledge.

Pinar, W. F. (2015). *Educational experience as lived.* New York, NY: Routledge.

Pinar, W. F. (2019a). *What is curriculum theory?* (3rd ed.). New York, NY: Routledge.

Pinar, W. F. (2019b). *Moving images of eternity: George Grant's critique of time, teaching, and technology.* Ottawa, ON: University of Ottawa Press.

Roberts-Mahoney, H., Means, A. J., & Garrison, M. J. (2016). Netflixing human capital development: Personalized learning technology and the corporatization of K-12 education. *Journal of Education Policy, 31*(4), 405–420. doi:10.1080/02680939.2015.1132774

Robertson, S. L. (2005). Re-imagining and rescripting the future of education: Global knowledge economy discourses and the challenge to education systems, *Comparative Education, 41*(2), 151–170. doi:10.1080/03050060500150922

Sadowski, J. (2019). When data is capital: Datafication, accumulation, and extraction. *Big Data & Society, 6*(1), 1–12. doi:10.1177/2053951718820549

Said, E. (1993). *Culture and imperialism.* New York, NY: Random House.

Saltman, K. J. (2016). Corporate schooling meets corporate media: Standards, testing, and technophilia. *Review of Education, Pedagogy, and Cultural Studies, 38*(2), 105–123. doi:10.1080/10714413.2016.1155953

Schultz, T. W. (1953). *The economic organization of agriculture.* New York, NY: McGraw Hill.

Schultz, T. W. (1959). Investment in man: An economist's view. *Social Service Review, 33*(2), 109–117. Retrieved from www.jstor.org/stable/30016430

Schultz, T. W. (1963). *The economic value of education.* New York, NY: Columbia University.

Schultz, T. W. (1993). *Origins of increasing returns.* New York, NY: Blackwell Publisher.

Sen, A. (2002). *Rationality and freedom.* Cambridge, MA: Harvard University Press.

Slobodian, Q. (2018). *Globalists: The end of empire and the birth of neoliberalism.* Cambridge, MA: Harvard University Press.

Smith, A. (1789/1904). *An inquiry into the nature and causes of the wealth of nations.* London: Methuen.

Smith, G. D. (2006). *Trying to teach in a season of great untruth: Globalization, empire and the crises of pedagogy.* Rotterdam, Netherlands: Sense Publishers.

Smith, G. D. (2013). Wisdom responses to globalization. In W. F. Pinar (Ed.), *International handbook of curriculum research* (pp. 45–59). New York, NY: Routledge.

Spring, J. (2015). *Economization of education: Human capital, global corporations, skill-based schooling.* New York, NY: Routledge.

Spring, J. (2019). *Global impacts of the Western school model: Corporatization, alimentation, consumerism.* New York, NY: Taylor & Francis.

Steger, M. B. (2006). From market globalism to imperial globalism: Ideology and American power after 9/11. *Globalizations, 2*(1), 31–46. doi:10.1080/14747730500085049

Takayama, K. (2008). The politics of international league tables: PISA in Japan's achievement crisis debate. *Comparative Education, 44*(4), 387–407. doi:10.1080/03050060802481413

Taubman, P. M. (2009). *Teaching by numbers: Deconstructing the discourse of standards and accountability in education.* New York, NY: Routledge.

Tröhler, D. (2017). Educationalization of social problems and the educationalization of the modern world. In M. A. Peters (Ed.), *Encyclopedia of educational philosophy and theory.* doi:10.1007/978-981-287-588-4_8

Tröhler, D. (2020). National Literacies, or modern education and the art of fabricating national minds. *Journal of Curriculum Studies, 52*(5), 620–635. doi:10.1080/00220272.2020.1786727

Webb, P. T., & Gulson, K. N (2015). Policy scientificity 3.0: Theory and policy analysis in-and-for this world and other-worlds. *Critical Studies in Education, 56*(1), 161–174. doi:10.1080/17508487.2014.949812

Williamson, B. (2013). *The future of the curriculum: School knowledge in the digital age.* Cambridge, MA: MIT Press.

Williamson, B. (2018). Silicon startup schools: Technocracy, algorithmic imaginaries and venture philanthropy in corporate education reform. *Critical Studies in Education, 59*(2), 218–236. doi:10.1080/17508487.2016.1186710

Williamson, B. (2021). Digital policy sociology: Software and science in data-intensive precision education. *Critical Studies in Education, 62*(3), 354–370. https://doi.org/10.1080/17508487.2019.1691030

Wozniak, G. (1987). Human capital, information, and the early adoption of new technology. *The Journal of Human Resources, 22*(1), 101–112. doi:10.2307/145869

Zuboff, S. (2019). *The age of surveillance capitalism: The fight for a human future at the new frontier of power.* New York, NY: Public Affairs.

7 Extrapolated imperial nationalisms in global education policy formation

An historical inquiry into American and Scandinavian agendas in OECD policy

Christian Ydesen

1 Introduction

Education has always been associated with authority in one sense or another (Rury & Tamura, 2019), and it is where truths and worldviews are produced and where future members of communities are shaped. Ever since the emergence of modern nation-states in the 19th century, the shaping of education has been intertwined with national government agendas concerned with the production of the right type of citizen (Tröhler, Popkewitz, & Labaree, 2011). In addition, education serves as a foreign policy instrument associated with the geopolitical priorities of nation-states. In particular, the geopolitical dimension of education became abundantly clear during the bi-polar era of the Cold War (Grek & Ydesen, 2021).

The implication is that the state and its authority are recurring companions of education and the way we perceive and understand the very role and *modus operandi* of education – even under the reign of globalization (Tröhler, 2020). As contended by Sassen, "the epochal transformation we call globalization is taking place inside the national to a far larger extent than what is usually recognised" (cited in Ozkirimli, 2017, p. 2). Historical research has found that the very workings of contemporary global education emerge from historical trajectories and antecedents consisting of styles of reasoning, technologies, institutionalizations and research fields affiliated with the construction of nations and nation-states over the last couple of centuries in general and during the Cold War period in particular (e.g. Bürgi, 2017; Cardoso & Steiner-Khamsi, 2017; Elfert & Ydesen, 2020; Tröhler & Maricic, 2021; Ydesen & Andreasen, 2020).

In this respect, Tröhler (2020) persuasively argues that the Programme for International Student Assessment (PISA) operated by the Organisation for Economic Cooperation and Development (OECD) in a tri-annual cycle since 2000, has "a national background, namely the United States, which educationalized the Cold War, implemented school reforms and developed a test system that was intended to ensure the effects of these reforms. It was this national model that was globally extrapolated via the OECD, and now pretends to be global – instead of imperial" (pp. 21–22). From this point of view, PISA – and other global education

DOI: 10.4324/9781003137801-10

programmes and initiatives – can be understood as reflections of extrapolated nationalisms that act imperially by offering naturalized meaning, orientation and direction to actors working to shape education in both local, regional, national and global contexts (Antonsich & Skey, 2017).

Connecting with the theme of the *World Yearbook*, this chapter adds to our understanding of the complexity of global education policy formation by historically exploring the ways in which national agendas and their extrapolated nationalisms have been embedded in, reproduced and promoted via global and international education agendas. It is a prism to deal with the complexity of policy formation within the global scenario where recent research has shown that a host of actors, agendas and technologies associated with IOs, philanthropic foundations, private edu-businesses and powerful governments struggle to set the scene (Lewis, 2020; Mundy, Green, Lingard, & Verger, 2016; Tröhler & Lenz, 2015; Ydesen, 2019). By historically studying the extrapolation of nationalisms in global education policy formation, the aim of this chapter is to transcend the traditional division between local, regional, national and global contexts and bring them into one analytical lens to tease out the imperial energy that frames and shapes globalization and national education systems.

The overall hypothesis of the chapter is that imperially extrapolated nationalisms cut across global arenas – practically, discursively and ideologically – and that these nationalisms generate meaning, orientation and direction for the formation of policy instruments with a global reach. In other words, the imperial energy of nationalisms emerges from the authoritative scripts engraved in nationalisms containing naturalized values defining boundaries of normality and deviance and/ or on-track development and off-track development. Overall, the chapter demonstrates how imperial nationalisms are reproduced and filter into the formulation and launch of new educational programmes and the concrete development of tools and practices within these programmes.

1.1 Approaching the study of nation-states and nationalisms in the global arena

Looking at the influence of states in the shaping of education beyond their own borders, it is a common feature in the international relations literature to view international organizations (IOs) as instruments "used by their members for particular ends" (Archer, 2001, p. 135) to promote foreign policy interests. However, this is not to say that IOs do not have agency of their own (Barnett & Finnemore, 2004). In many ways, IOs serve as arenas or catalysts for the confluence of interests and agendas – both external and internal. In the case of states, Centeno (2021) points out that they mainly try to increase their influence in two ways; firstly, by exerting "pressure on agenda-setting through funding," and secondly, by seeking "to influence knowledge production" (p. 6; see also Rutkowski & Engel, 2010). While the former mechanism is quite straightforward and amounts to what Kjell Eide[1] (1990) calls the promotion of "national pet projects" (p. 16), the latter hinges on nation-states being closely involved in the development and formation of programmes and initiatives "either by providing staff and consultants to the organisation, or by supplying national expertise through studies and reviews" (Centeno, 2021, p. 113). While such mechanisms for the export of national agendas can be made the object of empirical research, it is necessary to also develop a sensitivity for the more subtle and reproductive mechanisms behind the extrapolation of imperial nationalisms.

Emerging in the intersections between practice, discourse and ideology, nationalism essentially asserts that the nation and the state correspond (Gellner, 1983). To understand the reproduction and extrapolation mechanisms of nationalism, Ozkirimli (2017) contends that nationalism finds relevance "as the fundamental organizing principle of interstate order, as the ultimate source of political legitimacy, as the taken-for-granted context of everyday life and as a readily available cognitive and discursive frame to make sense of the world that surrounds us" (p. 2). In that sense, there is no contradiction between a focus on national agendas and their influence on global actors and the study of nationalism as discursive formations with ideological components as the hotbed for the recurring reproduction of nationalism.

1.2 Selecting an analytical focus – the OECD, United States and Scandinavia triangle

Since the establishment of the Organisation for European Economic Cooperation (OEEC) in 1948, which morphed into the OECD in 1961, the organization has gradually increased its work in education. During the Cold War, the OECD was an arena where agents from Western capitalist states could meet, seek inspiration and coordinate policies and positions in the wider global – and highly antagonistic – policy space (Schmelzer, 2016). As pointed out in a Danish country response to OECD educational activities in 1980, "The OECD is the only organization where all the advanced industrialized countries can co-operate effectively in education and within which such cooperation takes the unique form of relating education to the broader social and economic context."[2] However, while the OECD may be viewed as an actor in its own right, the funding, formulation and execution of OECD programmes and initiatives are inconceivable without the many partners involved, including member and non-member states affiliated with the OECD, other IOs, edu-businesses, universities, think tanks and a host of experts. In this sense, the OECD is also an arena of struggles and disputes which – apart from external partners – also include the agendas and priorities of internal offices, departments and branches (Sorensen, Ydesen, & Robertson, 2021).

To investigate to what extent national agendas frame and shape globalization, this chapter explores the positions taken up by two reference societies – the US and the Scandinavian states – that actively sought to influence global education through the OECD. Together they have played important roles in the development of policy instruments under the OECD umbrella. These two reference societies have often been antagonistic in terms of approaches and priorities in the shaping of OECD policy instruments. In his exposition of the OECD history in education, Papadopoulos (1994) writes about two opposing camps: "on the one side, the neoconservatives, dominated by Reaganite and Thatcherite views of society, and on the other, the 'egalitarians,' largely represented by the Scandinavian model of society" (p. 181). In this sense, the chapter employs a contrasting epistemology.

Clearly, some OECD member-states have emerged more powerful than others in setting the rules of the game in the OECD arena. Going back to the channels of influence pointed out by Centeno earlier, namely the funding track and the knowledge production track, the two selected cases stand out. As a powerful financial contributor, the United States is, in many ways, in a league of its own since its percentage share is normally more than double that of any other member-state (Centeno, 2021).

It means that the United States has carried enormous weight in terms of defining the OECD's approach to education in general and its programmes in particular. For instance, in the 1960s, one of the key national agendas of the United States was the search for new scientific methods for developing and optimizing educational policies and practices (Bürgi, 2019; Elfert & Ydesen, 2020). In this sense, the United States used the OECD as an arena for advancing this agenda – hinging on human capital theory – feeding into OECD programmes and setting a standard for and in exchange with other member-states (OECD, 1961; Becker, 1964). Another example stems from the 1980s, when the United States effectively threatened to withdraw financial support for the OECD Centre for Educational Research and Innovation (CERI) if a programme for the development of international comparative indicators was not launched (Grek & Ydesen, 2021).

While the United States has been key in both OECD funding and knowledge production, the Scandinavian countries also stand out as member-states that are willing and committed to engaging with and influencing knowledge production processes in the OECD arena. According to Eide (1990), the Scandinavian states have punched above their weight in the historical development of the OECD's work in education. In her document analysis of the 2013 OECD reviews of evaluation and assessment in education, Prøitz (2015) finds that "the simple word count showed that Norway, Sweden and Denmark were mentioned frequently, both individually and together as a Nordic cluster of countries, when compared with that of other more prominent countries within the field of assessment" (p. 78).

These observations indicate that Denmark, Norway and Sweden historically have served as reference societies in the OECD arena and that they – like the United States – have had the self-confidence to engage with global education issues from an understanding that their model of society was a model worth following by other nations and states.[3]

2 Theoretical underpinnings, methodology and analytical strategy

As argued in previous text, the analytical pursuit of the chapter is a historical analysis of discourses of extrapolated nationalisms and their imperial energy between

Scandinavia, the United States and the OECD in the shaping and development of global policy instruments. In defining policy instruments, I lean on the work of Simons and Voß (2018) who define policy instruments as "programmes, initiatives, and technologies containing scripts for reordering society" and which "gather a constituency comprised of practices and actors oriented towards developing, maintaining and expanding a specific instrumental model of governing" (p. 31). Some examples of OECD policy instruments are the programme for Educational Investment and Planning launched in 1962, the Education at a Glance reports published annually since 1992, PISA and the OECD Learning Framework 2030.

As often pointed out in the literature on nationalism, the study of nationalism can be a difficult undertaking because the phenomenon itself is elusive – both dynamic and static, and both responsive and resilient at the same time (Antonsich & Skey, 2017; Ozkirimli, 2017). I, therefore, search for nationalisms in published historical documents and in the minutiae of selected archival sources from the Danish National Archive in Copenhagen, the US National Archive in Virginia, the OECD Archive in Paris and a private archive generously made accessible by Mats Ekholm, Swedish member of the OECD Centre for Educational Research and Innovation (CERI) governing board 2000–2009. In addition, the analyses draw on interviews with retired officials who disclose information and perspectives that cannot be found in the traditional written or published sources.

This analysis focuses on two important and historically intertwined trajectories in OECD history reflecting agendas from American and Scandinavian actors, i.e. the development of comparative indicators and the development of evidence-based policy research (EPBR). Both of these agendas can be understood as policy instruments with a global reach. Within these instruments and their historical context, I will search for discourses reflecting the constructions of nation, nationalism and the nation-state. For this step, I draw on critical discourse analysis (CDA). As described by Anderson and Holloway (2018),

> CDA in education policy research is . . . concerned with how power and related relations (e.g. ideologies) in the real world are reflected, reproduced, or resisted in micro-textual sites such as policy documents, often focusing on issues of control.
>
> (p. 5)

However, in order to fully grasp the ideological dimension of OECD policy formation, it is helpful to remember that the *D* in *OECD* stands for *development*. According to Singh, "technocrats and international organizations [were] charged with a development mandate after World War II" (cited in Auld & Morris, 2021, p. 2; see also Gilman, 2003). Singh argues that the implication was that half the world's population was identified as "developing" and that this ideological narrative has been institutionalized and re-interpreted by different IOs. The role and significance of the development narrative within the OECD may be understood as an expression of what Beckert (2020) called "promissory legitimacy," which is established through discursively stated claims on the future regarding anticipated developments or by the concept of "anticipatory global governance" developed by John Berten and Matthias Kranke (2019). The latter point out that "international organisations (IOs) are especially active in authoritatively delineating certain visions – that is, specifying certain versions of the future but not others" (p. 1). In this sense, a focus on the notions of development in OECD policy instruments creates a rudder with which to navigate the imperial policy formations where the negotiations, struggles and trajectories of nationalisms and globalization take place.

3 Nationalism in the development of comparative indicators

The OECD has promoted a vision about indicators being the core pillars of effective and optimal education policies for decades. In the candid words of the former director of the OECD Centre for Educational Research and Innovation (CERI), Ron Gass: "You know, the OECD is full of indicators, you can't do anything unless you have an indicator these days."[4] In the opening address at the second General Assembly of the OECD Project on International Education Indicators (INES), held in Lugano-Cadro, Switzerland, in September 1991, Thomas Alexander (1994), director of the OECD Directorate for Education, Employment, Labour and Social Affairs (DEELSA), made a general claim about the value of international comparisons within national education politics:

> The general wave of educational reforms that has been apparent in most of the OECD Member countries since the 1980s and which is characterized by an overriding concern with the effectiveness of schools seems to have brought with it a new interest in comparability issues. International comparisons of educational conditions and performance are now perceived as a means of adding depth and perspective to the analysis of national situations. References to other nations' policies and results are beginning to be routinely used in discussions of education, and comparability now belongs with accountability to that changing set of driving words which shape the current management paradigm of education.
>
> (p. 17)

The discourse focuses on comparability as a means of achieving effective schools along with perspective and depth on the national situation. Comparability is portrayed as a one-size-fits-all tool that promises comparable nation-states the ability to gauge the state of their education systems, i.e. a measure of their level of development in relation to ideals about effectiveness understood in an economic sense.

In the United States, the interest in indicators surged with the publication of the report *A Nation at Risk* in 1983, which developed risk indicators as representations of US students' performance in national and international tests (Morgan, 2009). The report triggered broad public concern about education and initiated a push for closer monitoring of the education system and a search for a point of orientation that would provide indications of improvements (or deteriorations).

The answer was found in the Secretary of Education's "Wall Chart" that compared states' educational performance. It could provide US states with knowledge about their comparable performance and aggregate information about national performance. According to Bryk and Hermanson (1993),

> The Wall Chart prompted the CCSSO [The Council of Chief State School Officers] to begin work on a fairer set of indicators and to create the State Educational Assessment Center. In the following year the National Research Council recommended that data collection and reporting be reorganized under a stronger federal agency. International efforts on educational indicators received a boost in 1987 with U.S. government support for a cross-national indicator project within the OECD in Paris.
>
> (p. 451)

The quote indicates a strong American provenance of the OECD's work on comparative indicators, and the link with the *A Nation at Risk* report suggests a strong link with an American national agenda in general and geopolitical concerns associated with the Cold War in particular (Krejsler, 2020). The archival documents from the INES project provide ample evidence for this connection, which is supported by the fact that the American members of INES promoted American experiences with indicators as a learning example for the development of international indicators. In his paper to the INES general assembly, Rolf K. Blank from the CCSSO argued that

> Lessons learned through the development of State-by-State education indicators in the U.S. can be useful for considering key issues for implementing indicators that involve different governments and in identifying important steps for building a co-operative system for collecting and reporting data.[5]

Here, indicators are discursively portrayed as the necessary conditions for constructing a co-operative and international collecting and reporting system; more specifically a system ideologically moulded into the image of the United States and reproducing American nationalism – i.e. a domestic political agenda extrapolated to the international level revolving around assumptions that the world is measurable, that indicators are objective, meaningful and transferable instruments and that states are a meaningful organizing principle for monitoring education internationally.

Another indication can be seen in the funding for the INES project, which came not only from the OECD itself but also from the US National Center for Educational Statistics. However, it is important to note how the development of indicators in the INES programme was not an American agenda alone. Apart from the United States, France, Italy and Austria also hosted meetings for the central project work.[6] Thus, a picture can be drawn of multiple nation-states taking an interest in the development of comparative indicators. As recently pointed out by Grek and me (2021), different standpoints and national agendas could come together in a shared space for the creation of a "new indicator measurement infra-structure" (p. 7).

Zooming in on the nature and content of American nationalism, Eide (1990) contends that by the mid-1980s, the United States changed its role in the educational collaboration of the OECD

> to aggressive missionary activities, characterized by "the fight against communism" and religious fundamentalism. In the eyes of the new US delegates, Western Europe mainly consisted of semi-communist countries, and the Nordic countries were definitely behind the iron curtain. This policy was pursued with a strong power language, attacks upon the education sector within the OECD Council, and threats to withdraw from CERI.
>
> (p. 48)

Eide's candid contention reflects the ideological content in what can be understood as American nationalism containing a taxonomy of development placing the United States on top and a will and determination to push American agendas in the OECD arena. But the quote also reflects a somewhat shifting approach to both content and deliverance. Shifting administrations had different priorities and as emphasized in my interview with Jørn Skovsgaard,[7] the personality, ambition, ability and preferences of the American representatives also played a role for the nature, conviction and strength of US agendas in the OECD.

According to an interview with Ron Gass, reflecting on the 1980s work on indicators in the OECD in general and the US role in particular, a picture can be drawn of a heavy American hand prompting the OECD to launch a comparative indicators programme.[8] This observation testifies to the distinct geopolitical and economic components of the education indicator programme to a large extent orchestrated and led by the national agendas of the United States (as also suggested by Eide). It largely confirms Tröhler's (2020) interpretation mentioned earlier. In his report for the OECD from the American Educational Research Association conference held in Boston, April 12–14, 1990, Alan Gibson, Her Majesty's Inspectorate, Department of Education and Science, United Kingdom contends that

> the experience of the USA, as evidenced in the AERA [American Educational Research Association] sessions concerned with American activity, may be seen from the point of view of the ensemble of OECD countries as a "natural experiment" capable of informing the protocols and planning for the use of EIs [education indicators] on an international scale.[9]

The discourse is clearly that the American experiences with indictors constitute a valuable – and even natural – learning reservoir for OECD countries and a translation to the international domain. The American power position in the development of OECD practices and setting of standards is unambiguous and so is the imperial energy surrounding that power position.

Regardless of Eide's critical points in 1990, the Scandinavian countries seem to have been more or less on board with the US-driven agenda in CERI. This is visible when we look into the engine room of the INES project, which was essentially the process leading up to the development of PISA. CERI managed the project through four networks and one technical group. The networks came together initially through a collaborative consortium of countries:

- Network A: Educational Outcomes (chaired by the United States),
- Network B: Education and Labour Market Destinations (chaired by Sweden),
- Network C: Features of Schools (chaired by the Netherlands), and
- Network D: Attitudes and Expectations of Education System Users (chaired by the United Kingdom).[10]

Denmark, Norway and Sweden – along with some 15 other countries – took an active part in Network A, which was regarded as the most important network in the INES project. The ideology of establishing certainty about the state of national education systems via the use of comparative indicators seems to have enjoyed broad support and engagement from OECD member-states. Nevertheless, there was a bone of contention between the United States and a number of other OECD member-states. According to Skovsgaard, the Scandinavian countries – along with the Netherlands and Austria – pushed for the inclusion of an indicator for foreign language proficiency in PISA, but this suggestion was heavily resisted by the United States. According to Skovsgaard's reading of the negotiations, the Americans felt that English was the global *lingua franca* and that the inclusion of such an indicator would be a national embarrassment for the United States, jeopardizing the discursive development hierarchy in the OECD. Eventually, Andreas Schleicher, the Director for the OECD Directorate of Education and Skills, argued that adding a foreign language component would be too expensive. And so again, the United States seems to have exerted its imperial power when it comes to determining the content of a key education policy instrument.

4 Nationalism in the development of evidence-based policy research

Closely intertwined with the agenda of developing comparative indicators was the agenda of establishing quality in education. Within the OECD arena, the United States pushed to make quality a focus for the OECD's work on education in the 1980s (Eide, 1990), particularly the quality of educational research and what it had to offer policymaking. According to Gass reflecting back on the situation in the 1980, "the Americans were very active in terms of OECD Education. At a certain point in time, it was the Neo-conservatives, Reagan, etc., and they had a very different view of how policies were made – I sum it up by saying: It's a 'what-works' view."[11]

In 1995, CERI published a report on *Educational Research and Development: Trends, Issues and Challenges*, which derived from a 1990 OECD Ministers of

Education meeting where the need to strengthen education's knowledge base was strongly emphasized.[12] This endeavour resembles the development of comparative indicators because the discussion quickly evolved into debates about the criteria – or indicators – of good-quality education research. How could education research be ranked, and was there a gold standard? The big debate was about whether EBPR was confined to randomized control trials or whether other sources of evidence could be used (Hansen, Rieper, & Bhatti, 2006).

At its October 2003 meeting, the OECD/CERI Governing Board endorsed a CERI project on EBPR:

> The Governing Board agreed that policy makers in education need to be able to draw on the evidence of good, rigorous research to a much greater extent than is currently possible. It was agreed that it would be very useful to arrive at a clearer understanding of the need for, and constraints on, EBPR. It also asked the Secretariat to explore the reasons and sources of resistance to EBPR. There is a substantial need for clarification of the methods available to build EBPR, how they have been applied in practice (or not) in different countries, and to which policy questions each can best be applied.[13]

The launch of the CERI project on EBPR reflects an open and explorative approach to the topic that allowed different participating member-states to contribute. Between 2004 and 2006, four OECD conferences on EBPR in education were held.[14] In terms of extrapolated nationalism, the first conference entitled "OECD – U.S. Meeting on Evidence-Based Policy Research" held in Washington, D.C., is particularly interesting because it contains a clash of agendas between the United States and the Scandinavian countries in terms of how to understand EBPR. In my interview with Mats Ekholm, former Director-General in the Swedish Ministry of Education, he explained,

> I remember well that there was a stormy meeting in Washington where we Europeans pointed out that the Americans were almost crazy because they strongly claimed evidence-basing as the only true religion in the educational field. . . . Nor were the Americans interested in the learning that takes place in schools outside the school subjects, such as the development of independence, solidarity, tolerance.

The conference itself was organized by CERI in cooperation with the US Education Department's Institute of Education Sciences and the American organization Coalition for Evidence-Based Policy, dedicated to increasing government effectiveness through the use of rigorous evidence about "what works"[15] (Elvbakken & Hansen, 2019). It is a clear indication of the strong US involvement in the issue of EBPR. One of the speakers at the conference was Jon Baron from the Coalition for Evidence-Based Policy. Baron contended that evidence-based policy research in education is needed because of the American experience with the difficulty of improving performance in spite of large financial injections. As in the case of comparative indicators, we see clear signs of a US national agenda being pushed in the OECD and used as an argument for which path to follow and how to understand EBPR. Baron advocated the use of randomized trials and argued that they are the gold standard in many other areas such as medicine.[16]

In a session entitled "Comparing Experiences: Various approaches to evidence-based policy research in OECD member countries," the delegate from International Association for the Evaluation of Educational Achievement (IEA) Lars-Henrik Schmidt, Dean of the Danish School of Education, expounded that in a Danish context, the concept of evidence-based education must be qualified and that it cannot be reduced to randomized control trials (RCTs). Schmidt argued that educational research is a practised form of knowledge unable to escape different kinds of beliefs. According to the note about the conference, the Q&A session following Schmidt's talk reflects that many conference participants found Schmidt's presentation very provocative (ibid.).

However, the critical reflections from Scandinavian delegates were far from over. Mats Ekholm criticized the conference's one-sided focus on RCTs. He found that there was a certain dogmatism where everyone must be strong believers in RCTs, which, he contended, are only one way to gather systematic knowledge. It is noteworthy that Jørn Skovsgaard from the Danish Ministry of Education approved of Ekholm's speech, agreeing that there is a need to develop the toolbox with a plurality of evidence types. Ole-Jakob Skodvin, a representative of the Norwegian Ministry, stressed that he also believed that a more holistic approach is needed and that there is a need to take into account that contexts and approaches vary between countries (ibid.).

After these comments, a few of the participants referred to "the Nordic Coalition." For example, Tom Schuller talked about "the US/Scandinavian dialogue," and Bob Boruch portrayed the Nordic countries as 'special cases,' arguing that these countries have relatively homogeneous populations and public databases with a lot of microdata on the individuals, minimizing the need for control groups compared to other countries (ibid.).

Thus, the OECD conference gives the impression of a discrepancy between the Scandinavian and American participants on methodology. The Americans seemed to value RCTs and methodological rigour within the framework of a classical positivist paradigm, while the Scandinavian contributions stated the need for methodological pluralism or a 'toolbox approach.' In my interview with Jørn Skovsgaard, he explained that

> The Americans were very frustrated with some of us because we did not buy into their agenda and we were very critical of their bombastic behaviour. They came up with a somewhat violent rhetoric, such as that their proposal based on 'randomised controlled trials' was 'a gold standard' and they talked about a 'coalition of the willing.'

In his paper for the conference, Ekholm argued that the lessons learnt by Sweden and other countries with different kinds of educational research "need to be illuminated when a new step is taken in the use within educational systems of evidence-based policy research."[17] Interestingly, Ekholm's point follows the same discursive structure as Baron's argument mentioned earlier, hinging on an assertation of national experiences and thereby also an ideological idea – an imperial taxonomy of development – about which paths to follow in the development of educational research.

The debate taking place in the OECD arena between an American and a Scandinavian agenda in terms of EBPR is essentially a dispute over which education research practices should be prevalent in the OECD's work on education. The issue at stake is what kinds of knowledge and experiences deriving from national contexts should be recognised in the OECD arena. It carries implications in terms of relevancy and, at the ideological level, also how the very development of desirable education systems should be understood and achieved.

5 Concluding discussion

The hypothesis of the chapter has been that extrapolated nationalisms cut across global arenas – practically, discursively and ideologically – and that this nationalism generates imperial meaning, orientation and direction for the formation of policy instruments with a global reach.

Analysing the interactions between Scandinavia, the United States and the OECD in relation to the two policy instruments, comparative indicators and EBPR, has demonstrated a strong presence of US nationalism in both cases. This nationalism filters into the launch and formulation of new programmes and the concrete development of tools and practices within these programmes. Discursively the nationalism is underpinned by American practical experiences but also needs and agendas emerging from the federal organization of the American education system and a taxonomy of development reflecting the Cold War terminology of the First, Second and Third World. In this way, the nationalism discursively affirms the organization of the American nation-state and the superiority of the American nation, and it positions other systems in an inferior or at least potentially problematic position. It is a nationalism building on geopolitical priorities of wanting to excel over other nation-states and to create better rooms for manoeuvre in the future global scene as a result of other countries following the US lead and allowing themselves to be moulded in the American image. This twin discourse of nationalism – one inward-looking and one outward-looking – reveals a clear ideological component in terms of ideas about a desirable education system and how to organize and build such a system.

In the case of Scandinavia, we see some of the same mechanisms. Generally, the Scandinavian countries have taken a leading role in the history of the OECD's educational work, often playing the card of offering more socially balanced agendas. In a geopolitical lens, the Scandinavian position – although not always perfectly aligned between the Scandinavian nation-states – offered an intermediate station between communism and capitalism during the Cold War era. Historical evidence suggests that the notion about a Scandinavian bloc in the OECD was underpinned by other countries having an idea about a Nordic model of education (Eide, 1990). For instance, in the 1970s, the Scandinavian countries stood out by refusing to accept the idea that public expenditures on education should necessarily be reduced, thus affirming the discourse about the Scandinavian nation. The ideological content of such a position revolved around redistribution mechanisms of goods and the promotion of education as a public good and a vehicle for building societal coherence.

Analysing the practice, discourse and ideology surrounding the development of comparative indicators and the EBPR instrument clearly suggests that the meaning, orientation and direction in the development of policy instruments may be very different and even reflect deep disagreement in terms of practice, discourse and ideology. One bone of contention was the inclusion of a language proficiency indicator in PISA. In the 2004 EBPR conference, the sea ran high and in my interview with Ekholm, he recalls how the acrimonious debate led him to "torment the US delegation by pointing out that their state had disregarded the evidence put forward by the UN delegation led by Hans Blix showing that Iraq had no production of nuclear weapons when it justified its attack on Iraq." Perhaps this argument did not have anything to do with education as such, but it is a reflection of a clash in terms of ideology and national agendas, given that Blix was a Swedish national and Ekholm found the analogy useful to express what was at stake in the discussions about EBPR in education.

Looking across the two policy instruments of the analysis it is important to pay homage to the very different historical contexts. The development of the comparative indicator instrument was initiated during the Cold War with a strong sense of community among Western nation-states. While the development of the EBPR initiative took place in an atmosphere of the Iraq war (2003–2011), which created a division between the 'coalition of the willing' and the rest (Sweden belonging to the latter, Denmark belonging to the former). It is this context that may explain Ekholm's argument and Skovsgaard's discursive terminology when he talks about the American attempt to build a 'coalition of the willing' in EBPR in education. These contextual observations may carry some explanatory power in understanding the different stances between the US and Scandinavia in the two instrument cases treated here.

In terms of education policy formation, the analysis of extrapolated nationalism in these two cases based on two very different reference societies suggests that the US was able to push imperial nationalism both through the funding lever and the knowledge production lever, while Scandinavia generally only used the latter. Nevertheless, both reference societies took up assertive stances affirming and building their relevance as nations and nation-states. But it is important to note that the extrapolation of nationalism in international fora also carries a feedback mechanism to the host country. One example is the acrimonious debate at the 2004 EBPR conference which – in a contextual and discursive perspective – reflects the reputation and authority surrounding nation-states and their agendas and determines the latitude offered to national representatives. In this sense, engaging with international fora like the OECD is tantamount to holding a mirror up in front of nation-states.

This point finds relevance in terms of understanding how policy instruments are designed and how they are practiced and enacted. The extrapolation of nationalism inherent in the initiative, development and enactment of policy instruments offers guidelines for meaning, orientation and direction, but these guidelines – and the imperial energy surrounding them – may be distinctly curbed in the interactions with other extrapolations of nationalism determined by the context, reputation and authority surrounding nation-states and their agendas. In this sense, analysing the extrapolation of nationalism in an international arena serves as a constructive prism for transcending the traditional division between local, regional, national and global contexts and thereby asks new questions as to the workings of global education policy formation.

Notes

1 Between 1961 and 1964, Kjell Eide (1925–2011), a Norwegian social economist, headed the OECD's work on education planning, and he served as the first board chairman of the Centre for Educational Research and Innovation (CERI) after the formal establishment in 1970.
2 Education Committee, Governing Board, Review and Forward Planning of OECD Educational Activities – Country Responses, Denmark, May 1980, ED(80)10/05; CERI/CD(80)14/05, OECD Archive, p. 2.
3 It should be duly mentioned that Finland rose to prominence as a Scandinavian reference society following its high ranking in PISA results in the 2000s.
4 Interview with Ron Gass conducted in Paris, 22 August 2017, by Dr. Maren Elfert and PhD fellow Trine Juul Reder. The data was collected under the auspices of the project "The Global History of the OECD," hosted by Aalborg University, Denmark, with Christian Ydesen as the PI.
5 Paper entitled "International Education Indicators: developing and implementing education indicators" written by R. K. Blank, Council of Chief State School Officers, U.S.A., General Assembly of the INES Project, Conceptual and Theoretical Aspects, Indicators, Reporting and Rationality, September 1991, CERI/INES(91)14, OECD Archive, Paris.
6 Project on International Educational Indicators (INES Project): Review of Preliminary Results and Proposal for Future Work, October 1989, CERI/CD(89)12, OECD Archive, Paris, p. ii.
7 Senior Advisor, Danish Ministry of Education, member of CERI Governing Board and member of INES network A (since 1996) and the INES Strategic Management Group
8 Interview with Ron Gass (see footnote 4)
9 Working paper, INES Project, Educational Indicators at the 1990 AERA, CERI/INES/COG/90.04, 17 September 1990, OECD Archive, Paris
10 International Educational Indicators (INES), CERI/CD (91)10, 28 October 1991, OECD Archives, Paris.
11 Interview with Ron Gass (see footnote 4)
12 Emerging issues in Evidence-based Policy Research in Education, Draft, CERI, 2005, Private Archive.
13 OECD-CERI, Evidence-based Policy Research: extracted comments, Prepared for the OECD/US Seminar on Evidence-based Policy Research, 19–20 April 2004, Washington DC, Private Archive.
14 OECD-U.S. Meeting on Evidence-Based Policy Research in Education, Washington 19–20 April 2004; Evidence-based policy research: The interaction between policy makers and research in education, Stockholm 27–28 January 2005; Linking Evidence

to Practice, The Hague, 14–15 September 2005; Final Workshop for Evidence-based Policy Research in Education, London, 6–7 July 2006.
15 http://coalition4evidence.org/mission-activities/ (accessed 3 March 2021).
16 Note about OECD conferences on Evidence-Based Policy Research entitled 'Notat om OECD-konferencer om EBPR,' Department of Political Science, University of Copenhagen, November 2005, Private Archive. The document is an extended summary of the document 'OECD (2004) OECD-U.S. meeting on evidence-based policy research in education. In: Forum proceedings, OECD, Paris, 19–20 April.' This original source document has been impossible to obtain either via the OECD archive or interlibrary loan.
17 Ekholm, M. 'Evidence-based policy research – some Swedish lessons', Private Archive, p. 5.

References

Alexander, T. J. (1994). Introductory address. In A. Tuijnman & N. Bottani (Eds.), *Making education count: Developing and using international indicators* (pp. 13–19). Paris and Washington, DC: OECD Publications and Information Centre.

Anderson, K. T., & Holloway, J. (2020). Discourse analysis as theory, method, and epistemology in studies of education policy. *Journal of Education Policy, 35*(2), 188–221. doi:10.1080/02680939.2018.1552992

Antonsich, M., & Skey, M. (2017). Introduction: The persistence of banal nationalism. In M. Skey, & M. Antonsich (Eds.), *Everyday nationhood: Theorising culture, identity and belonging after banal nationalism* (pp. 1–13). Palgrave Macmillan UK. doi:10.1057/978-1-137-57098-7_1

Archer, C. (2001). *International organizations.* New York, NY: Routledge.

Auld, E., & Morris, P. (2021). Humanitarian assessment: Tracing the OECD's evolving narratives within a global development complex. *Globalisation, Societies and Education* (forthcoming).

Barnett, M. N., & Finnemore, M. (2004). *Rules for the world: International organizations in global politics.* New York, NY: Cornell University Press.

Becker, G. S. (1964). *Human capital: A theoretical and empirical analysis, with special reference to education.* New York, NY: National Bureau of Economic Research.

Beckert, J. (2020). The exhausted futures of neoliberalism: From promissory legitimacy to social anomy. *Journal of Cultural Economy, 13*(3), 318–330. doi:10.1080/17530350.2019.1574867

Berten, J., & Kranke, M. (2019, June 26–29). *Studying anticipatory practices of international organizations: A framework for analysis.* Paper presented at 6th European Workshop in International Studies, Krakow.

Bryk, A. S., & Hermanson, K. L. (1993). Educational indicator systems: Observations on their structure, interpretation, and use. *Review of Research in Education, 19*(1), 451–484. doi:10.3102/0091732X019001451

Bürgi, R. (2017). *Die OECD und die bildungsplanung der freien welt: Denkstile und netzwerke einer internationalen bildungsexpertise.* Berlin: Verlag Barbara Budrich.

Bürgi, R. (2019). Learning productivity: The European Productivity Agency – An educational enterprise. In C. Ydesen (Ed.), *The OECD's historical rise in education: The formation of a global governing complex, global histories of education* (pp. 17–37). London and New York, NY: Palgrave Macmillan.

Cardoso, M., & Steiner-Khamsi, G. (2017). The making of comparability: Education indicator research from Jullien de Paris to the 2030 sustainable development goals. *Compare:*

A Journal of Comparative and International Education, 47(3), 388–405. doi:10.1080/0305 7925.2017.1302318

Centeno, V. G. (2021). The OECD: Actor, arena, instrument. *Globalisation, Societies and Education, 19*(2), 108–121. doi:10.1080/14767724.2021.1882958

Eide, K. (1990, March 26–30). *30 years of educational collaboration in the OECD.* International Congress Planning and Management of Educational Development, Mexico. Retrieved from http://unesdoc.unesco.org/images/0008/000857/085725eo.pdf

Elfert, M., & Ydesen, C. (2020). The rise of global governance in education: The OEEC and UNESCO, 1945–1960. In K. Gram-Skjoldager, H. A. Ikonomou, & T. Kahlert (Eds.), *Organizing the world – International organization and the emergence of international public administration 1920–1960* (pp. 73–89). London and New York, NY: Bloomsbury.

Elvbakken, K. T., & Hansen, H. F. (2019). Evidence producing organizations: Organizational translation of travelling evaluation ideas. *Evaluation, 25*(3), 261–276. doi:10. 1177/1356389018803965

Gellner, E. (1983). *Nations and nationalism.* Oxford: Blackwell Publishing.

Gilman, N. (2003). *Mandarins of the future: Modernization theory in cold war America.* London: Johns Hopkins University Press.

Grek, S., & Ydesen, C. (2021). Where science met policy: Governing by indicators and the OECD's INES programme. *Globalization, Societies and Education, 19*(2), 122–137. doi:10 .1080/14767724.2021.1892477

Hansen, H. F., Rieper, O., & Bhatti, Y. (2006). *Evidensbevægelsens udvikling, organisering og arbejdsform: En kortlægningsrapport.* Kbh.: AKF-Forlaget.

Krejsler, J. B. (2020). Imagining school as standards-driven and students as career-ready! A comparative genealogy of US federal and European transnational turns in education policy. In G. Fan & T. S. Popkewitz (Eds.), *Handbook of education policy studies: School/university, curriculum, and assessment, volume 2* (pp. 351–383). Singapore: Springer. doi:10.1007/978-981-13-8343-4_19

Lewis, S. (2020). *PISA, policy and the OECD: Respatialising global education governance through PISA for schools.* Singapore: Springer.

Morgan, C. (2009). *The OECD programme for international student assessment: Unravelling a knowledge network.* Saarbrucken: VDM Verlag.

Mundy, K., Green, A., Lingard, B., & Verger, A. (2016). Introduction: The globalization of education policy – key approaches and debates. In K. Mundy, A. Green, B. Lingard, & A. Verger (Eds.), *The handbook of global education policy* (pp. 1–20). Chichester: John Wiley & Sons, Ltd.

OECD. (1961). *Policy conference on economic growth and investment in education: Washington, 16th – 20th October 1961,* Paris: OECD Publishing.

Ozkirimli, U. (2017). *Theories of nationalism.* London: Macmillan Education UK. Retrieved from https://ebookcentral.proquest.com/lib/[SITE_ID]/detail.action?docID=6234664

Prøitz, T. S. (2015) Uploading, downloading and uploading again – concepts for policy integration in education research. *Nordic Journal of Studies in Educational Policy, 2015*(1), 70–80. doi: 10.3402/nstep.v1.27015

Rury, J. L., & Tamura, E. H. (Eds.). (2019). *The Oxford handbook of the history of education.* Oxford: Oxford University Press.

Rutkowski, D., & Engel, L. C. (2010). Soft power and hard measures: Large-scale assessment, citizenship and the European union. *European Educational Research Journal, 9*(3), 381–395. doi:10.2304/eerj.2010.9.3.381

Schmelzer, M. (2016). *The hegemony of growth. The making and remaking of the economic growth paradigm and the OECD, 1948–1974.* Cambridge: Cambridge University Press.

Simons, A., & Voß, J.-P. (2018). The concept of instrument constituencies: Accounting for dynamics and practices of knowing governance. *Policy and Society, 37*(1), 14–35. doi:10.1080/14494035.2017.1375248

Sorensen, T. B., Ydesen, C., & Robertson, S. L. (2021). Re-reading the OECD and education: The emergence of a global governing complex – an introduction. *Globalisation, Societies and Education, 19*(2), 99–107. doi:10.1080/14767724.2021.1897946

Tröhler, D. (2020). Nation-state, education and the fabrication of national-minded citizens (introduction). *Croatian Journal of Education, 2*, 11–27. doi:10.15516/cje.v22i0.4129

Tröhler, D., & Lenz, T. (2015). *Trajectories in the development of modern school systems.* New York, NY: Routledge.

Tröhler, D., & Maricic, V. (2021). Data, trust and faith: The unheeded religious roots of modern education policy. *Globalisation Societies and Education, 19*, 1–16. doi:10.1080/14767724.2021.1872371

Tröhler, D., Popkewitz, T., & Labaree, D. F. (2011). Introduction: Children, citizens, and promised lands: Comparative history of political cultures and schooling in the long 19th century. In D. Tröhler, T. Popkewitz, & D. F. Labaree (Eds.), *Schooling and the making of citizens in the long nineteenth century: Comparative visions* (pp. 1–27). New York, NY: Routledge.

Ydesen, C. (2019). The formation and workings of a global education governing complex. In C. Ydesen (Ed.), *The OECD's historical rise in education: The formation of a global governing complex, global histories of education* (pp. 291–303). London and New York, NY: Palgrave Macmillan.

Ydesen, C., & Andreasen, K. E. (2020). Historical roots of the global testing culture in education. *Nordic Studies in Education, 40*(2), 149–166. doi:10.23865/nse.v40.2229

8 Indexical traces of the real

Teaching in the techno-nation-state

William F. Pinar

While still specific to each nation – even to each locale – curriculum worldwide has in common its technologization, a globalizing trend driven by standardized assessment, accelerated by the cancellation of in-person schooling in many countries during the COVID-19 crisis. Technologization is recoding the human subject – already reduced to "the learner" and to "human capital" – as datum, dubbed "data colonialism" by Couldry and Mejias, who define the term as "what happens when life becomes the input of capitalism and becomes organized through data relations" (2019, p. 57). What is the connection between technologization and historical colonialism? "If historical colonialism was an appropriation of land, bodies, and natural resources," Couldry and Mejias (2019, p. 85) explain, "data colonialism can be understood as an appropriation of social resources . . . [that] operates in ways that replicate relations that re-create a colonizing form of power." Even when physically free, we can, they are suggesting, become psychologically enslaved, ensnared in the screen of our handheld devices.

As raw material for capitalist production – one hundred years ago the automobile assembly line was the main metaphor for the curriculum, producing children as products – "data colonialism brings extraction home, literally into the home and the farthest recesses of everyday life" (Couldry & Mejias, 2019, pp. 136–137). Technology and social media specifically constitute, Han (2017, p. 8) asserts, "digital panoptica, keeping watch over the social realm and exploiting it mercilessly." Exploitation of bodies but also the dissolution of subjectivity, as social media infiltrates our psyche, polarizing politics, incurring interpersonal violence. With the omniscient screen, its camera and recording capability, technological visuality insinuates itself inside the intimacy of interiority. No longer even apparently non-political (Bowers, 2016), technological infrastructure commands attention, and with attention, compliance, so insidiously that Han (2017, p. 14) alleges that "now the subjugated subject is not even aware of its own subjugation." In fact, we are even optimistic: techno-utopianism is pervasive, especially in education.

Any conception of a curriculum as an ongoing complicated conversation is eclipsed by "adaptive" learning software that can, Williamson (2017, p. 7) reports, semi-automate the "allocation" and "personalization" of "content" according to each student's "data profile." Now and then blur, evident in Reese's (1997, p. 114) summary of what happened to students in Germany 90 plus years ago: "With little

DOI: 10.4324/9781003137801-11

awareness of what was happening, children became part of an inhuman machinery, well-functioning, but with stunted souls." Today children become post-human subjects recoded according to software, i.e. "formats structuring data help shape who we are" (Koopman, 2019, p. vi).

Consider the association with colonialism and its restructuring of subjectivity. Like historical colonialism, Couldry and Mejias (2019, p. 85) continue, datafication structures how the "colonized think of themselves, legitimizing . . . a specific conceptualization of time and space that ends up universalizing a specific worldview." The prospect of a "universal homogenous state" precedes the present moment (see for example, Pinar, 2019, pp. 10, 106), but never before have they seemed so material. No longer only a matter of black skin and white masks (Fanon, 1967), all children who are connected can become concealed behind data, masked as numbers. "Big Data," Han (2017, p. 12) warns, is reducing children and adults "into *things*, which can be quantified, measured and steered." Academic study as (even relatively) autonomous and socially inflected self-formation had long ago disappeared from many schools, but now study becomes cramming aided by pharmaceutical intervention (Ellison, 2015) with neurological consequences (Brody, 2016).

Datafication can be considered the governance structure of the techno-nation-state, seducing its own (de)sexualized or "asexual" (Richardson, 2018, p. 88) citizenry submerged in software, spellbound by the spectacle of the screen. "Now," Han (2017, p. 59) alleges, "numbers and data are not just being absolutized – they are becoming sexualized and fetishized," so that "dataism is displaying libidinal – indeed, pornographic – traits." "Dataists mate with their data," he suggests, becoming "datasexuals" (2017, p. 59) who find data "sexy" (2017, p. 60).

Not only can physical intimacy become virtual – in one sense it was always: recall that for Freud sex was primarily a matter of fantasy – physical classrooms are being replaced by virtual ones, especially during the COVID-19 pandemic but perhaps also post-pandemic, if Crow and Debars (2020) are right about the "fifth wave" of not only higher education. On Zoom, classrooms become waiting and break-out "rooms" as TV acting threatens to replace teaching and as coursework becomes more infotainment than intellectual engagement with knowledge of most worth. Embodied educational experience is eclipsed by staring at the screens of devices, screens into which children and teachers can disappear. That can constitute a welcome absorption in learning, but it could also represent submergence, a form of subjection, as Han (2017, p. 18) accuses: Now "motivation, projects, competition, optimization and initiative represent features of the psycho-political technology of domination that constitutes the neoliberal regime."

Entrepreneurship replaces education; autonomy is relocated from the political into the decidedly undemocratic economic sphere. "As an 'entrepreneur of himself,' the neoliberal achievement-subject engages in auto-exploitation willingly – even passionately," Han (2017, p. 27) points out, adding: "The self-as-a-work of art amounts to a beautiful but deceptive illusion that the neoliberal regime maintains in order to exhaust its resources entirely." An overstatement, but Han is not entirely mistaken.

1 Techno-nation-state

Historically, as Daniel Tröhler (2020) points out, the nation has been conceived as a cultural thesis about belonging: commonality, inclusion and exclusion. In our era, it is possible to argue that the concept is being cannibalized by technologization, simulations of commonality created by aggressive acts of exclusion, evident in unequal access to computers and the Internet, but also in violent video games, politically polarized exchanges, in cults like QAnon. What is shared in common now is staring at screens, forced to comply with whatever software specifies. Anyone who has a device and is connected to the Internet becomes its de facto citizen; anyone who has no access becomes, in effect, stateless, implied in a news report issued during the COVID-19 pandemic.

While educators and middle-class parents debated the merits of online learning, Gettleman and Raj (2020) reported that in many poorer countries hundreds of millions of children lacked computers or access to the Internet; these children lost access to schooling altogether. Gettleman and Raj also reported that unemployed, economically desperate parents pressed their children into labour: mining sand in Kenya, labouring on cocoa plantations in West Africa, being painted silver and posing as living statues begging for money in Indonesia. This worldwide surge in child labour erased recent gains in school enrolment, literacy, social mobility and children's health: "All the gains that have been made, all this work we have been doing, will be rolled back, especially in places like India," lamented Cornelius Williams, a UNICEF official (quoted in Gettleman & Raj, 2020, p. A1). "Child labor is just one piece of a looming global disaster," Gettleman and Raj (2020, p. A1) continue, as "severe hunger is stalking children from Afghanistan to South Sudan." United Nations officials reported a rise in forced marriages for girls and child trafficking generally, especially across Africa and Asia; teen pregnancies in Uganda increased during pandemic-related school closures; in Kenya "many families" forced their teenage girls into sex work to feed the family (Gettleman & Raj, 2020, p. A5). All the while the pandemic and the inequitable distribution of vaccines threaten, maybe "most of all," those 70 million refugees, "the least likely to have soap and water, food and medicine" (Dorfman, 2020, p. 50).

As these reports confirm, being "offline" condemns one not only to non-connectivity but to civic non-existence, as child labour and sex trafficking replace schooling. Online and connected, the privileged still suffer subjection: involuntary citizenship in a transnational state structured by software, animated by images and sounds, protocols posing as academic instruction. The device is the apparatus by which the techno-nation-state installs its hegemony, a techno-political system once parading as direct democracy. While humanity continues "to create and posit things," human beings are also "posited by things, because that is what [we] essentially are by nature" (Marx quoted in Strathausen, 2017, p. 311). Our humanity (including our capacity to create things) is also interwoven with our inhumanity (our capacity – and our created things' capacity – to kill us, physically and spiritually). As this news report demonstrates, the most vulnerable of human beings – children – can be victimized by adults' desperation, their caretakers' inhumanity.

But a totalizing determinism won't do; without humanity and our agency, there can be no politics, no history, no science. Without that empty subjective space within us and between us and the world – the space of non-coincidence (Pinar, 2019, p. 17, p. 99) – we can only coincide with what is, as the early Marx also knew (see Strathausen, 2017, p. 311).

In the new millennium, then, the nation-state mutates into not only a marriage of the two (nation and state) but also their fusion in software. Online learning creates (supra)national citizens, instilling (supra)national literacies and loyalties, submerged in software, spellbound by the Medusa-like stare of the screen. These could be called the techno-dynamics of nation-building, interpolating a (supra) national identity accented by avatars, passports, usernames and passcodes, soulless citizens of nowhere, as humanity flees the plundered earth for the Cloud. The eschatological confidence of Christians is secularized as techno-utopianism.

The nation-state's emphasis upon its exceptionality, sometimes associated with its (often imagined) ethnic purity and distinctiveness, with the mythologization of its history and future, goes global, one nation worldwide, united by software. (Does the eruption of old-style nationalism in America, Brazil, China, Hungary, Poland, Russia, Turkey and elsewhere constitute blowback?) Many nations' sense of uniqueness had been corroded by post-1960s demands for "development," then often associated with the USA but now also with China, the World Bank, the Organization for Economic Cooperation and Development. Now development denotes technologization, infrastructure designed to connect markets, globalizing not only trade and capital but cyberculture as well. The very concept of globalization (see the Tröhler introduction to this volume) obscures the nationalism, imperialism and colonialism embedded within it. Despite blowback (right-wing populism and other forms of nationalism), globalization continues, especially as technologization, evident in the datafication of education.

2 A techno-totalitarian state of mind

"Schools" are being converted into "data-production centers," Williamson (2017, p. 6) begins, as "students" are subjected to "data mining" and "data analytics" technologies that "trace their every digital move." So-called data brokers, he continues, "collect, curate and aggregate" this information, then "sell it back to education stakeholders" (2017, p. 7). Children had already been reduced to "learners," organic elements of human capital, "inner-focused individuals whose own self-responsibility, competence, and well-being – their deep inner soul, interior life, and habits of mind – have been fused to the political objective of economic innovation" (Williamson, 2013, p. 83). *Innovation* has become an Orwellian word for exploitation.

What roles do teacher-citizens play in this "datafication of social life?" (Williamson, 2017, p. 71) Educators are reduced to "data entry clerks" (Williamson, 2017, p. 82), technicians who survey student learning (Williamson, 2017, p. 82), themselves subjects of "digital governance," compelled to "provide detailed and 'intimate' data" concerning "performances," available for "public display and scrutiny" (Williamson, 2017, p. 82). Soon enough teachers may be replaced, as "pedagogy" becomes a function of "automated machines," "teacher bots" and "cognitive tutors" – what Williamson (2017, p. 7) terms "computerized software agents designed to interact with learners, conduct constant real-time analysis of their learning, and adapt with them."

These developments document the "datafication" of education, its recodification as "quantifiable information" stored in "databases" for "measurement and calculation" (Williamson, 2017, p. 9). Even one's private self becomes quantified, with sensor-enabled devices tracking one's movements, sleep patterns, feelings and sexual activity (Williamson, 2017, p. 28), "emptying the self of any and all meaning" as the "self gets broken down into data until no sense remains" (Han, 2017, p. 60). "The reason both traditional surveillance and datafied tracking conflict with notions of freedom," Couldry and Mejias (2019, p. 155) explain, "derives from something common to both: their invasion of the basic space of the self on behalf of an external power." That external power is software.

Composed in code, software is a set of instructions, structured and operationalized through algorithms, what Williamson (2017, p. 53) summarizes as the conversion of "inputs" into "output[s]." Code makes software "work" (Williamson, 2017, p. 53). Code programmes reality, co-opting our "agency (who does what), materiality (what we can touch, see and hear), and sociality (how we form attachments and collective belonging)" (Williamson, 2017, p. 56). Williamson (2017, p. 56) sees software as a "substrate," but there's nothing "underlying" about it, as – by his own admission – code structures "our personal perceptions, sensations and transactions, and it crystallizes new social formations, publics and groups." Never "innocent," Williamson (2017, p. 56) concedes, code "derive[s] from the worldviews of its originators and that are projected on to its recipients." Projected and *installed* he might have added, as they become internalized psychically (Han, 2017, p. 12) – "we are soothed by data that calm us into stillness and eventually into unthinking sleep" (Koopman, 2019, p. vi) – and enacted behaviourally, a scale of structuration Williamson does acknowledge: "code . . . augments and ultimately *produces* collective political, cultural and economic life" (2017, p. 56). Software engineers and programmers not only operate "technical systems," Williamson (2017, p. 57) allows, but also "social outcomes." In effect, they codify what used to be called society.

Algorithms, Williamson (2017, p. 58) continues, ensure "social ordering, governance and control," what he (2017, p. 61) characterizes as an "algorithmic ideology." That ideology means that "coders . . . select our values for us and potentially prioritize the interests of private technology companies over public interests and concerns" (Williamson, 2017, p. 61). There's no "potentially" about it, as "private technology companies" usurp "public interests" and in so doing constitute themselves as *de facto* officials of the techno-nation-state, structuring, governing and directing "citizenry," a concept now virtual – no longer exclusively geographical or ethnic or mythological.

Ideological control can seem almost complete, as education conceived as one of the humanities – even as a social science – is replaced by the so-called educational 'data sciences," derived from the psychological and cognitive "learning sciences" (Williamson, 2017, p. 103; see also Taubman, 2009). One of these – psycho-informatics (Koopman, 2019, p. 19) – deploys "data mining" and "machine learning" to "detect, characterize and classify behavioral patterns" (Williamson, 2017, p. 107). "Education data science," Williamson (2017, p. 107) explains, translates into the "unprecedented tracking of student behaviors and actions through big data and their analysis through algorithmic techniques of data mining and machine learning." Once associated with emancipation (for example, Gordan, 1993), education becomes exclusively technical, sealed within software, the architecture of which constitutes one worldwide panopticon, the techno-nation-state.

Learning analytics software is designed to track individual students in "real time," to predict "future progress," surveillance in service to the optimization of "learning" (Williamson, 2017, p. 108). The assumption is that "students' access to knowledge" can become a function of "automated, algorithmic processes and techniques" (Williamson, 2017, p. 111). Understanding seems incidental, assessment is all, as what is sought are technologies that will "make emotional measurement and management possible" (Williamson, 2017, p. 124). One is reminded of Goffman's (1961) concept of the total institution, the "possibility of turning, or being turned, from a live person into a dead thing, into a stone, into a robot, an automaton, without personal autonomy of action, an *it* without subjectivity" (Cohen & Taylor, 1972, p. 109). That panopticon was – is – the prison, now also a metaphor for the techno-nation-state.

Measurement and management will be encoded in new "devices and platforms that measure and intervene in the body, behaviour and mood of the learner," Williamson (2017, p. 124) warns. Such a totalizing scale of measurement and intervention will not be limited to "learners." As Williamson (2017, p. 130) appreciates: "Data-driven persuasive technologies . . . confer upon citizens particular ways of thinking and behaving – in other words, for educating citizens to participate in the dominant governing styles of society." That "society" is virtual not actual, its "styles" software designed, homogenous, standardized – what George Grant knew would be "a universal tyranny, destined to eradicate the historic aspirations of the Western world and particularly its North American experiments" (Pinar, 2019, p. 106). Citizenship in such "society" is ensured by seduction, not spectacle.

Such seduction starts early, embedded in "affective computing, biosensor and biometric technologies for measuring children's moods [that] have been developed for schools," including devices "designed to detect excitement, stress, fear, engagement, boredom and relaxation directly through the skin" (Williamson, 2017, p. 134). Such internally installed surveillance should ensure compliance, colonization (to invoke the Mejias and Couldry analogy) rationalized by "growth mindsets research" associated, Williamson reports, with behavioural economics and its subset nudge theory; in its integration of research from psychology, neuroscience and economics, such "research" promises to "address shortcomings in individuals' decision-making processes" (2017, p. 141). Williamson (2017, p. 142) cites ClassDojo, an app that enables teachers to "collect, store and visualize data" about the children in their classroom. According to its website (www.classdojo.com/),

ClassDojo is installed in 95% of US schools, what Williamson (2017, p. 145) subsumes in a totalizing "governmentalization of behavior change." That government is the world's new (if officially unrecognized) universal state, a total institution, a techno-nation-state.

So, you see that the datafication of education extends well beyond students' learning, implementing what Williamson (2017, p. 146) worries is a "biopolitical strategy" to produce "pathology-proofed" citizens capable of coping with the "stresses and anxieties themselves caused by government policies and capitalist culture combined." Not only "pathology-proofed" but also "emotionally maximized" as "personal well-being is understood to be the prerequisite for the development of productive human capital under conditions of digital capitalism" (2017, p. 146). Not only nurture but nature is targeted: "educational genomics" draws on data "about the human genome to identify particular traits that are understood to correspond with learning," so that corporate employees – not academic specialists – can develop curriculum according to each child's "DNA profile" (Williamson, 2017, p. 155). "Neurocomputation" connects "neuro-scientific expertise with technical development, commercial ambitions and governmental objectives," Williamson (2017, p. 156) continues, providing infrastructure for "neuroeducation," based on the "brain-based nature of learning," disclosed through "advanced brain scanning and imaging techniques" (2017, p. 159). The applications include "computer-based brain-training programs, multi-modal forms of virtual reality designed to stimulate regions of the brain associated with learning, and the design of 'human-like' artificial tutoring agents" (Williamson, 2017, p. 159). No more teachers' pension payments, no more school buildings (each requiring upkeep); the screen at which the child stares provides all: total control for the sake of "learning."

Williamson reports that Pearson is proposing to "bypass the cumbersome bureaucracy of mass standardized testing and assessment . . . and instead focus on . . . the AI-enhanced classroom," providing "detailed and intimate analytics of individual performance, which will be gained from detailed modelling of learners through their data" (2017, p. 164). In Pearson's plan "educational systems" are recast as "neurocomputational networks where brain-based technologies will perform a constant measurement and management of learning environments and of all those individuals who inhabit them" (Williamson, 2017, p. 164). Like Pearson, IBM operates on the assumption that "human qualities can be augmented, strengthened and optimized via intelligent machines in order to deal with technical and economic demands" (Williamson, 2017, p. 167). In 2016, IBM and Pearson partnered their "cognitive computing and AIEd project," Williamson (2017, p. 168) reports, operationalizing the view that the brain is "mental software" that requires "being updated all the time" in order to stay aligned with an "increasingly networked social and technical environment" that is itself "retooling" the brain (Williamson, 2017, p. 170). It is retooling psycho-social life too, as sociality shifts from its civic associations with historic nation-states to citizenship in a transnational techno-state – that universal homogenous society George Grant and others had feared, one we are now forced to embrace.

3 Digital citizenship

"Digital citizenship" (Williamson, 2017, p. 177) in the techno-nation-state – materialized through machine-machine connections in the Cloud – seems to be also a state of mind. Rather than becoming, say, cosmopolitan – a citizen of the actual world – living online implies citizenship in the Cloud, stateless in its historic sense, without rights or protection (Strathausen, 2017, p. 306). While Williamson (2017, p. 177) emphasizes the "do-it-yourself (DIY) potential of citizens to participate in the production of new public services, create new value-producing projects, and contribute to the cultural dynamics of cities and regions," one is also obligated to acknowledge the erasure of "public services," as the very concept of the "public" dissolves, not into separate or even micro-publics but into websites, non-places of propaganda, pornography and other forms of distraction sometimes so engrossing that children and their caretakers disappear into the screen for hours, even days.

The technologization of the K-12 curriculum, Williamson (2017, p. 177) explains, is "designed to sculpt and model a form of subjectivity that is deemed appropriate to contemporary digital citizenship." Once again associating agency (as with his reference to DIY) with technologization, Williamson (2017, p. 179) cites the "UK Code Club initiative" – an "after-school coding class run by volunteer programmers" – that communicates the "constructionist idea that young people should learn to program the computer rather than be programmed by it." (Isn't programming the other side of the same coin as being programmed, still stuck inside software?) The UK computing curriculum was the result, Williamson (2017, p. 183) notes, of a "series of lobbying and campaigning activities involving private sector, public sector and civic sector organizations." The Oracle Corporation invested over $200 million in the US Computer Science for All initiative; in 2016 it announced a $1.4 billion investment to produce "software, curriculum and professional development" for European Union computer teachers (Williamson, 2017, p. 188). Oracle is not alone, as Google and Microsoft have also made significant investments installing the computing curriculum. The computing curriculum is not only a specific curriculum but a synecdoche for civic society, now a vast virtual space structured by tracking, trafficking, profiling, profiteering.

"[L]earning to code is not a neutral, decontextualized or depoliticized practice," Williamson (2017, p. 192) acknowledges, "but shaped, patterned, ordered and governed by powerfully commercial coded infrastructures." They are "commercially coded infrastructures" that dictate what people learn, corporate forms of (pseudo)public pedagogy (Burdick & Sandlin, 2013) that parody both terms, atomizing hundreds of millions cybercitizens "into filter bubbles and echo chambers where," Williamson (2017, p. 202) knows, "access to information, culture, news and intellectual and activist discourse is being curated algorithmically, sometimes via computational propaganda and fake news."

Except by poverty and corresponding non-connectivity, is voluntary non-citizenship in the techno-nation-state possible? Is subjective non-coincidence with technology possible even when imprisoned inside it? Strathausen (2017, p. 297) answers affirmatively, insisting on "the conceptual irreducibility of humans to things." What about the ontological irreducibility of humans to things? In answering that question other figures are not so confident, among them George Grant (Pinar, 2019, p. 96, p. 109 n. 4, p. 171). Is disappearance into devices inevitable? Can one exceed one's image on – fusion with – the screen? Online, is subjective presence possible?

4 Being online

Non-coincidence – open inner space – seems to me to be the issue here, as the "self's minimal integrity is the boundedness that constitutes a self as a *self*," by which Couldry and Mejias (2019, p. 156) mean that inner space of separation from (non-coincidence with) what is that provides the "materially grounded domain of possibility that the self has as its horizon of action and imagination," e.g. that "open space in which any given individual experiences, reflects, and prepares to settle on her course of action." Couldry and Mejias (2019, p. 161) caution: "By installing automated surveillance into the space of the self, we risk losing the very thing – the open-ended space in which we continually monitor and transform ourselves over time – that constitute us as selves at all." This space of non-coincidence – an inner empty space wherein one comes to form as an individual through relationships with self and others (including non-human animals and objects) – is the prerequisite for forming a self-conscious relationship with devices, what Couldry and Mejias (2019, p. 204) characterize precisely as "living with an intimate enemy." Since the device declines negotiation, this relationship requires separation for the sake of self-preservation, for freedom, a political concept with its subjective substrate.

As if originating in that empty inner space, the human "voice" – that "unmodulated, nonpredictive accounting of experience, once valued as part of social life" (as Couldry and Mejias characterize it) – is "excluded from Big Data analytics" (2019, p. 148). The self splinters as it is quantified, facilitating an "absor[ption] [of] human life into an external totality – the apparently self-sufficient world of continuous data processing" (Couldry & Mejias, 2019, p. 156). Without freedom there can be no ethics, as "ethics must start out from an understanding of the self" (Couldry & Mejias, 2019, p. 151). While the self is social, it can also be asocial, solitary, a private self, continuous through changing circumstances, including a changing self; subjective coherence comes from non-coincidence with the self itself, enabled by solitude, privacy, meditation (Kumar, 2013). While "all values, such as privacy, are socially negotiated," Couldry and Mejias (2019, p. 183) allow, "there is something distinctively complex about privacy and, specifically, the importance of privacy to autonomy (understood as the capacity to 'find one's own good in one's own way')." Lured by technologization, many might have lost their way: "we must acknowledge that we are, most of us, deeply complicit in the order of data colonialism, whether we like it or not" (Couldry & Mejias, 2019, p. 194). But any "reimagining of our existing relations to data is much more than saying *no*," Couldry and Mejias (2019, p. 198) caution, concluding:

Rather than silence, it is better, as we stand to the side of data colonialism's road, to affirm what we know: the minimal integrity of the self that cannot simply be delegated or outsourced to automatized systems; that the new social order being built through data will produce patterns of power and inequality that corrode all meaningful practices of freedom; and that these contradictions with important values can still, for now at least, be seen for what they are (2019, pp. 214–215).

Lucidity and "critique" would appear to be humanity's "last stand" (see Koopman, 2019, p. 180). It's already too late, Han (2017, pp. 6–7) tells us: "[n]o resistance to the system can emerge in the first place," he declares, explaining that "under the neoliberal regime of auto-exploitation, people are turning their aggression *against themselves*," an "auto-aggressivity [that] means that the exploited are not inclined to revolution as much as depression." It is as if we realize – at least subliminally – that "communication and control have become one, without remainder. Now, everyone is his or her own panopticon" (Han, 2017, p. 40). "[W]e have become our data," Koopman (2019, p. ix) concludes.

There may be no escape, but there is life in prison – this one virtual not physical, less awful than an actual prison of course, but confinement nonetheless, involuntary citizenship in a techno-nation-state that online learning and many forms of employment require. As in actual imprisonment, actions and relationships are strictly structured, now by software rather than prison-building architecture and prison-guard protocols. In both actual and technological prisons subjective presence – being there, *Dasein*, subjective presence (Gumbrecht, 2004) – remains, if overdetermined by software and screen. Altering our relationships with our devices may be insufficient to challenge the techno-nation-state – as Couldry and Mejias insist – but it seems hardly irrelevant to "living with an intimate enemy." It may be the only move to make.

Caution is constantly required, as life in prison can be toxic, dangerous physically and psychologically, triggering depression (as Han emphasizes) and aggression, the latter self-directed against oneself or others, or by others against oneself. Deleuze and Guattari's assertion resonates here: "We do not lack community. On the contrary, we have too much of it. We lack creation. We lack resistance to the present" (quoted in Koopman, 2019, p. 192). In a "total institution" – a totalitarian state – what resistance is possible?

Koopman (2019, p. 193) poses that question this way: "What is resistance in a present saturated by data?" He continues: "What could it even mean to be against information today?" (2019, p. 193). It is "our functional universal" (2019, p. 191): "To take a loud stand against data," Koopman (2019, p. 193) imagines then stops himself: "the very idea is incoherent, impossible, incredible. We live within a data episteme and under a power of information. We are informational persons" (2019, p. 193). Acknowledging that "resistance can [only] be conducted *within* the operations of infopower," Koopman (2019, p. 191, p. 194) fastens his attention onto "infopower" and recommends "repurposing and releveraging information for alternative designs," noting that "in their formats (which are also our formats) are already contained decisions and pathways that will entrench specific informational subjectivities for decades to come." With inner struggle, including detachment from devices, becoming subjectively present within them, we may not in every instance be *reduced* to information, however channelled through information we must be.

What evidence do I offer for that assertion? It is anecdotal, autobiographical, my first experience of teaching online that occurred during the pandemic: fall term 2020. There were 25 enrolled, too many to encounter each student each session. Despite the physical isolation in which Zoom meetings occur, a certain simulation of subjective presence – through dialogical encounter between human subjects (through but not reduced to the machine-machine interface characteristic of dataism) – can occur, as I was able engage each student who appeared solo on the screen, their voices and images constituting "indexical traces of the real," as if "they have a power that energizes reality itself" (Koepnick, 2020, p. 118). Subjective presence – an opportunity afforded, even encouraged, by appearing solo on the screen in the midst of others – is a "power" that can dissipate in an actual classroom, a setting where one's individual voice can be modulated (even muted) by the psycho-social press of other physically present students. In my fall 2020 online course, students' assignments – I asked each to quote a passage from the assigned reading, explain why s/he chose that passage, then pose a question, 100 words in total – focused each of us on the text (yes, information but also analysis) filling the shared screen, "recall[ing] and rework[ing] a long pictorial tradition in which reading [and speaking] w[ere] encoded as spiritual communication – initially with God, then later as literary exaltation" (Koepnick, 2020, p. 119).

No literary exaltation or communication with God I admit, but still there was, to my astonishment, a simulated sense of being subjectively present. That subjective presence was imagistic and auditory, contained within the screen, confined to the Cloud, but – as Koepnick denotes (if in a different context) – an "indexical trace of the real." The (illusory) privacy of the encounter was accented by the imagistic details of our separate settings: to my left side was a ceiling-to-floor painting, books piled high on a table in behind me, books on shelves behind that. When she spoke to me, one student sat on an overstuffed couch, stroking her cat and sipping tea, the pot resting on the table in front of her, a landscape painting on the wall behind her. (When the background is bare – as YouTube Zoom videos often recommend – the figure dominates the ground completely, amplifying that person's presence imagistically.) The illusion of privacy even intimacy – as if I had been invited into the student's home to chat – simulates subjective presence as it insulates one from the pull of that differentiated materiality that is the physically populated seminar room in Scarfe Hall (where I teach when I teach in-person), distracting in its dullness and lack of character, slightly claustrophobic when a window is blocked or absent altogether.

In physical and virtual classrooms there can be absent any sense of an "outside" that the painting (in my study now studio) and the couch and cat (in the student's living room) register. That appearance of parole – overstated as the prison analogy must seem – reminds that there is material natural reality outside. When embedded – "entrenched" is Koopman's more military word, "internalized psychically" is Han's observation – in the screen, there may be no outside, only a series of images and sounds, even when one closes the computer, even when one does walk outside. Despite the totalization technology triggers, Strathausen (2017, p. 295) stays insistent, telling us that "the main characteristic of organic life is the emergence of new and unforeseen systemic effects." Despite being potted in non-organic "soil"? There *is* life in the prison that is the techno-nation-state, but what kind of life is it?

5 Conclusion

As intrusions of the techno-nation-state inside our homes, inside ourselves, devices materialize the most recent iteration of an transhistorical trend toward technologization – George Grant associated it with modernity itself (Pinar, 2019, p. 8, p. 17) – that was already educationally embedded in 20th-century models of in-person professionalism that tended to standardize teaching practice, now conceived as "best practices" (http://geiendorsed.com/blog/inspiration/10-best-practices-of-highly-effective-teachers/). Within this macro-trend there have been efforts at resistance and reform, among the most memorable the progressive education movement in the United States 100 years ago (Pinar, 2010), today scattered throughout the world (for examples see: Thapan, 2015, p. 147; www.bbc.com/news/world-europe-39889523). Parole may be impossible, but simulations of subjective presence through dialogical encounter remain possible, if threaded through the software from which Zoom profits.

The question of the human subject recurs. Hanafi (2017, p. 97) is clear that the "subject . . . is still the battlefield between threatening and threatened authority versus freedom;" she recommends that "both left and right, if capable of it, should relaunch the normativity of politics and law against the deviations of the economy and technology." Casting economism and technologization as "deviations" seems hopeful indeed, as Wittgenstein's sense of foreboding seems to me more sensible: "It isn't absurd, e.g., to believe that the age of science and technology is the beginning of the end for humanity; that the idea of great progress is a delusion, along with the idea that the truth will ultimately be known. . . . It is by no means obvious that this is not how things are" (quoted in Monk, 1990, p. 485).

While waiting, one can still study and teach. There remain indexical traces of the real in the techno-nation-state, including the presence of the human subject, even – especially – on Zoom. As Hanafi (2017, p. 85) appreciates: "[I]t is precisely the presence or absence of the political centrality of the subject and its equal dignity that makes the difference." That centrality has been – is – often ignored in the physical classroom. But fall term 2020, contra critique and common sense, it was simulated onscreen, if in short segments, traces of the real. Or so it seemed.

References

Bowers, C. A. (2016). *Digital detachment. How computer culture undermines democracy*. New York, NY: Routledge.

Brody, J. E. (2016, May 31). Tear your eyes away from the computer. *The New York Times*, CLXV(57,249), D5.

Burdick, J., & Sandlin, J. A. (2013). Learning, becoming, and the unknowable: Conceptualizations, mechanisms, and process in public pedagogy literature. *Curriculum Inquiry, 43*(1), 142–177.

Cohen, S., & Taylor, L. (1972). *Psychological survival: The experience of long term imprisonment.* New York: Vintage.

Couldry, N., & Mejias, U. A. (2019). *The costs of connection. How data is colonizing human life and appropriating it for capitalism.* Sanford, CA: Stanford University Press.

Crow, M., & Debars, W. (2020). *The fifth wave: The evolution of American higher education.* Baltimore, MD: The Johns Hopkins University Press.

Dorfman, A. (2020, December 3). Songs of loss and reinvention. *The New York Review of Books, LXVII*(19), 49–50.

Ellison, K. (2015, November 24). Treating A.D.H.D. electronically. *The New York Times, CLXV*(57,060), D6.

Fanon, F. (1967). *Black skin, white masks* (C. L. Markmann, Trans.). New York, NY: Grove Weidenfeld.

Gettleman, J., & Raj, S. (2020, September 28). Virus closed schools, and world's poorest children went to work. *The New York Times, CLXX*(58,830), A1, A5.

Goffman, E. (1961). *Asylums.* New York, NY: Anchor Books.

Gordon, B. (1993). Toward emancipation in citizenship education. In L. Castenell, Jr. & W. F. Pinar (Eds.), *Understanding curriculum as racial text* (pp. 263–284). Albany: State University of New York Press.

Gumbrecht, H. U. (2004). *Production of presence. What meaning cannot convey.* Stanford, CA: Stanford University Press.

Han, B-C. (2017). *Psycho-politics. Neoliberalism and new technologies of power.* London: Verso.

Hanafi, Z. (2017). Left and right: Why they still make sense. In George Edmondson and Klaus Mladek (Eds.), *Sovereignty in ruins: A politics of crisis* (pp. 63–99). Durham, NC: Duke University Press.

Koepnick, L. (2020). Face time with Hitler. In J. A. Thomas & G. Eley (Eds.), *Visualizing fascism: The twentieth-century rise of the global Right* (pp. 111–133). Durham, NC: Duke University Press.

Koopman, Colin. (2019). *How we became our data: A genealogy of the informational person.* Chicago, IL: University of Chicago Press.

Kumar, A. (2013). *Curriculum as meditative inquiry.* New York, NY: Palgrave Macmillan.

Monk, R. (1990). *Ludwig Wittgenstein. The duty of genius.* New York, NY: Penguin.

Pinar, W. F. (2010). The eight-year study. *Curriculum Inquiry, 40*(2), 295–316.

Pinar, W. F. (2019). *Moving images of eternity: George Grant's critique of time, teaching, and technology.* Ottawa: University of Ottawa Press.

Reese, D. (1997). Emancipation or social incorporation: Girls in the *Bund Deutscher Mädel.* In H. Sünker & O. Hans-Uwe (Eds.), *Education and fascism: Political identity and social education in Nazi Germany* (pp. 102–120). London: Routledge Falmer.

Richardson, D. (2018). *Sexuality and citizenship.* Cambridge: Polity.

Strathausen, C. (2017). Thing politics and science. In G. Edmondson & K. Mladek (Eds.), *Sovereignty in ruins: A politics of crisis* (pp. 292–317). Durham, NC: Duke University Press.

Taubman, P. M. (2009). *Teaching by numbers: Deconstructing the discourse of standards and accountability in education.* New York, NY: Routledge.

Thapan, M. (2015). Curriculum and its possibilities: Schooling in India. In W. F. Pinar (Eds.), *Curriculum studies in India: Intellectual histories, present circumstances* (pp. 141–161). New York, NY: Palgrave Macmillan.

Tröhler, D. (2020). National literacies, or modern education and the art of fabricating national minds. *Journal of Curriculum Studies, 52*(5), 620–635. doi:10.1080/00220272.2020.1786727

Williamson, B. (2013). *The future of the curriculum. School knowledge in the digital age.* Cambridge, MA: The MIT Press.

Williamson, B. (2017). *Big data in education. The digital future of learning, policy and practice.* London: Sage.

Part III

Imperial policies and resurgences of nationalism

9   In the name of the nation

PISA and federalism in Australia and Canada

Sam Sellar, Bob Lingard and Edda Sant

This chapter examines how the Organisation for Economic Cooperation and Development's (OECD) Programme for International Student Assessment (PISA) has contributed to the reworking of relations between globalization and different nationalisms. PISA is an international large-scale assessment (ILSA) of the reading, mathematical and scientific literacies of students who are approximately 15 years of age. The OECD first conducted PISA in the year 2000 and has expanded the programme across subsequent triennial assessments (2003–2018) to include young people in nearly 80 countries. PISA is arguably the most prominent and influential ILSA today and has had significant policy impact, driven in large part by media representations of rankings that emphasize nation-to-nation comparison between participating countries (Martens & Niemann, 2013; Baroutsis & Lingard, 2017). In this chapter, we analyze two national cases – Canada and Australia – that each have federal systems in which states or provinces have primary responsibility for schooling. We address the following research question: How has PISA contributed to the emergence of national imaginaries of schooling in Australia and Canada?

A brief historical reflection on the development of PISA is necessary to understand how the programme has shaped both national imaginaries and the global education policy field. In 1983, amidst growing concerns about educational standards in US schooling, the A *Nation at Risk* report announced that the US's "once unchallenged pre-eminence in commerce, industry, science, and technological innovation is being overtaken by competitors throughout the world" (The National Commission on Excellence in Education, 1983, p. 5). The anxieties evident in A *Nation at Risk* echoed those of the US's earlier '*Sputnik* moment,' which had previously drawn attention to the need for greater investment in education, with a renewed focus on mathematics and science. The report lamented the "rising tide of mediocrity that threatens our very future as a Nation and a people" (The National Commission on Excellence in Education, 1983, p. 6). Seeking better information for benchmarking educational performance internationally, the US later advocated for the development of PISA and the OECD's Indicators of Education Systems (INES) initiative, which inform the OECD's annual publication of comparative international educational statistics in its Education at a

DOI: 10.4324/9781003137801-13

Glance reports (Henry, Lingard, Rizvi, & Taylor, 2001). While the OECD is the most visible proponent of PISA today, the US played a central role in driving the development of the programme, and it thus reflects a national agenda that was globalized through the subsequent work of the OECD and participation by other countries.

Important shifts occurred in global education policy during the 1990s, and the OECD's education work played an important role in these developments. This was a period of renewed globalization in which the numbers and comparisons generated by the OECD's work contributed to the emergence of a global education policy field (Lingard & Rawolle, 2011; Rutkowski, 2007), and the OECD and other and international organizations began to play a significant role in articulating education and economic policy. Much of the literature examining PISA over the past two decades has emphasized the OECD's role in the global governance of education (e.g. Sellar & Lingard, 2014; Kallo, 2009; Martens & Jakobi, 2010), complemented by a focus on top-down global effects on national policy making in education (Beech & Larsen, 2014; Larsen & Beech, 2014; Lingard, 2021b; Sellar & Lingard, 2013).

Perspectives on PISA from both policy and academic standpoints have begun to shift. The results of the 2016 UK 'Brexit' referendum and the election of Donald Trump to the US Presidency in 2016 manifest the resurgence of nationalisms and ethnonationalisms in the Anglosphere, while other parts of the world, such as Latin America, had already experienced a re-nationalization trend during the previous decade (Sant & Gonzalez, 2018). The prevailing consensus regarding the triumph of economic globalization was challenged by new foreign policy approaches, an emergent anti-multilateralism and changes to trade relations prompted by Brexit and Trump. The fracturing of this consensus continued with the disruption to global flows caused by the COVID-19 pandemic (Appadurai, 2020). At the same time, PISA appears to have passed its zenith and has confronted growing critique from participating nations, including from the US (Schneider, 2019; Lingard, 2021a). Some of these critiques have focused on the rapid expansion of PISA to create new programmes and assessment domains, which potentially undermine its rigour and value for participants, particularly developed nations. PISA 2021 has also been postponed until 2022 due to the pandemic, and a new set of education policy problems has emerged with the closure of schools globally and the move to online teaching. Clearly, the attention given to the global policy field over the past three decades requires rebalancing with national perspectives, which is a key objective of this volume.

Our aim in this chapter is to examine the influence of PISA in Australia and Canada from 2000 to the present, in order to analyze its contribution to the emergence of national imaginaries of schooling. In the next section, we introduce the theoretical framework for our analysis, drawing on theories of the nation-state, globalization and federalism. We then analyze our two case studies of the impact of PISA within federal education systems to demonstrate how PISA has reworked state/province/federal relations and its uses to advance the distinct yet complementary projects of states and nations. We draw on interviews with policymakers and analysis of documents, including PISA reports produced by the OECD and the national agencies that manage the assessment.

1 Theoretical framework

Nations and the nation-state

In line with the broader framing of this volume, we assume the nation to be a discursive practice. Theory and research, within and beyond the field of education, often employ different paradigms for the study of nationhood (e.g. Smith, 2000; Özkırımlı, 2017; Sant & Hanley, 2018), but the mere existence of paradigms suggests that nationhood operates as a contested social construct (Özkırımlı, 2017). As a discursive practice, the nation functions as an "empty signifier" (Laclau, 2007a, p. 69), which is both limited and open. The nation requires the presence of an excluded Other; yet, the nation is also open to the pressure of distinctive competing discourses, each of them with a different image of this Other (Sant, 2019). By recognizing the contested meanings of the 'nation,' and that struggle over meaning takes place in policies, we aim to avoid assumptions that could otherwise condition our analysis of the idea of nationhood.

In the context of nation-states, the nation functions as a mutual ally of the state. Prior to the emergence of nation-states, kings often claimed legitimacy as a divine right (Kelly, 2005). In his classic, *The King's Two Bodies*, the historian Ernest H. Kantorowicz (1967/1999) described medieval kings as entities with two bodies: a transcendent or political body and a natural/mortal body, with the power (or sovereignty) of the latter derived from the ahistorical nature of the former. In a context in which states attempted to react against and appropriate religious authority (Brown, 2014), nation-states 'inherited' the king's two bodies. The nation became the 'soul' or 'enduring' body from which state sovereignty emerged, and the state became the container for the nation. Indeed, today the relationship between nation and state operates at the level of what, following Derrida (2006), we could describe as spectrality (Cheah, 1999). The nation constitutes the spirit, providing transcendence and legitimacy to the state. State sovereignty arises precisely from its appeal to the nation. Yet, the nation, as previously stated, is 'empty.' Derrida (2006) explains:

> For there is no ghost, there is never any becoming-specter of the spirit without at least an appearance of flesh, in a space of invisible visibility, like the disappearing of an apparition. For there to be ghost, there must be a return to the body, but to a body that is more abstract than ever.
>
> (p. 157)

The ghostly nature of the nation requires "flesh" to manifest; it "can exist only through its parasitic attachment to some particular body" (Laclau, 2007b, p. 72). This ghostly nation takes the shape of state structures – the technical and institutional bodies that administer the impossible fullness of the 'spiritual' nation.

Anderson (1996) uses the simile of the haunted house (the nation) that can only manifest through old switchboards (the state) (see also Cheah, 2003). This spectral relation is, therefore, symbiotic. The nation requires a state to manifest its presence; the state requires a nation to legitimize its power. Through nation-building, the empty shell of the state structure attempts to give itself a soul (Fanon, 1963).

The increasing complexity of national-global relations

Rather than a globalism-nationalism binary, what we see today are much more complex interactions between processes of nationalization and globalization. According to Brown (2014), the accelerating processes of globalization have generated a situation in which political sovereignty is increasingly migrating from states to international economic and governance institutions and to entrepreneurial decision makers. Simultaneously, processes of deterritorialization have led to disjunctive relationships between the 'the state' and 'the nation,' with some 'nations' searching for 'states' and others spreading through existing state boundaries with migration and the emergence of new diasporas (Appadurai, 2006). Moreover, states seek to manage the deterritorializing desires produced by global flows of technology, media and money, and the loss of some economic sovereignty, by reterritorializing desire onto new ideas of nationhood as an expression of cultural sovereignty (Deleuze & Guattari, 1987). Appadurai argues that today, given demographic diversity, the state and the nation have become the project of each other, with the hyphen in 'nation-state' indicating the somewhat attenuated relationship between the two.

The recent erosion of nation-state sovereignty has had a strong impact on citizens' perceptions of their ability to influence increasingly important phenomena such as global capital, climate change, transitional terrorist networks and, more recently, the global COVID-19 pandemic (Brown, 2014). Paradoxically, the 2008 financial crisis, the rise of cultural diversity and the commodification of democratic politics have contributed to a resurgence of nationalist and ethnonationalist political discourses (Mouffe, 2018). As Sassen (2013) points out, "[t]he issue here is not one of nationalism versus globalism, but one of complexity" (p. 26).

Federalism and its manifestations in Canada and Australia

Federalism refers to a structure of government with two layers, for example, a federal or national government and state or provincial governments. This structure allows for unity and diversity within a given nation. A formal Constitution outlines the division of powers and defines powers for each layer of government. So, for example, Section 51 of the Australian Constitution outlines the powers of the federal government with those not listed remaining residual powers of the states and territories. A federal government structure differs from a unitary form of government such as in New Zealand, where there is one layer of government covering the entire nation. As Wallner (2018, p. 81) observes, "Federal systems are centred on the principle of 'shared-rule' and 'self-rule,' where political and societal actors attempt to find a balance between the value and benefit of independent decision-making and central oversight, contrasted with the value and benefit of independent decision-making and sub-national autonomy."

Australia and Canada are both federations, but federalism works very differently in each case. In both, though, education is the responsibility of the lower tiers of government; in Canada, the provinces and territories, and in Australia, the states and territories. These differences reflect varying histories and demographics. Politics and changing circumstances, for example globalization and emergent new nationalisms, affect the workings of federalism and particularly the changing roles of the national government. The balance between centralization and decentralization, and the relations between the national tier of government and the states, provinces and territories, fluctuates and changes. As a generalization, over time the national government in federal states has tended to wield more influence. This is absolutely the case in relation to Australia but not so in relation to Canada, where a multinational nation with recognized First Nations and a Francophone province, Quebec, has resulted in a form of federalism that limits centralization and the increased influence of the national government. Wallner (2018) refers to the centralizing trend in federalisms as a trend towards the shared rule of education, an observation that applies to Australia and, to a much lesser extent, Canada. The two federalisms thus work in different ways, and this is particularly the case in respect of education policy and centripetal forces in these federalisms.

2 The Australian case

Australian federalism in education

While education is a Constitutional responsibility of the states and territories in Australia, there has been increasing federal government involvement, particularly since the 1970s. During the Second World War, the federal government took over income tax-raising powers from the states. This has resulted in Australian federalism manifesting the highest degree of vertical fiscal imbalance of any federalism, with the federal government having the resources and the states having responsibility for expensive services such as schooling, health and policing. Furthermore, under Section 96 of the Constitution, the federal government has the capacity to make specific purpose grants to the states. This situation and changing geopolitical framing since the 1970s have seen an ever-increasing involvement of the federal government in schooling in Australia, functioning at times through funding-compliance trade-offs and at other times through explicit policy developments. In the mid-1970s enhanced federal involvement was focused on achieving equity. Subsequently, in the context of neoliberal globalization and an economistic, human capital reframing of the purposes of schooling, there was further centralization in Australian schooling. This occurred under federal Labor governments from 1983 to 1996 and again from 2007 to 2013.

It was during this second period of Labor governments that the momentum towards centralization and more national involvement reached its peak. Labour's so-called education revolution saw *inter alia* the creation of a national curriculum, national testing and national standards for teachers. This centralization was achieved through agreements between the federal government and the states and territories made at the Intergovernmental Council in Education, consisting of all the Ministers of Education. The national agenda in Australia might be best described as a "federally driven yet collaborative intergovernmental reform" (Wallner, Savage, Hartong, & Engel, 2020, p. 254). The national agenda has been managed by a new body, the Australian Curriculum, Assessment and Reporting Authority (ACARA), established in 2008 and co-owned by the federal, state and territory governments.

These national policies were both a response to and an articulation of globalization, as well as being an expression and constitution of the nation in changing geopolitical circumstances. Gerrard and Farrell (2013, p. 5) have eloquently grasped this situation in their observation that "the development of a national curriculum has been framed both as an instantiation of nationhood and a devoted gesture to the global network of educational practices (e.g. PISA, OECD . . .) within which local schooling practices are increasingly interpellated." One can see the close interweaving of the global and the national in this set of national policies. With globalization of the economy, nations lost to varying degrees sovereignty over their economies. In this context, Appadurai (2006, p. 23) noted that "[t]he nation-state has been steadily reduced to the fiction of its ethnos as the last cultural resource over which it may exercise full dominion." That reality also formed a backdrop to the Labor governments' national agenda, particularly the national curriculum, as did a human capital framing of education as one central economic policy still controlled by the nation (Savage, 2016; Lingard, 2018). At the same time, these national policies were a response to what was perceived to be Australia's declining performance on international large-scale assessments, including PISA.

These changes in the functioning of Australian federalism in education have to be seen against the varying impacts of globalization, including new spatialities (Amin, 2002). Regarding the latter, we have seen some rescaling of politics to regions and international organizations, and centripetal forces and rescaling pressures within most federal political structure, evidenced in a strengthening of federal presence in schooling policies.

Australian participation in PISA

Substantial involvement in and with the OECD has been important to Australia as a mid-range international nation. Australia joined the OECD in 1971, ten years after its creation in 1961, and has played an important role in the work of the OECD – and that work has had a substantial impact on policy making. In Australia, the significance of the OECD in general, and specifically in education, is demonstrated by a number of facts and has been expressed in our interviews with Australian policy makers (particularly federal) since the turn of the century. Many of these interviewees have noted 'Australia punching above its weight at the OECD' with the corollary that the OECD's work has had more impact in Australia than in many other nations.

Two Australians have headed Education at the OECD. Professor Barry McGaw was the first director of the stand-alone Directorate for Education created in 2002. The Australian Council for Educational Research (ACER) has played a significant role in designing and developing PISA. It is significant that Professor McGaw was a major player in the federal Labor government's national agenda (2007–2013), and he was the first Chair of ACARA. The current chair of the PISA Governing Board is a Senior Australian public servant, Michelle Bruniges, who is now head of the federal Department of Education, Skills and Employment. It is significant that Bruniges has defended the expansion of main PISA against criticisms coming from the federal department of education in the US (see Lingard, 2021a). A former Australian politician has been appointed the Secretary-General of the OECD from June 2021.

In research conducted on the OECD since the late 1990s, we have found that, particularly up until 2009, PISA had much more policy salience in Australia than in the UK and the US (Sellar & Lingard, 2013). This Australian positioning *vis-a-vis* the OECD must be kept in mind when considering its role in the constitution of a putatively national system of schooling in Australia. We see in this relationship an interesting interweaving of policy actors and institutions: the global in the nation and the nation in the global.

In the first two PISA assessments conducted in 2000 and 2003, Australia performed strongly. The media coverage was very positive, so that, for example, the headline in the *Canberra Times* regarding Australia's performance on the 2003 PISA, proclaimed that "Australia's education system gets full marks" (December 13, 2004). What is significant to observe here is the use of "Australia's education system," when at that time there was no national curriculum nor national testing. Rather, each state and territory constructed its own curricula and assessment regimes, yet the reporting on PISA performance was as if there was an Australian system of schooling. We argue that PISA reporting helped discursively to constitute the imaginary of an Australian schooling system.

From PISA 2006 onwards, Australia's performance declined. The federal Labor government elected in 2007 used this decline as one rationale for its 'education revolution' (Savage, 2021), which included the creation of the national curriculum and national testing. These developments helped constitute the notion of a national schooling system, as did reporting on PISA results. It should be noted, though, that all of the states and territories from the first PISA in 2000 have over-sampled so that comparisons can be made between these jurisdictions. This is unusual amongst federations. However, media reporting still talks of Australia's performance on PISA. This neglects the reality of different levels of performance by the states on PISA; so, for example, the Australian Capital Territory performs very well, while the Northern Territory performs poorly. The aggregation of scores at the national level underpins the description of decline in Australia's overall performance.

Shanghai's stellar performance on PISA 2009, outperforming Finland, caused a PISA shock in Australia (Sellar & Lingard, 2013). This shock was amplified by the publication in 2012 by the think tank, the Grattan Institute, of a report, *Catching*

Up: Learning from the best school systems in East Asia (Jensen, Hunter, Sonneman, & Burns, 2012). The report basically reflected on the PISA 2009 results and the outstanding performance of many Asian schooling systems. The headline concerning the report in the national newspaper, *The Australian*, stated, "Lessons from Asia show the way forward for our schools" (February 17, 2012). The other national newspaper, *The Financial Review*, ran with the headline "Asian education goes to the top of the class" (February 18, 2012).

The then Australian Prime Minister, Julia Gillard, formerly federal Minister for Education, noted in relation to *The Australian's* story on the Grattan Institute report:

> Four of the top performing school systems in the world are in our region [based on PISA results] . . . . On average, kids at 15 in those nations are six months ahead of Australian kids at 15 and they are a year in front of the OECD mean. . . . If we are talking about today's children – tomorrow's workers – I want them to be workers in a high-wage economy where we are still leading the world. I don't want them to be workers in an economy where we are kind of the runt of the litter in our region and we've slipped behind the standards and the high-skill, high-wage jobs are elsewhere in the region.
>
> (Franklin, 2012, p. 1)

This is a significant set of observations. It expresses a human capital version of the purposes of schooling, which was also a significant rationale for the Labor government's (2007–2013) national schooling agenda. It also reflects Australia's pivot towards Asia in the so-called Asian century, and it shows the significance of the OECD's PISA in constituting a national view of schooling as well. In this case, despite the Constitutional reality, involvement in PISA and the OECD's education work, and the move to a national curriculum and national testing in schooling, together helped discursively constitute a national imaginary of schooling.

3 The Canadian case

Canadian federalism in education

The Canadian writer, Mavis Gallant, once suggested that "a Canadian is someone who has a logical reason to think he [sic] is one" (Gallant, 1981, p. xiii). Gallant grounds her vision of Canadian national belonging in rationality – in this case, a discussion of Canada's conferral of citizenship by birth – rather than shared ancestry, language, culture or beliefs. A similar view was expressed by Canadian Prime Minister, Justin Trudeau, in an interview with the *New York Times* magazine, where he suggested that:

> There is no core identity, no mainstream in Canada. There are shared values – openness, respect, compassion, willingness to work hard, to be there for each

other, to search for equality and justice. Those qualities are what make us the first postnational state.

(Lawson, 2015, para. 46)

Both Gallant and Trudeau point to the basis of Canadian national identity in shared rights and responsibilities, in contrast to the European model based on "territorialized notions of cultural belonging" (Soysal & Soyland, 1994, p. 3). Soysal and Soyland define postnational citizenship as conferring "upon every person the right and duty of participation in the authority structures and public life of a polity, regardless of their historical or cultural ties to that community" (p. 3). While cultural and ethnic nationalisms clearly play important roles in Canadian history, modern Canadian nationalism is predominantly an inclusive, civic nationalism.

Canadian federalism is also an exception to the centripetal forces evident in many federal schooling systems in the context of globalization. This reflects the idiosyncratic nature of Canadian federalism, with schooling policy jealously guarded by the provinces as their domain of governance, which reflects the Constitutional reality. Additional factors in Canadian federalism have been the recognition of First Nations and the existence of a single Francophone province, Quebec. The provinces have considerable autonomy in respect of taxation, along with "a robust system of unconditional equalisation to redistribute funds throughout the federation" (Wallner, 2018, p. 83). Unlike Australia, in Canada there is real fiscal federalism. While there is no federal presence in schooling and no federal department of education, there have been moves toward horizontal alignment across the education policies of the provinces in relation to testing and curriculum, which has been driven by the provinces themselves. The Council of Ministers of Education (CMEC) facilitates some cross-nation developments, including the Pan-Canadian Assessment Program (PCAP), but there is no national curriculum. Schooling is quite centralized within each province under the oversight of provincial Ministries of Education, such that Wallner (2018, p. 83) describes the Canadian federal system of schooling "as deconcentrated rather than decentralised." Globalization has not affected the federal functioning of schooling in Canada as it has done in Australia with the growth of national policies. Cross-nation developments in Canadian schooling have resulted from horizontal alignments across provinces and not through vertical integration.

Canadian participation in PISA

Canada is the only OECD member country that does not have a national Ministry of Education and thus constitutes an interesting case study of 'national' participation in PISA. Provincial participation is coordinated at a federal level by CMEC. This case study draws on CMEC reports and an interview conducted in 2016 with a key informant from CMEC. We also draw on previous analyses of the media and policy impacts of Canadian PISA 2012 performance (Sellar & Lingard, 2018).

CMEC is an intergovernmental body that was established by the provinces and territories in 1967 to provide national leadership in education in Canadian federalism. The aims of CMEC include supporting national policy debate, support for initiatives that are of mutual interest to provinces and territories, and coordination between national education organizations and the federal government, as well as serving as "an instrument to represent the education interests of the provinces and territories internationally."[1] Provinces have pursued a collaborative approach to assessment for some time, and CMEC has been central in developing this agenda, as our informant explained:

> [Provinces] had a very strong interest in assessments since the beginning of the organization. We instituted a national assessment. At the time it was called the Student Achievement Indicators Programme. It's morphed into the Pan-Canadian Assessment Program, and we manage this on their behalf from beginning to end. Development, administration, reporting, and so on.

The School Achievement Indicators Programme (SAIP) was established in 1993 and was replaced by the Pan-Canadian Assessment Programme (PCAP) in 2007. PCAP is a sample-based assessment of reading, mathematics and science aligned to curricula. Curricula vary in each province and territory, although common approaches are fostered by mechanisms such as the Western and Northern Canadian Protocol (WNCP). PCAP has been conducted with grade 8 students (~13 years) every three years since 2007, but it has not had a significant impact on provincial and national policy debate.

With the emergence in the 1990s of new international large-scale assessments, our informant explained that the provinces approached CMEC to coordinate their participation.

> [With] the increased interest in international assessments, the provinces asked us to co-ordinate multi-provincial efforts and participation. PISA is a pretty good example, where technically each province could possibly participate in PISA, and they do that in [the IEA's] TIMSS or in PIRLS, . . . but when there's a critical mass of provinces interested, then they ask the secretariat to co-ordinate their participation. That's what we do in the case of PISA.

Canada oversamples for PISA in order to disaggregate province-level results and enhance their relevance for the decision making of provincial ministries. CMEC, with partner agencies that have changed over time (e.g. Statistics Canada), has managed this participation on behalf of ministries. Our informant explained:

> CMEC [is] the conduit for provincial participation in terms of payment, but also expertise, review of items, development and administration. In addition to administering the assessment itself, we're asked to come up with reports. The ministries use that mainly for their own internal research. Very rarely will they publish something that is related to PISA or another international assessment.

The CMEC PISA reports focus on comparing provincial performance and Canadian average performance, including in relation to the performance of other countries and systems. However, there is some slippage between discussion of the performance of Canadian students and performance at a provincial level, suggesting a view of Canadian education as a homogenous space in relation to this assessment. This translation of provincial performance into a representation of national performance is much stronger in the OECD's PISA reporting, which focuses mainly on Canadian average performance with disaggregation between provinces occurring only in less prominent sections of the PISA reports.

Canada was ranked second in the PISA 2000 assessment of reading literacy behind Finland, and this generated a narrative about the high quality of many provincial education systems and international interest in Canadian education policies and practices. Indeed, Alberta performed more strongly in reading literacy than Finland, with British Columbia, Quebec, Manitoba, Saskatchewan performing better than all other participating countries other than Finland. In her analysis of media coverage of Canada's performance in PISA 2000, Stack (2006) demonstrates how the PISA results were used by governments and the media to represent students as homogenous groups that reified regional stereotypes and generally accepted the strong performance of 'Canada' at face value. This coverage of the first PISA results helped to establish both national narratives about performance across Canada, but also a narrative about Canadian performance and the quality of Canadian schooling systems, which elided the differences emphasized in sub-national comparisons and other important contextual information for interpreting the results. The image of 'national' student performance was thus established on the basis of diverse data emerging from different provinces.

Media coverage and interpretation of PISA remained relatively consistent until 2013, when the provincial and national narratives regarding PISA shifted following the reporting of the PISA 2012 results, which focused on mathematics literacy. Mathematics was first assessed as a major domain of PISA in 2003, and it was the major domain for a second time in 2012. The publication of results in December 2013 thus provided the first opportunity to properly compare mathematics performance over time. Canadian provinces had performed well in 2003, with a national average score of 532, and all provinces performed at or above the OECD average. By 2012, the Canadian national average score had decreased to 518, and all but two provinces – Quebec and Saskatchewan – saw significant declines.

Canada's mathematics performance in 2012 made the headlines nationally. For example, *The Globe and Mail* reported on the day of the PISA release that "Canada's fall in math-education ranking sets off alarm bells" (December 3, 2013), and the editorial in the same issue was titled "Quebec adds, Canada subtracts on its math scores" (December 3, 2013). As our CMEC informant noted, the PISA 2012 results gave rise to policy debate about mathematics curricula and pedagogies at a provincial level, but also across Canada more generally:

> It's been attributed, by both the media and experts in ministries, to how mathematics is taught. The debate between sticking to the core of mathematics versus going to Discovery math has raged here for a number of weeks, if not months, after the release of the results. . . . It is influencing the revision to

curricula in a number of provinces where they want to put back some "back to basics" math, but certainly not to shift altogether there.

Provincial participation in PISA, facilitated by an intergovernmental body, thus gave rise to national media coverage and policy debate about the state of 'Canadian' mathematics education (see also Sellar & Lingard, 2018).

4 Discussion

In both cases, we can see how state infrastructures, namely collaboration in respect of assessment, provide a basis for building a national identity for schooling. These national imaginaries have emerged partly through involvement in PISA and the statistical work undertaken to construct national performance as a unit of comparison that can be glorified or scandalized (Steiner-Khamsi & Waldow, 2018). Both cases thus demonstrate the role of PISA in what Appadurai (1996) described as the increasingly embattled relationship between nation (culture, demography) and state (government apparatuses of politics and policy) inside nation-states. PISA, as a surrogate measure of the quality of potential human capital, contributes to both processes simultaneously by promoting the globalizing logics of human capital and magnet economies, while helping to constitute new ideas about national projects of schooling. If we think in terms of Anderson's (1996) metaphor of the haunted house to describe the relationship between the nation-state, PISA operates as a visitor that activates the switchboards to animate the house, that is, the nation.

In the Australian case, there is a federal infrastructure for education, including an intergovernmental council comprising all education ministers, ACARA and a national ministry, but the OECD's education work and narratives about Australian schooling shaped by declining PISA performance have influenced the development and use of this infrastructure to establish national curriculum and national assessments. The achievement of a national curriculum, national testing and national standards for teachers in Australia's federal system demonstrates how the federal government, working collaboratively with the states and territories, helped create a *de facto* national schooling system. This was enabled to some extent by the idiosyncratic character of Australian federalism, with extensive vertical fiscal imbalance almost creating mendicant states and territories, at the same time as globalization precipitated centripetal pressures in schooling policy. The national government manages the economy, while the human capital construction of schooling, promoted by the OECD, almost demands an enhanced federal government presence in schooling policy and its economization, but always mediated by federalism. Reporting of Australia's PISA performance has also contributed to the creation discursively of a national imaginary of schooling. Also important here have been effects of globalization, namely, the loss of economic sovereignty and complementary stress on national ethnos, as argued by Appadurai (2006), demonstrating the nation and the state as the project of each other. The international education work of the OECD has helped constitute the globe as a commensurate space of measurement of comparative school performance, which has been legitimated by the work of the nation.

The Canadian case is interesting because it is the only OECD member without a national governing body in education. With no federal Ministry of Education, CMEC has played an important role in coordinating national involvement in PISA that has enabled Canadian schooling performance to emerge in the form of a statistical average across provinces. The constitution of a national schooling imaginary has been made possible by the reporting of PISA results that, in some cases, represent Canadian students as a homogenous group celebrated or problematized as a matter of national pride or concern. Whilst Canada presents itself as a post-national state, it still requires a national imaginary to function. The empty space of the Canadian 'nation' is not filled with references to an ethnic or cultural nation (ancestry or traditions), but with a civic culture and values which privilege diversity and multiculturalism. The national imaginary of Canadian schooling thus responds to this civic construction of nationhood. 'National' schooling performance appears as the 'soul' of the educational infrastructure, which is firmly grounded in provincial systems. The soul, as a representation of a non-existent national schooling system, is praised or blamed for the performance of the different state parts. The ontotheological relation between the nation and the state functions in such a way that it benefits from a context of global competition, whilst sustaining supra- and intra-national claims of sovereignty (e.g. First Nations, Quebec, globalism).

5 Conclusion

In this chapter, we have analyzed the cases of Australian and Canadian participation in PISA to demonstrate how national imaginaries of schooling have a 'ghostly' nature insofar as they are primarily symbolic, yet this presence rests upon the material work of states and provinces. We have shown how PISA contributes to the development of these imaginaries by enabling students educated in different educational systems under different curricula to become represented as a 'national student body,' and how the data infrastructures of federal states and provinces give 'flesh' to otherwise non-existent national schooling systems. PISA, along with other policy tools and institutions of global governance, offers an additional legitimization particularly for federal nation-states. Regardless of whether these states are potentially 'threatened' by internal processes of state-building (e.g. Quebec in Canada) or not (e.g. Australia), human capital framings of global education policy create opportunities for the nation-state to present itself as a single entity unifying its two bodies. Without the opposition that these spaces facilitate, "the elements constituting popular unity would disintegrate and its identity would fall apart" (Laclau, 1990, p. 32). The imagined nation needs the state and its educational apparatuses to exist as much as the states and provinces need the nation to legitimize their sovereignty. Only insofar as the global education race exists, facilitated by international large-scale assessments such as PISA, can the bodies and souls of national schooling manifest in Australia and Canada as they have over the past two decades. Paradoxically then, the very processes of globalization that have reworked national education policy since the 1990s have also potentially abetted the return, or the new constitution, of national imaginaries of schooling in both contexts.

Note

1 www.cmec.ca/11/About_Us.html

References

Amin, A. (2002). Spatialities of globalization. *Environment and Planning, 34*, 385–399.

Anderson, B. (1996). *Imagined communities*. London: Verso.

Appadurai, A. (1996). *Modernity al large: Cultural dimensions of globalization*. Minneapolis: University of Minnesota Press.

Appadurai, A. (2006). *Fear of small numbers: An essay on the geography of anger*. London: Duke University Press.

Appadurai, A. (2020). Coronavirus won't kill globalization. But it will look different after the pandemic. *Time Magazine*. Retrieved May 9, 2001, from https://time.com/5838751/globalization-coronavirus/

Baroutsis, A., & Lingard, B. (2017). Counting and comparing school performance: An analysis of media coverage of PISA in Australia, 2000–2014. *Journal of Education Policy, 32*(4), 432–449.

Beech, J., & Larsen, M. A. (2014). Replacing old spatial empires of the mind: Rethinking space and place through network spatiality. *European Education, 46*(1), 75–94.

Brown, W. (2014). *Walled states, waning sovereignty*. Brooklyn, NY: Princeton University Press.

Cheah, P. (1999). Spectral nationality: The living on [sur-vie] of the postcolonial nation in neocolonial globalization. *boundary 2, 26*(3), 225–252.

Cheah, P. (2003). *Spectral nationality: Passages of freedom from Kant to postcolonial literatures of liberation*. New York, NY: Columbia University Press.

Deleuze, G., & Guattari, F. (1987). *A thousand plateaus: Capitalism and schizophrenia*. Minneapolis: University of Minnesota Press.

Derrida, J. (2006). *Specters of Marx: The state of debt, the work of mourning and the new international*. London and New York, NY: Routledge.

Fanon, F. (1963). *The wretched of the earth* (Vol. 36). New York, NY: Grove Press.

Franklin, M. (2012, February 24). We risk losing education race, PM warns. *The Australian*. Retrieved May 9, 2021, from www.theaustralian.com.au/national-affairs/education/we-risk-losing-education-race-julia-gillard-warns/news-story/a2dd64e2aa9e372429dfdfa7d001a166

Gallant, M. (1981). *Home truths: Selected Canadian stories*. Toronto: Macmillan of Canada.

Gerrard, J., & Farrell, L. (2013). 'Peopling' curriculum policy production: Researching educational governance through institutional ethnography and Bourdieuian field analysis. *Journal of Education Policy, 28*(1), 1–20.

Henry, M., Lingard, B., Rizvi, F., & Taylor, S. (2001). *The OECD, globalization and education policy*. Oxford: Pergamon Press.

Jensen, B., Hunter, A., Sonneman, J., & Burns, T. (2012). *Catching up: Learning from the best school systems in East Asia*. Melbourne: Grattan Institute.

Kallo, J. (2009). *OECD education policy. A comparative and historical study focusing on the thematic reviews of tertiary education.* Jyväskylä: Finnish Educational Research Association.

Kantorowicz, E. H. (1967/1997). *The king's two bodies: A study in mediaeval political theology.* Princeton: Princeton University Press.

Kelly, M. J. (2005). Pulling at the threads of Westphalia: Involuntary sovereignty waiver-revolutionary international legal theory or return to rule by the great powers? *UCLA Journal of International Law & Foreign Affairs, 10*(2), 361.

Laclau, E. (1990). *New reflections on the revolution of our time.* London: Verso.

Laclau, E. (2007a). *On populist reason.* London: Verso.

Laclau, E. (2007b). *Emancipation(s).* London: Verso.

Larsen, M., & Beech, J. (2014). Spatial theorizing in comparative and international education research. *Comparative Education Review. 58*(20), 191–214.

Lawson, G. (2015, December 8). Trudeau's Canada, again. *The New York Times Magazine.* Retrieved May 9, 2021, from www.nytimes.com/2015/12/13/magazine/trudeaus-canada-again.html

Lingard, B. (2018). The Australian curriculum: A critical interrogation of why, what and where to? *Curriculum Perspectives. 38*(1), 55–65.

Lingard, B. (2021a). Enactments and resistances to globalizing testing regimes and performance-based accountability in the USA. In S. Grek, C. Maroy, & A. Verger. (Eds.), *World yearbook of education 2021: Accountability and datafication in the governance of education.* London and New York: Routledge.

Lingard, B. (2021b). Globalisation and education: Theorising and researching changing imbrications in education policy. In B. Lingard (Ed.), *Globalisation and education.* London: Routledge.

Lingard, B., & Rawolle, S. (2011). New scalar politics: Implications for education policy. *Comparative Education, 47*(4), 489–502.

Martens, K., & Jakobi, A. P. (2010). *Mechanisms of OECD governance. International incentives for national policy-making?* Oxford: Oxford University Press.

Martens, K., & Niemann, D. (2013). When do numbers count? The differential impact of the PISA rating and ranking on education policy in Germany and the US. *German Politics, 22*(3), 314–332.

Mouffe, C. (2018). *For a left populism.* London: Verso Books.

Özkırımlı, U. (2017). *Theories of nationalism: A critical introduction* (3rd ed.). Basingstoke, Hampshire: Palgrave Macmillan.

Rutkowski, D. J. (2007). Converging us softly: How intergovernmental organizations promote neoliberal educational policy. *Critical Studies in Education, 48*(2), 229–247.

Sant, E. (2019). National myths and democratic history education: Secondary students' discursive construction of Catalan nationhood. *Pedagogy, Culture & Society, 29*(2), 173–191.

Sant, E., & Gonzalez, G. (2018). Latin America. In I. Davies, L. C. Ho, D. Kiwan, C. Peck, A. Peterson, E. Sant, & Y. Waghid (Eds.), *The Palgrave handbook of global citizenship and education* (pp. 67–82). London: Palgrave Macmillan.

Sant, E., & Hanley, C. (2018). Political assumptions underlying pedagogies of national education: The case of student teachers teaching 'British values' in England. *British Educational Research Journal, 44*(2), 319–337.

Sassen, S. (2013). Land grabs today: Feeding the disassembling of national territory. *Globalizations, 10*(1), 25–46.

Savage, G. (2016). Who's steering the ship? National curriculum reform and the reshaping of Australian federalism. *Journal of Education Policy. 31*(6), 833–850.

Schneider, M. (2019). Is PISA a victim of its own success? IES head calls for change. *Education Week*. Retrieved May 9, 2021, from www.edweek.org/policy-politics/opinion-is-pisa-a-victim-of-its-own-success-ies-head-calls-for-change/2019/01

Sellar, S., & Lingard, B. (2013). Looking East: Shanghai, PISA 2009 and the reconstitution of reference societies in the global education policy field. *Comparative Education, 49*(4), 464–485.

Sellar, S., & Lingard, B. (2014). The OECD and the expansion of PISA: New global modes of governance in education. *British Educational Research Journal, 40*(6), 917–936.

Sellar, S., & Lingard, B. (2018). International large-scale assessments, affective worlds and policy impacts in education. *International Journal of Qualitative Studies in Education. 31*(5), 367–381.

Smith, A. D. (2000). *Myths and memories of the nation.* New York, NY: Oxford University Press.

Soysal, Y. N., & Soyland, A. J. (1994). *Limits of citizenship: Migrants and postnational membership in Europe.* Chicago, IL: University of Chicago Press.

Stack, M. (2006). Testing, testing, read all about it: Canadian press coverage of the PISA results. *Canadian Journal of Education/Revue canadienne de l'éducation, 29*(1), 49–69.

Steiner-Khamsi, G., & Waldow, F. (2018). PISA for scandalisation, PISA for projection: The use of international large-scale assessments in education policy making – an introduction. *Globalisation, Societies and Education, 16*(5), 557–565.

The National Commission on Excellence in Education. (1983). *A nation at risk: The imperative for educational reform* (GPO Publication No. 065-000-00177-2). Washington, DC: U.S. Government Printing Office.

Wallner, J. (2018). Federalism and education: The Canadian case. In K. Wong, F. Knupling, M. Kolling, & D. Chebenova (Eds.), *Federalism and education: Ongoing challenges and policy strategies in ten countries.* Charlotte, NC: Information Age Publishing.

Wallner, J., Savage, G., Hartong, S., & Engel, L. C. (2020). Laboratories, coproducers, and venues: Roles played by subnational governments in standards-based reform in four federations. *Comparative Education Review, 64*(2), 249–268.

10 Infrastructuring the nation

Examining the role of national large-scale assessments in Russia

Nelli Piattoeva and Nadezhda Vasileva

The end of nationalism has frequently been envisaged by both researchers and politicians, but it remains a supreme force in contemporary societies (Bieber, 2018). Nor has globalization abolished nations, but it has transformed the means and forms of nation-building (Kraemer, 2019). Nationalism is expressed in political and ideological realms, and manifested through economy, culture, education, sport and everyday life in the so-called banal, that is, unnoticed ways (Billig, 1995). Many embodiments of banal nationalism have not yet been identified (Laruelle, 2019), yet they reproduce the idea of homogenous nations and an image of the world as politically divided into cohesive but mutually exclusive national communities. Research on nationalism has also maintained that nations are never ready, so to say, but need to be continuously remade. We focus on one of the arenas of national reproduction – formal schooling – whose role in shaping future generations and the making and maintaining of nationalism has been and remains paramount (Tröhler, 2020).

Our specific case is the policy of governing formal schooling by means of nationwide large-scale assessment (NLSA), which in the Russian context takes the form of a compulsory graduation examination called the Unified State Exam (USE) in the last year of school education. The exam constitutes one of the most important education policy reforms in recent years, aimed at standardizing the curriculum implementation and the evaluation of education quality through annual, nationally designed testing of individual learning achievements. The data produced by the examinations is aggregated to render legible and governable a range of actors beyond individual students, such as teachers or various levels of educational administration (e.g. Piattoeva, 2015). The USE was introduced as an experiment in a handful of Russian regions in 2001 and then gradually expanded, becoming mandatory across the country in 2009 (Andrushchak & Nathov, 2012; Drummond & Gabrscek, 2012; Luk'yanova, 2012; Piattoeva, 2015; Solodnikov, 2009). In 2019, approximately 750,000 examinees took part in USE in 85 regions of Russia and 54 foreign countries (Agranovich, 2019). They were required to pass two compulsory subjects, namely Russian language and mathematics, in order to obtain the certificate of completed secondary education (*attestat*), and other optional subjects required for entering tertiary education in the study field of their choice.

DOI: 10.4324/9781003137801-14

The implementation of large-scale testing processes in education, such as NLSA, relies on existing and generates novel bureaucratic and digital infrastructures defined in our study as digitally mediated arrangements of humans, processes, procedures, tools and technologies that produce, use, transport and store examinations, data and information generated thereon (Hartong & Piattoeva, 2021). Moreover, the standardized assessment itself serves as an infrastructure that builds the state's presence into and enables it to exercise power over a vast territory and the lives of its population to craft a nation and mark its territory. In contrast to the prevailing image of infrastructures as neutral, we study them as playing significant, but often neglected, roles in forging spaces and national identities. This interest is embedded in the larger question of how nationalism and nation-states are reproduced in digitally mediated societies (cf. Szulc, 2017; Skey, 2020). Our argument is that the coming together – the infrastructuring of – diverse socio-material-discursive elements in the infrastructure of the Russian NLSA contributes to (no less than) both nationalizing the Russian territory and territorializing (that is, bordering) the Russian nation.

1 Nation-state as a sociomaterial and technoscientific accomplishment

In 2014, in order to understand the rise and effects of national large-scale assessments in Russia, one of the authors interviewed a number of officials and experts responsible for the assessments. One of her interviews was with an official of Rostelecom, the largest telecommunications and digital service provider in Russia. At the time of the interview, the administration of the large-scale assessment was changing rapidly, particularly to strengthen the procedural side of the exam. Rostelecom was working across the Russian territory to realize the state's aim of making the exam procedure and evaluation more standardized and transparent, and in their words more objective and fairer, by digitalizing the delivery of exam questions and answers, and by installing a system of video surveillance to examination sites (see Piattoeva, 2016).

When asking the respondent about future plans for collaboration between the Ministry of Education and their company, the discussion focused on the challenges of installing optical fibre cable in the zones with permafrost. As the state strives to enable Internet access to all corners of the country, including remote, sparsely populated regions with particularly challenging climatic conditions, expensive satellite connections make way for cables laboriously laid underground. These concrete material efforts are also necessary to administer NLSA under standardized conditions. Thus, the implementation of NLSA by digital means does not only enable the state to deliver education, and to collect data on a large segment of its population and one of its vital systems, but it contributes overall to its material presence across a vast territory.

Building roads, power stations, transforming nature and linking different corners to the political centre through a chain of communication media, the state orchestrates the processes of standardization and centralization of a common

ulture to craft a nation (Williams & Smith, 1983). In this chapter we under-
tand *nation-state* as a political principle that equates *state* as the governing
apparatus of a bounded territory, with *nation* as an imagined cultural community
(Gellner, 1983; Anderson, 2006). Thus, nation-state is a contingent and vulnerable accomplishment – an ongoing process of nation-state building rather than
an achieved fact (Kymlicka & Straehle, 1999; also Kuzio, 2001), dependent on
continuous strategic and habitual reproduction across public and private domains
(Brubaker, 1996; Malešević, 2019).

In societies saturated with and connected through global digital technologies,
the bundle of state, territory and nation becomes uncertain in new ways (Möllers,
2021). Thus, states increasingly remobilize scientists and engineers for a "territorializing project" to transform the boundless, global information infrastructure into
a bounded national territory, or what Norma Möllers calls a digital territory as a
nationalized information infrastructure (ibid., pp. 3–4). This process entails both
material and moral aspects, that is, creating a material network that circumscribes
a digital national territory and imbuing that network with normative ideas about
the nation and its people. The digital territory follows but is not necessarily limited
by the topographical borders of the state's sovereign territory, as we will also show
in the empirical part of this chapter – and this is a particularly interesting aspect
in the modern world, where populations move (and borders shift, as in the case
of Russia), but where states have not lost their interest in re-territorializing these
populations in flux.

Our overall theoretical approach to infrastructure as nationalizing and territorializing projects builds on understanding the exercise of power and governance as
discursive, sociomaterial and technoscientific, that is, as relying on and deploying
heterogeneous materials from data, bureaucracy and cables to various forms of
technology and scientific knowledge to shape the conditions of political possibility
and forms of collective life. Joyce and Mukerji (2017) use the term *logistical power*
to describe how the state performs itself impersonally across many sites – a state
of things, literally, that takes multiple shapes as it enlists different material means.
What the state largely does is to move information through things (Joyce & Mukerji, 2017, p. 15). It continuously reinvents itself by changing the lines of communication and solutions to the distance problem (ibid.). Thus, "the power of
the state is mostly experienced outside discourse and below the level of conscious
awareness, in the habitus, and the shared practices of life created by logistical
governance" (ibid., p. 3). "Hegemonic strategies, at once material and symbolic,
produce the idea of the state while concretizing the imagined community of the
nation by articulating spatial, bodily and temporal matrixes through the everyday
routines, rituals, and policies of the state system" (Alonso, 1994, p. 382).

The material infrastructures of the state thus enable the daily preservation and
reproduction of the bond between the people and the authority, and the nation
itself. One of the ways in which the state has developed and exercises its power
is through various types of infrastructure – from electricity supply to post offices
and schools. Infrastructures that connect different locations (Larkin, 2008) allow
the nation to function as an organized entity (DeLanda, 2006) and create "the

conditions in which the nation as a concept and a sensation can be narrated and internalized by individuals" (Taylor, 2015, p. 63). The sense of national belonging is thus generated by inhabited infrastructures as these give rise to shared practices and habitus (Taylor, 2015). Infrastructure is constituted by the normative bureaucratic and discursive order that regulates a certain bounded territory. At the same time, infrastructure takes part in the reproduction of this normative order. In particular, infrastructure relays normative ideas about a given state's envisaged national identity and the ideal characteristics of its nationals that are entwined with the territorialization of information infrastructure (Möllers, 2021). These assumptions "normalize moral judgments about who counts and who does not, who may be sanctioned or punished, and who may be ignored or forgotten" (Möllers, 2021, p. 6).

To summarize, the following analysis presents NLSA as an infrastructure of nation-state building in two intertwined ways. First, by expanding and refining its technological and bureaucratic constitutive elements, the Unified State Exam enables the territorialization of the nation by both marking its borders and establishing a particular kind of centripetal geography and dense connectivity. Second, it enrols and puts into motion concrete normative narrations and symbols of the nation, thus performing the state's nationalizing policies with the objective of fostering cultural homogeneity (Brubaker, 1995).

We are working with diverse materials from existing research on the Internet, media and education policy in Russia to first-hand resources, such as policy documents across relevant policy sectors and media sources (newspaper articles, news reports and press releases) that help us to gradually build up a picture of current developments and debates. In order to accommodate different perspectives on the examination, we selected several media resources that serve various audiences and ideological positions. We have analyzed materials published in *Rossiyskaya Gazeta* (Russian Newspaper), the official organ of the government; *Novaya Gazeta* (New Newspaper), known for its oppositional agenda; financial and business resources such as *Vedomosti* (Reports), *RBK* and *Kommersant* (Merchant), covering commercial agendas and materials published specifically for teachers and educators in *Uchitel'skaya Gazeta* (Teachers' Newspaper) and *Vesti Obrazovaniya* (Education Reports).

Based on the preliminary analysis of the collected data, we selected three empirical examples to illustrate the mechanisms of nationalization and territorialization via the Unified State Exam (USE) infrastructure described earlier. Instead of trying to condense the recent history of USE, we develop our argument through these three cases in which, for various reasons, the construction of USE infrastructure was abrupt, and therefore its traces are more apparent. We examine the expansion of USE to the annexed territory of the Crimean Peninsula, the extension of USE to remote areas of the Russian Far North and the administration of NLSA to students of the Russian-speaking diaspora abroad. Taken together these examples enable us to show how the Russian state makes itself present in uncertain territories, where the process of nation-state building is ongoing, using the infrastructure of USE and USE as an infrastructure. Together, these cases demonstrate how digital nfrastructures enable a centrifugal link between the centre and peripheries, while also constructing the borders, imageries and ideals of the nation.

2 Russian education, politics and national idea through the prism of digitalization

This section contextualizes the case of NLSA in Russia and illustrates the close interrelationships of education policy, nationalism and digitalization policy. The implementation of the Unified State Exam has been a part of a complex and multilateral reform of the Russian education system and society. After the collapse of the Soviet Union in 1991, Russia's new state authorities initiated intensive nation-building, based on three strategic developments, namely Russian idea, strong state and efficient economy (Budnitskiy, 2018; Tolz, 2001). The "Russian idea" is a set of traditional cultural repertoires that before 2012 included patriotism, great power status (the idea that Russia was and will remain a great nation), statism (the representation of state and its institutions as having an exceptionally important role in the life of the country and its people) and social solidarity (the idea that collectivism has always prevailed over individualism) (Budnitskiy, 2018). Whereas Dmitri Medvedev's time in office, which is the period when USE became compulsory and expanded, could be characterized by technocratic ideals of effective governance and standardization, after 2012 and the re-election of Vladimir Putin, Russian politics and identity discourse mostly took on distinctly moral, religious and civilizational dimensions (Budnitskiy, 2018; Makarychev & Medvedev, 2015; Østbø, 2017; Stepanova, 2015). The strong state and efficient economy presuppose multiple layers of effective infrastructures encompassing the entire country. The infrastructures of electricity, bureaucracy and the Internet, materialized in cables, wires and expanding legislation to underpin these, connect settlements and enable inhabitants to participate in national activities and rituals such as, for example, voting, taking the national exam or watching the traditional New Year's greetings from the president. Without electricity and the Internet, the functioning of the technology necessary to administer the USE and transfer the data that it generates would be simply impossible.

Russia is the most extensive territory in the world and encompasses very diverse and challenging natural conditions. There are persisting divides in the country in regional economic and social development, leading to multiple inequalities between industrial and rural centres, between the more densely populated Western and the more sparsely populated Asian territories, which all influence the quality of available telecommunications infrastructure while at the same time highlighting the role that information infrastructure and technologies should play in a country of such size and diversity (Vartanova, 2020). "Territorial immensity, as well as weakness of the federal budget make it impossible to build roads linking isolated regions to more developed centres. So the construction of "information highways" is often at the heart of the debate on Russian development and territorial cohesion" (Kolarova, Samaganova, Samson, & Ternaux, 2006, p. 886).

The Russian state pays special attention to the Internet, which on the one hand is seen by the authorities as a source of national progress and sovereignty, but on the other hand is framed as a threat, often seen as coming from the West (Budnitskiy, 2018). Russia's development of the Internet remains a combination of both national and global features. The Soviet Union was in the frontline of developing the first Internet network (cf. Peters, 2016). Since then, even though these first attempts did not take root and the Western Internet took precedence, Runet – the Russian-speaking Internet – has maintained and developed many national features (Laruelle, 2020). One important feature is the availability of domestic software and the presence of professional software and communications developers that make Russia more independent of foreign technologies (Biagioli & Lepinay, 2019). At the same time, the ownership of the main companies supplying electricity and connectivity is largely state-based or in the hands of the political elite's immediate circles (Pallin, 2017; Lonkila, Shpakovskaya, & Torchinsky, 2020).

While aiming to increase Internet access, retaining central control over information on the Internet has been a priority for the Russian state authorities (Kreitem, Ragnedda, & Muschert, 2020, p. 7). Control over the Internet is often justified by reference to information sovereignty and the protection of national interests, particularly in the context of mounting tensions with the West (Laruelle, 2020). For example, the 2008 Strategy of Information Society Development, adopted towards the very end of Putin's second presidential term, stated that one of the goals for information and communication technologies is the "preservation of the culture of the multinational Russian people, strengthening of moral and patriotic principles within the public consciousness, development of the system of cultural and humanitarian education" (Russian Ministry of Digital Development, Communications and Mass Media, 2008, p. 2). The coming together of digitalization and education – and viewing these as constitutive elements of a unified country and culture – is manifest in the adoption of documents such as the Federal Programme for the development of the Unified Information and Education Space (2001–2005) (Russian Government, 2001). At the same time, recent state programmes on the development of information society and digital economy also emphasize Russia's ambition to become a world leader in digital matters. Overall, technological modernization is a central element in bolstering Russian sovereignty, including its cyberspace, and the project of constructing and communicating an identity of a great digital power (Budnitskiy, 2018): "Russia's internet governance discourse uses the language of territorialized sovereignty, which bounds a cultural and national space that tolerates no foreign interference" (ibid., 2018 p. 16).

3 The expanding infrastructure of the Unified State Exam (USE) territorializing the Russian nation

USE enrols and relies on multiple elements: infrastructures such as electricity and the Internet, roads, the network of schools and examination points, even post offices; bureaucratic procedures, instructions, legislation and protocols that structure the exam; objects such as textbooks, forms, video surveillance cameras, numerical scores etc.; human actors who develop the content of the exam, control and perform maintenance on technical equipment, participate in and are affected by exams and the data produced thereon. Since the experimental phase in the early to mid-2000s, the requirements for infrastructure and technical equipment that assist the exam significantly changed, expanded and standardized (see e.g. Piattoeva, 2015; 2016). In this section, we explore how infrastructures underpinning NLSA and the infrastructural affordances of the examination contribute to the physical and symbolical bordering of the nation.

In the example of the USE, we can observe how mandatory practices such as national educational assessments increase the need to develop infrastructure, mostly the Internet, in places that are remote from central, urban Russia. Thus, inaccessible territories, such as the Arctic, are integrated among other things through the USE exam and its expanding infrastructure. However, some areas are still inaccessible to infrastructure for technical reasons, especially areas where Northern nomadic ethnic groups live and move. Students belonging to these ethnic groups are required to synchronize their distinct, nomadic way of life with the rest of Russia in order to prepare for and participate in the exam. They leave their parents, who move across a vast territory during the year, for special boarding schools (Liarskaya, 2005; Zhuravel, 2018), provided with teachers and equipment, plugging them into the infrastructure, if it cannot reach them in their home environments.

The political annexation of the Crimean Peninsula in 2014 provides an empirical illustration of state control over infrastructures and their importance for territorialization. The infrastructural development of the Peninsula started immediately after annexation, when Rostelecom laid a fibre-optic communication line along the bottom of the Kerch Gulf. The then Prime Minister Medvedev stated, "It is unacceptable that information and documents related to the administration of the territory by two constituent entities of the Federation, including information of a confidential nature, are transmitted using the capacities of outsiders, that is, foreign telecommunications companies" (Noviy, 2014). Rostelecom bought out the lines of Ukrainian operators which previously provided communications to Crimea. Miranda Media, a 100% subsidiary of Rostelecom, became the key telecommunications company on the peninsula. In addition to the Internet and communications, Crimea also found itself without electricity, since electricity was supplied to the region by Ukraine. In May 2016, an *Energomost* (Energy Bridge) to Crimea started operating at full capacity: "More than 800 km of power transmission lines of 220 and 500 kV voltage class have been built, four circuits have been laid along the bottom of the Kerch Gulf, each consisting of four cable lines, with a total span of 230km" (Ministry of Energy, 2016). This example shows how the state mobilized material resources to extend and secure Russia's national information infrastructure to the annexed regions.

The first implementation of the Unified State Exam (USE) in Crimea took place in 2014, immediately after the annexation of the peninsula. In a month after the annexation, the Russian parliament accepted changes to the law "On education" to integrate the educational systems of the annexed territories into the

Russian educational system (Russian Federation, 2014). Until 2019, participation in USE was voluntary for school graduates, however. This five-year period served as preparation for a gradual transition of the school system from the Ukrainian to the Russian curriculum and aligning school infrastructure with Russian standards (TASS, 2016). In 2019 and 2020, graduates of the peninsula were formally placed in the same conditions as other Russian examinees, with USE as the mandatory examination format.

The idea of the Russian nation and the wider civilizational concept of the *Russkii Mir* (Russian World) are discursively represented as transcending the Russian state borders through Russian language and culture, orthodoxy and the diaspora (Budnitskiy, 2018; Blakkisrud, 2016; Laruelle, 2015; Tsygankov, 2014). The infrastructure of USE also extends beyond the official territory of the Russian state to other 54 counties (Agranovich, 2019), in which the exam can be taken, for instance, in the buildings of Russian embassies as extensions of Russian territory. These nodes of the infrastructure reach out particularly to Russian speakers abroad, merging Russia's foreign and education policies and constructing a particular ideal of the Russian nation, to which we return in the next section.

The concept of the "Russian school" operates within the framework of the state policy to support "compatriots" abroad. One of the tasks of the Russian school abroad is the formation of a positive attitude towards modern Russia among the younger generation (Russian President, 2015a). In addition, the activities of these schools contribute to the promotion of Russian educational technologies, teaching and upbringing methods, and the scientific and methodological developments among teachers. The implementation of education in the Russian language abroad is aimed at strengthening the position of the Russian language, the spread of Russian culture in the world and the growth of Russia's cultural and political influence: "In modern conditions, the demand for and prevalence of the language abroad are the most important indicators of the authority of the state and its influence in the world" (Russian President, 2015b). Therefore, supporting the Russian language is an important aim of Russian foreign policy and an instrument of cultural diplomacy (cf. Mäkinen, 2016). Special emphasis is placed on strengthening the position of the Russian language in the CIS countries,[1] as many of their residents speak Russian as (one of) their language(s).

Following the Euromaidan,[2] Ukrainian revolution in 2014 and war between pro-Russian separatists and the Ukrainian forces, the provinces of Donetsk and Luhansk proclaimed independence and established a People's Republic whose status has not been acknowledged by the international community. Since "independence," both territories adopted Russian education standards, including its grading system, textbooks and the primacy of Russian language as the language of instruction. As Donbass and Luhansk remain liminal spaces of statehood, and their infrastructural bases are incomplete, USE cannot be implemented on their territories, but there are a number of special arrangements to connect students to the USE infrastructure. Exclusive transportation organized by the republican administration enables school graduates to travel to and participate in the exam in the neighbouring Russian city of Rostov-On-Don. Moreover, an agreement between the

epublics and the Russian administration guarantees unrestricted border crossing
or the examinees during the official examination period (Durnev, 2019).

Modern infrastructure intertwines with and is in many ways critical for the
national state's ambition to reproduce – and at times reimagine – the nation in
he digital age. Moreover, the design of the infrastructure, the way it is used and
ts ownership reiterate a certain national normative order, to which we turn next.

4 Normative ideas about citizen and nation

The infrastructures that enable the implementation of the national educational
project such as NLSA have become an important channel that implicitly and
habitually relays national ideals and symbols to its participants and seeks to shape
their identities. The NLSA is riddled with national symbols that manifest the
national character of the examination experience. The exam sheets, for instance,
display Russian national symbols such as the double-headed eagle and the tricol-
our palette that refers to the Russian state flag. Even the Internet portal of the
exam that assembles key information for the examinees, their families and the
organizers of the exam across the country is distinctly white-blue-red. Another
banal flagging of the nation (cf. Billig, 1995) appears when students present their
passports at the examination to prove their identity. The exams begin with a pass-
port check, which marks a rare moment in school life when students use their
passports, making concrete to them their citizenship and formal belonging to a
certain nation-state.

Moral dimensions, according to Möllers (2021), refers to normative ideas about
a given state's imagined national identity that are entwined with the territorialization of information infrastructure. She claims that the moral dimensions of territorialization projects are important because they "(a) justify state intervention
and guide if, when, and how they intervene; and (b) normalize moral judgments
about who counts and who doesn't, who may be sanctioned or punished, and
who may be ignored or forgotten." She further quotes Benjamin (2016, p. 151) to
highlight that normative ideas are uneven; that is, they are imagined to benefit
some and not others, and they produce distinctions that reproduce familiar lines
of domination. For instance, a commonly circulated image in the official media
is that of a student who received the highest score. These school graduates as
ideal future citizens may be called the "golden hopes of Russia" (Vesti Novosibirsk,
2019), described as hardworking, purposeful and honest. As a result, the whole of
Russia is said to open up to these graduates as they can potentially apply to and be
enrolled at any university in Russia.

One major concern that underpins the Unified State Exam (USE) is testing mastery of the Russian language as the state language and in the words of Vladimir
Putin, "the natural spiritual skeleton of our entire multinational country" (RBK,
2017). Even though people in Russia speak 150 languages, only Russian is mandatory and in fact possible as the language of USE. The Soviet and Russian states
have pursued the goal to build a unified identity that would encompass and unite
the population of a "multinational" country by different means. The terminology

of the multinational and multi-ethnic deployed by the authorities signifies, first, reproduction of the controversial Soviet legacy of "institutionalized multiethnicity" (Tishkov & Olcott, 1999, pp. 64–67), that is, decoupling citizenship and nationality (see Brubaker, 1996; Piattoeva, 2009). Second, it demonstrates different co-existing visions of what Russian nationhood should entail. The notion of *rossiiane* expresses the nation as a community of citizens regardless of their ethnic affiliation who are united by allegiance to the political institutions of the Russian Federation. The understanding of Russia as a community of Russian speakers brings Russian speakers living in the former Soviet states into the realm of the Russian nation. Another interpretation extends the Russian nation to the borders of the former Soviet Union but contains a Slavic bias, limiting itself to ethnic Russians, Ukrainians and Belorussians (Tolz, 2001). Despite the apparent differences, all these versions attest to the centrality of the Russian language either as a language of civic and political participation or as a marker of a common cultural and linguistic identity. All school graduates, regardless of their ethnic or cultural origin, must pass the Russian language exam in order to get the certificate of completed secondary education (*attestat*). Moreover, average scores in Russian attract the attention of national officials as they annually compare the quality of school education across the regions.

Additionally, since 2018, the status of school education in native languages other than Russian has changed to voluntary (Russian Federation, 2018). This amendment supports a gradual reduction in the numbers of students who study their native languages because they prefer, as it is written in the media, to devote more effort to learning Russian, which is the language of USE (Smolin, 2018; Urchenko, 2017). The future career aspirations of students are represented as dependent on their Russian language proficiency, whereas the use of native languages is shifting to the private domain. In this manner, mastery of the Russian language marks belonginess, defines the borders of Russian statehood and dictates how far or where the infrastructure of NLSA may expand.

The structure and content of the national exam are standardized under the auspices of the aim to provide equally fair conditions to all examinees across the country. This intention also determines the standardization of students' preparation for the exam and the development of a set of basic textbooks which, according to the words of the head of the state Duma Committee on security and anti-corruption Yarovaya, "eliminate existing discrimination of children, inequality in preparation for the exam" (Vedomosti, 2015). In particular, history textbooks have been revised to provide a uniform view of Russian history. The NLSA functions as an infrastructure of conveying a common "desired past," which students have to learn when preparing for this exam. Moreover, the "correct" knowledge of the past should be complemented with the recognition of the priority of history in the determination of Russia's present and future. In a television news report about the school graduate who got the maximum score for three exams, the student explained her interest in history using the idea that she attributed to Gumilev: "History is the present, and what we consider the current moment does not exist at all. History gives the most complete understanding of what is happening in the world, what is happening in Russia. After all, you need to know the fate of our nation, how it developed"[3] (Rossiya 1, 2018). In 2020, the updated Russian Constitution incorporated the Eurasian ideals of common destiny and common history of people living in the territory of contemporary Russian Federation and introduced the idea of an "historical truth" that requires protection in different fora (State Duma, 2020).

5 Conclusions

In everyday life, the nation often operates "just beneath the surface, underpinning the social order without requiring, or even permitting, much tinkering" (Fox, 2017, p. 26; Millei, 2019, p. 2). The metaphor of nationalism being "beneath the surface" or "grounded" is helpful in understanding how continuous reproduction of nationhood operates in current times marked by both technological progress in digitalization and new capacities of the governing bodies to make their population legible for governance through expert and technoscientific means, such as NLSA, as illustrated in the chapter. The elementary infrastructures that NLSA relies on are functioning Internet and electricity. These infrastructures are literally laid underground – under the sea, thick layers of permafrost or bare asphalt – but their geography is far from arbitrary (Starosielski, 2015). Studying how NLSA technical infrastructure expands, we directed our attention to both the centralization in the geography of these infrastructures and their active role in territorializing – bordering – the nation. However, territorialization along the topographical borders of the state is complemented by possibilities for NLSA to spill over the borders and territorialize the nation digitally. The banality of such infrastructures, that is, their muteness and embeddedness in everyday life and their seemingly apolitical nature as "mere" technological material easily veil their political role in reproducing the nation-state.

The infrastructure of the Unified State Exam (USE) is complex and includes different elements ranging from electricity to Russian foreign policy. What we have shown in the chapter is how infrastructure enables the state and the nation to endure through reforms. Nations continue to thrive in and through education, but they do so also in the emerging educational cyberspace that is often imagined as a space of global flows and the retreat of the nation (cf. Szulc, 2017). Aronczyk (2017) calls this the logic of substitution, where globalization and the processes associated with it – such as digitalization – are perceived as substituting for national thinking and being. She appeals to a logic of accumulation to highlight how global processes interact with and even enable the survival of nationalism. We have shown how USE enacts territorialization along Russia's official and aspired or imagined borders and national moral ideals. The focus is on Russia's own history and destiny as the cornerstones of the official identity discourse and the articulation of the nation as a community of many ethnicities and cultures united by a common past. Moreover, Russian language and state patriotism are all present in and relayed by USE infrastructure. These intersect with the ideas that Russia's "real" borders are not confined to those accepted by the international community and are disseminated through the Russian language and culture, orthodoxy and the Russian-speaking diaspora (cf. Blakkisrud, 2016; Laruelle, 2015; Tsygankov, 2014).

Recent scholarship, particularly that foregrounding materiality in understanding social phenomena, has been paying attention to how national forces and affects circulate. In some ways, they have challenged or extended classical studies on nationalism, particularly on banal nationalism or the imagined community thesis. Instead of grounding nationalism in discourses and ideologies as well as individual or collective bodies and artefacts, their focus lies in the processes of emergence of nationhood with material elements not just containing or reflecting the nation but generating it. This is why an infrastructural perspective and a focus on infrastructures is productive and necessary: to understand how, in the words of Merriman and Jones (2017, p. 601), "the material and affective qualities of infrastructures become associated with particular geographies" and thus enable the nation to endure and be experienced both individually and collectively. It is "through material objects and practices that national genealogies are created and inhabited" (Zubrzycki, 2017, p. 16).

Researchers of education policy principally view the recent rise and spread of NLSAs as a manifestation of the globalization of education policies and practices. Within this view, the means that enable the actual implementation of the assessments, whether policy, expertise or digital infrastructures, act as relays in and of the globalizing education space and its largely permeable borders. In contrast, we show how NLSAs rely on and enable the (re)construction of state-centric nationhood in Russia. NLSAs do not only become incorporated into an environment where nation-ness is an endemic condition, but reproduce a view of the world as one of existing or aspiring nations and a view of nations as real entities with defined borders and shared attributes.

Notes

1 CIS (Commonwealth of Independent States) – a regional intergovernmental organization that unites nine post-Soviet states: Armenia, Azerbaijan, Belarus, Kazakhstan, Kyrgyzstan, Moldova, Russia, Tajikistan, Uzbekistan.
2 Euromaidan was a wave of demonstrations in Ukraine (November 2013 – February 2014) that were sparked by the Ukrainian government's decision to suspend the signing of an association agreement with the European Union, instead choosing closer ties to Russia and the Eurasian Economic Union.
3 Lev Gumilyov was a Soviet historian, ethnologist and anthropologist. He developed the ideas of Eurasianism – the national metanarrative about the exclusiveness of Russia, whose territorial size and location in space are the drivers of the country's mission in the world, and of the nature of its state and culture (Laruelle, 2019). Russia is interpreted by this tradition as a unique country that is neither solely Europe nor Asia but Eurasia. The news report was broadcast on the TV Channel *Rossiia* 1 – a state-owned television company.

References

Agranovich, M. (2019, June 24). The results of the main wave of USE are summed up. *Rossiyskaya Gazeta*. Retrieved from https://rg.ru/2019/06/24/podvedeny-itogi-osnovnoj-volny-ege.html [In Russian].

Alonso, A. M. (1994). The politics of space, time and substance: State formation, nationalism, and ethnicity. *Annual Review of Anthropology, 23*(1), 379–405.

Anderson, B. (2006). *Imagined communities: Reflections on the origin and spread of nationalism.* London and New York: Verso Books.

Andrushchak, G., & Nathov, T. (2012). The introduction of USE, strategies of graduates and accessibility of higher education. *Voprosy Obrazovaniya, 3,* 64–83.

Aronczyk, M. (2017). Narratives of legitimacy: Making nationalism banal. In M. Skey & M. Antonisch (Eds.), *Everyday nationhood. Theorising culture, identity and belonging after banal nationalism* (pp. 241–258). London: Palgrave Macmillan.

Benjamin, R. (2016). Catching our breath: Critical race STS and the carceral imagination. *Engaging Science, Technology, and Society, 2,* 145–156. doi:10.17351/ests2016.70

Biagioli, M., & Lepinay, V. A. (2019). Russian economies of code. In M. Biagioli & V. A. Lépinay (Eds.), *From Russia with code: Programming migrations in post-Soviet times* (pp. 1–36). Durham: Duke University Press.

Bieber, F. (2018). Is nationalism on the rise? Assessing global trends. *Ethnopolitics, 17*(5), 519–540.

Billig, M. (1995). *Banal nationalism* (1st ed.). London: Sage.

Blakkisrud, H. (2016). Blurring the boundary between civic and ethnic: The Kremlin's new approach to national identity under Putin's third term. In P. Kolstø & H. Blakkisrud (Eds.), *The new Russian nationalism: Imperialism, ethnicity and authoritarianism 2000–2015* (pp. 249–274). Edinburgh: Edinburgh University Press. doi:10.3366/edinburgh/9781474410427.003.0010

Brubaker, R. (1995). National minorities, nationalizing states, and external national homelands in the new Europe. *Daedalus, 124*(2), 107–132.

Brubaker, R. (1996). *Nationalism reframed: Nationhood and the national question in the new Europe.* Cambridge: Cambridge University Press.

Budnitskiy, S. (2018). *Digital nationalisms: Identity, strategic communication, and global internet governance* (PhD thesis). Carleton University.

DeLanda, M. (2006). *A new philosophy of society: Assemblage theory and social complexity.* London: Continuum.

Drummond, T. W., & Gabrscek, S. (2012). Understanding higher education admissions reforms in the Eurasian context. *European Education, 44*(1), 7–26.

Durnev, D. (2019, February 10). "Going both ways": Where do university entrants from Donetsk and Luhansk go? *Novaya Gazeta.* Retrieved from https://novayagazeta.ru/articles/2019/10/02/82210-i-nashim-i-vashim [In Russian].

Fox, J. (2017). The edges of the nation: A research agenda for uncovering the taken-for-granted foundations of everyday nationhood. *Nations and Nationalism, 23,* 26–47. doi:10.1111/nana.12269

Gellner, E. (1983). *Nations and nationalism.* Oxford: Basil Blackwell.

Hartong, S., & Piattoeva, N. (2021). Contextualizing the datafication of schooling – a comparative discussion of Germany and Russia. *Critical Studies in Education, 62*(2), 227–242.

Joyce, P., & Mukerji, C. (2017). The state of things: State history and theory reconfigured. *Theory and Society, 46*(1), 1–19.

Kolarova, D., Samaganova, A., Samson, I., & Ternaux, P. (2006). Spatial aspects of ICT development in Russia. *The Service Industries Journal, 26*(8), 873–888.

Kraemer, K. (2019). Longing for a national container. On the symbolic economy of Europe's new nationalism. *European Societies, 22*(5), 529–554. doi:10.1080/14616696.2019.1694164

Kreitem, H., Ragnedda, M., & Muschert, G. W. (2020). Digital inequalities in European post-Soviet states. In S. Davydov (Ed.), *Internet in Russia. Societies and political orders in transition* (pp. 3–15). Cham: Springer.

Kuzio, T. (2001). Historiography and national identity among the Eastern Slavs: Towards a new framework. *National Identities, 3*(2), 109–132.

Kymlicka, W., & Straehle, C. (1999). Cosmopolitanism, nation-states, and minority nationalism: A critical review of recent literature. *European Journal of Philosophy, 7*(1), 65–88.

Larkin, B. (2008). *Signal and noise: Media, infrastructure, and urban culture in Nigeria*. Durham: Duke University Press.

Laruelle, M. (2015). *The "Russian world": Russia's soft power and geopolitical imagination*. Center on Global Interests. Retrieved from www.google.com/search?q=from+http%3A%2F%2Fglobalinterests.org%2Fwp-content%2Fuploads%2F2015%2F05%2FFINAL-CGI_Russian-World_Marlene-Laruelle.pdf&rlz=1C5CHFA_enRU862RU862&oq=from+http%3A%2F%2Fglobalinterests.org%2Fwp-content%2Fuploads%2F2015%2F05%2FFINAL-CGI_Russian-World_Marlene-Laruelle.pdf&aqs=chrome..69i57.787j0j7&sourceid=chrome&ie=UTF-8

Laruelle, M. (2019). *Russian nationalism: Imaginaries, doctrines, and political battlefields*. Oxon: Routledge.

Laruelle, M. (2020). Afterwords. In S. Davydov (Ed.), *Internet in Russia. Societies and political orders in transition* (pp. 295–298). Cham: Springer.

Liarskaya, E. (2005). Northern residential schools in contemporary Yamal Nenets culture. *Sibirica: Journal of Siberian Studies, 4*(1), 74–87. doi:10.1080/13617360500070889

Lonkila, M., Shpakovskaya, L., & Torchinsky, P. (2020). The occupation of Runet? The tightening state regulation of the Russian-language section of the internet. In M. Wijermars & K. Lehtisaari (Eds.), *Freedom of expression in Russia's new mediasphere* (pp. 17–38). Oxon: Routledge.

Luk'yanova, E. (2012). Russian educational reform and the introduction of the unified state exam. A view from the provinces. *Europe-Asia Studies, 64*(10), 1893–1910.

Makarychev, A., & Medvedev, S. (2015). Biopolitics and power in Putin's Russia. *Problems of Post-Communism, 62*(1), 45–54.

Mäkinen, S. (2016). In search of the status of an educational great power? Analysis of Russia's educational diplomacy discourse. *Problems of Post-Communism, 63*(3), 183–196.

Malešević, S. (2019). *Grounded nationalisms: A sociological analysis*. Cambridge: Cambridge University Press.

Merriman, P., & Jones, R. (2017). Nations, materialities and affects. *Progress in Human Geography, 41*(5), 600–617. doi:10.1177/0309132516649453

Millei, Z. (2019). Pedagogy of nation: A concept and method to research nationalism in young children's institutional lives. *Childhood, 26*(1), 83–97. doi:10.1177/0907568218810078

Ministry of Energy of the Russian Federation. (2016). *Brief information about the project to build an energy bridge from the UES of Russia to the Crimean Federal district*. Ministry of Energy of the Russian Federation. Retrieved from https://mobile.ruscable.ru/article/1440/ [In Russian].

Möllers, N. (2021). Making digital territory: Cybersecurity, techno-nationalism, and the moral boundaries of the state. *Science, Technology, & Human Values, 46*(1), 112–138.

Noviy, V. (2014, March 25). Connected by a single network. *Kommersant*. Retrieved from www.kommersant.ru/doc/2437318 [In Russian].

Østbø, J. (2017). Securitizing "spiritual-moral values" in Russia. *Post-Soviet Affairs, 33*(3), 200–216.

Pallin, C. V. (2017). Internet control through ownership: The case of Russia. *Post-Soviet Affairs, 33*(1), 16–33. doi:10.1080/1060586X.2015.1121712

Peters, B. (2016). *How not to network a nation: The uneasy history of the Soviet Internet*. Cambridge, MA: MIT Press.

iattoeva, N. (2009). Citizenship and nationality in changing Europe. A comparative study of the aims of citizenship education in Russian and Finnish national education policy texts. *Journal of Curriculum Studies, 41*(6), 723–744.

iattoeva, N. (2015). Elastic numbers: National examinations data as a technology of government. *Journal of Education Policy, 30*(3), 316–334.

iattoeva, N. (2016). The imperative to protect data and the rise of surveillance cameras in administering national testing in Russia. *European Educational Research Journal, 15*(1), 82–98.

RBK. (2017, July 20). Putin spoke about the spiritual skeleton of Russia. *RBK*. Retrieved from www.rbc.ru/rbcfreenews/5970bfd79a79475b5e46ec28 [In Russian].

Rossiya 1. (2018, July 5). *A schoolgirl from Konakovo scored 300 points on the unified state exam* [Video]. Retrieved from www.youtube.com/watch?v=sBltHtRkiQg [In Russian].

Russian Federation. (2014). Federal Law "On the peculiarities of legal regulation in the field of education due to the admission of the Republic of Crimea to the Russian Federation and the formation of new subjects within the Russian Federation – The Republic of Crimea and the City of Federal Sevastopol and on amendments to the Federal Law "On Education in the Russian Federation," no. 84-FZ. Retrieved from www.consultant.ru/document/cons_doc_LAW_162566/ [In Russian].

Russian Federation. (2018). Federal law "On Education in the Russian Federation," no. 273-FZ. Retrieved from www.consultant.ru/document/Cons_doc_LAW_146342/f8ff-02b9fd1f82762dda491ad2a9a1e3072a2c97/ [In Russian].

Russian Government. (2001). Federal programme for the development of the unified information and education space (2001–2005), no. 630. Retrieved from http://docs.cntd.ru/document/901796094 [In Russian].

Russian Ministry of Digital Development, Communications and Mass Media. (2008). *Strategy of information society development in the Russian Federation*. Retrieved from http://minsvyaz.ru/uploaded/files/strategiya_razvitiya_inf_obschestva_1.pdf [In Russian].

Russian President. (2015a). *The concept of "Russian school abroad"*. Retrieved from http://kremlin.ru/acts/news/50643 [In Russian].

Russian President. (2015b). *The concept of state support and promotion of the Russian language abroad*. Retrieved from http://kremlin.ru/acts/news/50644 [In Russian].

Skey, M. (2020). *Nationalism and media*. Retrieved from https://stateofnationalism.eu/article/nationalism-and-media/

Smolin, O. (2018, May 9). The law on national languages is a step in the right direction. *Vesti obrazovaniya*. Retrieved from http://vogazeta.ru/articles/2018/9/5/edpolitics/4556-zakon_o_natsionalnyh_yazykah__shag_v_pravilnom_napravlenii [In Russian].

Solodnikov, V. V. (2009). The unified state examination experiment: Halfway to the finish line. *Russian Education & Society, 51*(3), 9–24.

Starosielski, N. (2015). *The undersea network*. Durham: Duke University Press.

State Duma. (2020). *New text of the Constitution as amended in 2020*. Retrieved from http://duma.gov.ru/news/48953/ [In Russian].

Stepanova, E. (2015). 'The spiritual and moral foundation of civilization in every nation for thousands of years': The traditional values discourse in Russia. *Politics, Religion & Ideology, 16*(2–3), 119–136.

Szulc, L. (2017). Banal nationalism in the Internet age: Rethinking the relationship between nations, nationalisms and the media. In M. Skey & M. Antonsich (Eds.), *Everyday nationhood. Theorising culture, identity and belonging after banal nationalism* (pp. 53–74). London: Palgrave Macmillan.

TASS. (2016, June 29). The Federation Council allowed Crimean graduates not to take the unified state exam in 2017 and 2018. *TASS*. Retrieved from https://tass.ru/obschestvo/3416235 [In Russian].

Taylor, D. (2015). Plugging in: Power sockets, standards and the valencies of national habitus. *Journal of Material Culture, 20*(1), 59–75.

Tishkov, V., & Olcott, M. B. (1999). From ethnos to demos: The quest for Russia's identity. In A. Åslund & M. B. Olcott (Eds.), *Russia after communism* (pp. 61–90). Washington, DC: Carnegie Endowment for International Peace.

Tolz, V. (2001). *Inventing the nation: Russia*. London: Arnold.

Tröhler, D. (2020). National literacies, or modern education and the art of fabricating national minds. *Journal of Curriculum Studies, 52*(5), 620–635.

Tsygankov, A. P. (2014). *The strong state in Russia: Development and crisis*. Oxford: Oxford University Press.

Urchenko, V. (2017, November 29). The "sun" of the Russian world. The Tatar language has lost its compulsory status in the Republic's schools. *Novaya Gazeta*. Retrieved from https://novayagazeta.ru/articles/2017/11/29/74733-solntse-russkogo-mira [In Russian].

Vartanova, E. (2020). The Internet in the structure of the Russian media system. In S. Davydov (Ed.), *Internet in Russia. Societies and political orders in transition* (pp. 17–37). Cham: Springer.

Vedomosti. (2015, December 5). Yarovaya's draft law on basic textbooks submitted to the State Duma. Retrieved from www.vedomosti.ru/politics/news/2015/05/12/zakonoproekt-yarovoi-o-bazovih-uchebnikah-vnesen-v-gosdumu [In Russian].

Vesti Novosibirsk. (2019, June 27). Golden hopes of Russia: Students who received 100 points on the unified state exam were awarded in Novosibirsk [Video]. Retrieved from www.youtube.com/watch?v=syj-8eSZJt0 [In Russian].

Williams, C., & Smith, A. D. (1983). The national construction of social space. *Progress in Human Geography, 7*(4), 502–518.

Zhuravel, V. (2018). Rights of the indigenous peoples of the Russian Arctic: Problems and solutions. *Arctic and North, 30*, 76–96. doi:10.17238/issn2221-2698.2018.30.76 [In Russian].

Zubrzycki, G. (2017). *National matters: Materiality, culture, and nationalism*. Stanford, CA: Stanford University Press.

11 Nationalism, populism and education in a globalizing India

Fazal Rizvi

Many theorists of globalization over the course of 1990s – especially those David Held and Anthony McGrew (2003) refer to as 'hyperglobalists' – regarded the nation-state as a passing force. They suggested that since the nation-state is a relatively recent historical phenomenon, there is no reason to assume it will continue to perform a coordinating role in social formations, as a means of mass identification and mobilization. It is a product of modernity, of the economic, political and social transformations that are no more than 250 years old. Nation-states, they suggested, were no longer essential for managing economic relations. In his book, *The End of the Nation State*, Ohmae (1996) presented perhaps the most extreme version of this thesis, insisting that nation-states were no longer required to perform the functions vital to capitalist global economy: financial investment was no longer geographically bounded; industries were more global in orientation; the new developments in technology allowed for the production of goods and services across national borders; and the patterns of consumption had now become globally stretched. These developments had given rise to a new logic of capitalism in which transnational corporations and international organizations had acquired more power than the nation-states. While Ohmae celebrated these developments, critics of globalization, such as Hardt and Negri (2000, p. 9), noted that globalization necessitated the reconstitution of "the legal territorial basis of sovereignty," leading decisively to the diminution in the authority of the nation-states, reducing their capacity to control what happens under their purview.

While in the 1990s there might have been a degree of plausibility to these claims about the decline in the authority of the nation-states, a quarter of a century later, there is now little empirical evidence to show that the significance of nations and nationalism has declined. The power of nationalism in upholding the emotional bonds that people continue to have to national traditions and sentiments remains strong. This realization points to the veracity of Smith's (1995) account of nationalism, which suggests that the crucial legacies of the memories and traditions of ethnicities that predated the nation-states continue to play a powerful role in the political organization of social relations. Similarly, Castells (2004) suggests that far from weakening nationalism, globalization is accentuating it, as people cling to their cultural traditions, as a way of coping with and negotiating the disruption and dislocation caused by global forces. They moreover display a great deal

DOI: 10.4324/9781003137801-15

of political resistance to the ways in which globalization is often represented a inevitable, with an agency of its own.

Arguably, this anti-globalization politics opens up a space in which populist leaders and parties are able to exploit feelings of economic and cultural uncertainties. Their populism can thus be viewed as a political contrivance that involves the opportunistic deployment of traditional and new narratives of nationalism in the exercise of power through the alignment of these narratives to the work of the institutions of nation-states, such as education. However, the ways in which these narratives of nationalism are utilized vary greatly across time and space, revealing the different forms that populism can take. In this way, while, in recent decades the rise of right-wing populism has been evident across the world, it does not exhibit the same attributes with respect to nationalist narratives (Rizvi, 2021).

This points to the need to view nationalism and populism as concepts that are different but related. The temptation to conflate the two concepts is understandable since both revolve around claims of sovereignty of 'the people,' leading some to view populism as 'a kind of nationalism' (Stewart, 1969, p. 183). In this chapter, I want to argue that this conflation should be resisted, enabling us to understand how in recent decades nationalist sentiments have been rearticulated through populist politics that have included attempts to re-make the nation-state and its key institutions, as well as the relationship between the state and civil society. To illustrate my argument, I focus on the case of India, demonstrating how nationalist narratives are deployed in the service of right-wing populist politics, promoting a particular understanding of national belonging, privileging the political claims of a specific group of people, while side-lining others. In so doing, I show how education plays a role in the populist promotion of ethno-nationalist discourses.

1 Contested nationalisms in colonial India

As is clear from the papers included in this volume, the concepts of nations and nationalism are far from straightforward. Both the meaning and historical origins of these concepts are highly contested. In his influential work, Smith (1995) defines nations as sociobiological formations that have ethnic origins. Authors such as Hastings (1997) in contrast deny any intrinsic link between ethnicity and nations, viewing them instead as a product of social, economic and political transformations begun with the industrial revolution. A nation, Hastings (1997, p. 10) argues, is "formed from one or more ethnicities it possesses or claims the right to political identity and autonomy as a people, together with the control of specific territory," while nationalism invokes a sense of normative belonging. And while nationalism only became a key theoretical category in the western political thinking in the late 19th century, it existed as a powerful reality in many places long before then (Pryke, 2009). It drove the need to create a 'nation-state' that involved an administrative and legal infrastructure through which political authority is exercised. Nation-states, once created, in turn, promote a sense of nationalism in the populations residing within their borders, sometimes through force but more often through various ideological means, including systems of schooling.

This suggests the relationship between nationalism and nation-states to be complex one, both historically inherited and politically constructed. Nor are nation-states unchanging social entities. Hobsbawm (1992, p. 10) has made this point powerfully. He argues that the idea of nations as a natural, God-given way of classifying human beings, with an inherent political destiny, has always been a myth. Similarly, nationalism, he notes, "takes pre-existing cultures and turns them into nations, sometimes invents them, and often obliterates pre-existing cultures." In short, "for the purposes of analysis nationalism comes before nations." Gellner (1964, p. 167) has similarly noted that "nations do not create nationalism; it is the other way around: nationalism creates nations." He insists that "nationalism is not the awakening of nations to self-consciousness: it invents nations where they do not exist" (p. 168). Nationalism thus plays an important role in imagining, creating or preserving a nation-state – in ensuring that the people who live within the borders of a nation-state view those borders as legitimate; have a deep affective sense of belonging to a nation-state; are prepared to abide by its rules and regulations; and agree for their behaviours to be rewarded or sanctioned by its social and political institutions.

Given such high stakes, debates about the imaginary of the nation (Anderson, 1991) in the colonized parts of the world for most of the 20th century were understandably intense and highly consequential. This was particularly the case in British India, which was never a single coherent social or political unit, but consisted in a multiplicity of nations, ethnicities, religions, cultures and political systems (Copland, 1997). The borders across the various jurisdictions within India were highly contested, so the assumption that various ideological, economic and religious divides in India could have been easily reconciled was at best ambitious. What kind of postcolonial nation India might become was therefore a question that lay at the heart of the Indian struggle for freedom. Among other issues that preoccupied the leaders of the freedom movement were the competing conceptions of nationalism. For example, in the 1920s, as the Indian nationalist movement was entering its mass phase, different possibilities of nationalism were hotly debated. Mahatma Gandhi, for example, emphasized the emancipatory potential of nationalism, while Rabindranath Tagore drew attention to the aggressive possibilities inherent in it, pointing to the risks associated with the conflating of nationalism with patriotism (Seth, 2007, p. 163).

Passionate, and often violent, debates about the politics of cultural and religious difference threatened to derail the prospects of an independent India. A number of imaginaries of India were debated, including a nation that celebrated its local forms, inspired by Mahatma Gandhi's commitment to the principles of peace and social cohesion across India's diverse cultural traditions. It stood in contrast to a modernist image of postcolonial India that expressed the aspirations of the Indian middle class, which saw great value in maintaining some of the colonial institutions from which they had benefitted greatly. They believed that if India were to become an economically independent and strong nation, it had no other choice but to pursue the path to modernization through industrialization, which included the necessity of mass schooling.

Other more intense debates about Indian nationalism centred on issues of religious identity. The Hindu nationalists, for example, traced their nationalism to the Vedic times (1500–500 BCE). This perspective found its political expression in the 1925 creation of Rashtiya Sawyamsevak Sangh (RSS), a tightly disciplined organization that was inspired by fascist ideologies of Hitler and Mussolini. One of its prime ideologues, V. D. Savarkar, spoke of the need to reassert the purity of the Indian nation and its culture (Sharma, 2007). Some Indian Muslims too believed that their political autonomy could not be guaranteed without the creation of a new nation in those parts of British India where Muslims were a majority. The Indian Muslim League (IML) was created in 1906 to promote the nationalist interests of India's Muslim communities (Khan, 2017). Both RSS and IML eventually came to believe that the competing political claims of India's various ethnic, caste, regional and religious communities could not be reconciled. This eventually led to the separation of India into two nations: one Muslim and the other Hindu.

The question of how it became impossible for the competing visions of India to be resolved has been widely debated by historians (Khan, 2017). A popular line of thinking points to the mischievous role played by the British colonial authorities. This suggests that the political debates among the leaders of the independence movement took place under the conditions created by colonial authorities. The British were never innocent bystanders in these debates, but they encouraged both Hindus and Muslims to demand their own separate space to which they had a distinctive sense of belonging, building upon the ethno-nationalist traditions that had already existed in India. These traditions had been reproduced over generations through the separate value systems which the young learned both at home and in schools. Under the British rule, no attempt was made to create a singular unified system of education. Each region and religion had its own way of inculcating the young into its own distinctive norms of sociality, in its own vernacular language. To promote its Hindutva ideologies, RSS created its own schools, while Muslim leaders relied on their own system of religious schools, the *Madrassas*, to institutionalize their political legitimacy (Bello, 2019).

Despite these religious divisions, upon independence, the dominant form of anti-colonial nationalism in India derived its credo from an equally strong secular tradition, represented by such historical Indian figures as Ashoka, who was inspired by the teachings of Buddha, and Akbar, a Mughal emperor committed to the cause of inter-religious harmony. In both its ideological articulation and political practice, this secular tradition recognized the inevitable multicultural and multi-religious character of Indian society, and therefore aspired to an independent nation-state that stood for non-discrimination on the grounds of caste, creed and religion. To justify this position, Indian political leaders often pointed to the Hindu religious scriptures and the teachings of the 19th century social reformers to argue for the principles of mutuality, hospitality and reciprocity developed among the people through intercultural and inter-religious interactions. Equally, they were influenced by European ideas of secularism and liberalism, since they believed these ideas to provide a space for dissent and discussion, and the resolution of inter-faith conflicts. In his analysis of nationalist thought in India,

Chatterjee (1993), for example, has shown how the dominant strand of Indian nationalism was thus derived from Western thought, though transformed as it was deployed in the service of anti-colonial thinking (p. 5).

Education is an institution where the processes of this transformation continue to be most visible, particularly in India's elite schools at which many of its postcolonial leaders were educated, including India's first prime minister, Jawaharlal Nehru and his sons. One such school is the Doon School. Established in 1935, the Doon School provided an education in the tradition of British public schools that mimicked some of the British ruling class manners for which such schools are still well known. An ethnography of the school by Sanjay Srivastva (1998) points to an institution that still embraces the colonial understanding of what constitutes educational excellence, seeking to develop subjectivities that are characterized by "practical minds, solid builders and sane opinions" needed to create a new confident India (Srivastva, 1998, p. 20). Its graduates are expected to make a contribution to build a nation-state that is industrialized and modernized, but that is also embedded within the India's distinctive traditions of secularism. The school thus represents a nationalist project that recognizes its own ambiguity across its modernist sanguinity and the pitfalls of modernity to which Tagore was so alert.

In this way, as Chatterjee (1993, p. 6) notes, Indian postcolonial nationalism has been sutured through an intricate relationship of both borrowing and difference. He speaks of an 'ideological sieve' through which anti-colonial nationalists filtered European ideas, drawing a distinction between "nationalism as a political movement that challenges the colonial state, and nationalism as cultural construct which enables the colonised to posit their difference and autonomy" (Loomba, 1998, p. 190). The former is derivative, but the latter needs to draw its energies from a wide variety of sources. In meeting the requirements of governance, a postcolonial nation-state inherits a range of institutional practices and norms, but also needs to express new expectations and realities. Accordingly, the Indian Constitution was conceived as an instrument embodying the democratic-secular-liberal principles that institutionalize a political system based on fundamental civic rights like freedom of speech and expression, as well as a sense of pluralism which serves as a check on the possibilities of a rampant nationalism turning into a form of 'majoritarianism' in which the rights of minorities are discarded or marginalized.

2 Weakening of civic pluralism

For more than three decades after independence in 1947 India promoted a form of nationalism based on what Girvin (2020) refers to as 'civic pluralism' whereby the state sought to accommodate a diverse set of ethnic and linguistic demands through a consensual federal system. The outcome was a complex asymmetrical federalism that sought to accommodate but also actively oppose the demands of right-wing nationalist movements that continued to exist in one form or another (Guha, 2012). Upon independence, the version of Indian nationalism that was celebrated involved forging of a nation in which diverse castes, cultures and religions were encouraged to live in harmony with each other. In 1948, the first prime minister of India, Jawaharlal Nehru, insisted that "all of us, to whatever religion we may belong, are equally the children of India with equal rights, privileges and obligations" (quoted in Clarke, 2017, p. 104). Indians were encouraged to regard India as a more enlightened nation than Pakistan, which in 1947 had become a Muslim-majority state that defined itself as an Islamic Republic, celebrating its presumed homogeneity (Mukta, 2000).

In post-colonial India, education played a major role in promoting the secular form of nationalism in several ways through a variety of means, both formal and informal. The British had left India in a parlous state, with schooling provided for only a fraction of the Indian population. In 1950, more than 80% of Indians lacked basic literacy and numeracy skills (Ghosh, 2007, p. 35). In the 1950s and 1960s, the Indian government invested heavily in expanding educational opportunities, introducing adult literacy programmes. It established universities and research institutes to develop skills relevant to the aspirations of national development (Agarwal, 2007). At the same time, the principles of secularism, pluralism and social justice were incorporated in both the formal curriculum, but also in the symbolic practices of the informal curriculum. Textbooks in subjects such as history and social studies were revised to reflect narratives of Indian nationalism. Rituals such as flag-raising and singing of the national song became a required practice in all schools (Shukla, 1997). A programme called 'National Cadet Corps' was developed by the Indian armed forces in order to develop national sensibilities among the Indian youth, with the expectation that all Indian students needed to develop a sense of duty to safeguard the unity of the fledgling nation (Ghosh, 2007).

Despite this imperative, the nationalist educational project in postcolonial India was contradictory in many ways. Perhaps, most significantly, the Indian state declared Hindi as a national language, despite it being a minority language in India. As Alok Rai (2001) points out, this policy was tied to a politics that privileged the Hindi-speaking parts of India, which was no more than 20% of the Indian population. Schools were encouraged to replace English with Hindi as the medium of instruction to display their patriotism. An asymmetry of power inherent in this approach was felt acutely in many parts of India, including West Bengal, Tamil Nadu and Kerala. Similarly, the cultural rituals associated with the hidden curriculum in India mostly used Hindu symbols, contradicting the state discourses of pluralism and secularism. Indeed, as Srivastva (1998) notes, at the Doon School, the meaning ascribed to the idea of 'the Indian tradition' universalizes the matrix of Hindu aesthetics, side-lining other religious practices. The Doon School's discourse of secularism thus continues to have the form of what Srivastva (1998, p. 114) refers to as 'Hindu contextualism.'

These contradictions were clearly borne out of a certain majoritarianism. However, they also contained certain seeds of populism. Not surprisingly, by the mid-1970s, India's postcolonial settlement of civic pluralism began to fracture. Under the leadership of Nehru's daughter, Indira Gandhi, the government faced numerous crises, relating to its failure not only to deliver on the economic promises it had made to the masses but also to meet the cultural goals of a social cohesive society. In many parts of India, strong separatist sentiments began to emerge, hreatening India's national unity. The nationalist narrative upon which India had gained its independence began to lose some of its credibility. To meet the challenges, Mrs. Gandhi turned to a range of populist measures that have often been historically deployed in times of crises.

While such measures are not new, their application is often specific to particular conditions and possibilities. Populism involves mobilizing people in a common project either in a sense of grievance or with the promise of a more meaningful and productive future, or indeed both. It variously functions as a political ideology, strategy, worldview, discourse, political style and logic (Mudd & Kaltwasser, 2017). Often also it deploys a particular narrative of nationalism, to express a sense of dissatisfaction with the *status quo*, while highlighting the unity of 'the people' in the service of some broader political agenda. In this way, while the concepts of nationalism and populism are related in various ways, they are not interchangeable. Although populism usually operates in a national context, it also signifies a politics through which a national narrative is defined and enacted in acquiring and preserving power. It is an idea centred on the nodal points of 'the people' and the 'the elite' that are assumed to exist in an antagonistic relationship.

Accordingly, Mrs. Gandhi sought to identify her government with 'the people' by both creating a sense of national crisis, as well as pointing to numerous enemies – some real, others imagined – who were held as responsible for her government's failures. An aspect of her populist politics harnessed national sentiments, blaming Pakistan for its attempts to destabilize Indian sovereignty and regional separatist movements for undermining India's unity (Guha, 2012). Her positive reform proposals focused on the eradication of poverty, especially among the rural poor, arguing that her party, the Indian National Congress (INC), had always championed the ordinary people. In education, it expanded measures to provide greater access to education, especially for girls and the rural communities. However, these programmes ultimately benefitted not the Congress, but the Hindu right (Swamy, 2018), as the right was able to better capture the affective mood of the country. Exasperated with continuing lack of success, the INC government turned to various authoritarian measures, most notoriously a sterilization programme that sought to bring India's exploding population under control (Gupte, 2015). These measures proved to be widely unpopular.

Even as Indira Gandhi abandoned some of her authoritarian policies a few years later, the damage had been done. This was so because the Congress Party's approach to politics, as Bello (2019, p. 75) observes, had become "synonymous with the bureaucratic control of the economy and overregulation – the so called License Raj," which had led not only to economic stagnation but also widespread corruption. In the late 1980s, the Indian economy was near collapse. While it had long resisted foreign intervention in its domestic policy processes, it now had little option but to accept the rescue packages offered by the World Bank and the International Monetary Fund, under the conditions that it would pursue a rigorous programme of structural adjustment. The programme of economic liberalization that followed from 1991 included measures to reduce the fiscal deficit, a new market-friendly industrial policy, reductions in tariffs, as well as policies that encouraged private investment in insurance, banking, telecommunications, air travel, and in the services sectors, including education.

These measures were designed to take advantage of developments in the globalization of economy. They were embraced wholeheartedly by not only the India's middle and corporate classes but also foreign investors who had long projected possibilities of enormous profits in India, but were scared away by India's continuing commitment to economic planning processes controlled by the state, as well as its unwieldy and often cumbersome bureaucratic culture. The Indian diaspora, in particular, supported economic liberalization with much enthusiasm, blaming vested interests, which they believed included politicians, bureaucrats, academics and local entrepreneurs, for keeping India's command economy going, preventing it from realizing its boundless potential. Indian diaspora economists at leading universities in the US and UK, such as Bhagwati (2007), argued that globalization could provide India a 'circuit breaker' to forge a new economy that was not trapped within the postcolonial nationalist discourses but in the possibilities of economic globalization as a positive force.

In this way, globalization and economic liberalization unsettled India's hard-won secular nationalist imaginary forged historically in the struggle against the colonial rule, and in the processes of postcolonial national formation. And while hyper-globalist sentiments have never captured popular imagination in India, the political transformations have nonetheless created an oppositional space in which new nationalist discourses have found a home. It has become possible for new discourses of nationalism to be deployed in the service of a more radically new imaginary of the nation, no longer tied to the assumptions of civic pluralism. The Hindu right in India now promotes a discourse of nationalism it had long favoured, within the possibilities of a populist politics that has not only harnessed anti-globalization sentiments but has also portrayed the nation in distinctively new ways. Paradoxically, it has taken credit for the benefits that economic liberalization has brought to the urban middle class, while laying the blame for the continuing plight of the rural poor at the feet of the Congress Party. Indeed, as the Indian economy expanded at an unprecedented rate to over 6% per year during the last decade of the 20th century, some began to refer to this achievement as 'the Hindu rate of growth' (Guha, 2012, p. 695).

The impact of globalization on India may be described in terms of its economic, cultural and political dimensions, each contradictory in its own way. So while economically, India's economy has grown rapidly, the prosperity it has brought to Indians has been at best uneven. As Dreze and Sen (2013) have argued, India's economic success represents an 'uncertain glory,' which has created some very rich people, produced a reasonably well-off entrepreneurial middle class, focused on the global IT industry in particular and eradicated extreme poverty. At the same time, however, economic globalization has increased the divide between rich and poor, with a rising GINI index. Globalization has created conditions of precarious work and economic uncertainties and anxieties. The agricultural sector has been corporatized, leaving farmers without a sense of social belonging and economic security. Culturally, globalization has enabled Indians to forge transnational links hat were once difficult to establish. However, it has also created a culture of onsumerism, with goods and services for sale that only a few can afford. Many in ndia also feel that their cherished cultural values and traditions are now threat-ned by the encroaching global commodity culture. The Hindu right has seized upon these concerns in order to reassert the primacy of its cultural symbols and values in re-defining Indian nationhood.

Politically, these developments have altered India's self-image, enabling it to play a more significant role in international relations and to enjoy the status that a country of nearly 1.3 billion clearly deserves. Many of its institutions, includ-ng education, have become stronger as a result of its engagement with global nstitutions. However, globalization has also opened a space in which the Hindu right has become more politically strident, especially with the support of the suc-cessful Indian diaspora abroad, which has not hesitated in promoting its own ver-sion of 'long-distance nationalism' (Skribis, 2017). In line with the global rise of populism (Moffit, 2017), India has witnessed the development of a new political discourse that accepts the benefits of economic globalization but also allows the fears and anxieties associated with its cultural dimensions to be stoked (Pathak, 2006). This discourse reasserts the glories of an India past, couched in essentialist terms. It ties the cultural risks associated with a globalizing India to the alleged deficiencies of a secular India. This has enabled the new nationalist politics to be articulated in populist terms, with the definition of 'the people' of India defined narrowly, privileging those who belong to a particular religion, caste and ethnicity, while marginalizing those who are viewed either as the underserving 'others' or the manipulative 'elite.'

3 Rise of right-wing populism

As I have already noted, criticisms of secularism are not new in India; they date back to the 1920s (Anand, 2016). However, in recent decades, such criticisms have become more visible, used to mask some of the deeper political interests and prejudices. In ways that are common to populists around the world, explicit attempts are now made in India to privilege particular forms of social bonds by constructing those who can be portrayed as the untrustworthy and dangerous 'others.' This was most evident in a relentless campaign to demolish the Muslim Babri Mosque and replace it with a Hindu Mandir at a site that many Hindus claim to be the birthplace of one of Hinduism's most revered gods. Over the years there have been regular demonstrations in support of religiously inspired claims and conspiracy theories that allege that Muslims, who make up around 15% of India's population, disrespect various Hindu religious symbols, such as the cow. Muslims are often assumed to be 'anti-national,' clandestinely sympathetic to the interests of India's great rival, Pakistan.

In opposition, Bharatiya Janata Party (BJP) was not only highly effective in sponsoring its own brand of ethno-nationalist identity politics but also in mobi-lizing people's sense of grievance against the entrenched power of institutions, both state and non-state, national and global. However, when it won the national elections in 2014, it needed to develop more complex ways of articulating its populism. In Modi, it found a prime minister who has proven to be a shrewd politician, and who now commands much electoral support. As a teenager, Modi was a member of RSS, and he continues to be committed to some of its core ideological principles. These include the idea that the essence of being an Indian lies in an intimate sense of belonging to a sacred geography that shares the inheritance of its Vedic ancestors. This Hindutva ideology views Indian citizenship as a biological community that entails a shared culture. Those who do not share this culture are assumed not to be 'real' Indians (Harriss, 2015). In government, while Modi does not articulate such extreme ethno-nationalist views in any explicit terms, his millions of followers have little doubt that he subscribes to them. They point to his symbolic politics, the manner in which he acts and refers to the rights and responsibilities of citizenship.

A key ingredient in Modi's continuing electoral success is thus his populist style, which consists of his identification with 'the people' and his characterization of the corrupt 'elite,' especially those associated with the old bureaucracy and the intellectuals committed to the Nehruian social democracy. His political authority lies in his claims to morality and direct democracy, and in his capacity to invariably put the blame for any failure on others, behaving as though he were still in opposition, continuing to polarize the community, seeking to mobilize political conflict. Modi's approach to populism is thus consistent with Muller's (2016, p. 43) contention that "populists combine the constant creation of pressure with an aesthetic production of 'proximity to the people.'" Modi's populist style assumes that the state rightfully belongs to 'the people' of whom he is a champion. In this way, an attempt is made to obliterate any clear-cut distinction between the state and the civil society. Modi is also adept in exercising political power through 'mass clientelism' (Muller, 2016, p. 22), which consists of exchanging material and non-material favours for mass political support.

For BJP, this approach to populist politics is backed up with a well-planned presidential-style political campaign around Modi himself (Chhibber & Verma, 2014). His populist projection of the nation involves a style that is performed and enacted across various political and cultural contexts. Social media plays a crucial role in the performance of this form of populism (Moffit, 2017). Bello (2019) has provided a most insightful analysis of India's distinctive brand of populism, as it is represented in the popular media. It involves three overlapping components. The first cultivates a pro-growth image, designed to win over investors, disarm the sceptics and give the appearance of supporting the middle class. The second seeks to normalize Hindu nationalist discourses, transforming the public discursive space in an attempt to define an exclusive national imaginary. And finally, every attempt is made to disparage and denigrate the critics of BJP's ideological agenda, especially if the critics happen to be the minorities.

Beyond the discursive realm, the Modi regime has not been shy in wielding legal and extra-legal power. Legally, BJP has introduced various measures to constrain democratic conventions and has even used investigative agencies and the armed forces to silence its critics, as is the case, for example, in the contested state of

Kashmir, where the region's distinctive legal status has been abolished. BJP has also introduced laws that redefine citizenship in ways that arguably discriminate against Muslims (Varughese, 2019). A controversial new federal law, for example, entitles non-Muslim migrants and refugees from three Muslim-majority countries in India's neighbourhood to apply for citizenship if they can show that they are subjected to religious persecution. The law, however, does not extend this right to Muslims.

Extra-legally, almost every form of surveillance, intimidation and infiltration used by the RSS vigilante groups has been overlooked in an evolving synthesis of Hindutva ideology and populism (Yadav, 2017). This synthesis, according to Jeffrelot (2017, p. 2), dates back to the inception of RSS – "intended to transform society from the inside by infusing in it its own sense of discipline which it thought was necessary to defend the Hindus more effectively." RSS thus sees no real distinction between society and the state, regarding the state as an expression of the society at large. According to this Hindutva *doxa*, social order and harmony are only possible when the law and public policy encapsulate the 'general will' of the people defined, of course, in terms of its own distinctive imaginary of India. Indian populism thus operates not only through the instruments of state power, but, much more profoundly, through the transformation of the civic space, in which practices of 'banal nationalism' (Billig, 1995) acquire greater significance than formal articulations of public policy. This realization is helpful in understanding how populist politics in India has involved attempts to reshape the purposes and practices of education.

4 Populist politics and education

Under the BJP government, the politics of education in India has been contradictory in many ways. On the one hand, the government remains committed to the social justice goals of educational reform, articulated in India's constitution, reinforced in its Right to Education Act in 2010. Recently, its National Education Policy (Department of Human Resource Education, 2020) has reiterated the role of education in promoting a socially inclusive society. The policy recommends investing heavily in programmes that seek to increase educational opportunities for the poor and the under-served communities. It promotes the progressive notion of child-centred education, along with pedagogic reforms designed to lift educational standards in disadvantaged communities. Its progressive agenda is, however, located within a populist vision of developing "an India-centric education system that contributes directly to transforming our nation sustainably into an equitable and vibrant knowledge society by providing high-quality education to all" (p. 1).

The ideological use of the idea of 'India-centric' in NEP's vision is deliberate, designed to signal BJP's complex relationship to the processes of globalization, on the one hand, and narrowly framed nationalism, on the other. While the government accepts that economic globalization has brought many benefits to India, it is deeply suspicious of globalization's cultural dimensions. Whenever politically convenient, it does not hesitate to mobilize an anti-globalization rhetoric to assert its nationalist credentials. And while its reform agenda in education has embraced several of the prescriptions of what Sahlberg (2011) refers to the 'Global Educational Reform Movement' (GERM) – including privatization, corporatization and an emphasis on assessment and accountability – its educational discourses are hostile to sentiments that are not aligned to Hindutva's sense of moral, cultural and ideological legitimacy (Flaten, 2017). Accordingly, it has attempted to change the school curriculum to reflect the self-image of India as a Hindu nation, especially in subjects such as literature, history and social studies. It has also spoken out against the socially democratic discourses of post-independence India that articulate the values of secularism and pluralism.

While, in formal policy enactments, the BJP government has not entirely been able to overhaul the pluralist and secular vision of India, it has been remarkably successful in creating a civic space in which Hindutva ideology has gained considerable ascendency. This success is due largely to a populist politics that is based not so much on government edicts but on the manner in which ideological sentiments have gradually crept into the everyday discourses and practices of most social institutions, including education. Encouraged by the authority of the state, civic organizations associated with the Hindu right, including RSS, have been given greater latitude in advancing their ideological agenda than those non-government organizations that are opposed to it. The right-wing organizations have become increasingly strident, often acting with impunity in asserting the primacy of Hinduism in prescribing the role of education in re-making of the Indian society. Highly influential Hindu groups have, in recent years, flooded the government with recommendations that blur the line between the state and Hinduism. As Gahlot (2015, p. 2) reports, "One proposal recommends eliminating English as a compulsory language in schools. Another recommends studying mathematics as discussed in the Vedas, the oldest Hindu scriptures." A new symbiotic relationship has thus emerged between the state and the civil society, asymmetrically leaning towards the right.

Along with major Hindu nationalist organizations, the government has been particularly harsh on intellectuals who have dared to provide alternative narratives of Indian history, culture and politics. For example, it has attacked educational institutions which it regards as hostile to its Hindu national imaginary, most recognizably in ugly incidences at the Jadavpur University Campus in Kolkata, Jawaharlal Nehru University, Delhi University and the University of Hyderabad (Kumar, 2020). The Hindu organizations and the state have worked together to embolden right-wing student activists on campuses by encouraging them to demand courses that celebrate India's image as a Hindu nation. Professors known for their progressive and radical views have frequently been harassed, especially those who profess secular neo-Marxist beliefs, such as the historian, Irfan Habib, as well as those whose scholarship focuses on the contribution of Muslims and other minorities to India, such as Romila Thapar (Flood, 2015). The Hindu civic organizations have also threatened the closure of departments that do not

ow their ideological line. Many critics of the Hindutva ideology have simply been
silenced into submission.

Symbols of Hindu nationhood are now visible on campuses throughout India,
to an extent they had never been before; and the assumption that public higher
education is a secular site for critical examination of cultural traditions is now
widely scoffed, if not crushed – if not by the government then certainly by its
proxy organizations. Wishing not to be portrayed as authoritarian, the state does
not wish to be seen to be silencing the voices of dissent by public intellectuals, but
nor does it discourage the increasingly confident and ubiquitous right-wing media
from doing so. Public broadcasting has been starved of funds, replaced by noisy
cable stations on which debates over public policy invariably favour the right-wing
populist opinion. Wishing to carry favour with the government, the owners of the
cable stations give ample opportunities to the vociferous right-wing public intellectuals and activists to shout down the voices of opposition. Media thus plays
an important role in creating and sustaining the conditions under which Indian
populist politics thrive.

The media has also played a role in steering popular culture in India toward
the sentiments associated with the Hinduva ideology of what it means to be a
citizen of India, who can expect to enjoy the protection of the state and what are
the responsibilities of citizenship. In the 1950s, Bollywood, India's most extensive
and influential mirror to popular sentiments, promoted a postcolonial vision of an
egalitarian and pluralist India. Fifty years later, populism demands representations
of an India that is transnationally connected on the one hand and grounded in
Hindu mythologies and religious symbols on the other. Far too frequently, in popular media, minorities have either become invisible or are portrayed as enemies of
the nation. Athavala (2019) has shown how the rise of jingoist Hindi cinema has
paralleled BJP's ascent to power, as Bollywood producers have taken heed of the
advice of senior government ministers who have called for the need to show history from an 'Indian' standpoint, so that 'ordinary Indians' can relate to it and can
be proud. Other sites of popular culture have also been affected by the relentless
advocacy for Hindu imageries and icons in the public space.

Schools in India have been deeply affected by this transformation of the civic
space, reshaping teacher and student identities, their sense of belonging in historical time and cultural space. As is globally the case, youth culture in India is
unquestionably affected by cultural globalization in metropolitan areas in particular. But what is also clear is that the young in India now engage with cultural
globalization through the ideological prism created by the rising tide of Hindu
nationalism, enacted through populist politics. While they are seduced by American consumer culture, the young nevertheless also espouse an ideological commitment to the nation, shaped in the idioms of Hindu nationalism (Berti, Jaoul, &
Kanungo, 2019). Their teachers seldom challenge these idioms either because
they fear being branded 'too political' or because they share the Hindu narratives of the nation themselves. At the same time, as the Indian system of school
education, under the global influence of neoliberalism, has become increasingly

privatized, the more instrumental goals of education are now ascendant, leaving little space for critically oriented citizenship education.

5 Conclusion

In this chapter, I have used the illustrative case of India to examine the complicated relationship between nationalism and populism. The temptation to conflate the two concepts is understandable since they both revolve around the claims of sovereignty of 'the people.' However, I have argued that while nationalism is an ideology, populism is a mode of politics, the practices of which can vary a great deal across time and space. Some three decades ago, it was widely believed that the forces of globalization were likely to weaken nationalist ideologies. The rise of right-wing populism in countries such as India has, however, demonstrated this assumption to be mistaken. On the contrary, the primacy of the nation has been revived in determining economic, cultural and political priorities. This is clearly evident in India in the ways in which Hindu nationalist narratives are deployed in the service of a right-wing populist politics, promoting a particular understanding of national belonging, privileging the political claims of a specific group of people, while side-lining others. This politics has undermined the culture of civic pluralism that the architects of independent India had hoped to promote, partly through education. Over the past decade, education has instead been expected to play a different role in the populist promotion of an ethno-nationalist narrative of India.

References

Agarwal, P. (2007). *Indian higher education: Envisioning the future.* New Delhi: Sage.
Anand, D. (2016). *Hindu nationalism in India and the politics of fear.* London: Palgrave Macmillan.
Anderson, B. (1991). *Imagined communities: Reflections on the origin and spread of nationalism* (revised ed.). London: Verso.
Athavala, S. (2019). Bollywood, a propaganda tool: Mughals were bad, Hindutva is great, but these movies are historically wrong in. *The Logical Indian.* Retrieved from https://thelogicalindian.com/exclusive/bollywood-propaganda-mughals-hindutva/
Bello, W. (2019). *Counter revolution: The global rise of the far right.* Rugby Warwickshire, UK: Practical Action Press.
Berti, D., Jaoul, N., & Kanungo, P. (Eds.). (2019). *Cultural entrenchment of Hindutva: Local mediations and forms of convergence.* London: Routledge.
Bhagwati, J. (2007). *In defence of globalization.* London: Oxford University Press.
Billig, M. (1995). *Banal nationalism.* London: Sage Publications.
Castells, M. (2004). *The power of identity, the information age: Economy, power and identity* (2nd ed.). Oxford: Blackwell.
Chatterjee, P. (1993). *The nation and its fragments: Colonial and postcolonial histories.* Princeton, NJ: Princeton University Press.
Chhibber, P., & Verma, R. (2014). An ideological consolidation of the right: BJP 2014 Modi's wave. *Economic and Political Weekly, 49*(39).
Clarke, S. (2017). *Competing fundamentalisms: Violent extremism in Christianity, Islam and Hinduism.* Louisville: Westminster John Knox Press.

Copland, I. (1997). *The princes of India in the endgame of empire 1917–1947*. Cambridge: Cambridge University Press.

Department of Human Resources Education. (2020). *National education policy 2020*, New Delhi: Government of India.

Dreze, J., & Sen, A. (2013). *An uncertain glory: India and its contradictions*. Princeton, NJ: Princeton University Press

Flaten, L. T. (2017). Spreading Hindutva through education: Still a priority for the BJP? *India Review, 16*(4), 377–400.

Flood, A. (2015, October 13). Intellectuals will be silenced': Historians express fears of Indian government In *The Guardian*. Retrieved from www.theguardian.com/books/2015/oct/30/indian-historians-romila-thapar-irfan-habib-protest-government

Gahlot, M. (2015, March 19). India's new school textbooks favor Hindu nationalist themes, making minorities uneasy. *The Washington Post*. Retrieved from www.washingtonpost.com/national/religion/indias-new-school-textbooks-favor-hindu-nationalist-themes-making-minorities-uneasy/2015/03/19/30b5dad6-ce4a-11e4–8730–4f473416e759_story.html

Gellner, E. (1964). *Thought and change*. London: Weidenfeld & Nicholson.

Ghosh, S. C. (2007). *History of education in India*. New Delhi: Rawat Press.

Girvin, B. (2020). From civic pluralism to ethno-religious majoritarianism: Majority nationalism in India. *Nationalism and Ethnic Politics, 26*(1), 27–45.

Guha, R. (2012). *India after Gandhi: The history of world's largest democracy*. New Delhi: Picador.

Gupte, P. R. (2015). India: "The emergency" and the politics of mass sterilization. *Asian Studies*. Retrieved from www.asianstudies.org/wp-content/uploads/india-the-emergency-and-the-politics-of-mass-sterilization.pdf

Hardt, M., & Negri, A. (2000). *Empire*. Cambridge, MA: Harvard University Press.

Harriss, J. (2015). Hindu nationalism in action: The Bhartiya Janata Part and Indian politics. *South Asia: Journal of South Asian Studies, 38*(4).

Hastings, A. (1997). *The construction of nationhood: Ethnicity, religion and nationhood*. Cambridge: Cambridge University Press.

Held, D., & McGrew, A. (Eds.). (2003). *The global transformation reader* (2nd ed.). Cambridge: Polity.

Hobsbawm, E. (1992). *Nation and nationalism* (2nd ed.). Cambridge: Cambridge University Press.

Jeffrelot, C. (2017). Over to the Vigilante. In *Carnegie endowment for international peace*. Retrieved from https://carnegieendowment.org/2017/05/13/over-to-vigilante-pub-70028.

Khan, Y. (2017). *The great partition: The making of India and Pakistan*. New Haven, CT: Yale University Press.

Kumar, S. (2020). Campus attacks by nationalists and police alarm India's scientific community. *Science*. Retrieved from www.sciencemag.org/news/2020/01/campus-attacks-nationalists-and-police-alarm-india-s-scientific-community

Loomba, A. (1998). *Colonialism/postcolonialism*. London: Routledge.

Moffit, B. (2017). *The global rise of populism: Performance, political style and representation*. Stanford, CA: Stanford University Press.

Mudd, C., & Kaltwasser, C. R. (2017). *Populism: A very short introduction*. London: Oxford University Press.

Mukta, P. (2000). The public Face of Hindu nationalism. *Ethnic and Racial Studies, 23*(3).

Muller, J-W. (2016). *What is populism?* London: Penguin.

Ohmae, K. (1996). *The end of the nation-state: The rise of regional economies*. London: Harper-Collins.

Pathak, A. (2006). *Modernity, globalization and identity: Towards a reflexive quest*. New Delhi: Aakar Books.

Pryke, S. (2009). *Nationalism in a global world*. London: Palgrave Macmillan.

Rai, A. (2001). *Hindi nationalism*. New Delhi: Orient Longman.

Rizvi, F. (2021). Populism, the state and education. *Globalisations, societies and education*. doi :10.1080/14767724.2021.1910015

Sahlberg, P. (2011). *Finnish lessons: What can the world learn from educational change in Finland?* New York, NY: Teachers College Press.

Seth, S. (2007). *Subject lessons: Western construction of colonial India*. Durham, NC: Duke University Press.

Sharma, S. R. (2007). *The life and works of V D Savarkar*. New Delhi: Book Enclave.

Shukla, S. (1997, July) Nationalist educational thought. *Economic and Political Weekly, 119*, 1825–1828.

Skribis, Z. (2017). *Long-distance nationalism: Diasporas, homelands and identities*. London: Routledge.

Smith, A. (1995). *Nations and nationalism in a global era*. Cambridge: Polity.

Srivastva, S. (1998). *Constructing post-colonial India: National character and the doon school*. London: Routledge.

Stewart, A. (1969). The social roots. In G. Ionescu & E. Gellner (Eds.), *Populism: Its meaning and characteristics* (pp. 180–195). London: Weidenfeld & Nicholson.

Swamy, A. (2018, May). Hindu nationalism in India a century in the making. *East Asia Forum*. Retrieved from https://www.eastasiaforum.org/2018/05/15/hindu-nationalism-in-india-a-century-in-the-making/

Varughese, A. (2019. India's new citizenship act legalizes a Hindu nation. *The Conversation*. Retrieved from https://theconversation.com/indias-new-citizenship-act-legalizes-a-hindu-nation-129024

Yadav, Y. (2017). What is to be done? *India Seminar*. Retrieved from india-seminar.com/2017/699/699_yogendra_yadav.htm

12 Cuban education in the Cold War

National independence within international socialism

Tom G. Griffiths and Euridice Charon Cardona

The massification of education as a global phenomenon was succinctly expressed in the United Nations (1948) Declaration of Universal Human Rights' inclusion of the Right to Education (Article 26) as both a fundamental human right in and of itself, and a means to achieve other human rights. Education, along with health care, secure housing and employment, became part of the Cold War battleground. The battleground was acute in the context of post-WWII decolonization and the struggles for national liberation and independence, whereby the absence of these basic social services and the legacies of this absence were associated with Western, colonial and capitalist domination. Even as universal public education, as part of a modern welfare state, became entrenched in 'developed' capitalist countries located in the Global North, former colonies had experienced extreme levels of inequality and inequity with respect to access to education and all that comes with the attainment of educational credentials.

The significance of the mass education project in the context of the Cold War, and within historical socialism generally, is apparent here. Identified global purposes of mass education to simultaneously produce 'good workers' and 'good citizens' were a significant feature of what Wallerstein's (1995, 2005) world-systems analysis sets out as the socialist variant of the shared national modernization and development project, aspiring to and promising a future of material abundance. In the case of Cuba education was, amongst other things, called upon to produce skilled disciplined workers to drive economic innovation and development; to form citizens loyal to the socialist State, Party and committed to the international socialist cause, including anti-imperialist, antiracist, political and social movements; to demonstrate the superiority of socialism, and to recruit international support for socialist states and projects. These objectives were consistently infused with and/or presented as expressions of promoting students' 'love for the *patria* (homeland),' with national independence and social justice for all defining features of the independent Cuban nation. Gott (2005), for example, concluded his volume with a note that Fidel Castro and the Revolution "engendered in the Cuban people an intangible but real sense of pride in their nation" (p. 319), producing "fresh generations of well-educated citizens . . . possessed of a developed sense of patriotism, with pride in their country's long history and the achievements of its people" (p. 32).

DOI: 10.4324/9781003137801-16

The dynamic developed in this chapter is one of continuity of a longer-standing cultural project to define and construct a sense of Cuban national identity, and efforts to appropriate and present this project in terms of the socialist political project and its reconstruction of the Cuban State. The inherited cultural project invokes historical efforts striving for political independence under the banner of *Cuba Libre* – free (*libre*) from colonial and foreign domination. This historical narrative, in turn, is linked in official statements and policy to the Revolutionary and to 1960–1961 socialist political trajectory. Cuba's socialist project is constructed as at least fulfilling, if not more profoundly embodying, core aspects of the historical project of national political independence and liberation, and an accompanying reconstruction of the identity of the Cuban nation. The historical project of national political independence and liberation – tracked back to the wars of liberation against Spanish rule and José Martí's dream of *Cuba Libre* – became redefined in socialist terms of equality, of social justice, of international solidarity and at the same of national unity around the reconstructed Cuban nation-state and the Communist Party.

This dynamic is developed over four sections. The first explores the narration of the historical struggle for political independence and equality, and the socialist project characterized by the project for rapid economic development. Next, we review the more 'open' and 'radical' period of the 1960s itself that provided significant space for debating and creating an authentically Cuban socialist project, and corresponding foreign policy, within the international socialist movements. The third section contrasts this with the distinctive turn to Soviet alignment and 'institutionalization' of the Revolution, elaborating some of the negative social and cultural consequences and their educational manifestations. In the concluding section we reflect on Afro-Cuban identities in Revolutionary and Cold War Cuba, as illustrative of the limited space that the invocations for political unity provided for multiple social and cultural expressions and identifications. The exhorted unity of the nation, the Party, the State quickly discouraged mobilizing on any other grounds or identities, impacting on the (re)founding of the Cuban nation.

1 The Cuban revolution as national liberation struggle for political independence

The Cold War dynamics and influence are reflected in expressions about the Cuban education project, its purpose, structure and curricular contents. The early period and 1960s are generally seen as one of experimentation and debate, seeking to describe and construct an authentically, distinctive, radically independent Cuban socialism. A combination of internal and international events led to a shift to alignment with the Soviet Union in the 1970s, with major consequences for the intellectual and political debate, and for the socialist state and its institutions such as education. This alignment carried through to Cuba's 'Rectification of Errors and Negative Tendencies' campaign that commenced in 1985–1986, returning to some critique of the Soviet models that had been applied (see for example Azicri, 1992).

We acknowledge the popular nature of the Cuban Revolution that involved several years of both urban and guerrilla struggle against the Batista dictatorship that had seized power in Cuba in 1952 (Fernández Guevara, 2019) and which culminated in the collapse of Batista's government and the formal beginnings of Cuba's revolutionary (and socialist) project from January 1, 1959 (see for example Chomsky, 2011; Gott, 2005; Kapcia, 2005; Veltmeyer & Rushton, 2013). As much of the scholarship cites, the popularity of Fidel Castro and the July 26 Movement that overthrew Batista and assumed power in 1959 was beyond question. Indeed, support was so overwhelming that even the US agencies identified Fidel Castro and the Revolution's popularity as major barrier to their efforts to destabilize and ultimately replace the new government with one more amendable to United States interests (for succinct accounts of US intelligence reports for example, see Gleijeses, 2002, 2013).

Gott (2005) argues that "Cuba under Castro became a Communist country where nationalism was more significant than socialism, where the legend of Martí proved more influential that the philosophy of Marx" (pp. 148–149). He adds that Fidel, and the Cuban Revolution, managed to keep "the twin themes of socialism and nationalism endlessly in play" (p. 149). The nationalism referred to here is the idea of the free and independent Cuban nation-state, fused with the socialist political project within the Cold War context. Much of the literature about Cuba and the Cuban Revolution conflates the project for political independence and sovereignty with the cultural project of the Cuban nation, under the single reference to 'national independence' or 'national liberation.' For example, Veltmeyer and Rushton (2013) cite Fidel and Che to characterize the Revolution as "fundamentally a struggle for national liberation – to liberate the country from imperialist exploitation and oppressions – and a class struggle against class exploitation and the oppressive oligarchical regime set up to enforce this exploitation" (p. 218). Morales Domínguez's (2013) characterization of the revolution, along these lines, presents it as "a continuation of multiple wars for national independence and sovereignty" (p. 109).

The historical struggle alluded to here also included conflicts that went back almost a century, such as the 10-year war that began in 1868, mobilizing Cuban *Mambises* (liberation fighters), and which was defeated by the Spanish and followed by internal divisions that, as Morales Domínguez (2013) describes, frequently involved racial and racist divisions within anti-colonial movements. The liberation movement rejected the concept of race as a tool used by the Spanish colonial powers to divide it, presenting racism as a "sin against the life of the would be nation" (Ferrer, 1999, p. 25). This struggle both against slavery and racism made the liberation movement a "mythic project that armed black, white, and mulatto men together to form the world's first raceless nation" (Ferrer, 1999, p. 25). Kapcia (2009) similarly notes how some black Cubans in this period saw rebellion as "a struggle for racial equality as well as national liberation" (p. 11), inspired by the mulatto general of the Liberation Army, Antonio Maceo. He goes on to argue that in the late 19th century it was Jose Martí who "managed to fuse the movement's disparate nationalism and its growing radicalism into a vision of

Cuba Libre that went beyond political independence to advocate a socially equal Cuba" (Kapcia, 2009, p. 13).

In this history we encounter the calls first for "Independence or Death" and "Liberty or Death" from Antonio Maceo, leading the Liberation Army in 1868 (see Maceo, 1968 (1878)). Calling upon liberated slaves to join the struggle and "march together to emancipate the homeland as soldiers of the Liberation Army" (cited in Limia Díaz, 2021), Maceo's invocations were integrally bound up with Martí and his expressed struggle to fight (to the death) both against colonial rule and Yankee imperialism, and for *Cuba Libre*. Limia Díaz (2021) notes that on March 4, 1960, for the first time, Fidel used the phrase that synthesized these sentiments: *Patria o Muerte* ("Homeland or Death"). Later that year Fidel added *Venceremos!* ("We will be victorious!"), and later still the characteristic three-part slogan that came to end his speeches and those of other Cuban leaders: *Socialismo o Muerte! Patria o Muerte! Venceremos!* This sort of fusion of the socialist state with the Cuban nation generated a particular Cuban patriotism and socialist nationalism.

These sorts of patriotic expressions of the homeland, and love for the homeland, were incorporated into educational policy as values or morals to be promoted in students. From the earliest days both the provision of education, and the formal policy intention to utilize the institution of schooling for the goals of the new government, were made clear. In February 1959, the revolutionary government decreed a Fundamental Law: Family and Culture, which included a commitment to provide "universal education without prejudice" in the face of high levels of illiteracy and sharp educational inequalities within and between rural and urban populations (Gobierno Revolucionario, 1959, pp. 6–7). Law 561 followed to provide formal education for the identified 1.6 million school-age children without access to schooling, via the appointment of 4,000 primary school teachers and an interim plan to build 10,000 classrooms (Gobierno Revolucionario, 1960).

Amongst these rapid expansion measures, Law 680 in the same year declared that the expanding school system must promote in students "a spirit of Cuban identity . . . love of the homeland and its democratic institutions" (Gobierno Revolucionario, 1960, p. 23). Such policy intentions were grounded in an acknowledgement that schooling, as a state institution, was and should be "an instrument of the social objectives of the nation" (MINED, 1960, p. 36). Thus, prior to the socialist character of the revolution being formally declared, the Ministry of Education was calling on teachers to educate students "conscious of the necessity to transform the economic and social structures of Cuba" (MINED, 1960, p. 58). Cuban education was to have an explicit role in shaping people's formation as Cuban citizens; their understanding of the country and its social, political and economic situation; and in supporting the unfolding project of the Cuban Revolution. These expressions invoked Martí's ideal of building *la patria* with and for all Cubans (de la Fuente, 2001).

De la Fuente (2001) also notes the early, and we argue consistent, call for unity as part of the appeal for building the nation (in effect, for building the socialist state), citing Raul Castro's speech on May Day 1959, in which he affirmed that 'the Unity of all people is as important to the revolution as the integration of all Cubans is to the nation" (p. 268). Here again we see clear signs of the conflation of the Revolution with the nation, effectively articulating the unity of the population in their support for the Revolution's political project and its advancement, as synonymous with building the Cuban nation. Proposals for this sort of political formation in schooling, in the early 1960s, included the use of units of work like "Study more in order to better serve our socialist homeland," for which the Ministry provided an extensive list of required readings (MINED, 1963, p. 7). These were accompanied by prescribed focus questions for teachers to discuss with students; for example, "Why does the working class need the leadership of a Marxist-Leninist party?" (MINED, 1963, p. 59). At the same time, the Ministry of Education warned against the passive and uncritical transmission of such knowledge, in favour of a socialist pedagogy that included the "active intervention" of students (MINED, 1965, pp. 3–4). Alongside the political units of study for inclusion in secondary schools, others focused on guiding students towards specific vocations, in accordance with the independent national development project. For example, a work unit entitled "Exploring our occupational preferences" called on teachers to encourage students' interest in vocations identified as "most necessary to the construction of socialism" (MINED, 1963, p. 45).

A key educational ritual of presenting primary school students in their first year of schooling with their *pañoleta* (scarf or kerchief), which had been carried out by an earlier iteration of a Cuban Communist Party in the 1930s, was recreated in 1962, initiating students into the Union of Cuban Pioneers. As de las Nieves Barrios Sánchez (2014) recalls, the ceremony was accompanied by singing the national anthem, while the blue and red *pañoletas* were explained to students by reference to the colours of the Cuban flag, with blue evoking the colour of the sky of the *patria*, and red the blood shed by national heroes and martyrs for the cause of Cuban independence and liberty. After Che Guevara's defeat and death in Bolivia, the slogan for the Pioneers changed from *Pioneers Always Ready* to *Pioneers for Communism! We will be like Che!*, highlighting Che's internationalism, sacrifice and work ethic, as something to which all should aspire. Such patriotic symbols and activities included a pledge to the flag and commemorations of the death of key pre- and post-1959 historical figures, and of course the ever-present figure of Jose Martí in all Cuban schools. These activities illustrate the Revolution's efforts to (re)create the imagined, politically independent, Cuban nation, as "loyalty to patriotic symbols legitimized the existence of the new order and government, based in the preservation of ideals forged during the struggle against Spanish colonialism" (De las Nieves Barrios Sánchez, 2014, p. 10).

Che Guevara advanced the idea of consciously educating the *hombre nuevo* (the 'new man and woman') for the envisaged socialist and communist Cuba, and so began the idea of developing students' revolutionary consciousness in a meaningful way to support the use of moral over material incentives (Guevara, 1964b, p. 6). These interventions connected with Guevara's (1964a) elaboration of the role of individuals and politically conscious human agency in the construction of socialism and communism. Che warned against the production of "docile employees of the official line" (Guevara, 1964a, p. 10) in favour of the *hombre nuevo* with heightened political consciousness, including a sense of international solidarity that extended beyond the limited visions of the Soviet Union. Education Minister Armando Hart (1962) had similarly stressed the crucial role of the school in the desired political formation, asserting that "the environment that we create in each school will decide whether an individual that is formed in the school moves towards Marxism-Leninism or counter-revolution. . . . This is a fundamental truth" (p. 24).

These political commitments came to be expressed in organizational and curricular terms, reflected in the official affirmation that "Cuba persists in her aim to develop a new concept of education . . . in order to bring about the formation of the new man, a man of conscience and knowledge, needed by our country" (MINED, 1967, p. 3). The primary means of developing the consciousness of the *hombre nuevo* was through the concept of work-study, involving school students in some form of productive labour, first as Schools *to* the Countryside and then the mass programme of full boarding schools *in* the countryside. Fidel had noted in 1966 that "the aspiration of our society, of our Revolution, is that one day both manual and intellectual work will be realised by practically everyone" (Castro, 1966, in Castro, 1972, p. 2). Incorporating manual productive labour into formalized schooling was to be the mechanism for this formation. It was the envisaged vehicle to develop students' moral and ideological formation toward an imagined future in which social status and wage differentials between mental and manual labour occupations would disappear. In Che Guevara's idealized vision, through this form of education "work loses the obsessive character which it has in the capitalist world and becomes a welcome social duty which is carried out joyfully" (cited in Figueroa, Prieto, & Guitérrez, 1974, pp. 4–5).

The intended moral and ideological formation, and identification with the independent, socialist, nation-state, was also envisaged as coming through students' direct participation in the nation's economic development plans and projects, particularly in the field of agricultural production for the population. This in turn was expressed as a key dimension of the general polytechnical education of the population, helping to convince students of "the need to attain the technical development that will facilitate and increase the plans of food production" (MINED, 1967, p. 30). Implicitly and explicitly, the new model consolidated the concept of the national development project and its advance as a defining characteristic of the independent, socialist, Cuban state and Cuban nation.

Cuban education was directly linked to the project of independence and liberation, and breaking historical relations of economic and political dependence, first from Spanish colonial rule and then from United States neo-colonial domination. Students would not only directly contribute to production, but through their vocational specialization and training, they would contribute to future productivity advances of the country. From a world-systems perspective, the strategy was to develop the country's human capital as rapidly as possible, as a precondition for rapid, 'catch-up' style economic growth and development (e.g. Wallerstein, 2005). This broad characteristic of historical socialism is well expressed, for example, in

Khrushchev's (1956) exhortations that the Soviet Union's socialist development model would see the country rapidly overtake the capitalist model and deliver an "abundance of food and consumer goods" (p. 11). Speaking at an Inter-American economic and social council meeting in Uruguay in August 1961, Che Guevara similarly projected rapid growth rates of 10–15% p.a. for the next 20 years in Cuba, and per capita income to match that of the United States (cited in Brundenius, 1984, p. 48). Cuban education and work-study was thus tasked with developing students' "reverence towards work [and] . . . devotion to the common good" (MINED, 1960, p. 59) as required for the catch-up national development project, freed from the constraints and exploitation of foreign powers and foreign capital.

In April 1961, the United States' CIA-backed invasion of Cuba at the 'Bay of Pigs,' deploying Cuban exiles, was rapidly defeated, succinctly described by Chomsky (2011) as "just one in a long, dreary list of U.S. invasions and occupations of their countries, largely unknown in the United States itself" (p. 68). The events were the context for Fidel's proclamation of *Patria o Muerte*, cited previously. The CIA's 'Operation Mongoose,' which followed the failed invasion, escalated "punitive economic sabotage operations" like a series of attacks on the *Matahambre* copper mine, the third of which occurred in October 1962, "just as President Kennedy was announcing the presence of Soviet missiles on the island, and denying that Cuba could possibly have any need to defend itself from U.S. aggression" (Chomsky, 2011, p. 81). The Cuban Revolution was now projecting the Cuban nation in terms of its independent socialist political project and its triumphant resistance to CIA-backed imperialist intervention. As Gott (2005) concluded, "Castro had harnessed his revolutionary chariot to the powerful forces of a renewed Cuban nationalism and was beyond challenge" (p. 191).

2 An independent Cuban socialism

The October 1962 Missile Crisis was a crucial marker of Cuba's Cold War relations, and of Cuba's role in this global context, with the confrontation with the United States and threat of the Cold War becoming nuclear war. Crucially, the unilateral decision by Khrushchev to remove the nuclear weapons from Cuba, without consulting the Cuban government, provoked anger and distrust within Cuba. The affront to Cuba's newly found political independence was sharp, undermined by the fraternal Soviet Union. Moreover, Gleijeses (2002) documents how the accompanying concession or "pledge" by the United States not to invade Cuba if the missiles were removed was never formalized, and that the broad conditions that President Kennedy put forward for such an agreement left the possibility for a future invasion open. These world-shaking events occurred in a context of rich intellectual debate within Cuba about the nature and practices of its socialist project, seeking to carve out a clear position of independence from the United States, and from the Soviet Union and any further or future efforts from the socialist world to restrain the island.

The intellectual climate of Cuba in the 1960s is eloquently described by a key protagonist, Marxist scholar Fernando Martínez Heredia (2018), who offers a profound insight into the richness of the intellectual climate and discussion of the 1960s and how Cuba's revolutionary project might construct its own socialist path and project. Martínez Heredia (2018) was recruited to the University of Havana's Philosophy Department, which had been charged with teaching Marxist philosophy to students in all programmes in the university, as part of the intended political and ideological formation of the population and its professionals. The course began with the Soviet "Konstantinov manual" (p. 67), but he recalled that "by 1964 we understood that . . . the students deserved better" (p. 68). While Cuba's National Directorate of the Party schools had suggested a course on "Dialectical and Historical Materialism," Martínez Heredia and the department that he directed from September 1966 instead created their own course on the "History of Marxist Thought" and their own textbook that compiled the works of 27 authors from across the world, including some who "said things that we didn't agree with" (p. 71).

Martínez Heredia's (2018) reflections make clear that in this more radical and open period of debate in Cuba, he and his colleagues experienced opposition from those "committed to Soviet-style Marxism," and that they "had to deal with the avalanche of 'Marxism-Leninism' which had fallen on us since 1961. . . . But the visible predominance of Cuban socialism from 1965 favoured us" (p. 76) (for a review of the shifting space for such debate in Cuba see Griffiths, 2019). The project of defining an independent Cuban socialism, tied to the historical struggle for independence, was further advanced by the group's publication of the journal *Pensamiento Crítico*, from 1967. The editors noted in the first issue that the journal sought "to respond to Revolutionary Cuba's actual need for information about current developments in political and social thought," and that it would include "unedited articles from Cubans and foreigners, and the reproduction of selected articles from the most diverse publications in the world" (Consejo Editorial, 1967, p. 1).

This sort of open intellectual climate sought to articulate an authentically "Cuban socialism," connected to and simultaneously maintaining and an actively independent position within the international socialist camp, advancing the interests of 'underdeveloped' countries across the world. For example, when speaking to the Economic Seminar of Afro-Asian Solidarity in Algeria, Che Guevara publicly asserted that the Soviet concept of "mutually beneficial trade" between underdeveloped countries and the more 'developed' Soviet Union was "immoral" since it was by definition "based upon an unequal law of value and of international relations which are a product of that law" (cited in James, 1970, p. 132). In other words, such trade relations were cast as continuing the extraction of surplus value from the dependent and relatively underdeveloped country, now channelled to socialist USSR. Guevara argued that "the development of the countries who are now starting on the road to liberation should be paid for by the socialist countries" (cited in Domínguez, 1989, p. 66). He similarly went on to publicly accuse the USSR and its allies of effectively acting as "accomplices of imperialist exploitation" in their demand for any return on assistance for underdeveloped countries, adding that they had a "moral duty" to end this "tacit complicity with the exploiting countries of the West" (cited in Domínguez, 1989, p. 67).

In a similar fashion, speaking at an event to mark the formation of the Cuban Communist Party (PCC) in October 1965, Fidel proclaimed that "we will never ask anyone's permission to do something . . . to go somewhere . . . to befriend a party or a people" (Castro, 1965, p. 57). The sub-text here was Cuba's support for revolutionary and guerrilla movements internationally, sometimes at direct odds with the Soviet position. In 1967, Fidel championed Cuba's independent ideological credentials and its support for revolutionary movements, and he denounced (the then Soviet position) of an alternative peaceful and parliamentary road to socialism (see Castro, 1967; Primer Congreso de Solidaridad de los Pueblos de América Latina, 1968). This posed a direct challenge to the Soviet Union's support for the communist party in Venezuela's programme for a peaceful transition to socialism, while Cuba supported armed guerrillas opposing both the Venezuelan government and the pro-Soviet communist party. Anderson (1997, p. 533) concluded on this point that Cuban support for revolutionary guerrilla movements abroad came to be seen, or at least presented as, part of the project of Cuban socialism at home. This merged with the constructed cultural vision of the Cuban nation, defined by such international solidarity and support for others' projects for political independence and national development (e.g. Hickling-Hudson, Corona González, & Preston, 2012).

Concrete statements and actions like these gave tangible substance to the ideas of an independent Cuban socialism, to political independence even within the socialist camp amidst Cold War tensions. International solidarity abroad was as a defining feature of independent socialism at home, advancing corresponding causes for national independence and liberation from the legacies of colonialism and capitalist exploitation and domination.

3 The Soviet turn/institutionalization

In 1968 Cuba launched its 'Revolutionary Offensive' that nationalized over 50,000 remaining small (non-agricultural) businesses, driven by efforts to further advance the consciousness of the *hombre nuevo* (Domínguez, 1989; Rodríguez García, 1990). By this time, however, Cuba's independent foreign policy positions and actions had exacerbated tensions and negatively impacted on trade relations with the Soviet Union, compounding problems of worsening economic conditions and shortages at home. Gleijeses (2002) for example noted that "most Latin American Communist parties, Moscow's loyal followers, had come to resent Havana's encouragement of armed struggle in the hemisphere, irrespective of their wishes" (p. 29). In October 1967, Cuba had sent a lower-level Minister to lead the Cuban delegation to the 50th anniversary of the October Revolution, effectively boycotting the established inter-socialist protocols (Gleijeses, 2002, p. 218).

Diplomatic and political tensions, coupled with domestic problems, culminated in a decisive turn toward formal alignment with the Soviet Union. Wallerstein (1994) describes 1968 as a 'world revolution,' and a marker in the demise of the shared culture of liberalism across capitalist and socialist countries. The 1968 Soviet invasion of Czechoslovakia added to the new social movements' rejection of US imperialism and capitalist alienation, and of the bureaucratic, authoritarian Soviet alternative. Against expectations, Cuba's independent socialist project formally supported the Soviet action. It "provided the opportunity" (Gleijeses, 2002, p. 220) for the country to improve relations with the Soviet Union and to begin to improve and stabilize social and economic conditions at home. Martínez Heredia (2018) similarly highlights how the "severe economic shortages" (p. 77) impelled Cuba toward the USSR and the CMEA. This decisive shift, arguably, involved consideration of Cuba's future independence and vulnerability to a military invasion from the United States, in the sense that support for Soviet action in Prague carried a commitment to reciprocal military support from the Soviet Union to defend Cuba in the event of a future imperialist attack.

A period of political and economic reform followed, referred to as the institutionalization of the revolution, along Soviet lines and models. The official line invoked the need to "overcome the so-called errors of idealism of the previous phase, mainly the desire to advance too rapidly" (Martínez Heredia, 1991, p. 28). Full membership of the CMEA followed, along with conventional methods of economic planning and accounting reintroduced under the centralized System of Economic Management and Planning. The shift away from Che's more radical and idealistic approach of the 1960s to a more gradual approach to economic development, and the construction of socialism and communism in Cuba, was clear. Citing the preceding economic turmoil, Gleijeses (2002) surmised that "Cuba adopted the Soviet economic model. It was inefficient and wasteful, yet it was a dramatic improvement" (p. 223).

On the cultural and intellectual front, the early 1970s involved the imposition of a dogmatic political orthodoxy in accordance with the official Soviet line, and with no tolerance for any 'deviationism.' *Pensamiento Crítico* was shut down in August 1971 as part of a "strong ideological regression and a profound breakdown in social theory . . . embracing the institutions and beliefs of 'actually existing socialism' in so many fields" (Martínez Heredia, 2018, p. 78). Martínez Heredia (1995) described the mandated Soviet model of Marxism-Leninism as "a tragic use of the name of one of the greatest fighters for freedom and liberty in the twentieth century – [being] dogmatic, impoverished, dominating, authoritarian, exclusive" (p. 22). The 1971–1976 period came to be known within Cuba as the 'grey quinquennium.' Even the sympathetic account of Kapcia (2014) described this as the period of the "most Stalinist approach to culture" (p. 135) in the Cuban Revolution's history.

This "Stalinist approach to culture" had direct impacts on educational policy and official prescriptions for the political and moral formation of the youth. For example, the infamous First Congress of Education and Culture held in 1971 set out restrictive prescriptions towards all aspects of national cultural life in adherence with the rigid Soviet orthodoxy. These extended to detailed prescriptions of acceptable and correct behaviour for students, down to the level of appropriate musical tastes (no bourgeois Beatles), dress and hair styles for the youth (see Castro, 1971; MINED, 1971a, 1971b). They extended to definitions of "anti-socialist and deviant behaviour, specifically targeting homosexuality" (Kapcia, 2009,

). 61), which in turn contributed to a purge of gays within public institutions and positions of influence. Socialist discipline, rather than rebelliousness, was the dominant theme for the youth.

Disciplined manual labour was further promoted in the consolidated polytechnical and work-study model of schooling, leading to a major expansion of (both lower and pre-university) full boarding secondary schools *in* the countryside. A 1973 Ministry of Education Resolution 126–73 established, for the first time, a sequence of secondary school subjects dedicated to students' political education and formation: "Communist Morals" for year 10 and "Marxism-Leninism" for year 11 (Fernández, 1973). A special group of the Central Committee of the PCC was established to oversee the creation of curriculum materials and texts for full implementation by the 1974–1975 school year, and a special commission was established to analyze and revise the syllabus and teaching in preparation for the new subjects and the broader Marxist-Leninist orientation of all curriculum contents (Fernández, 1974).

In 1975 a detailed five-year plan for the improvement of the structure and content of general education was finalized and a programme for its implementation mandated (Fernández, 1975). The single, core curriculum established for the subsystem of general education further revised the secondary school political subjects and added a third to the primary curriculum, as follows: 1) "Political life of my homeland" for year 4; 2) "Fundamentals of political knowledge" for year 9; and 3) "Fundamentals of Marxism-Leninism" for year 12 (Fernández, 1975). Seven years later, well after the end of the restrictive 'grey' period, the Cuban Ministry of Education continued to call on Cuban teachers to struggle against all "ideological deviationism," particularly "anti-sovietism" (Ministerio de Educación, 1982, p. 36). The curriculum materials that Cuban Marxist scholars and intellectuals had resisted in the 1960s were institutionalized as the vehicle for students' political formation and their identification with the socialist nation.

The First Congress of the Communist Party of Cuba in 1975 further entrenched the broad educational policy. Schooling and the work-study principle focused on education's capacity to "prepare skilled workers . . . with the qualifications needed for them to assume the responsibilities that our economic, social, and scientific-technical development demands" (PCC, cited in Kolésnikov, 1983, p. 264). With respect to the cultural project of creating a distinctive sense of the Cuban nation, under such conditions, the reformed Cuban Constitution adopted in 1976 affirmed that work-study in and for the *patria* could "inculcate a high sense of socialist patriotism and proletarian internationalism" (PCC, cited in Kolésnikov, 1983, p. 264).

Cuba's independent socialist project now invoked a more rigid Soviet conception of the transition to socialism and communism, under the vanguard leadership of the PCC and its construction and consolidation of the socialist State and its institutions. The adoption and adherence to Soviet prescriptions was not absolute, however, as its ongoing support for international struggles and political movements such as in Angola and other parts of the African continent demonstrate (see Gleijeses, 2002, 2013).

4 Race, racism, Cuban education and the Cuban nation

We conclude this chapter with a return to some reflections on the question of race and racism in Cuba. We do this here to illustrate how the revolutionary project of constructing an independent Cuban nation effectively subsumed such dimensions of social and cultural life of the nation into the political and ideological prescriptions of the PCC and the socialist state and its requirement for formal political unity. The renowned Cuban anthropologist Fernando Ortiz (2014 [1939]) had famously defined the Cuban identity using the metaphor of a traditional Cuban soup, *Ajiaco*, a tropical melting pot of cultures, described as "exogenous streams – white, black, and yellow; of immigrants, interests, and ideas – [which] ceaselessly arrive, stir, and get dissolved in the Cuban broth, delaying the consolidation of a definitive and basic national homogeneity" (p. 478). Cuba and Cuban education in the Cold War arguably set out to consolidate a national homogeneity, but one defined in terms of Cold War politics, of the Party, its vanguard leadership, and the State, with no real space for even a politically progressive mobilization and identification based on African descent.

Some of these tensions and complexities are evident in symbolic, and authentic, acts of international solidarity within Cuba for the jailed African-American political activist Angela Davis. Students engaged in writing letters and postcards calling for her release, and they participated in subsequent meetings when she visited Cuba. Seidman (2020) for example considered the associated and iconic Cuban artwork depicting images of Angela Davis on postcards and billboards in Havana, in which her "Afro" hairstyle, as a symbol of black resistance and affirmation of African women's identity, contrasted with Cuba's position discouraging references to a corresponding Afro-Cuban identity. As Seidman (2020) notes, "both counter-cultural long hair and overt symbols of blackness were discouraged on the island, and the Afro falls squarely into both subversive categories" (p. 22).

The limited space for explicit Afro-Cuban identification and mobilizing, and indeed the active discouragement of such overt cultural expressions, does not negate the major advances against historical racism and its real, material, social and economic consequences in Cold War Cuba. These advances included access to and performance within formal education systems and subsequent representation across professions, something that wealthy and 'developed' countries of the core continue 60 years later to struggle with. De la Fuente (2001), for example, highlights how the "nationalization of private schools in July 1961 destroyed one of the most enduring pillars of racism in Cuban society . . . [since] most of these schools were segregated" (p. 275). The highly successful popular literacy campaign of the same year also brought basic literacy to the most marginalized sectors of the population, and "brought Cubans of different social backgrounds together" (de La Fuente, 2001, p. 275).

On the one hand, the project to eradicate or transcend historical racism in Cuba clearly referenced the 19th century liberation struggles that had sought to "create a new 'historical consciousness' that gave Africa and its descendants the place they deserved in the formation of the Cuban nation" (de la Fuente, 2001,

p. 287). For Morales Domínguez (2013) one of the Revolution's greatest achievements was that it "gave us a nation that gradually started to be for all" (p. 117). Critically, he argues that just as the 19th-century liberation movements struggled to resolve the question, in Cold War Cuba of the 1960s "other 'ghosts' got in the way," including "a revival of the age-old fear that a debate on race would seriously jeopardize Cuban unity," which was prioritized above all else in the face of United States hostility (p. 117). More pessimistically, de la Fuente (2001) concludes that "the [subsequent] lack of public debate about race and racism facilitated the survival and reproduction of the very racist stereotypes that the revolutionary leadership claimed to oppose. Historically, a unique opportunity had been lost" (p. 295).

Morales Domínguez (2013) concludes that "racism is to be blamed three times over for the unsuccessful attempt to found our nation" when the Spanish were defeated but victory was handed to the "Yankee imperial eagle's clutches in spite of all the blood that Cuban whites, blacks, and mestizos alike had shed for our independence" (p. 113). The three contributing dimensions of racism were its deployment to generate fear of national unity, to promote divisions within the rebellion, and to exclude non-whites from joining the Cuban nation. The ongoing political fear of division manifest itself as "a widespread aversion to recognizing its existence and tackling the subject as a part of the reality of our life" (Morales Domínguez, 2013, p. 114).

This sort of critique, after more than 50 years of Cuban socialism, reflects a deeper problem of the Cuban Revolution and Cuban education's emphasis on promoting an ideal of a single Cuban identity, of a sense of Cubanness, and accompanying calls for unity that was silent on the question of racial identities and differences. Indeed, the conflating of the cultural project of the founding the Cuban nation with the project of political independence, of Cuban and then Soviet-aligned socialism (as an expression of Cuban independence to determine such alliances), also meant silence on other dimensions of social and cultural identification and difference, suppressed amidst universalized services and calls for unity.

The Cold War context, the constant actual and threat of United States' aggression against Cuba, coupled with its geographical vulnerability, made the centrality of calls for 'national unity' understandable if the independent/pro-Soviet socialist project was to survive. The political and cultural projects were a continuation of a longer historical struggle. Political independence won through, and it was to be maintained and consolidated by national unity and loyalty to the Revolution, the State and the Party, in the face of adversity, of open hostility, and in the face of internal opposition that periodically left the island. Political independence emerged through a project of rapid, catch-up, national economic development that would overcome the dependent relationships of the past. Independence in these terms required a well-educated, disciplined workforce to deliver the requisite national development and a population educated about the historical struggles on which their current realities and the Cold War dynamics were grounded.

The Cold War, and Cuba's position within the Soviet Bloc, shaped the Cuban educational response from 1959, prioritizing human capital formation and politically loyal citizens for national development. The achievements of Cuban

214 Tom G. Griffiths, Euridice Charon Cardona

education within the conventional terms of mass and equitable participation, and of human capital formation, maintained throughout the various stages of the Cuban revolution, are remarkable. As an independence and liberation project, it is clear that discussion and debate about the (re)construction of the Cuban nation and the complex identifications and of its members must reckon with the Cold War expressions and limitations with respect to the cultural project, and continue to push beyond the bounds of ritualized and restricted political unanimity as national identity.

References

Anderson, J. L. (1997). *Che Guevara: A revolutionary life*. London: Bantam Books.
Azicri, M. (1992). The rectification process revisited: Cuba's defense of traditional Marxism-Leninism. In S. Halebsky & J. M. Kirk (Eds.), *Cuba in transition: Crisis and transformation* (pp. 37–54). Boulder, San Francisco and Oxford: Westview Press.
Brundenius, C. (1984). *Revolutionary Cuba: The challenge of economic growth with equity*. Boulder and London: Westview Press.
Castro, F. (1965). En el Acto de presentación del Comité Central del Partido Comunista de Cuba. In *Discursos: Fidel Castro* (Vol. tomo I, pp. 35–58). La Habana: Editorial de Ciencias Sociales.
Castro, F. (1967). Este continente trae en su vientre una Revolución: Tendrá un parto mas o menos difícil, pero inevitable . . . *Bohemia*, (33), 29–40.
Castro, F. (1971). *La Escuela en el Campo y el Congreso Nacional de Educación y Cultura: texto de las intervenciones de Fidel en las inaguraciones de las escuelas secundarias básicas en el campo "Ceiba Uno", "Primer Congreso" y "19 de Abril"*. Retrieved from La Habana: CDIP.
Castro, F. (1972). *Fidel: Escuela al Campo y en el Campo 1966–72* (Document No. 12452). Retrieved from La Habana: CDIP
Chomsky, A. (2011). *A history of the Cuban revolution*. West Sussex: John Wiley & Sons.
Consejo Editorial. (1967). Nota editorial. *Pensamiento Crítico*, (1), Inside cover.
de la Fuente, A. (2001). *A nation for all: Race, inequality, and politics in twentieth-century Cuba*. Chapel Hill and London: The University of North Carolina Press.
De las Nieves Barrios Sánchez, M. (2014). Pionero soy: de corazón. *Cubahora: Primera revista digital de Cuba*. Retrieved from www.cubahora.cu/sociedad/pionero-soy-de-corazon
Domínguez, J. I. (1989). *To make a world safe for revolution: Cuba's foreign policy*. Cambridge, MA: Harvard University Press.
Fernández, J. R. (1973). Resolución Ministerial 126/73: Sobre la formación ideológica. *Educación, III*(10), 80–82.
Fernández, J. R. (1974). Resolución Ministerial 02/74: Sobre una comisión para analizar y revisar la enseñanza de marxismo-leninismo. *Educación, IV*(13), 103–104.
Fernández, J. R. (1975). Resolución Ministerial 210/75: Sobre el perfeccionamiento de la estructura y el contenido de la educación general. *Educación, V*(18), 104–110.
Fernández Guevara, D. J. (2019). Constructing legitimacy in "stone" and "words" during Cuba's second republic: Building and contesting Fulgencio Batista's José Martí. *History and Memory, 31*(2), 117–154.
Ferrer, A. (1999). Cuba, 1898: Rethinking race, nation, and empire. *Radical History Review*, (73), 22–46.
Figueroa, M., Prieto, A., & Guitérrez, R. (1974). *The basic secondary school in the country: An educational innovation in Cuba*. Paris: The UNESCO Press.

Gleijeses, P. (2002). *Conflicting missions: Havana, Washington, and Africa, 1959–1976*. London: The University of North Carolina Press.

Gleijeses, P. (2013). *Visions of freedom: Havana, Washington, Pretoria, and the struggle for Southern Africa, 1976–1991*. Chapel Hill: University of North Carolina Press.

Gobierno Revolucionario. (1959). Ley Fundamental: De la Familia y la Cultura. *Gaceta Oficial*, (13), 6–8.

Gobierno Revolucionario. (1960). *Reforma Integral de la Enseñanza – Leyes: 559–561–680: Textos completos ajustados a la Gaceta Oficial*. La Habana: Editorial Luz-Hilo.

Gott, R. (2005). *Cuba: A new history*. London: Yale University Press.

Griffiths, T. G. (2019). Socialism in Cuba: Debate and socialist renewal for the twenty-first century. *International Critical Thought*, 9(2), 236–253.

Guevara, C. (1964a). El Socialismo y el hombre en Cuba. *Nuestra Industria Económica*, (5), 3–14.

Guevara, C. (1964b). Sobre el sistema presupuestario de financimiento. *Nuestra Industria Económica*, (5), 3–23.

Hart, A. (1962). *Sobre organización y trabajo en el Ministerio de Educación*. La Habana: MINED Departamento de Publicaciones.

Hickling-Hudson, A., Corona González, J., & Preston, R. (Eds.). (2012). *The capacity to share: A study of Cuba's international cooperation in educational development*. New York, NY: Palgrave Macmillan.

James, D. (1970). *Che Guevara: A biography*. London: George Allen and Unwin.

Kapcia, A. (2005). Educational revolution and revolutionary morality in Cuba: The 'New Man', youth and the new 'Battle of Ideas'. *Journal of Moral Education*, 34(4), 399–412.

Kapcia, A. (2009). *Cuba in revolution: A history since the fifties*. London: Reaktion Books.

Kapcia, A. (2014). *Leadership in the Cuban revolution: The unseen story*. London: Zed Books.

Khrushchev, N. S. (1956). *Report of the central committee of the communist party of the Soviet Union to the 20th Party Congress*. Moscow: Foreign Languages Publishing House.

Kolésnikov, N. (1983). *Cuba: Educación popular y preparación de los cuadros nacionales 1959–1982*. Moscú: Editorial Progreso.

Limia Díaz, E. (2021, February 20). Ante la memoria de nuestros abuelos y padres. *Juventud Rebelde: Diario de la Juventud Cubana*.

Maceo, A. (1968 [1878]). Independencia o Muerte, Libertad o Muerte, Patria o Muerte. *Pensamiento Crítico*, (12), 86–101.

Martínez Heredia, F. (1991). Cuban socialism: Prospects and challenges. *Latin American Perspectives*, 18(2), 18–37.

Martínez Heredia, F. (1995). Izquierda y marxismo en Cuba. *Temas: Cultura Ideologia Sociedad*, (3), 16–27.

Martínez Heredia, F. (2018). Thinking for ourselves. *Interview by Emir Sader. New Left Review*, (110), 57–82.

MINED. (1960). *Mensaje educacional al pueblo cubano*. La Habana: Cultural S.A.

MINED. (1963). *Plenos estudiantiles – Programa de actividades en la Escuela Secundaria Básica*. La Habana: Talleres Tipograficos.

MINED. (1965). *Primer Seminario de Unidad del Sistema Nacional de Educación* (Document No. 5224). Retrieved from La Habana:

MINED. (1967). *Cuba 1967 – the educational movement: Report to the XXX international conference on public instruction convoked by the OIE and the UNESCO*. Havana: Ministry of Education.

MINED. (1971a). *Congreso Nacional de Educación y Cultura: Dictamenes y Resoluciones, Temas 1–3*. La Habana: Instituto Cubano del Libro.

MINED. (1971b). *Congreso Nacional de Educación y Cultura: Memorias.* La Habana: Instituto Cubano del Libro.

Ministerio de Educación. (1982). VI Conferencia de Ministros de Educación Pública de Países Socialistas. *Educación, XII*(44), 33–39.

Morales Domínguez, E. (2013). *Race in Cuba: Essays on the revolution and racial inequality.* New York, NY: Monthly Review Press.

Ortiz, F. (2014 [1939]). The human factors of cubanidad. *HAU: Journal of Ethnographic Theory, 4*(3), 445–480.

Primer Congreso de Solidaridad de los Pueblos de América Latina, L. H. (1968). *América Latina: Educación y Cultura – Tomo I.* La Habana: Ediciones Políticas.

Rodríguez García, J. L. (1990). *Estrategia del desarrollo económico en Cuba.* La Habana: Editorial de Ciencias Sociales.

Seidman, S. (2020). Angela Davis in Cuba as Symbol and Subject. *Radical History Review,* (136), 11–35.

United Nations. (1948). *The universal declaration of human rights.* Retrieved from www.un.org/en/documents/udhr/index.shtml

Veltmeyer, H., & Rushton, M. (2013). *The Cuban revolution as socialist human development.* Chicago, IL: Haymarket Books.

Wallerstein, I. (1994). The agonies of liberalism: What hope progress? *New Left Review,* (204), 3–17.

Wallerstein, I. (1995). *After liberalism.* New York, NY: The New Press.

Wallerstein, I. (2005). After developmentalism and globalization, what? *Social Forces, 83*(3), 1263–1278.

Part IV

Paradoxes, inconsistencies and a self-reflection

13 Cosmopolitan nationalism and global citizenship rhetoric

Analysis of policies and curricula in South Korea, Israel and the United States

Miri Yemini, Laura Engel, Moosung Lee and Claire Maxwell

National education systems were developed in conjunction with the establishment and consolidation of modern nation-states, with schools tasked to teach and embed state-based narratives of belonging through rituals, languages, studies of religion and particular historical accounts (Green, 1997). All of these narratives speak to the notion of a continuously forming, accepted history of a place, which cements the idea of the 'nation-state' and of a shared and non-disrupted recounting of its formation and meaning (Tamir, 2020). These dynamics are especially complex in federal and semi-federal systems or in cases of conflict-ridden societies, when centralized nation-building attempts are resisted 'from within' by populations that may seek to make claims for autonomy or independence by proposing the establishment of regional or local schooling that articulates an alternative narrative of the nation-state and its history (Engel, 2016). Moreover, processes 'beyond the nation-state' are increasingly affecting the organization of education, curricula, imagined futures and constitution of individual school populations (van der Wende, 2007). While many benefit from new possibilities being made available beyond the nation-state, such opportunities are not equally available, and some people/groups prefer to stay closely connected to their nation-state. These contradictory yet powerful imperatives, which come from 'above' and from 'below,' are being played out within education.

Nationalism in this chapter refers to the building and sustaining of the common 'we,' based on joint cultural and political narratives of a group of people concentrated in a certain territory who believe they share joint histories and common destinies (Engel, 2016; Tamir, 2020). While traditionally this process has been nurtured by local symbolism, we argue that recently nationalism has been revived through the state-led fusion of global voyages into various aspects of national policy making; or in other words, in the cultivation of the political 'we' through a process we call 'cosmopolitan nationalism.' Cosmopolitan nationalism arguably demands the rewriting of the social contract in the educational sphere through transformation of national education policies and curricula so they comply with the globally oriented agenda imposed on, adapted by and consequently adopted by nation-states. We argue that nationalism, at least the way it is interpreted,

DOI: 10.4324/9781003137801-18

facilitated and practiced in schooling, is actually in some cases better described as 'cosmopolitan nationalism,' meaning that the sense of a joint past and present can be only sustained by co-imagining a cosmopolitan anchoring of being and behaving. This cosmopolitan nationalism is not banal, drawing on Billig (1996); rather, it exploits the global dimension to sustain and strengthen the national dimension.

In this chapter we explore through case studies of three countries the differing but also common ways cosmopolitan nationalism is being practiced within education today, through the prism of Global Citizenship Education (GCE). The 'global turn' in education (Goren, Yemini, Maxwell, & Blumenfeld-Lieberthal, 2020), a process initiated since the 1980s, has been further embedded by UNESCO's announcement in 2016 that GCE would become one of its Sustainable Development Goals (SDGs – 4.7). In particular, while schools were formerly entrusted with the responsibility of promoting a nationalistic agenda, nowadays a greater number of schools are adopting a cosmopolitan narrative, aimed at preparing students to participate in a more global world (Oxley & Morris, 2013). These globally oriented curricula foci are often grouped under GCE (Yemini, Tibbitts, & Goren, 2019). Broadly stated, GCE can be described as curricular contents and programmatic initiatives aimed at preparing students to function in a global society through the development of an understanding of global issues, empathy for people of different origins, a multi-cultural appreciation and global skill sets (Dill, 2013). GCE-related content can be diverse and may include, among other issues, knowledge of other cultures, education towards proactive protection of human rights and environmental awareness. At the same time, GCE is also focused on preparing students for the modern, globalized workforce (Myers, 2016). Many countries now promote GCE as a goal of schooling in general and specifically within subjects such as civics and social studies; many others offer variants of GCE, such as 'Global Dimension' and 'Global Awareness' studies (Oxley & Morris, 2013).

At the same time, policy-makers have continued to look and even travel beyond their national borders in an effort to locate and borrow international 'best practices' in education. Among the different educational discourses borrowed and traded across boundaries is GCE, now widely supported as a positive, necessary curricular focus. Sometimes GCE is incorporated into broader processes of internationalizing the curricula or adopting internationalized curricula, as happens with the International Baccalaureate (IB) (Prosser, 2018). In other instances, GCE is integrated through global assessments such as the OECD's PISA 2018 focus on global competence (OECD, 2018). In yet other cases, nationally instituted forms of citizenship education have now been replaced by GCE.

Arguably, these developments directly contravene the initial purposes of nationally organized education provision – to promote a national, coherent, state-based system of belonging (Resnik, 2019). And yet, as these processes and dynamics play out in different ways, the assumed binary between cosmopolitanism and nationalism becomes blurred. Rather, we see a complex and simultaneous overlay of nationalistic and globalist orientations within schooling.

Additionally, other factors affecting GCE vary widely and straddle global-national-subnational-local dimensions. Such factors include the ever-increasing movement of people between borders for temporary and permanent stays, rising aspirations for international mobility for (higher) education, stakeholders with varied interests demanding 'fit-for-purpose' curricula provision, different arrangements regarding who is responsible for schooling across countries and what is actually offered in schools. Frequently, the transformations are class-based, with access to the benefits of a globalized curriculum limited largely to higher socio-economic classes. Therefore, it is critical that the concept of 'cosmopolitan nationalism' is a multi-level and multi-dimensional framework through which to explore and better explain the constitution, implementation and practices of education found across the world.

We argue that in view of the increasing dominance of nationalistic sentiments and political power in the last decade (May, Byrne, Holmes, & Takhar, 2020), alongside the implications of border closures experienced during the COVID-19 outbreak, our understanding of how nationalism and education intersect requires re-examination. While nowadays, some interpret nationalism simply as xenophobia, we claim that nationalism (in its primordial forms and in its contemporary resurgence) is based on globalist rationales. Education systems are therefore struggling to make sense of what they must do for the sake of the nation-state and for its individual residents (citizens and non-citizens alike). The confusion will be further exacerbated if and when the world is able to move beyond or learn to live to COVID-19, which has disrupted schooling in most countries for significant periods of time. The apparent tension between the global and the local in education has already been studied extensively (see, for example, the *World Yearbook of Education 2005*). However, new challenges in education exacerbate the tensions in both directions, towards greater globalization and regional patriotism simultaneously (Billig, 1996; Fox & Van Ginderachter, 2018; Kymlicka, 2001). Often, internationalization is advocated by various stakeholders for the sake of the state's own development and competitiveness. This idea that internationalization will 'save the nation-state' comes in many guises with multiple outcomes. As such, it deserves renewed attention.

This volume aims to provide visibility to the variety of ways in which the national imagination has become embedded in, and promoted by, education in the era of globalized schooling. We understand the concept of cosmopolitan nationalism as located at the core of concurrent, and at times, conflicting pressures within national education structures promoting internationalization and a global gaze. At the same time, countries have to retain national/local cultures and histories, promote their economic development and build social cohesion amongst a continually diversifying citizenry. Sometimes these pressures work in concert (educating future workers who will be flexible, able to compete in a global economy and directly involved in sustaining their nation's development), while in other instances they seem mutually contradictory (for instance, the possibility that creating global citizens may undercut the primary loyalties citizens have towards their own countries). Similarly, while international organizations and systems of global governance have increased their influence in national and local education systems, some nation-states integrate these global dimensions to meet nationally oriented agendas. Cosmopolitan nationalism is the direct and overall outcome of these various pressures, a continuous effort performed by the nation-states and their agencies to promote the development of a common, national political 'we' that nonetheless has to, and wishes to, engage with global forces.

In this chapter we further develop the concept of cosmopolitan nationalism and empirically examine its potentiality for understanding current developments in three countries. In what follows we present examples of current developments in South Korea, Israel and the US to illustrate how specific policy trends and initiatives are integrating 'the global' within 'the national' and to consider what implications this has for the kinds of education being provided and the relations of (in)equality they foster. We undertake this analysis to illustrate how other scholars of education might draw on this concept of 'cosmopolitan nationalism' in their own work (as Wright et al., 2021 recently did). We have chosen to focus on these three countries as they represent a diversity of governmental regimes (unitary, adversary, federal), histories (relatively recently established counties or ones with trajectories over centuries), cultural influences (Confucian, Middle Eastern, Westernized), population heterogeneity, size and education system performance according to international measures. Despite these notable differences, each system is actively struggling with increasing pressures from within to address persistent inequalities and has undertaken significant investments of resources and policies aimed at internationalising the national education system.

1 The Korean case

Over the last two decades, South Korea (hereafter Korea) has encountered a "new" diversity moulded by a continuous growth of immigrants and interracial/ethnic marriage families.[1] The emergence of this new diversity has brought multiculturalism to the front stage of policy discourses in recent years (Lee & Cha, 2018) in two distinctive ways. On the one hand, multiculturalism has been endorsed as facilitating the pursuit of social justice and diversity. On the other hand, multiculturalism has been supported to acculturate ethnic minorities into the Korean society for the sake of advancing the nation-state's stable socio-economic development and maintaining strong national identity (Yuk, 2016). Running in parallel is a desire to promote global citizenship through education and Korea as a leading nation in this area. Consequently, such a political move has resulted in GCE becoming a key education agenda (Pak & Lee, 2018).

This emerging phenomenon originated in the 2012 Global Education First Initiative (GEFI), introduced by UN Secretary-General Ban Ki-Moon. The initiative focused on three priorities: *put every child in school, improve the quality of learning and foster global citizenship* (United Nations, n.d.). GEFI was welcomed by a group of 16 UN-member 'champion countries,' which alongside Korea included mostly Global South countries and a few Global North countries (e.g., Australia, Denmark, the US). Not surprisingly, the former group were particularly focused on the first two priorities, which reflect Education For All (EFA), aspiring that all children should have access to primary education by 2015. In contrast, the latter group of countries were invested in promoting official development assistance (ODA) and global partnerships/collaborations in education. Notably, Korea, meanwhile, concentrated considerable efforts on the GEFI's third priority – integrating global citizenship in its policies and curricula.

There are two major reasons for Korea to pay special attention to fostering global citizenship. At the micro level, Ban Ki-Moon, the UN Secretary-General, played a crucial role in promoting the idea within Korean policy circles. Since Ban was the first Korean to hold the top leadership role in the UN, he has had a powerful impact on Korean society. The 2015 World Education Forum, which was held in Korea, provided a political opportunity for Ban and the conservative-led Korean government to demonstrate leadership on global educational issues in the eyes of the Korean public. The Korean government proposed GCE as a key education agenda to display its educational innovation and to position "itself to be a global leader in GCE" (Cho & Mosselson, 2018, p. 861; Pak & Lee, 2018). Subsequently, the Korean government developed several GCE initiatives, including a revision of its national curriculum to reflect GCE under a broader policy goal of articulating "Korean Education that Harmonizes with the World" (as per the title of a Ministry of Education publication, 2018).

At the macro level, stakeholders in Korea generally embrace education policy measures which include the prefix *global* (Pak & Lee, 2018). Both the Ministry of Education and local education authorities have come to see GCE as assuring safe passage of proposed policy initiatives. Historically, many parents and students in Korea have been frustrated with features of the national education system such as the exam-oriented school culture, rote learning and severe academic pressure (cf. Kim, 2016; Seth, 2002). Therefore, central and local educational authorities have tended to be cautious about launching any new initiatives. However, they have learned, through experience, that using policy lexicon including *global* (such as global citizens, global leaders, global competences and global competitiveness) is one proven way to safeguard their policy agendas (Pak & Lee, 2018).

Given this context, the third GEFI priority – fostering global citizenship – was quickly translated into policy measures in Korea. Indeed, prior to GEFI in 2012, GCE was not a major policy direction for education reform in Korea. Rather, civil society organizations such as World Vision were the major players that engaged in GCE-related curricula or activities (Sim, 2016). Since 2012, however, a state-led model of GCE has been hastily developed. The government played an important role in encouraging schools to offer GCE activities, mainly integrated into social studies and school-based extracurricular activities, as part of the national curriculum. To this end, the government has focused on professional development programmes for teachers to implement GCE in their schools. Specifically, in 2015 the Ministry of Education initiated the 'GCE Lead Teacher (LT) Programme,' which aimed to provide knowledge and skills for selected teachers nationwide (Pak & Lee, 2018). The Ministry of Education also established a strong partnership with the Asia-Pacific Centre of Education for International Understanding (APCEIU) as an in-service teacher training institute for GCE. As of 2018, the GCE Lead Teacher (LT) Programme has produced 240 National LTs and approximately 2,500 Regional LTs.

Once teachers complete the GCE LT programme offered by UNESCO-APCEIU, they can use the title 'National LTs,' and are then expected not just to implement CGE activities in their school but also to design and operate Regional LT training programmes in their respective regional municipality (Pak & Lee, 2018).

As a centralized and input-driven strategy, this is a typical state-led initiative for school change. Yet GCE in Korea is viewed as a 'soft' state-led initiative for two reasons. First, although it has been actively promoted by the central government with designated resources, it is not compulsory. GCE is only encouraged as part of other existing subjects or school-based extra-curricular activities. While schools with a focus on GCE activities can obtain additional resources from the Ministry of Education (Cho et al., 2016), the implementation of GCE in schools is entirely voluntary. Second, the outcome of GCE is neither closely monitored nor critically reflected on in evaluating school-level performance.

Indeed, the Korean government's adoption and adaptation of GCE initiatives to local contexts can be characterized as cosmopolitan nationalism, given the following features. First, the state-led GCE aims to imbue 'the global' into its national curriculum explicitly, while it intends to locate Korea in the position of a leading nation in the global policy discourse of GCE. As an analogy, this move is like a nation vying to host the Olympic Games in the spirit of cosmopolitan friendship and global solidarity, while intending to bolster its own visibility and leadership in organizing the global event and beyond. Through implementing GCE, the Korean government reinforces the feature of the national political 'we.'

Second, the state-led GCE has an ambivalent feature, straddling cosmopolitanism and nationalism. On the one hand, the Korean government's justification for GCE as a policy measure for school change and innovation has been based on GCE's reputation as a highly rationalized global education agenda endorsed by credible international organizations pursuing cosmopolitan spirits, such as the UN and Oxfam. On the other hand, the implementation of GCE on the ground, within Korean schools, is based on an instrumental purpose to 'fix' certain problems facing the domestic education system, such as mitigating exam-oriented school culture and offering more meaningful educational experiences for students through a variety of GCE activities, instead of rote learning.

In sum, the state-led GCE in Korea shows how cosmopolitan features can be infused into national education systems so as to promote national interests and enhance visibility in global education governance, but also to solve the state's own domestic education problems with cosmopolitan elements embedded in GCE.[2] In this regard, the Korean case sheds light on cosmopolitan nationalism by illuminating how nationalistic motivation and justification within the process of the 'global turn' can instrumentalize (and possibly appropriate) educational ideas imbued with cosmopolitanism (Maxwell, Yemini, Engel, & Lee, 2020).

2 The Israeli case

One of the main tensions shaping the Israeli education system since the turn of the century is the pressure from the government to become more globally competitive

(Yemini, Bar-Nissan, & Yardeni, 2014), accompanied by simultaneous pressures to further embed the Jewish religion across the system[3] (Sabbagh, 2019). These obviously counter-acting forces shape the forms of education provision offered today and significantly affect the pathways of social mobility made possible for the various groups in Israel – in terms of outcomes, exposure to global issues and integration.

Israel has no formal internationalization policy and no explicit formal instructions for integration of GCE, but several documents engaging with possible future developments in this direction were published in 2016. At the same time, the Ministry of Education (MOE) has been widely criticized for the country's low scores in internationally comparative examinations and the perceived lack of readiness of its young people for the so-called globalized workplace, which is claimed to endanger the country's existence in light of prolonged conflict with neighbouring Arab states (Yemini & Gordon, 2017; Yemini, Bar Nissan, & Yardeni, 2014). The building of the "imagined community" (Anderson, 1983) is particularly challenging in a conflict-ridden state like Israel, since too many conflicting narratives of the historical foundation coexist. Hence, the nation-state must straddle a form of cosmopolitan nationalism in seeking to meet these challenging and conflicting needs. To illustrate the ways cosmopolitan nationalism operates in Israel, we focus on a secondary analysis of a key document published by the Israeli MOE in 2016 (Dvir, Maxwell, & Yemini, 2019), which aimed to set the agenda for the future development of the education system. This document (and the process underpinning its development) was the first time the MOE officially engaged with global dimensions within education, where it identified 'glocalism' (MOE, 2016) as one of the six pillars of a future-oriented pedagogy. However, the way it approached this objective and the final articulation of what this meant illustrates the restricted spaces within which internationalization can take place, as the nationalist tendencies continue to have a firm hold on the education system.

In 2016, the MOE published its first official declaration that school curricula and practices should have a global dimension. As stated in the document, this global dimension actually involves preparedness for global competition, while also strengthening national identification and knowledge of the 'world' (in essence of the Global North). Moreover, while the initial aim was to ensure compliance with the Organisation of Economic and Cooperative Development's (OECD) promotion of global competencies, given the way the policy was developed (through a relatively lengthy consultation process involving a wide range of actors), the MOE's final definition of 'glocalism' was rather vague; namely, "[t]he learner develops a systemic understanding of the environment, from the local level to the global one, and generates complex identity and consciousness that consists of a harmonious mix of global and local components and values" (MOE, 2016, p. 19).

We suggest that such a conceptualization of how the global should be integrated into the national is an articulation of a form of cosmopolitan nationalism – an awareness of, and affinity for, the global, which must always be achieved within the confines of a local frame (thus necessarily restricting its potential effect). Furthermore, such 'internationalization' has no 'policy teeth,' as it is not enshrined in curricular content and allows the different sectors of the Israeli education system to engage with and implement this principle in their own way. To date, the MOE has not issued any more specific guidance on how glocalism is to be worked into everyday practices. As we argue in Dvir and colleagues (2019), this situation has led to an uneven implementation of the policy, leading to a further embedding of the lines of stratification found across the system, whereby the secular sector embraces the new doctrine, while the religious and Palestinian Arab segments are less invested and also have less expertise to integrate it into their curricula.

GCE offers an additional obvious mechanism through which to develop and implement the principle of glocalism within Israel. While the MOE has not directly promoted GCE as a concept, GCE is a measurable SDG that will be considered in upcoming international comparative assessments. However, to date, GCE has been rather underdeveloped in Israel, especially within the formal curriculum. Until recently, the stated aims of the official civics curricula made no mention of the term itself; nor did the term appear in policy reform documents. Nevertheless, the curricula for civics education and geography do seem to be moving towards the inclusion of topics associated with environmentalism and human rights that could fall under the construct of GCE. Contents associated with GCE could theoretically appear in curricula for other subjects that are naturally affiliated with global contents, such as history and languages (namely English), but they do not yet do so. While some programmes are run primarily by NGOs in schools, these are usually extra-curricular programmes and remain rare.

Despite the potential for GCE to become incorporated within Israeli curricula, it remains a fairly underdeveloped area of the provision of education, in comparison to other countries, such as South Korea and Canada, for example (Buckner & Russell, 2013; Ramirez & Meyer, 2012). In studies seeking to examine how teachers from various education sectors (Goren, Maxwell, & Yemini, 2019) who work in schools with different socio-economic catchment areas (Goren & Yemini, 2017) interpreted the term, stark differences were found. Among marginalized groups (Palestinian Arabs), GCE is seen as offering a way of securing a sense of belonging to a global society. For already well-resourced social groups (the Jewish secular sector), GCE is viewed as a way of promoting global futures. Meanwhile, among the Jewish religious minority in Israel, GCE is seen as a threat to national identity and religious values. Furthermore, teachers' perceptions of their students' physical mobility and of the imagined futures they attribute to their students shape GCE teaching. Therefore, teachers' own experience of the global and their perceptions of their students strongly shape how GCE might be delivered. These differences are again reinforced as middle-class, more secular families extend their children's engagement with 'the global' through other activities (extra language lessons, travel abroad etc.).

A symbolic commitment to GCE has become embedded in the state's apparatus, through its principle of glocalism. However, its non-statutory status means that GCE is interpreted and implemented unevenly and varyingly in the segmented Israeli education system, with 'the global' being made more available to some groups than others. The concept of 'cosmopolitan nationalism' helps to make sense of this situation – where gestures towards cosmopolitanism are made, but national politics and long-standing stratifications continue to make cosmopolitan orientations and futures only available to those with the most resources.

3 The US case

Similar to Korea and Israel, GCE has continued to grow in significance within US education policy discourse, though in practice has remained disjointed and unequal. Over the past three decades, education stakeholders at local, state, and federal (national) levels have advocated for educational reforms to align with the changing global world (Stewart, 2009). Taking a cosmopolitan nationalism lens, it is possible to frame the extent to which these multiple levels simultaneously adopt, adapt and promote ideas of global citizenship, and how they are situated within national dynamics (Engel, Fundalinski, & Cannon, 2016; Frey & Whitehead, 2009; Parker, 2011). For example, since the 1980s, the federal government, 50 states and local districts have increasingly circulated and helped to centralize ideas and ideologies about 'global competence' in response to economic and demographic shifts (Fowler, 2013). Additionally, fervent concerns were voiced over the stagnation of US students' global competitiveness spurred by the 1983 A Nation at Risk report, continuing in 2002 with the No Child Left Behind Act and more recently, the Every Student Succeeds Act (Engel & Siczek, 2017). Discourses of 'falling behind' educationally and economically are well-articulated in the US Department of Education's international education strategy document (originally published in 2012; re-released in 2018). Analysis of the 2012 strategy suggests an overarching idea that global competence is a vehicle for enhancing individual and national competitiveness, taking precedence over other values, such as collaboration both within an increasingly diverse US society and with other people/countries around the world (Engel & Siczek, 2017). Here, *cosmopolitanism* is understood more instrumentally as opposed to more humanistically (Parker, 2011).

While there is an increasing policy discourse surrounding GCE in the US, forms of GCE vary greatly across districts and states. Within the US, the growing attractiveness of global competence (along with an unfettered educational marketplace) has fuelled a significant growth of international schooling and, in particular, the use of IB as an alternative to the local curricula. The IB has grown so significantly over the past two decades that in several states (e.g., Florida, Ohio, Virginia and Maryland) the IB's growth has far out-paced its growth in whole countries and regions of the world (Bunnell, 2010). Of particular concern, these changes are adding to and affecting the reproduction of social inequalities. For example, and in contrast to other systems, the IB in the US has been utilized as a mechanism of reforming schools labelled as underperforming (Bunnell, 2010). About half of these schools are designated as Title I, indicating that they enrol higher proportions of students from lower-income households (IB, 2012). In these contexts, the IB can be used as a 'rebranding' mechanism aimed at attracting middle-class families seeking internationalized educational approaches to enhance their children's cosmopolitan capital (Weenink, 2008). The IB is also used as an educational approach within schools for 'talented and gifted' children (Conner, 2008), further contributing to the stratification of the US population. Considering the varied ways that the IB is used by the different levels of education governance across the US, in some instances it may be disrupting patterns of stratification (the solution for a failed school, attracting the middle classes to state education), while in others it could extend them (offering multiple 'tracks' within the same school).

Additionally, in the US, GCE has been linked to and even conflated with multicultural education (Pashby & Engel, 2020). The US has a large and increasingly diverse population of roughly 330 million inhabitants, and non-white students now outnumber white students in public schools around the country. Of course, multiculturalism is not a new feature of the US system, and in fact it is among the most central characteristics of a US national identity. There are deeply fractured and debated ideas about who the "we" is within the US national context, and who has the power to define and to embody that common national "we." Among the most illustrative and poignant examples of this point are the events of January 6, 2021 – the storming of the US Capitol – and its aftermath, revealing the tensions between the US as the imagined melting pot of ideas, peoples and cultures, and its historical and present-day legacies of white hatred, white supremacy and exclusionary political processes.

Historically, public schooling has tended to follow a more subtractive approach toward cultural and linguistic diversity in favour of unifying the diverse population around specific national values, ultimately preferring the dominant European white culture (Sleeter & Grant, 1987). Multicultural education was an approach that sought to alter this dynamic by cultivating "an appreciation of diversity, social justice and human rights, equal opportunities and equitable power distribution" as a set of values shared across the US population (Kolar, 2010, p. 18). And yet, the launch of and the backlash against the 1619 project have laid bare the tensions in who defines and who gets included (or excluded) in the telling of the US national story. These debates illustrate the divergent views of how US history should be taught and the extent to which race and racial identity is centred in conversations about national identity and belonging.

Since the turn of the 21st century, scholars have increasingly advocated for greater synergies between multicultural education and GCE (Kolar, 2010) and reframed the cultural diversity within US society more globally (Banks, 2004). The reasons for this shift are both ideological and pragmatic, such as the advancement of humanistic and participatory democratic values and intercultural communication skills now required in the job market. To that end, interestingly, there appear to be similarities with Korea in the lacing of cosmopolitan elements in discourses of multiculturalism. We note in both cases that cosmopolitan nationalism becomes a way to make sense of the consequences of repurposing multiculturalism as a skill required for competitiveness in a global marketplace. Specifically, cosmopolitan nationalism conceptually assists in pulling apart the conflated discourses of global, national and intercultural education and making sense of complex dynamics, such as the ways that broader cosmopolitan orientations can in fact sidestep local and national expressions of intolerance and racial discrimination (Dower, 2008; Pashby, 2009).

While the illustration of the growth of the IB offers a rather complicated picture of how a cosmopolitan-inflected curricular change could disrupt or reinforce uneven opportunities for social mobility along race/ethnic and social class lines, we are also witnessing potential disruptions to the rural/urban divide across the US, led by the turn to the global. However, again, the interpretation of such cosmopolitan forms of innovation becomes usurped by local and nationalistic political ideologies, particularly in the wake of the Trump Administration's America First agenda. In rural communities, which have experienced intensive job losses and economic slow-down in the wake of the globalized knowledge-based economy, cosmopolitanism on the one hand has been viewed as an opportunity for economic revitalization (e.g., in Ohio and North Carolina), while on the other hand, has been resisted due to a concern about inter- and intra-state brain drain from rural communities to urban centres (e.g., in Indiana). How the global becomes integrated into the local varies hugely across different parts of the US, as do its effects on traditional social stratification processes. Applying the analytical lens of cosmopolitan nationalism to these developments helps make sense of these various articulations and consequences.

4 Concluding thoughts

Nationalism, as we have shown in this chapter, remains central to the making of education policies. As Tröhler (2020) stated, today perhaps more than ever "national path dependencies" (p. 14) shape educational realms in many places. The concept of cosmopolitan nationalism serves as a tool to examine how the global turn in education, articulated through the quest or pressure to internationalize, is taken up and implemented at the various levels of national education systems. Our analysis of such developments in three countries reveals that such educational innovations are heralded by policy-makers and practitioners as cosmopolitan in nature, internationally recommended and recognized, and critical to the preparation of the younger generations. And yet, as we also note, the application of the notion of cosmopolitanism in all three of the examples provided here is strongly instrumental and motivated by local and national concerns and priorities. Global features are embraced to reinforce the status of the nation. Global features are not only apparent in contemporary nationalism, but they are in fact the pillars that facilitate the continuous nurturing of nationalism. These priorities are local and diverse, as well as strongly embedded in the nationalistic rhetoric, aimed to improve particular nations' status and uniqueness. This is so even in the case of GCE, whose meanings and intended outcomes are shaped and regulated by global policies and international testing regimes (e.g., the PISA 2018 Global Competence). This underlying characteristic creates a rather uneven set of education programmes, which purport to be cosmopolitan, but in reality are nationalistic, particularly in their implementation (see, e.g., Engel & Siczek, 2017). Furthermore, the focus and knowledge base of GCE and global education remains rather unidirectional; hence, for example, despite the growing proportions of immigrant and refugees' children found attending local schools in many places, their cosmopolitan knowledge and experiences are rarely valued and integrated to create truly global classrooms which aim to make connections to global forms of belonging.

We found three common developments across our case studies. First, across all three countries, we found support for tackling the 'problem' of increasingly multicultural societies through the integration of internationally developed and recognized education models. As scholars previously noted (Dower, 2008; Pashby, 2009), discourses of global, national and intercultural education often overlap, making it difficult to tease apart the complex ways that schooling is framed as a mechanism for instilling tolerance, cohesion and mutual respect amongst increasingly diverse local and national populations within a nation-state. Since the state formation can no longer be based on internal cohesiveness, global models are imported to effectively mould the state's machinery (Tröhler, 2020). Simultaneously, these discourses also potentially overlook localized and nationalistic examples of intolerance, shifting focus instead to helping students procure the skills required in the workforce. It is possible, for example, for discourses surrounding GCE to advocate for universal values of humankind and global belonging, while practices oriented to national belonging allow for degrees of intolerance to persist (Engel, Rutkowski, & Thompson, 2019). Cosmopolitan nationalism, as a conceptual frame and analytical tool, may well assist in problematizing and illuminating these different discourses and dynamics across contexts.

Second, turning to 'the global' has also served as a way for state systems to attempt to more definitively tackle the perceived decline in the quality of educational provision and educational attainment outcomes – at both local and national levels. We found various examples of this tendency across the cases we reviewed. In Korea, for instance, the 'global' orientation in schooling was introduced partially in response to educational stakeholders' dissatisfaction with some traditional forms of teaching and learning in Korean schooling. Meanwhile in the US, 'global competence' has been broadly integrated into existing discourses of crisis in the 'failing' US education system, while also becoming increasingly attractive to middle and upper-middle class parents seeking advantages for their children in an ever more competitive educational marketplace. In Israel, the global element is linked to legitimization of the Jewish (and democratic) state. In all cases, education is seminal to the promotion of the nation-state.

Third, embracement of the cosmopolitan signs in policies and curricula (e.g., the IB, GCE) as a priority appears to be another way in which local and national governing bodies are seeking to reinstate their institutional legitimacy (for their citizens and for global audiences) as having the necessary expertise and leadership to tackle highly complex, globally oriented problems plaguing the system. In the Israeli case, for example, strong governmental support underlies such an objective, but the tensions between different fractions of Israeli society have resulted in the government introducing these cosmopolitan features in a seemingly consultative, open manner. Furthermore, under some circumstances governmental adoption of lobalism in education also comprises a direct ploy to gain greater technocratic ontrol, most prominently illustrated in the Korean case.

Traditionally, the inflection of cosmopolitanism into education has largely erved the needs of a small, already-advantaged minority. In each of the three ases discussed here, however, some evidence exists for a disruption to the rela-ionship between GCE and the persistence of inequality. For example, the rise nd growth of the IB and internationalized schooling as a turnaround strategy or 'failed schools' in the US has become a mechanism for attracting more afflu-nt, white parents.[5] Similarly, in Korea, the desire to be GCE global leaders has orced some change in the pedagogy promoted through the curriculum, from rote earning and exams to collaborative group work and communication skills. Thus, n conclusion, we offer the concept of cosmopolitan nationalism as a useful tool or our colleagues within the discipline to consider applying if they are seeking o understand how the global intersects with the local. It works as a framework which may offer a way to understand how the global may not always re-instate the relations of inequality found across most education systems.

Notes

1 This section is reconstructed from the third author's previous work (e.g., Maxwell et al., 2020; Park & Lee, 2018).
2 In our previous work, we suggested the introduction of the International Baccalaureate (IB) programmes into the national education system in Korea as another case of cosmo-politan nationalism (see Maxwell et al., 2020).
3 This section is reconstructed from the first author's previous work: e.g. Dvir et al., 2019.
4 Israeli public education is comprised of various 'sectors' serving its different populations: the Jewish religious sector, the Jewish secular sector, and the Palestinian Arab sector.
5 In recent years, the IBDP has been introduced to Korea and is portrayed in certain media and policy reports as a ready-made solution for fixing the persistent problems of the Korean schooling system. In this process, similar to the U.S. case, the IBDP has gained traction from middle-class parents given its track records as an internationally validated curriculum (Lee, Kim, & Wright, in press).

References

Anderson, B. (1983). *Imagined communities*. London: Verso.

Banks, J. A. (2004). Teaching for social justice, diversity, and citizenship in a global world. *The Educational Forum*, 68(4), 296–305.

Billig, M. (1996). *Banal nationalism*. Los Angeles, CA: Sage.

Buckner, E., & Russell, S. G. (2013). Portraying the global: Cross-national trends in text-books' portrayal of globalization and global citizenship. *International Studies Quarterly*, 57(4), 738–750.

Bunnell, T. (2010). The International Baccalaureate and a framework for class conscious-ness: The potential outcomes of a 'class-for-itself'. *Discourse: Studies in the Cultural Politics of Education*, 31(3), 351–362.

Cho, D., Kim, J., Lim, J., Lee, S., Jeong, H., Choi, J., Seong, S., Lim, M., & Shin, K. (2016). *Program development for global citizenship competence for secondary school students*. Seoul: Korean Educational Development Institute & Korea University.

Cho, H. S., & Mosselson, J. (2018). Neoliberal practices amidst social justice orientations: Global citizenship education in South Korea. *Compare: A Journal of Comparative and International Education, 48*(6), 861–878.

Conner, J. O. (2008). From international schools to inner-city schools: The first principles of the International Baccalaureate Diploma Program. *Teachers College Record, 110*(2) 322–351.

Dill, J. S. (2013). *The longings and limits of global citizenship education: The moral pedagogy of schooling in a cosmopolitan age.* London: Routledge.

Dower, N. (2008). Are we all global citizens or are only some of us global citizens? The relevance of this question to education. In A. A. Abdi & L. Shultz (Eds.), Educating for human rights and global citizenship (pp. 39–54). Albany, NY: SUNY Press.

Dvir, Y., Maxwell, C., & Yemini, M. (2019). "Glocalisation" doctrine in the Israeli Public Education System: A contextual analysis of a policy-making process. *Education Policy Analysis Archives, 27,* 124–134.

Engel, L. C. (2016). Defining and debating the common "we": Analyses of citizen formation beyond the nation-state mold. In J. Williams & W. Bokhorst-Heng (Eds.), *(Re)building memory: Textbooks, identity, and the pedagogies and politics of imagining community. Vol. 2: Textbooks, identity, nation and state* (pp. 345–353). Rotterdam: Sense Publishers.

Engel, L. C., Fundalinski, J., & Cannon, T. (2016). Global citizenship education at a local level: A comparative analysis of four US urban districts. *Revista Española de Educación Comparada,* (28), 23–51.

Engel, L. C., Rutkowski, D., & Thompson, G. (2019). Toward an international measure of global competence? A critical look at the PISA 2018 framework. *Globalisation, Societies and Education, 17*(2), 117–131.

Engel, L. C., & Siczek, M. (2017). A cross-national comparison of international strategies: National competitiveness or global citizenship. *Compare: A Journal of Comparative, 48*(5), 749–767.

Fowler, F. C. (2013). *Policy studies for educational leaders: An introduction.* Boston: Pearson.

Fox, J. E., & Van Ginderachter, M. (2018). Introduction: Everyday nationalism's evidence problem. *Nations and Nationalism, 24*(3), 546–552.

Frey, C. J., & Whitehead, D. M. (2009). International education policies and the boundaries of global citizenship in the US. *Journal of Curriculum Studies, 41*(2), 269–290.

Goren, H., Maxwell, C., & Yemini, M. (2019). Israeli teachers make sense of global citizenship education in a divided society-religion, marginalisation and economic globalisation. *Comparative Education, 55*(2), 243–263.

Goren, H., & Yemini, M. (2017). Global citizenship education redefined – A systematic review of empirical studies on global citizenship education. *International Journal of Educational Research, 82,* 170–183.

Goren, H., Yemini, M., Maxwell, C., & Blumenfeld-Lieberthal, E. (2020). Terminological "communities": A conceptual mapping of scholarship identified with education's "global turn". *Review of Research in Education, 44*(1), 36–63.

Green, A. (1997). *Education, globalization and the nation state.* London: Palgrave Macmillan.

International Baccalaureate. (2012). *Research brief: Title I IB schools (2009–2010).* Retrieved from www.ibo.org/globalassets/publications/recognition/title1schools-research_2012-1.pdf

Kim, Y. C. (2016). *Shadow education and the curriculum and culture of schooling in South Korea.* London: Springer.

Kolar, N. (2010). A comparison of multicultural education and international education in the United States. In B. Shaklee, & S. Bailey (Eds.), *Internationalizing teacher education in the United States* (pp. 17–40). Plymouth: Rowman & Littlefield Publishers, Inc.

ymlicka, W. (2001). *Politics in the vernacular: Nationalism, multiculturalism, and citizenship* (Vol. 157). Oxford: Oxford University Press.

ee, M., & Cha, Y. K. (2018). Editorial: A tale of two multicultural limbos: Damunhwa in South Korea and Zainichi Koreans in Japan. *Multicultural Education Review, 10*(1), 1–2.

ee, M., Kim, H., & Wright, E. (in press). The influx of International Baccalaureate (IB) Programs into local education systems in Hong Kong, Singapore, and South Korea. *Educational Review*.

Maxwell, C., Yemini, M., Engel, L., & Lee, M. (2020). Cosmopolitan nationalism in the cases of South Korea, Israel and the US. *British Journal of Sociology of Education, 41*(6), 845–858.

May, V., Byrne, B., Holmes, H., & Takhar, S. (2020). Introduction: Nationalism's Futures. *Sociology, 54*(6), 1055–1071.

MOE. (2016). *Future pedagogy establishing document*. Jerusalem: MOE.

Myers, J. P. (2016). Charting a democratic course for global citizenship education: Research directions and current challenges. *Education Policy Analysis Archives/Archivos Analíticos de Políticas Educativas, 24*, 1–19.

OECD. (2018). *The OECD PISA global competence framework*. Retrieved from www.oecd.org/pisa/Handbook-PISA-2018-Global-Competence.pdf

Oxley, L., & Morris, P. (2013). Global citizenship: A typology for distinguishing its multiple conceptions. *British Journal of Educational Studies, 61*(3), 301–325.

Pak, S. Y., & Lee, M. (2018). 'Hit the ground running': Delineating the problems and potentials in State-led Global Citizenship Education (GCE) through teacher practices in South Korea. *British Journal of Educational Studies, 66*(4), 515–535.

Parker, W. (2011). 'International education' in US public schools. *Globalisation, Societies and Education, 9*(3–4), 487–501.

Pashby, K. (2009). The Stephen Lewis Foundation's Grandmothers-to-Grandmothers Campaign: A model for critical global citizenship learning. *Critical Literacy: Theories and Practices, 3*(1), 59–70.

Pashby, K., & Engel, L. C. (2020). Global citizenship education and teacher education in North America: US and Canada. In C. C. Wolhuter & D. Schugurensky (Eds.), *Global citizenship education and teacher education* (pp. 233–249). London: Routledge.

Prosser, H. (2018). Elites go public? International Baccalaureate's decolonising paradox in Ecuador. In C. Maxwell, U. Deppe, H. H. Krüger, & W. Helsper (Eds.), *Elite education and Internationalisation* (pp. 229–245). Cham: Palgrave Macmillan.

Ramirez, F. O., & Meyer, J. W. (2012). Toward post-national societies and global citizenship. *Multicultural Education Review, 4*(1), 1–28.

Resnik, J. (2019). Struggling for recognition: Access to higher education through the International Baccalaureate. *Critical Studies in Education, 60*(3), 340–357.

Sabbagh, C. (2019). "Glocal" neoliberal trends in Israeli education: The case of religionization. *International Journal of Educational Development, 68*, 88–95.

Seth, M. J. (2002). *Education fever: Society, politics, and the pursuit of schooling in South Korea*. Honolulu, HI: University of Hawaii Press.

Sim, H. R. (2016). Global citizenship education in South Korea through civil society organizations: Its status and limitations. *Asian Journal of Education, 17*, 107–129.

Sleeter, C., & Grant, C. (1987). An analysis of multicultural education in the United States. *Harvard Educational Review, 57*(4), 421–445.

Stewart, V. (2009). Becoming citizens of the world. In M. Scherer (Ed.), *Supporting the whole child: Reflections on best practices in learning, teaching and leadership* (pp. 182–194). Alexandria, VA: ASCD.

Tamir, Y. (2020). *Why nationalism*. Princeton, NJ: Princeton University Press.

Tröhler, D. (2020). Nation-state, education and the fabrication of national-minded citizens (Introduction). *Croatian Journal of Education: Hrvatski časopis za odgoj i obrazovanje* 22(Sp. Ed. 2), 11–27.

United Nations. (n.d.). *Global education first initiative*. Retrieved August 19, 2021, from https://www.un.org/millenniumgoals/pdf/The%20Global%20Education%20First%20Initiative.pdf

Van der Wende, M. (2007). Internationalization of higher education in the OECD countries: Challenges and opportunities for the coming decade. *Journal of Studies in International Education*, 11(3–4), 274–289.

Weenink, D. (2008). Cosmopolitanism as a form of capital: Parents preparing their children for a globalizing world. *Sociology*, 42(6), 1089–1106.

Wright, E., Ma, Y., & Auld, E. (2021). Experiments in being global: The cosmopolitan nationalism of international schooling in China. *Globalisation, Societies and Education*, 1–14.

Yemini, M., Bar-Nissan, H., & Yardeni, O. (2014). Between "us" and "them": Teachers' perceptions of the national versus international composition of the Israeli history curriculum. *Teaching and Teacher Education*, 42, 11–22.

Yemini, M., & Gordon, N. (2017). Media representations of national and international standardized testing in the Israeli education system. *Discourse: Studies in the Cultural Politics of Education*, 38(2), 262–276.

Yemini, M., Tibbitts, F., & Goren, H. (2019). Trends and caveats: Review of literature on global citizenship education in teacher training. *Teaching and Teacher Education*, 77(1), 77–89.

Yuk, J. (2016). Analyzing the anti-multiculturalists' construction of the 'other' and the allotropic relationship between multicultural and anti-multicultural discourses. Korean Journal of Sociology, 50(4), 109–134. [written in Korean]. 육주원. (2016). 반다문화 담론의 타자 만들기를 통해 본 다문화-반다문화 담론의 협력적 경쟁관계. 한국사회학, 50(4), 109–134.

14 The imperial nationalism of human rights and genocide education laws

Cases from the United States

Hannah Spector

As declared by the US Department of State (2021), the United States has a "tradition of protecting and respecting human rights, both at home and abroad." This tradition is expressed in the two most significant documents in this nation-state's history: the Declaration of Independence and the Constitution; it is also communicated internationally in the Universal Declaration of Human Rights and the United Nations Declaration of Human Rights Defenders. The State Department also maintains that one of the ways human rights defenders can do their morally righteous work is by "educating and training others on human rights." Complementing this stance on human rights, the US Atrocities Prevention Board (2017) professes its commitment to the prevention of "mass atrocities against civilians" throughout the world. Mass atrocities are deemed the most serious international crimes – i.e., genocide, war crimes and crimes against humanity (United Nations, 2014). With these seminal national and international documents, the US – a nation-state that is comprised of a federation of states that constitute its institutionalized statehood – presents itself as a nation with cosmopolitan values. In this study, the 'nation' is understood to be a cultural thesis concerning belonging and commonality; the 'state' is a system of governance that exercises political power. As an instrument of state power, compulsory education on human rights and genocide helps buttress the aforementioned interests of the nation.

National interests can be seen in a collection of education legislation passed by state legislatures that speak the same discourse as the State Department does on the importance of safeguarding human rights and preventing mass atrocities. To date, 15 states within the US have amended their respective school codes to require in various capacities instruction on human rights and genocide, with more states promising to follow suit (PR Newswire, 2017). The majority of these laws place particular emphasis on educating American youth about the Holocaust and genocide. Though states are increasingly mandating instruction on this 'unthinkable' subject, these bipartisan-driven legislative acts have received slight attention in educational research. In her singular legal analysis on the subject, Bitensky (2018) refers to this "little noticed phenomenon in American law" (p. 51) as "an obvious good in itself and an opportune stiffening of society's shared moral backbone" (p. 54). A good that comes by way of a "growing and righteous vanguard of states" (p. 51) that mandate "education about the foulest crime of all."

DOI: 10.4324/9781003137801-19

This chapter takes a more self-critical view of the aforementioned statutes for several reasons to be developed in this analysis. First, research concerning a state's 'goodness' written from the perspective of a citizen working in and/or for that state ought to be looked at as suspect. This is particularly true of scholarship that comes out of the US pertaining to this state's questionable relationship with human rights (e.g., Human Rights Watch, 2020) and genocide (e.g., Herman & Peterson, 2010; Jones, 2004). Without paying heed to the atrocities perpetrated by one's own state, that state is surely to continue acting atrociously. Second, and related to the first, when particular genocides are named in the laws to be interrogated, they are ones that have occurred 'faraway,' been perpetrated by 'others,' and/or survivors were liberated by 'us.' In other words, examples of atrocious human behaviour are sought and found in distant places for educational purposes so as not to question US dignity. The laws that also require instruction on human rights do not reference particular violations. However, as genocide is comprised of the most heinous human rights atrocities, teaching the former is a sufficient and efficient way of accomplishing the latter.

Third, a vast majority of school codes across the US do not legally require instruction on African American history (King, 2017), which could include inquiry into the *legalized genocide of colored people*: "one person at a time, so as not to cause any alarm" (Crump, 2019, p. 5), and 27 states do not mention Native Americans in their K-12 curriculum (Janzer, 2019) – let alone the cultural genocide of indigenous populations in North America by settler colonialists (Kingston, 2015). This does not mean that teachers do not educate students on these or other dark parts of America's past or present – though such teachings have been deemed un-American by the highest levels of political office (see Waxman, 2020). The very thought that those states to require instruction on human rights violations would include examples that paint American goodness in a bad light would surely be deemed un-American too.

Fourth and last, while human rights as a concept is said to be inherent to all human beings, in and for the US, some humans and their rights count more than others. While the US as political institutionalization of a nation claiming to be moral is not alone in such moral duplicity, this nation-state presents itself as *the* beacon of goodness whose goodness is in need of being exported to 'bad' parts of the world. This goodness has been articulated in its foreign policy as "advancing freedom and democracy . . . to support democracy and human rights" (US Department of State, n.d.). That it has been advanced at times with "forceful diplomacy" (Heiss, 2002, p. 528) and military action that includes civilian casualties (Gibbons-Neff, 2020) is educationally irrelevant. While some have argued that American hegemony waned under the Trump doctrine of "America first" (Cooley & Nexon, 2020), state-based discourse on international human rights has been waxing as illustrated in the uptick of education legislation that speaks to their protection. As such, understanding the politics of rights is a key component of becoming educated on human rights. However, the human rights and genocide education laws emerging across the US do not heed a need for critical engagement with the nature of human rights as orthodoxy and (il)legitimate action. This may well be because genocide and its denial is, like human rights, a highly politicized subject. The politicization of both in and by the US for (imperial) nationalistic reasons is the central thematic of this chapter.

Though the universality of 'inalienable' human rights is often associated with cosmopolitanism (Spector, 2020), this chapter aims to interpret the aforementioned laws in terms of nationalism and its cultivation in education. And though there are social, cultural and political differences in various regions of this country where these laws are located, it is striking to observe such a similar value system across state statutes. While different words (*parole*) are used in the statutes, the discourse (*langue*) across laws is much the same. This sameness may be seen to attest to a national interest in educating American youth on human rights and genocide. Understanding the politics that undergird human rights and the genocidal designation will provide a foundation for interpreting these laws in nationalistic terms and with attention to imperialism. In the case of the US, nationalism is not separate from imperialism. As Weeks (1994) describes in his writings on "Americanism" (p. 486), "the nation cannot be understood apart from the development of the empire" (p. 490). That Americanism can be found in education laws that speak a cosmopolitan *parole* are part of the laws' duplicity. From an educational point of view, what is so remarkable about Americanism is that it can be legislated for school-based curriculum and instruction across states in such a way that the laws appear anti-nationalistic, anti-imperialistic, and do not mention the US at all.

The *parole* and *langue* of the laws will be examined in light of the ways that certain histories are remembered, and others are forgotten, as educational strategies for building nationalistic sentiment in American schools. That human rights must be protected and genocide need be denounced are universally commendable values. These values are also particular to the US, as the US has the power "as the world's ordering agent" (Wertheim, 2020, p. 7) to decide whose rights 'at home' and 'abroad' are worthy of protection and which atrocities are considered genocidal. I frame this study with the concept of banal nationalism (Billig, 1995), which is explicated in the following section. The document-based analysis of the laws will be undertaken in terms of what the *parole* says in each of the laws and what patterns (consistencies) or breaks in patterns (inconsistencies) can be found in the *langue*. I conclude with a reflection on why the imperial nationalism of these laws matter.

1 The banal nationalism of the world's most powerful nation-state

It is striking to observe how little attention has been paid to US nationalism in social science scholarship – "even from specialists in nationalism" (Billig, 2009, p. 351). Billig has expressed surprise and disappointment that "the world's most powerful nationalism – that of the United States" has not been taken up in the research. "Instead, it has been the less powerful nationalisms that have attracted attention." In speaking to Billig's observation, Szulc (2017) notes, "research on online banal Americanism as being reproduced in the US is virtually nonexistent" (p. 68). Educational research on US nationalism (banal or otherwise) does not appear much different in this regard. A look at the American Educational Research Association's annual meeting themes over the last several decades supports these perceptions as the words *nation, nationality* and *nationalism* are unapparent. Globally, however, studies in nationalism and education have been gaining attention as showcased in the thematic of the *World Yearbook of Education 2022.* With these observations in mind, this chapter of the *Yearbook* seeks to examine that which has been largely overlooked in educational research: the, at once, banal and imperial nationalism of the world's most powerful nation-state.

Considered "the best known single work in nationalism studies" (Breuilly, 2016, p. 625) is Anderson's book *Imagined Communities*. In it, Anderson (1983/2016) observes that "[n]ation, nationality, nationalism – all have proved notoriously difficult to define, let alone analyze" (p. 3). This is said to be the case despite the fact that nation-states exist everywhere, and nationalism has exerted tremendous influence throughout the modern world. This does not mean that articulations of nationalism have lacked. According to Berlin (1972), nationalism is "an enflamed condition . . . caused by wounds, some form of collective humiliation" (p. 17) "on the part of colonial peoples against their imperialist masters" (p. 20). Berlin seems to equate nationalist uprisings with feelings of inferiority. Nationalism arises in a people "who cannot boast of great political, military, or economic achievements" in the same way that those nation-states that deem themselves "rationalists and liberals" (p. 19) can. If one is to understand nationalism in this way, the US is not the first country that comes to mind and does not make an appearance in Berlin's essay on the subject. Anderson, too, pays little attention to the US.

In his review of Anderson's work, Goswami (2020) does not mention the US once. He does note, however, a peculiar irony that "research on nationalism and the nation form by historians is in relative decline, even as we are, almost everywhere, awash in nationalist populism" (p. 446). The US is one of those nation-states where national populism and "nativist discourse" (Bonikowski, 2019, p. 110) has been backed in recent years by a major political party. It would thus seem to follow that laws requiring schools to provide instruction on the importance of protecting human rights and preventing genocide would push back against the kind of isolationism, group hatreds and xenophobia that nationalism welcomes. And while nationalism does not always lead to genocide, genocide – which relies on ideology and terror to deny the humanity and, therefore, rights of different Others – has been a culminating expression of extreme nationalism.

Nationalism, however, does not always announce itself explicitly. Nor does it simply arise in a people who have been oppressed by an imperial power. According to Billig (1995), "established nations" – i.e., those nation-states that are "at the centre of things" (p. 5) above and beyond the fact of their institutionalized statehood – "never spoke with a straightforwardly simple voice" (p. 176) about their nationalism. Rather, the nationalism of "established" nation-states reveals itself through a "complex dialectic of remembering and forgetting" (p. 37) that not only involves "collective amnesia" toward "the violence which brought a ation into existence" and shared remembrance for "ideologically convenient acts from the past." The nation-state's present day is dealt with in much the same way. This dialectic is said to operate "mindlessly, rather than mindfully" vis-à-vis routinized remembrance days and flags that present themselves unobtrusively in public. These daily, mundane operations are said to "reproduce" nationalism in established nation-states (p. 39). However banal these "flaggings" might be, there need be only a conscious willingness to look toward the background or attend to the little words" (p. 174) to find the inculcating spirit of nationalism at work. Billig stresses that though these flaggings may be banal, banal nationalism is not benign as it "reproduc[es] institutions with vast armaments" (p. 7). These armaments are always "primed, ready for use in battle," as is support of their use when needed.

The nationalism of established nations also presents itself under the guise of cosmopolitanism. "'[W]e' are global citizens" (Billig, 2009, p. 351), and 'they' are still struggling to achieve (inter)national recognition. The nationalism of the world's most powerful nation-state also masks itself by speaking in terms of society. 'Our society' (Billig, 1995, p. 55) holds the same values as all civilized "societies" (p. 53). Should these unquestionable values ever be threatened, they are "worth the price of sacrifice" (p. 175). "Today," he adds, "claims about a 'world community' or a 'new global order' are being made on behalf of the most powerful nation. As they are made, so an identity of interests is asserted: 'our' interests are the interests of the whole world" (p. 176). These interests are spoken about in terms of rights: "'We' must recognize the rights of others, whilst speaking for these others, and while reminding 'ourselves' that 'we,' the greatest nation in history, stand for 'our' own interests" (p. 90). In the American context, imperialism and nationalism are inextricably linked. While American imperialism may go about its imperializing differently than previous imperialisms (e.g., Vogel, 2006), the US nevertheless seeks to "Americanize the world" (Weeks, 1994, p. 490). To think of the two (nationalism and imperialism) as being at odds with each other obfuscates what has taken place in and by the US politically and militarily since World War II. This obfuscation may have something to do with reasons why US nationalism has gone largely unexamined in social science research.

The nationalism of established nations in the West is examined in a number of ways that are tied to a "whole complex of beliefs, assumptions, habits, representations and practices" (Billig, 1995, p. 6) that are "reproduced in a banally mundane way." Key examples in Billig's study include "the structuring of newspapers" (p. 8), political discourse that is "continually reported in the mass media" (p. 11) and the words of influential philosophers that may appear at first glance to "possess a cosmopolitan broadness of spirit" (p. 12) but actually wave gently in support of their homeland (p. 174). However, there is little attention placed in Billig's work on nationalism that gets developed in schools. An obvious way that banal nationalism can literally be seen and heard and which Billig points to is in the routine of pledging allegiance to the US flag (p. 50). Some may see this action as patriotic and not nationalistic because it is not a "fanatical" or "irrational" thing to do (p. 56). Whether one calls the performance of the pledge patriotic or nationalistic, it is nevertheless banal because it is a physical and verbal activity built into the school day that is done somewhat mechanically.

As banal nationalism also works metaphysically, the pledge only reveal so much about the ways in which US nationalism operates at an educationa level. If banal nationalism can be seen by paying attention to the "little words" (p. 174), it also can be found in those words that are present (remembered) and absent (forgotten) in education laws that project cosmopolitan values but on closer inspection support American interests. While the *parole* within the laws is not the same in every state, a national identity can nevertheless be found in the *langue* across laws. This identity "celebrates itself" (p. 50) without ever mentioning the national self. It is a celebration in which the written words are neither dangerous nor irrational in a conventional nationalistic sense *a la* "the language of blood: a call to arms which can end in the horrors of ethnic cleansing" (Ignatieff as cited in Billig, 1995, p. 48). However, the unwritten words function by denying horrors of similar magnitude that have taken place 'at home' and/or by 'us' while supporting the imperial nationalistic interests of the world's most powerful nation-state.

2 A national identity that speaks without speaking of itself

When interpreting the laws in question, I look to the linguistic theory of *langue* and *parole*. In the Saussurian sense, communication is conceptualized as a two-tiered system. *Langue* is "an abstract and invisible layer of language" (Fendler, 2014, p. 17) that governs communication within a shared community such as a nation; *parole* is the idiosyncratic use of words. For Saussure, *langue* is more powerful and thus holds a more privileged position than *parole* as it is connected to the fact that humans have the capacity to create a language – i.e., "a system of distinct signs corresponding to distinct ideas" (Saussure as cited in Gordon, 2004, p. 78). Others see *parole* as an instantiation of *langue* or that *parole* reveals *langue* (see Gordon, 2004, p. 87). In each of these senses, there are nevertheless said to be "underlying patterns" (Fendler, 2014, p. 19) found in the *langue* more so than on the surface of the *parole*. These thoughts on communication inform this analysis given what is (not) included in the *parole* of the laws.

A note of interpretive caution is in order. Though there may be consistencies in the *langue*, consistencies do not presuppose, following Foucault (1972/2010), a totalizing "secret law" (p. 150) – unwritten by a secret society of legislatures – in which "the semi-nocturnal unity of an overall figure" (p. 152) is unveiled and "its truth is at last to be revealed" (p. 151). The application of a law into standards, resources, or practices may reveal inconsistencies, but these areas of education go beyond the scope of a limited analysis on education law. Here, I study laws that prescribe what American youth are to remember (the written word) and what they are to forget (the unwritten word) concerning human rights and genocide. After the laws are examined in groups based on features, a summative analysis of all the laws will be looked at in terms of the banal nationalism of American imperial nationalism.

The Holocaust as American memory

The laws in Florida, Texas and Indiana are grouped together because they have a relatively narrow and nearly identical educational focus. Schools are required to provide instruction on the Holocaust. In Florida, the Holocaust shall be taught for the purposes of encouraging tolerance of diversity in a pluralistic society and nurturing and protecting democratic values" (Education – K-20 . . ., 2002, 2.f.). Texas requires its schools "to educate students about the Holocaust and inspire in students a sense of responsibility to recognize and uphold human value and to prevent future atrocities" (An Act Relating to Holocaust . . ., 2020, Sec. 1.b.). The entire Indiana mandate states: "a study of the Holocaust in each high school United States history course" shall be included (An Act to Amend the Indiana . . ., 2020, Sec. 7.1.c.).

These statutes support Novick's (2000) argument that "the Holocaust is an American memory" (p. 15). Why is it an American memory? The *parole* indicates that the Holocaust must be remembered so that American youth learn about the importance of protecting democratic values and valuing all human beings. However, it is also politically advantageous to remember the horrors of the Holocaust because they help the US evade responsibility for what it "has done to blacks, Native Americans, Vietnamese, or others" as these wrongs are not nearly as wrong as what the Nazis did. Moreover:

> It is much easier to deplore the crimes of others than to look at ourselves. It is also true, however, that were the will there we could learn much about ourselves from the Nazi experience. Manifest Destiny anticipated nearly all the ideological and programmatic elements of Hitler's Lebensraum policy.
> (Finkelstein, 2003, p. 145)

With these inward-looking critiques in mind, the school codes in these particular states do not reference the persecution or destruction other groups in or by the US when speaking about what and who to value. Florida's statute that requires instruction on "the history of African Americans" (Education – K-20 . . ., 2020, 2.h.) states that slavery was simply an "experience" (g). The history of the Holocaust, on the other hand, is described as "a watershed event in the history of humanity, to be taught in a manner that leads to an investigation of human behavior . . . prejudice, racism, and stereotyping." Native Americans are not included in Florida education law. That the Holocaust became a legally required curriculum in Texas in 2019 – a state that has one of the largest Hispanic populations in the country (Krogstad, 2020) – is noteworthy given what is not written into the law's *parole* when educating on "human value." The documented human rights abuses taking place against Hispanic women and child refugees and asylum seekers in US Immigration and Customs Enforcement detention facilities in Texas and other neighbouring states on the US-Mexico border (Bochenek, 2018) are not found (and would not be found for nationalistic reasons) in US-based education law. Though Indiana's mandate leaves open what to teach about the Holocaust, this genocide is the only named event in the history of the world that has found its way into the Indiana education code. That it is to be taught in US history courses reinforces the notion that the Holocaust is an American memory. In short, the Holocaust is a distinct sign that, following Saussure, corresponds to a distinct idea about who is evil ('them') and where evil takes place ('abroad'). The 'who' and the 'what' of this evil is suggestive of who is good ('us') and where goodness resides ('at home').

The most important atrocity

The laws in Connecticut, New Jersey, Kentucky, Delaware, Oregon and Pennsylvania align with the argument that the Holocaust is an American memory as well. However, the statutes in these states also include a need for instruction on genocide, in general. Connecticut amended its mandated social studies curriculum to include: "Holocaust and genocide education and awareness" (An Act Concerning the Inclusion . . ., 2020, Sec. 1.A). The Holocaust is the only named event in history within the Connecticut education code. The New Jersey Commission on Holocaust Education (1991) is to assist "in the development and implementation of Holocaust and genocide education programs" (c). Kentucky has amended its education statutes and regulations to include:

> instruction on the Holocaust and other cases of genocide, as defined by the United Nations . . ., that a court of competent jurisdiction, whether a court in the United States or the International Court of Justice, has determined to have been committed.
>
> (Ann Klein . . ., 2020, 1.a.3)

The *parole* in the laws of Delaware, Oregon and Pennsylvania speak in more explicit terms about why Holocaust and genocide education is mandated in their states. Though Delaware requires instruction "on the Holocaust and genocide" (An Act to Amend Title 14 . . ., 2020, Sec. 1.A.1), the Holocaust "serves as a frame of reference" (b) when: preparing "students to be responsible citizens in a pluralistic democracy" (b.2.); reaffirming "the commitment of free peoples to never again permit such occurrences" (b.3.); protecting "international human rights for all people" (c.2). In Oregon, "[s]chool districts must provide instruction about the Holocaust and genocide" so that students are prepared to "confront the immorality of the Holocaust, genocide and other acts of mass violence" (An Act Relating to Instruction . . ., 2019, Sec. 2.1.a). School districts in this state also have a responsibility to "help students gain insight into the importance of the protection of international human rights for all people" (b) and to develop in students an understanding of the "responsibilities of citizens in democratic societies" (d).

The Pennsylvania mandate maintains that "the Holocaust and any other genocide perpetrated against humanity, including the Rwandan genocide and other genocides committed in Africa, Asia, and Europe" (An Act Relating to the Public School System . . ., 2020, Sec. 1554.3.b.1.ii.) are to be taught in this Commonwealth so that children will understand "the importance of the protection of human rights and the potential consequences of unchecked ignorance." As this mandate also requires instruction on the "post-World War II trials" (i.), students can learn that the US helped bring a genocidal regime to international justice and, thus, that the US takes seriously its commitment to defending human rights. It is a remarkably detailed directive that includes information on guidelines to help prepare educators to teach the mandate and a timeline for when the DOE should conduct its compliance study. Yet nowhere in the state's school code are Native Americans or African Americans referenced.

The *langue* in this second set of laws suggests that the Holocaust serves as the reference point when providing instruction on other genocides. Students are to learn about genocidal horrors that took place under a totalitarian regime as a strategy to reaffirm the US commitment to upholding human rights – a commitment that, in actuality, "fight[s] for our way of life" (Bush, 2006). Though "our way of life" is not communicated explicitly, given that the US is never mentioned in these laws, it may be taken as axiomatic that the values 'we' uphold should be valued by all. These values that are to be learned about at school are universally commendable because they attest to a cosmopolitan commitment to safeguarding freedom for all people and condemning "prejudice, racism, and intolerance" (An Act to Amend Title 14 . . ., 2020, Sec. 1.b.2) everywhere. 'We' know that this is what 'we' stand for because there are only two governing bodies in the world (the US and the UN according to Kentucky law) that are "competent" enough to determine who has committed genocide. That "U.S. political elites sold the United Nations to the public as a route to global peace, while all along wanting it as a cover for militarization" (Lebovic, 2020) is a subject for another study (see Wertheim, 2020); but that subject provides additional insight into the intersection between power politics and the genocidal designation. In short, genocide may be understood as a distinct idea that tells Americans who 'we' are as a nation (i.e., the morally righteous) and what 'we' stand for on the international stage (i.e., the protector of international human rights and preventer of rights violations throughout the world).

Funding certain memories

Enactment of the laws in Michigan and Colorado rely upon external funding. Both states also emphasize instruction on the same two genocides. In Michigan, "[s]tate funds shall not be used for the operations of the governor's council" (Governor's Council . . ., 2020, p. 13.) on genocide and Holocaust education. The council is charged with securing "private funding for the governor's council" (14.e.) and is responsible to provide education that "memorialize[s] the victims of the Holocaust" (14.d.i.) and "Armenian Genocide" (ii.). In Colorado, "[t]he State Board shall adopt standards . . . related to the Holocaust . . . including but not limited to the Armenian Genocide" (An Act Concerning Requiring . . ., 2020, Sec. 2.A.). However, standards are only to be adopted if "gifts, grants, or other donations" (c.) are received. What is not written into these laws may be one of the most telling aspect of them: understanding the role that funding plays may provide insight into which atrocities most often get remembered at school. On this note, it seems unlikely that instruction on "other acts of mass violence" (Sec. 1.2.a) that challenges the unwritten belief in 'our' goodness would be encouraged by the state (e.g., Schwartz, 2021) – even if there existed ample funding.

Genocide is a new phenomenon that occurs elsewhere – amendments indicate

The last set of laws to be examined concern likeminded amendments that have been made to a state's original mandate. In its original version, Rhode Island provided autonomy for its DOE to "develop curricular material on genocide and human rights issues" (An Act Relating to Education . . ., 2000, 4.i). In an amendment to this Act, a directive was added that the DOE develop genocide related materials on "the Holocaust, Armenia, Cambodia, and Darfur" (An Act Relating to Education . . . 2011, iii). By 2016, the DOE was charged with including resources on other "relevant genocides" in "Iraq, Rwanda, and Darfur" (An Act Relating to Education . . . 2016, i.). Like Rhode Island, Illinois and California have amended their mandates to include additional genocides in the curriculum. Illinois added to its Holocaust education mandate a unit of instruction that "shall include, but not be limited to, the Armenian Genocide, the Famine-Genocide in Ukraine, and more recent atrocities in Cambodia, Bosnia, Rwanda, and Sudan" (An Act to Add . . ., 2005, Sec. 27–20.3). The rationale for the update is to reaffirm the state's commitment to "free peoples . . . and a recognition that crimes of genocide continue to be perpetrated across the globe as they have been in the past." The original California statute required schools to provide instruction on "human rights issues, with particular attention to the study of the inhumanity of genocide, slavery, and the Holocaust, and contemporary issues" (An Act to Amend Section 51220 . . ., 1992, Section 51220, b.i.). In an amendment to that statute, "the Legislature encourages the incorporation of survivor, rescuer, liberator, and witness oral testimony into the teaching of human rights, the Holocaust, and genocide, including, but not limited to, the Armenian, Cambodian, Darfur, and Rwandan genocides" (An Act to Amend Section 51220 . . ., 2016, Sec. 1.b).

The *parole* of these state's respective amendments puts a spotlight on named "recent atrocities" that have taken place 'abroad.' It is as though atrocities prior to the 20th century and/or closer to or 'at home' have not occurred or are deemed irrelevant. On this note, the *parole* does not indicate whose acts of enslavement are to be taught. What makes the named genocides relevant? The *langue* signifies that it is those that transpired under communist regimes or have been classified as genocide by the US (Bush, 2007). In contrast to the atrocities that are to be learned about at school, "free peoples" are assumed to be 'us' and those who are like 'us,' which is different from 'them.' "Free peoples" do not engage in human rights violations. Thus, if certain violations of rights are to be taught, it could not be any that have taken place 'at home' or by 'us' because 'we' respect human rights throughout the world, as these education laws affirm. Survivors who speak at schools are most often Holocaust survivors who were liberated by the Allied Forces ('us') when 'we' defeated the world's most evil regime in history. That the oviet Union played a more comprehensive role in the defeat of the Nazis than id the US (Overy, 1997, p. 321) is a history made invisible in these laws as well.

Though the *parole* within New York's amended law is quite different from the thers' discussed in this grouping, the *langue* is similar:

> The regents shall determine the subjects to be included in such courses of instruction in patriotism, citizenship, and human rights issues, with particular attention to the study of the inhumanity of genocide, slavery (including the freedom trail and underground railroad), the Holocaust, and the mass starvation in Ireland from 1845 to 1850.
>
> (An Act to Amend the Education Law . . ., 2020, Section 801.3)

Here, genocide is described as an inhumanity. Instruction on slavery, however, must include particular ways that Americans fought for slaves' freedom. While it is not stated outright, slavery can be thought about in relation to patriotism because New Yorkers as part of the Union helped defeat the Confederates. What is not written may well be the most significant feature of this statute: American dignity is preserved even when referencing one of the two great stains in US domestic history.

This last set of laws has been examined together because the amendments made to them tell a similar story. Rather than becoming more self-aware of and reconciliatory toward a racist past 'at home' that persists in the present (Sugrue, 2020), the revised laws amplify the complex dialectic of remembering and forgetting (in)convenient histories that help shape a national identity with an international agenda. The amplification is in naming evermore mass atrocities that occur somewhere else and by others. These atrocities and the human rights violations that comprise them may be understood as a distinct sign in the Saussurian sense. Its signage points to the idea that the US respects human rights while others violate rights. This must be true because this is what the laws imply. It would be nonsensical to suggest otherwise.

Summary of findings

The education laws that have been examined in this analysis have been divided into groups based on communication patterns. I have argued that the *langue* in the first and second groupings underscore the belief that the Holocaust is an American memory as it reminds Americans to forget about the moral wrongs perpetrated 'at home' and/or by 'us' as those wrongs are not nearly as wrong as the one(s) to be learned about under the law. These mandates also promote the idea that the Holocaust is exceptional, and genocidal violence is at once new and common given its proliferation since World War II. The third grouping opens up questions regarding how funding and private philanthropy may contribute to what and who are valued when educating for genocide awareness. The fourth grouping of laws indicate that Americans must search way over there, there, and there to find egregious acts of human behaviour that are then used to teach American youth why freedom and democracy ('our way of life') must be defended. That defending 'our way of life' in the 21st century involves perpetrating war crimes in the name of democracy (Brecher, Cutler, & Smith, 2005) is beside the point. But then again, it is a key aspect of the imperial point. While the *parole* across laws may be read as cosmopolitan in a righteous vanguard sense, the *langue* should be understood as imperial nationalistic in a banal sense given the ritualistic remembering and collective forgetting that teachers are mandated to (re)enact. What is so brilliant about these laws is that they speak for the nation-state using *parole* that cleverly conceals the nation-state's interests. The absolute right to not name the US or the atrocious acts it has perpetrated frees up its "national identity . . . with its own past and own future destiny" (Billig, 1995, p. 70) to be manifestly without limits.

3   Imperial nationalism of (dis)remembrance

It is said that education on human rights assists with the fight against their violations, and education on genocide can help end genocide. It would thus seem to follow that laws requiring schools to provide instruction on a subject of such grave importance in the world should be understood as a sign of universal moral progress. Indeed, the laws examined here have been celebrated as such by US state legislatures on the left and the right and by an expert in human rights law who sees in them the raising of a cosmopolitan consciousness in "the country and especially state lawmakers" (Bitensky, 2018, p. 54). These mandates are believed to be "the only real option . . . to grow an adult populace knowledgeable about genocide and [to become] well positioned to prevent it" (p. 58).

This analysis has taken a more self-critical perspective on this collection of laws given the underlying patterns found in the *langue*. These patterns indicate that the most horrific human behaviours occur in places far removed from the US and from those who are like 'us.' When educated about these yonder horrors, American youth are also to be reminded about what moral goodness looks like, where goodness resides and why it must be protected. That 'we' are good, and 'they' are evil must be true because the US is the leader of the free world, and 'our' world is worth fighting for. As the US is not only an established nation-state but has also been the primary ordering agent of the world, Americans do not necessarily learn or 'need' to learn in conventionally nationalistic ways what it means to be American. One place where national identity is flagged is in a wave of legislation that obliges schools to teach American youth about international human rights and genocide, one of the greatest crimes under international law. I have pointed to the ways in which the *langue* of these laws supports national interests particular to the US. These interests allow for wrongs of the most serious nature to be perpetuated 'here' and 'there' because they are obscured by a banner of freedom and democracy. Behind this unimpeachable banner moves a most dangerous form of nationalism.

In his opening remarks on banal nationalism, Billig (1995) looks to the context and content of words spoken by a sitting US president. From the Oval Office, George H. W. Bush announced to, and in the interests of, "the whole world" (p. 1) is rationale for leading a coalition of other states into the First Gulf War: "We have before us the opportunity to forge for ourselves and for future generations a new world order, a world where the rule of law, not the law of the jungle, governs the conduct of nations" (p. 1). As the dominant established nation-state, the US has been able to justify what it does for all to see from one of the world's most powerful settings, draped in American flags. The US also gives itself license to do its unspoken doings from the past and present, 'at home' and 'abroad' by way of little-noticed state laws that require schools to educate future generations of Americans on the need to defend human rights and prevent atrocious regimes from committing future atrocities. What kind of education could be any more exceptional?

Acknowledgement

I thank Laura Ax-Fultz, Associate Dean for Library and Information Services at Penn State Dickson Law, for her assistance with the legal citations and references.

References

An Act Concerning the Inclusion of Holocaust and Genocide Education and Awareness in the Social Studies Curriculum, Conn. Gen. Stat. § 10–18f (2020).

An Act Concerning Requiring the Satisfactory Completion of a Course that Includes Holocaust and Genocide Studies as a Condition of High School Graduation in Public Schools, Colo. Rev. Stat. § 22–2–127.3 (2020).

An Act Relating to Education, 16 R.I. Gen Laws § 16–93–1 (2000).

An Act Relating to Education, 16 R.I. Gen Laws § 16–93–1 (2011).

An Act Relating to Education, 16 R.I. Gen Laws § 16–93–1 (2016).

An Act Relating to Holocaust Remembrance Week in Public Schools, Tex. Educ. Code § 29.9072 (2020).

An Act Relating to Instruction in Public Schools about Genocide; Creating New Provisions; and Amending ORS 329.007, Or. Rev. Stat § 329.494 (2019).

An Act Relating to the Public School System, Including Certain Provisions Applicable as Well to Private and Parochial Schools; Amending, Revising, Consolidating and Changing the Laws Relating thereto, in Terms and Courses of Study, Providing for Holocaust, Genocide and Human Rights Violations Instruction, 24 Pa. Stat. § 15–1554 (2020).

An Act to Add Section 27–20.3 to "The School Code," 105 Ill. Comp. Stat. 5/27–20.3 (2005).

An Act to Amend Section 51220 of, and to Add Section 51226.3 to, the Education Code, Relating to Education, Cal. Educ. Code § 51226.3 (1992).

An Act to Amend Section 51220 of, and to Add Section 51226.3 to, the Education Code, Relating to Education, Cal. Educ. Code § 51226.3 (2016).

An Act to Amend the Education Law, in Relation to Instruction on the Subjects of Human Rights Violations, Genocide, Slavery and the Holocaust, N.Y. Educ. Law § 801 (2020).

An Act to Amend the Indiana Code concerning education, Ind. Code § 20-30-5-7 (2020).

An Act to Amend Title 14 of the Delaware Code Relating to Holocaust and Genocide Education, Del. Code tit. 14 § 4141 (2020).

Anderson, B. (2016). *Imagined communities: Reflections on the origin and spread of nationalism.* New York, NY: Verso. (Original work published 1983)

Ann Klein and Fred Gross Holocaust Education Act, Ky. Rev. Stat § 156.160 (2020).

Atrocities Prevention Board. (2017). Atrocity prevention. US Department of State. Retrieved from www.state.gov/atrocity-prevention/

Berlin, I. (1972). The bent twig: A note on nationalism. *Council on Foreign Relations, 51*(1), 11–30.

Billig, M. (1995). *Banal nationalism*. Los Angeles, CA: Sage.

Billig, M. (2009). Reflecting on a critical engagement with banal nationalism – Reply to Skey. *The Sociological Review, 57*(2), 347–352.

Bitensky, S. (2018). The plot to overthrow genocide: State laws mandating education about the foulest crime of all. *Marquette Law Review, 102*(1), 51–79.

Bochenek, M. G. (2018, February 28). In the freezer: Abusive conditions for women and children. *Human Rights Watch*. Retrieved from www.hrw.org/report/2018/02/28/freezer/abusive-conditions-women-and-children-us-immigration-holding-cells

Bonikowski, B. (2019). Trump's populism: The mobilization of nationalist cleavages and the future of U.S. democracy. In K. Weyland & R. Madrid (Eds.), *When democracy Trumps populism: Lessons from Europe & Latin America* (pp. 110–131). Cambridge, UK: Cambridge University Press.

Brecher, J., Cutler, J., & Smith, B. (2005). *In the name of democracy: American war crimes in Iraq and beyond*. New York, NY: Metropolitan Books.

Breuilly, J. (2016). Benedict Anderson's imagined communities: A symposium. *Nations and Nationalism, 22*(4), 625–659.

Bush, G. W. (2006, September 6). Bush: "Fighting for our way of life". *CNN*. Retrieved from www.cnn.com/2006/POLITICS/09/06/bush.transcript/index.html

Bush, G. W. (2007, May 29). *President Bush discusses genocide in Darfur, implements sanctions*. The White House President George W. Bush. Retrieved from https://georgewbush-whitehouse.archives.gov/news/releases/2007/05/20070529.html

Cooley, A., & Nexon, D. (2020, July/August). How hegemony ends: The unravelling of American power. *Foreign Affairs*. Retrieved from www.foreignaffairs.com/articles/united-states/2020-06-09/how-hegemony-ends

Crump, B. (2019). *Open season: Legalized genocide of colored people*. New York, NY: Amistad.

Education – Florida K-20 Education Code Created – General Amendments, Fla. Stat. § 1003.42 (2002).

Education – Florida K-20 Education Code Created – General Amendments, Fla. Stat. § 1003.42 (2020).

Fendler, L. (2014). *Michel Foucault*. New York, NY: Continuum.

Finkelstein, N. G. (2003). *The Holocaust industry: Reflections on the exploitation of Jewish suffering*. New York, NY: Verso.

Foucault, M. (2010). *The archaeology of knowledge and the discourse on language*. New York, NY: Vintage Books. (Original work published 1972)

Gibbons-Neff, T. (2020, May 7). U.S. military killed 132 civilians in wars last year, Pentagon says. *The New York Times*. Retrieved from www.nytimes.com/2020/05/07/world/middleeast/pentagon-civilian-deaths-afghanistan-iraq-syria.html

Gordon, W. (2004). Langue and parole. In C. Sanders (Ed.), *The Cambridge companion to Saussure* (pp. 76–87). Cambridge: Cambridge University Press.

Goswami, M. (2020). Benedict Anderson, *Imagined Communities* (1983). *Public Culture, 32*(2), 441–448.

Governor's Council on Genocide and Holocaust Education, Mich. Comp. Laws § 380.1168 (2020). Retrieved from www.legislature.mi.gov/(S(rx2pesp4ofpgydzpg05pp2n3))/mileg.aspx?page=getObject&objectName=mcl-380-1168

Ieiss, M. (2002). The evolution of the imperial idea and U.S. national identity. *Diplomatic History*, 26(4), 511–540.

Ierman, E. S., & Peterson, D. (2010). *The politics of genocide*. New York, NY: Monthly Review Press.

Iuman Rights Watch. (2020). United States: Events of 2019. *Human Rights Watch*. Retrieved from www.hrw.org/world-report/2020/country-chapters/united-states

anzer, C. (2019, November 29). States move to add Native American history to curriculum. *U.S. News & World Report*. Retrieved from www.usnews.com/news/best-states/articles/2019-11-29/states-move-to-add-native-american-history-to-education-curriculum

ones, A. (2004). *Genocide, war crimes and the West*. New York, NY: Zed Books.

King, L. J. (2017). The status of black history in U.S. schools and society. *Social Education*, 81(1), 14–18.

Kingston, L. (2015). The destruction of identity: Cultural genocide and indigenous people. *Journal of Human Rights*, 14, 63–83.

Krogstad, J. (2020, July 10). Hispanics have accounted for more than half of U.S. population growth since 2010. *Pew Research*. Retrieved from www.pewresearch.org/fact-tank/2020/07/10/hispanics-have-accounted-for-more-than-half-of-total-u-s-population-growth-since-2010/

Lebovic, S. (2020, October 19). Why is America the world's police? *Boston Review*. Retrieved from http://bostonreview.net/politics/sam-lebovic-stephen-wertheim-tomorrow-the-world

New Jersey Commission on Holocaust Education, N.J. Stat. §§ 18A:4A-2 (1991).

Novick, P. (2000). *The Holocaust in American life*. Boston, MA: Mariner Books.

Overy, R. (1997). *Why the Allies won*. New York, NY: W. W. Norton and Co.

PR Newswire. (2017, April 24). *Legislators in 20 U.S. states to introduce legislation on Holocaust and other genocide awareness and prevention*. Anne Frank Center for Mutual Respect. Retrieved from www.prnewswire.com/news-releases/legislators-in-20-us-states-to-introduce-legislation-on-holocaust-and-other-genocide-awareness-and-prevention-300443932.html

Schwartz, S. (2021, February 3). Lawmakers push to ban '1619 Project' from schools. *Education Week*. Retrieved from www.edweek.org/teaching-learning/lawmakers-push-to-ban-1619-project-from-schools/2021/02

Spector, H. (2020). Trends and typologies of cosmopolitanism in education. *Oxford Research Encyclopedia of Education*. New York, NY: Oxford University Press.

Sugrue, T. J. (2020, June 10). 2020 is not 1968: To understand today's protests, you must look further back. *National Geographic*. Retrieved from www.nationalgeographic.com/history/2020/06/2020-not-1968/

Szulc, L. (2017). Banal nationalism in the internet age: Rethinking the relationship between nations, nationalism, and the media. In M. Skey & M. Antosich (Eds.), *Everyday nationhood: Theorising culture, identity and belonging after banal nationalism*. London, UK: Palgrave Macmillan.

United Nations. (2014). *Framework of analysis for atrocity crimes: A tool for prevention*. United Nations Office on Genocide Prevention and the Responsibility to Protect. Retrieved from www.un.org/en/genocideprevention/documents/about-us/Doc.3_Framework%20of%20Analysis%20for%20Atrocity%20Crimes_EN.pdf

U.S. Department of State. (2021, January 20). *U.S. support for human rights defenders*. U.S. Department of State, Bureau of democracy, human rights and labor. Retrieved from www.state.gov/u-s-support-for-human-rights-defenders/

U.S. Department of State. (n.d.). *Advancing freedom and democracy*. U.S. Department o State, archived content. Retrieved from https://2009-2017.state.gov/j/drl/rls/afdr//index htm

Vogel, A. (2006). Who's making global civil society: Philanthropy and US empire in civi society. *The British Journal of Sociology, 57*(4), 635–655.

Waxman, O. (2020, September 17). Echoing decades of fighting over U.S. history class rooms, President Trump pushes for "patriotic education". *Time.* Retrieved from https:/ time.com/5889907/trump-patriotic-education/

Weeks, W. E. (1994). American nationalism, American imperialism: An interpretatior of United States political economy, 1789–1861. *Journal of the Early Republic, 14*(4) 485–495.

Wertheim, S. (2020). *Tomorrow, the world: The birth of U.S. global supremacy*. Cambridge MA: Harvard University Press.

15 Educating migrant children and women in the political projects of the welfare nation-state and secularization

The Danish "extreme case" in light of the French

Mette Buchardt

Those of the European populations with a migration history are frequently an object of public debate. People with a migration history have thus since the late 20th century functioned as a political demarcation line, making the question of the nation articulate. This includes the question of the varying degrees of 'nation-ness:' the belongings and ties to the nation within the population (e.g. Malešević, 2006), and thus the question of the internal borders of the nation-state with regard to its populations. Also, such debates have functioned as a passage for the question of religion to be articulated in public and political debates in the form of a special attention to the Muslim parts of the European population with a newer migratory history. Often such debates involve education: How to handle "bilingual students," "migrant students," "students with a different culture," "Muslim students" – categories that are often used as overlapping or even synonymously.

In 2018, a prohibition was passed in Denmark of the *niqaab*, a particular form of the Islamic hijab which, in addition to the hair, covers main parts of the face and is to be worn in public places, including educational institutions. It is one of the recent examples of legislation in the political reform process concerning migration-related phenomena.[1] The passing of the legislation was the culmination of a decade-long debate and was followed by more: Was it, for instance, fair to demand that teachers and fellow students should be able to see the full face of every student during teaching sessions? Was a ban rather a way to exclude niqaab-wearing female students, and thus Muslim women, from education? Or was the debate a problem in itself, diverting attention from more pressing school reform issues?[2] The legislation and the debate surrounding it share a resemblance with the French debate on the use of hijab in educational institutions from late 1980s onwards. This culminated in a ban against wearing religious symbols in public schools in 2004, something that scholars estimated has had severe consequences for the educational strategies and success of female students of Islamic affiliation (Abdelgadir & Fouka, 2020).[3]

These debates point to several features significant for the way migrants have been perceived across Europe from the late 20th century onwards: The political

DOI: 10.4324/9781003137801-20

reform debates on migrants and the public debates around them often focus on religion in a way that works in continuity with the nationality aspect, and often women and children are at the forefront of the debate, bringing the field of educa-tion as well as the question of educating to the centre of the nexus between nation, religion and migration. The chapter argues that the process of educationalization (cp. Tröhler, 2016) of migrant students and their families, which has taken place since late 20th century, should be understood in light of the mutual embeddedness of the political projects of the nation-state, of secularization and of welfare distri-bution, for which the conditions were laid out in late 19th-century social reform through education. And in continuation, that reforms and debates concerning migrants in schooling have not only contributed to transforming and sustaining religion as a political category, but are also making visible the religious aspirations of educational secularization.

Historically, children of migrants have under shifting guises been part of the state school systems since their formation across Europe during the 19th century as a political tool to create national cohesion. However, migration was not pre-dominantly perceived as an extensive national educational problem, something which is also not the case regarding the migration movements following WWI and II as well as decolonization (e.g. Sane, 1997).

In Northern Europe, however, this pattern changed with the guest-worker migration waves from South to North from the late 1960s. In the case of Den-mark, a Nordic welfare state with an ideology of universalist inclusion combined with national exceptionalism, "the migrant student" has in different forms ever since been regarded as a specific educational problem to the welfare- and nation-state project. As is the case in for instance France, this has been increasingly con-nected to what is in public political discourse often perceived as the problematic religious values and everyday behaviour of migrant students and their parents – as less secular than the modern nation-state and its citizens and as "religious" and "traditional" in a way which deviates from the nation and its school. Also, it has brought Muslims to the fore of debates about migration as well as on religion and other societal practices and institutions, just as it has foregrounded the question of migrant women and children in debates on migration.

The problematized character of "the too-religious migrant" for the political pro-ject of educational nationalism should, however, also be understood in light of the social-state and welfare-state project as it has evolved across Europe since late 19th century simultaneously and interlocked with the political projects of the nation-state and of secularization. This project – in its many e.g. European variants – developed as an answer to the so-called social question that domi-nated political discussions across the states of Europe from that time on: more specifically, the question of how to handle social difference while still maintain-ing social cohesion. Not least, schooling was in this context seen as an instru-ment for fighting poverty and ensuring universal social mobility (Buchardt, 2013). In the education reform waves that took place from late 19th century onwards, such goals interacted with the political nation-state project that aimed at creating national identification and cohesion as well as the granting and delimiting rights or citizens of the nation-state. Also, reworking of state-religion ties formed part of these educational reform waves, but different models were chosen. In for instance France, religion was separated from education, a reform process that started with school acts of the Third Republic in the early 1880s, whereas in Nordic states on their way from absolutism to parliamentarism, integration models were chosen, a process also starting out in late 19th century, as will be unfolded in the chapter. Solving the social question through education in other words overlapped and interacted with the political efforts of secularizing and nationalizing through education reform as central tools in modernizing the state on the road from monarchical absolutisms to different models of parliamentarism. This ended up with the state education political models for modern schooling that from late 20th century onwards increasingly reacted to the migrant students as representatives of an extraordinary and/or problematic degree of national-religious belonging, including lack of or too little national-religious belonging.

The purpose of this chapter is to analyze the perception and handling of "too religious" migrant students in light of the models of secularization, social reform and nation-states in their intertwinement. Firstly the chapter will sketch out the iconic model of secularization in France as it developed in the late 19th and early 20th century, often seen as an "extreme case" historically with regard to secularization reforms, and use it as a point of departure for unfolding the Nordic and Danish model of secularization and the way it has been attached to the nation- and welfare-state project through education in the same period. This will serve as a basis for understanding how the secularization model targets the question of migrants in national educational institutions. Then the focus in the chapter will turn to the Nordic case of Denmark, well known globally as a xenophobic "extreme case" and "Sonderweg," in order to explore how the public discovery of migrant women and children as objects for educational and other social reforms from especially the 1980s onwards rearticulated the project of secularization through the distinction between "tradition" tied to the cultural background of the migrant and "modernity," mainly tied to Denmark. Where religion was seen as the defining content of tradition that especially determined migrant women and children, modernity was revitalized and in more-or-less religiously leaning terms reattached to the nation-state. That means that I am comparing models of secularization across time in the way that I analyze the Nordic case of Denmark in light of a French perspective, describing the Danish "Sonderweg" by means of a single-case asymmetrical comparison with the French "Sonderweg" (Cady & Hurd, 2010; Kocka, 1999).

1 Methodology across historical contexts

The field of education is generally under-researched in the scholarship of nation-state building and nationalism. As pointed out by e.g. Tröhler (2020), education often appears in the margin as a taken-for-granted example not analyzed in depth. However, not least recent research has taken up the challenge to explore nation-state development through schooling, using for instance textbooks as sources (Gotling, 2020). Drawing on history of emotions and revisiting Billig's discourse psychological term of *banal nationalism* (Skey & Antonsich, 2017), Hoegaerts has reconstructed historical classroom practices as part of emotional embodiment of patriotism leading the national character building (Hoegaerts, 2020). In the same vein, but with a different empirical focus, we find for instance Eiranen's Helsinki-focused study of families as a breeding ground for nation-building and learning the nation-state (Eiranen, 2019).

The same pattern also by and large applies to research on secularization, where education figures as an example but is rarely studied as the main case (e.g. Dobb-elaere, 1987; Stark, 1999. This point is elaborated in Buchardt, 2021). Recently, Historian of Education Susannah Wright has, however, explored English anti-religious secularists investing in moral education and citizenship (2017). This can be seen as part of a new tendency to revisit the secularization as a powerful societal process which still impacts societies globally, something which scholar of German modern history Todd H. Weir (2015) has described as the history of secularism as ideology. This landscape of new secularism scholarship also features what could be defined as postcolonial and poststructuralist studies of secularization, where secu-larization is to be understood as a liberalist ideology spreading Western domina-tion outside as well as inside "the West" (e.g. Asad, 2003; Asad, Brown, Butler, & Mahmood, 2009). In line with this approach, scholar of French modern history and women's history Joan Wallach Scott has, as a critique of the "Clash of Civiliza-tions" paradigm and polemic, challenged what she understands as the claim that secularism guarantees gender equality and women's rights, arguing that secularism as played out in for instance the French Laïcité project in late 19th and early 20th century rather meant a modern sustaining of what she calls "a gendered divi-sion of labor" that "became foundational to (inseparable from) the Enlightenment vision of representative government and the imagined wholeness and racial purity of nations" (Scott, 2017, p. 88). In continuation, Scott interprets anti-Muslim laws and sentiment and the central role the discourse of the suppressed Muslim woman plays in this context as a continued dominance against women and the racial and religious other, in intersecting ways that Scott defines as "sexularism" (Scott, 2017, e.g. pp. 1–4, 179–183). Scott's analysis centres on "the extremity of the French case" concerning the veil, not least in the form of the hijab ban, as the extreme case example (Scott, 2017, p. 181). However, also Scott refrains from an analysis of the role of educational institutions towards which the religious symbol ban is directed. This lack of a detailed focus on the role of the education system in the nexus between secularization and the nation-state is what this arti-cle sets out to remedy, based on the thesis that education has been a crucial site for solving social problems during the modernizations of the European states from the late 19th century onwards in which the restructuring of the relation between state and religion was a central feature along with the establishment of the nation as part of the modernization of the state. Though research since the 1990s has challenged this presumed connection between the modern nation-state project and the project of secularization, this chapter is based on the assumption that these projects were intertwined (drawing on Brubaker, 2012), just as seculariza-tion and nation-state crafting intertwined with the solving of the social question, gain, resulted in different types of social- and welfare-state models. I hence use the conceptualization of welfare nation-states, drawing on welfare-state historians Pauli Kettunen and Andrzej Marcin Suszycki, who point out that nation-building processes in many states corresponded to the development of the welfare state and suggest that the migration waves which many Western European states were confronted with from the 1960s made the intertwinement and frictions between the social question and the national question visible (Kettunen, 2011; Suszycki, 2011). This chapter is in other words based on a methodology that understands welfare-state building, nation-state building and secularization, not as identical, but as overlapping political projects which served to modernize the state and integrate populations within it in new ways, compared to previous absolutist reigns. The chapter argues that education has been a main arena for these overlaps, and that the role ascribed to migrant children and women in late 20th- and early 21st-century education politics has revitalized these connections, but in ways which make only fully sense to understand in the perspective of late 19th-century European state modernizations.

In order to delve deeper into the forms of welfare nation-state secular politics that were pursued educationally with migrant students and their families as objects, I do, however, not conceptualize secularization as an ideology. As also pointed out by Weir (2015), many different ideologies have met in for instance secularizing efforts. When it comes to the question of education, the field is characterized by mixes and transformations that appear when social problems are defined as and sought solved by means of education – *educationalized* (Depaepe & Smeyers, 2008; Tröhler, 2016) – and forms of knowledge and politics are hence *pedagogized* (Bernstein, 1990, pp. 165–218; Buchardt, 2018), meaning instrumentalized into timetables, school subjects, institutional divisions and regulations, etc. In order to capture exactly that messiness, I will, besides the stipulated central policy, focus on the strategies pursued by meso-level actors (Luft, 2020): education professionals working in between research, education, media attention and popular publication efforts. A focus on the production of actors operating "in the middle ground between high culture or science and ordinary life" (Rabinow, 1989, p. 9) will thus provide access to the banal but powerful production of educational knowledge and strategies that have been part of setting agendas for the micropolitics of the classroom and well as for parliamentary law-making and rhetoric and public debate.

2 The Danish and French models of secularization and their reactions to the "too-religious migrants"

The education systems of Europe that from the late 20th century increasingly addressed and reformed in relation to migration had in the Nordic states, similar to France, their formative period in this late 19th-century social reform context which aimed to modernize the state institutions as well.

In the case of the Lutheran-dominated Nordic states Sweden and Denmark, this also resulted in educational reform work, in Sweden during the 1910s and in Denmark during the 1930s, when religious education underwent a scientific and historical turn, putting the nation and its "culture" in front of religious instruction and making it "objective" rather than confessional. In France, scholars of the new scientifically invested modernist theology, especially in the Protestant forms influenced reform efforts leading up to a series of reforms starting out in the early 1880s and culminating in 1905 with a complete separation of state and religion across institutional and political areas, from marriage laws to regulation of church property (Mayeur & Rebérioux, 1987; Cabanel, 2016; Buchardt, 2017).

Education was a major tool and point of departure in this context. While the final separation of religion and state was passed in France in 1905 under the so-called Laïcité Act, other separation laws had already been passed before, not least in the education act wave in the early 1880s under the Third Republic Minister of Education Jules Ferry (1832–1893). These reform waves separated religion and the school and made the topic of religion not only non-confessional but also abolished it as an independent school subject. With the education act passed in March 1882, religious instruction was thus removed from the timetable and replaced with a course on moral and civics education, and in the following decades clergy and other religious congregation members were gradually removed from teaching positions, something that was finally stipulated in 1904 (Singer, 1975; Mayeur, 2004; Mayeur & Rebérioux, 1987; Baubérot, 2010).

Behind the school secularization reforms was a heavy Liberal and social Protestant influence. In 1878, Ferry made Ferdinand Buisson (1841–1932) the director of primary education, a Liberal and social Protestant philosopher and later professor of education at Sorbonne. On this post he became a main force in developing the secularization laws for the school. In 1905, Buisson chaired the parliamentary committee to implement the complete separation of church and state (Singer, 1975; Cabanel, 2016).

A result was also that though religious instruction was as such abolished as a school subject, it did not mean that religion disappeared as school content. Instead religion as a historical and cultural phenomenon became a subtopic in e.g. history. The new moral and civics education course included along with duties to the nation also duties to God, denoting fundamental ideas recurring across and outside religious denomination (e.g. Mayeur & Rebérioux, 1987). The inspiration behind these curricular reform elements found support in Biblical Criticism, making religion and Christianity as history part of the civilization history, as well as in revolutionary Enlightenment deism and as such supporting the education into a universalist national self-perception of the future citizen of Third Republic France (Buchardt, 2020a, 2020b).

Turning to Denmark, the struggles over how to rework the relation between state and church had since the beginning of the 1890s had education as a central arena. Modernist liberal theologians had started debates about including the result of Biblical Criticism in the upper secondary school. Understanding Biblical history as the history of a people was from the outset a central endeavour, making it possible to relate it to the history of the Danish people. These efforts continued in early 20th century but did not succeed until the 1930s when the Social Democrats had taken office and the idea of "objective teaching" of religion gained a foothold.

his was based on the idea that the Biblical gospel – set free by "objective science" – should be made accessible in terms of cultural use through the understanding of he Bible as a history of distinct nations and their respective peoples. However, the fforts culminating in the 1930s had started out already in the late 19th century ind happened in exchange with and drawing on inspiration from reform efforts in ;weden, which had from 1919 taken a similar path (Buchardt, 2020a).

Though the French and the Danish models for secularization – the former a eparation model, the latter an integration model where the church is governed by he state and Christianity is a significant part of the national imaginary as "culture of the state" – in some senses seem radical opposites, a common main feature was rom the outset making religion part of the imaginaries of the nation as history and ext (Taylor, 2007). At the same time, secularity was made a signifier of the nation that again identified the nation with science-based modernity, not least pursued through education. Finally, the two models sprung from social question debates, and thus broader reform efforts aiming at bridging the gap between social difference and cohesion. Contrary to the situation in the US during the Cold War (e.g. Scott, 2017), Christianity did not play a significant role in US-leaning European states such as Denmark and France in the period as a freedom sign of the Western state, opposite the state-atheist dictatorships in the Eastern bloc. In the late Cold War years of the 1980s, migrants identified with Islam, covering a significant part of the migration-related populations in Denmark as well as in France, seem to have been granted the opposite role, namely as a foreign national-religious phenomenon, on the one hand in need of social reform, and on the other posing a threat to secular values. In this case the migrant women/children nexus and thus the migrant family can in both nation-state contexts be said to have become an educationalized object to secular reform, a move that at the same time served to revitalize national Christianity as modern and secular. This will in the following be elaborated and discussed with regard to the Danish extreme case from the discovery of the guest workers in the late 1960s, their children during the 1970s and in addition migrant women during the 1980s.

3 The Danish welfare nation-state discovers the migrants and their children: Late 1960s to the early 1980s

In Denmark, education political descriptions of migrant students – in macropolitical discussions as well as in the micropolitics of everyday life – have gone through a complex development. The first official formulation regarding so-called foreign children appeared in a departmental circular from the Ministry of Education in Denmark (Ministry of Education, 1970). Since then, categorizations have in varied wording related to the non-nationness of the children in question. In the late 1960s and early 1970s, the category that appeared frequently in e.g. communication between state bodies, early attempts to make teachers' guidelines, etc., was "foreign-worker children," describing the children in relation to the non-national guest-worker parents (although also children of e.g. refugees were included in the category). During the 1970s, the non-national mother tongue of the children came to the fore in the descriptions, such as "foreign language children" or "bilin-gual students," who in the late 1970s increasingly were described in light of their "different culture" and "other culture" in the meaning of different from and other than the "Danish culture," something that has figured prominently until the present (Buchardt, 2016).

What does run through this history of education political categorizations is, in addition, that the national and social deviance of the migrant student from the 1970s onwards has increasingly described them in terms relating to religion, making the juxtaposition between "Danish culture" and "Muslim culture" a frequent figure in political debate, and making "Muslimness" a quasi-national category, outside Danishness or even a Troyan horse within Danishness and thus a potential political and social security threat (Sheikh & Crone, 2012; Buchardt, 2014).

The emerging attention to "the guest-worker" question in the late 1960s, however, included neither children nor women. The arriving "guest workers" (*gæstearbejdere*) or "foreign workers" (*fremmedarbejdere*) were, despite the fact that guest workers were also female, by and large identified as male (Jønsson, 2013; Trige Andersen, 2013; Trige Andersen & Myong, 2015). In popular reception, such as newspapers and popular science magazines, they were connected to airports and railway stations and were thus seen as intonating a new modern and vibrant era, in similar ways as high-rises that were built in and around the capitol area in the same period, and thus as a sign of modernity (Trige Andersen, 2013; Buchardt, 2016). Their status was on the one hand defined as outside the *nation-state* due to conceptualizations such as "guest" and "foreign," while their status as "workers" on the other hand attached them to the social fabric of the *welfare-state* society. When public attention to migrants as more than guest-worker men grew during the 1970s, one of the first places for this to break through was in political debate on education, which also became a breeding ground for describing migrants, more specifically migrant children, in terms of cultural difference (Buchardt, 2016).

Early examples of this emerging pattern of explaining migrants as different from "Danish culture" are publications from the Copenhagen school *Sjæl-landsgades Skole*, where the municipality in 1971 had established an Office for Foreign Language Pupils (*Kontoret for Fremmedsprogede Elever*). Teachers and consultants from this environment became active in creating a body of knowledge through the publishing of articles in teachers' magazines, handbooks and supervision manuals. From the outset it was especially *Kineserbørn* ("China children" – i.e. Chinese-speaking pupils from migrant families that had arrived during the 1960s and were residing in the school district) whose culture and "milieu background" were described (e.g. Hill, 1971). However, in the first attempt to make more of a handbook in 1974, Islam was particularly emphasized as "dominating among foreign language pupils." "Seventy percent of the Yugoslavians who attend Copenhagen schools are Muslims," head teacher and school consultant Erik Odde argued (Odde, 1974, p. 29). Where the Chinese-speaking pupils were described culturally, but not through their religion, Islam was primarily depicted as culture congealed as habits and traditions. This way of describing "the foreign child as divided between two cultures'" – the traditional religious one and the Danish modern secular one – would come to dominate the following decades.

4 Children and women as reform objects: Mid-1970s to the early 1990s

From being understood mainly as linguistic strangers in the early 1970s, migrant children became during the 1970s increasingly associated with rural life and "traditional family patterns," just as juxtapositions between rural life and urban life and tradition vs. modernity became an increasingly used scheme for describing the deviant lifestyle of migrants in general. This language of description drew on a popularized concept of culture deriving from the cultural social sciences Cultural Sociology and Anthropology, but also echoing national romantic understandings of different cultures as the content of different nations. This line of knowledge transfer from for instance Weberian conceptualizations of tradition versus modernity to the use of culture as an explanatory social and pedagogical concept was no coincidence. The new growing field of professionals working with migrants and migrant children involved besides teachers, psychologists and linguists, students and scholars from or drawing on Cultural Sociology and Anthropology. At the same time the emerging use of the concept of culture in order to explain and reform migrants was criticized by some scholars from these scientific fields.[4]

In a report about Copenhagen Municipality's model for receiving migrant students, issued in 1976 and authored by psychology student Niels Bøgsted-Møller who was teaching newly arrived migrant students at Sjællandsgades Skole, parents of "foreign language pupils" were interviewed and categorized according to origin in either an area with a "strong religiosity in a more traditional sense" or "an area where religion and codes of conduct in society concurrently with advancing industrialization have gone through a re- and new interpretation more attuned to modern society" (Bøgsted-Møller, 1976, p. 55; Buchardt, 2012).

By 1980, culture as a category of explanation had also found its way to the ministerial level. The Ministry of Education hence published a special issue of *Uddannelse* (Education), bearing the title "New Danes. Cultural encounter or cultural clash," where "problems regarding cultural clashes" were considered just as severe as the language question (e.g. Bennedsen, 1980, p. 340).

The decade that followed brought a changed debate on what was increasingly labelled "Muslims" following the media attention on the Iranian revolution, the war in Lebanon and the Soviet occupation of Afghanistan (Würtz Sørensen, 1988; Pedersen, 1988). Conceptualizations connecting migrants to a "different culture," which was again connected to especially Islam, came to dominate politics and public discourse. In this climate, also migrant women were discovered by public, political and professional debate. The mainly left-intellectual daily *Information* (The Daily Information) launched a campaign featuring Muslim women in Denmark as specifically oppressed due to "Muslim culture" as its main theme. In the same period, the role of Muslim women in Soviet-occupied Afghanistan, more precisely in the areas dominated by the anti-Soviet Mujahedin fighters, was defended in the newspaper's coverage of the war (Würtz Sørensen, 1988; Pedersen, 1988; Buchardt, 2016).

This interest in women was not without connection to the fact that Copenhagen hosted the UN World Conference on Women in 1980 and that the second-wave feminist movement had attracted huge political and public attention since the mid-1970s, but it was also mirroring the complex ways international geopolitics were recontextualized in interior debate. For Danish foreign politics, Islam was due to the Danish NATO membership and thus US allegiance to be considered an enemy in places like Iran, but in continuation an ally when fighting the Soviet in Afghanistan.

An increasing and frictional attention to Muslim women that also occurred in pedagogical debate was one of the consequences (Buchardt, 2016). Historian of Education Ellen Nørgaard, who at the time was writing summaries of the press coverage of educational and pedagogical questions for *Dansk pædagogisk Tidsskrift*, estimated in May 1981 that there had never been written so much in the press about the teaching of migrant children as in the autumn and winter of 1980–1981 (Nørgaard, 1981). In the autumn of 1981, *Det Pædagogiske Selskab* conducted a symposium on "instruction of migrant children." Besides the question of language and language instruction, also the question of culture, especially in relation to "the girls," had according to the coverage of the symposium been on the agenda:

> It is clear that especially the girls must be taken into consideration, partly because the immigrants' cultural mobilization and their specificity center on the family and thus on gender roles, and partly because the girls' educational situation (also that of the Danish girls) demands such a high outcome from formal education.
>
> (JBP, HHH, 1981, p. 347)

During the Conservative-Liberal government (1982–1993), the ideological signals regarding education drew on the so-called canon approach, as known from the US. In the case of Danish education politics, this led to an increasing interest in "Danish culture." Also teaching professionals and scholars involved in education of migrants who engaged in multicultural and anti-racist education embraced culture as a pedagogical category. In the teachers' handbook *The multicultural school. About intercultural, anti-racist education*, religion was described as a resource for instruction; immigrant parents could e.g. be invited to school to give talks about Islam. Religion was, however, also described as a social problem and something which created "cultural clashes in school" (Clausen, 1986). Gender and sexuality loomed large in these descriptions, for instance by way of parents' attitude towards sex education and dress codes, areas which especially draw attention to women and girls. Islam had become a defining part of the cultural difference that separated migrants from the culture of the nation-state and its school, which was reversely framed as modern and thus secular as a presupposed way of "being Danish."

With the School Act of 1993 put forward by the new Social Democrat-headed government, the term *culture* entered the main purpose of schooling. The new opening paragraph, which still prevails in its basic form, stated that "The Folkeskole shall familiarize pupils with Danish culture and contribute to their understanding of other cultures" (The Act on the Folkeskole of 1993, §1.3). In the law remarks, Christianity was the only example given of "Danish culture" (Dupont & Holm-Larsen, 2004).

Culture as a category that connoted the nation and made "Danish culture" distinct from "other cultures" had thus found its way to the constituting paragraph defining the *Folkeskole*, the Danish primary and secondary school, in itself being a cornerstone in nation-building as well as a key welfare-state institution. Also the status of Christianity as the main content of "Danish culture" was stipulated. The ongoing definition and reform work targeting migrant children and women as belonging to a non-modern, non-Danish culture with Islam as its main content should be seen as building stones in the development.

In this way also the secularity of Denmark as a nation welfare state had become revitalized but in a way where secularity presupposed Christianity as part of the national culture. Just as scholars, as previously referred to, have drawn connections between the regulation of and interest in "Muslim women" in educational arenas in France from the late 20th century onwards and the French *Laïcité* model, the same can be said to be the case with regard to Denmark and its model of secularization with its insistence on Christianity as the culture of the nation, and the role ascribed to the "too-religious migrants" in the Danish state and its school.

5 Conclusion: The migrant student within the educational project of nation, secularization and welfare state

To sum up, in the "extreme case" of Denmark, culture in the presupposed meaning of traditionalism which again was connected to religion, in reality referring to Islam, became the central category of description of migrants. This scheme was not least played out and crafted in relation to children and women who were perceived as vulnerable objects, extraordinarily determined by and exposed to "traditionalism." Women and children with the migration category attached to them became part of a narrative in which they figured as objects being extraordinarily loaded with and determined by an allegedly non-secular, non-Danish traditional culture, and thus posing a threat, but also as potential objects to merciful attention and social reform. This process of explaining migrants at the same time reactivated the Danish model of secularization where religion in the form of Christianity was modernized into being key content of the nation-state.

This had consequences for the welfare-state model of education practiced in Denmark. While the welfare-state project relied on the dictum that "everyone" is included, in school and through attending school, the nation-state project at the same time distinguished in degrees of belonging, and degrees of secularity became a strong tool in this respect as a parameter of measuring of belongings. The narratives that developed ascribed migrants and thus also migrant students to a space outside "modernity," and thus outside the core of the Danish nation-state as a potential obstacle in the welfare state 'school for all.' This understand-ing of modernity was at the same time not anti-religious. Rather being modern was understood as having an appropriately secular attitude to religion, meaning a daily-life banal version of the Danish integration model of secularization, making Christianity not least a part of the national heritage and culture. The Danish ver-sion of the secularization model, with its impact of keeping religion as a cultural and historical heritage of the nation and thus as a tool serving the state, can in this context be said to on the one hand have fuelled the schemes to explain migrants as outside the modern space of national secularity. On the other hand, the handling of migrant students and of migrants in general can at the same time be said to have revitalized this modernist national secularity in which Christianity is a central signifier.

The Danish extreme case analyzed in comparison with the extreme case of France then opens the question of whether migrant students across Europe can thus be said to be placed within the frictions and interplay between social uni-versalism of the social state and welfare-state schooling "for all," one the one hand, and on the other: national border-making within the educational institu-tions. Also the comparison points out that "the too-religious" Muslim student has become a figure that reveals the secular or maybe rather the not-so-secular character of the welfare nation-state and its educational institutions.

Zooming out of the concrete case of how migrant students are perceived in this educational nationalism that has played out and been developed among not least the meso-level state crafters, commission members, journalists, scholars and education developers, text- and handbook authors, and education- and pedagogy associations, it becomes at the same time clear that education – being such a cen-tral area of political intervention in the late 19th century – is still a productive cor-nerstone in the welfare nation-state and secularization nexus. This intertwining of educational nationalisms and religio-nationalisms as components in the historical as well as the current attempts of 'solving the social question' needs to be increas-ingly questioned research-wise – not only concerning how these intertwined pro-jects have sought to reform migrants as well of the rest of the populations, but also with regard to how these projects together form conditions and produce formats for how to learn to become and perform as a citizen, be it with or without the not-so-universal rights of a citizen.

Notes

1 www.dr.dk/nyheder/politik/nu-er-det-vedtaget-fremover-udloeser-det-en-boede-baere-burka-og-niqab-paa-gaden, accessed January 4, 2021.
2 www.tv2lorry.dk/region-hovedstaden/ministerium-skoler-ma-godt-forbyde-niqab; www.folkeskolen.dk/60953/skolefolk-burkasnak-drukner-vigtig-debat-om-skolen, accessed January 4, 2021.
3 LOI n° 2004–228 du 15 mars 2004 encadrant, en application du principe de laïcité, le port de signes ou de tenues manifestant une appartenance religieuse dans les écoles, collèges et lycées publics (1), JORF n°65 du 17 mars 2004, www.legifrance.gouv.fr/jorf/

article_jo/JORFARTI000002020944 ["Law #2004–228 of 15 March 2004, concerning, as an application of the principle of the separation of church and state, the wearing of symbols or garb which show religious affiliation in public primary and secondary schools"]. In effect September 2, 2004. Accessed January 4, 2021.

An explicit example of the former is Rahbek Pedersen and Skutnabb-Kangas (1983, pp. 35ff.), whereas the cultural sociologist Jonathan M. Schwartz (e.g. 1977) is an example of the latter.

Bibliography

Laws, ministerial orders, etc.

Dupont, K., & Holm-Larsen, S. (Eds.). (2004). *Folkeskoleloven 2004: Sammenstilling, bemærkninger og gennemførelsesbestemmelser m.v.* [The Act on Folkeskolen 2004: Synopsis, remarks and rules for implementation]. Vejle: Kroghs Forlag.

Lov om folkeskolen 1993 (1994). [Act on the Folkeskole (The Danish Primary and Lower Secondary School) of 1993]. Copenhagen, Ministry of Education.

Ministry of Education. (1970). Cirkulære om undervisning i folkeskolen af udenlandske børn, November 30 (1970). [Departmental circular on the instruction of foreign children]. Copenhagen, Ministry of Education.

Printed sources and secondary sources

Abdelgadir, A., & Fouka, V. (2020). Political Secularism and Muslim Integration in the West: Assessing the Effects of the French Headscarf Ban. *American Political Science Review, 114*(3), 707–723. doi:10.1017/S0003055420000106

Asad, T. (2003). *Formations of the secular: Christianity, Islam, Modernity.* Stanford, CA: Stanford University Press.

Asad, T., Brown, W., Butler, J., & Mahmood, S. (Eds.). (2009). *Is critique secular? Blasphemy, injury, and free speech.* Berkeley, CA: Townsend Center for the Humanities/University of California.

Baubérot, J. (2010). The evolution of secularism in France. Between two civil religions. In L. E. Cady & E. S. Hurd (Eds.), *Comparative secularisms in a global age* (pp. 57–68). New York, NY: Palgrave Macmillan.

Bennedsen, D. (1980). Problemerne omkring de fremmedsprogede elever [The problems surrounding foreign language pupils]. "Nye danskere. Kulturmøde eller kultursammenstød" [New Danes. Cultural encounter or cultural clash]. *Uddannelse* (pp. 337–343), special edition, May–June. Copenhagen: Ministry of Education.

Bernstein, B. (1990). *Class, codes and control. The structuring of pedagogic discourse.* London and New York, NY: Routledge.

Bøgsted-Møller, N. (1976). *Kulturmøde i folkeskolen: En undersøgelse over fremmedsprogede elever i det københavnske skolesystem* [Cultural encounters in the Folkeskole: An examination of foreign language pupils in the Copenhagen school system]. Copenhagen: Københavns Kommunale Skolevæsen, Forsøgsafdelingen.

Brubaker, R. (2012). Religion and nationalism. Four Approaches. *Nations and Nationalisms, 18*(1), 2–20.

Buchardt, M. (2012). How did "the Muslim pupil" become Muslim? Danish state schooling and "the migrant pupils" since the 1970s. In J. S. Nielsen (Ed.), *Islam in Denmark. The challenge of diversity* (pp. 115–142). New York, NY: Lexington Books.

Buchardt, M. (2013). Religion, education and social cohesion: Transformed and traveling Lutheranism in the emerging Nordic welfare states during 1890s-1930s. In M. Buchardt, P. Markkola, & H. Valtonen (Eds.), *Education, state and citizenship* (pp. 81–113). Nordic Centre of Excellence NordWel. NordWel Studies in Historical Welfare State Research, Vol. 4.

Buchardt, M. (2014). *Pedagogized Muslimness: Religion and culture as identity politics in the classroom*. Religious Diversity and Education in Europe, Vol. 27. Münster, Berlin and New York, NY: Waxmann Verlag.

Buchardt, M. (2016). *Kulturforklaring. Uddannelseshistorier om muslimskhed* [Culture as explanation. Education histories about Muslimness]. Copenhagen: Tiderne Skifter.

Buchardt, M. (2017). Lutheranism and the Nordic states. In U. Puschner & R. Faber (Eds.), *Luther. Zeitgenössisch, historisch, kontrovers* (pp. 285–295). Frankfurt am Main: Peter Lang. Zivilisation und Geschichte 50.

Buchardt, M. (2018). The "culture" of migrant pupils: A nation- and welfare-state historical perspective on the European refugee crisis. *European Education, 50*(1), 58–73.

Buchardt, M. (2020a). Educational biblical nationalism. *Croatian Journal of Education, 22*(2), 133–150.

Buchardt, M. (2020b). Church, religion and morality. In D. Tröhler (Ed.), *Bloomsbury histories of education: The age of enlightenment* (Vol. IV, pp. 25–46). Bloomsbury Academic.

Buchardt, M. (2021, in press). The political project of secularization and modern education reform in "provincialized Europe". Historical research in religion and education beyond Secularization, R.I.P. *IJHE- Bildungsgeschichte*, No. 2.

Cabanel, P. (2016). *Ferdinand Buisson. Père de l'école laïque*. Genève: Labor et Fides.

Cady, K. E., & Hurd, E. S. (2010). Comparative secularisms and the politics of modernity. An introduction. In L. E. Cady & E. S. Hurd (Eds.), *Comparative secularisms in a global age* (pp. 3–24). New York, NY: Palgrave Macmillan.

Clausen, I. M. (1986). *Den flerkulturelle skole: Om interkulturel, anti-racistisk undervisning* [The multicultural school: About intercultural, anti-racist education]. Copenhagen: Gyldendal.

Depaepe, M., & Smeyers, P. (2008). Educationalization as an ongoing modernization process. *Educational Theory, 58*(4), 379–389.

Dobbelaere, K. (1987). Some trends in European sociology of religion: The secularization debate. *Sociological Analysis, 48*(1987), 107–137.

Eiranen, R. (2019). Emotional and social ties in the construction of nationalism: A group biographical approach to the Tengström family in nineteenth-century Finland. *Studies on National Movements, 4*(2019).

Gotling, N. (2020). National textbook narratives and historiography: Presenting a same that is never the same. *Croatian Journal of Education, 22*(2), 65–82.

Hill, S.-M. (1971). Kineserbørn i København – miljøbaggrund [China-Children in Copenhagen – Milieu Background]. *Fremmedsprogede elever, Læsepædagogen, 6*(1971), 15–16.

Hoegarts, J. (2020). Learning to love: Embodied practices of patriotism in the Belgian nineteenth-century classroom (and beyond). In A. Stynen et al. (Eds.), *Emotions and everyday nationalism in modern European history* (pp. 66–83). London: Routledge.

JBP, HHH. (1981). Kommunikativ kompetence. Symposium i Det Pædagogiske Selskab om undervisning af indvandrerbørn [Communicative competence. Symposium in The Pedagogical Society about instruction of immigrant children]. *Dansk pædagogisk Tidsskrift, 29*(8), 347.

Jønsson, H. V. (2013). *I velfærdsstatens randområde. Socialdemokratiets integrationspolitik 1960'erne til 2000'erne* [On the margins of the welfare state. Social Democracy's integration politics 1960s-2000s] (PhD dissertation). Department of History and Centre for Welfare State Research, University of Southern Denmark.

Kettunen, P. (2011). Welfare nationalism and competitive community. *NordWel Studies in Historical Welfare State Research*, 2(2011), 79–117.

Kocka, J. (1999). Asymmetrical historical comparison: The case of the German Sonderweg. *History and Theory*, 38(1), 40–50.

Luft, A. (2020). Religion in Vichy France. How meso-level actors contribute to authoritarian legitimation. *European Journal of Sociology*, 61(1), 67–101.

Malešević, S. (2006). *Identity as ideology. Understanding ethnicity and nationalism.* New York, NY: Palgrave Macmillan.

Mayeur, F. (2004). *Histoire Générale de l'Enseignement et de l'Éducation en France. De la Révolution à l'École Républicaine (1789–1930).* Paris: Perrin.

Mayeur, J.-M., & Rebérioux, M. (1987). *The third Republic from its origins to the Great War, 1871–1914.* Cambridge, UK: Cambridge University Press.

Nørgaard, E. (1981). "Skolen i pressen frem til ca. 1/3–81: Undervisning af indvandrerbørn, gæstearbejderbørn, fremmedsprogede børn" [Instruction of immigrant children, guestworker children, foreign language children]. *Dansk pædagogisk Tidsskrift*, 29(5), 200–204.

Odde, E. (1974). *Fremmedsprogede elever i danske skoler* [Foreign language pupils in Danish Schools]. Copenhagen: Lærerforeningernes Materialeudvalg.

Pedersen, L. (1988). Islam, muslimer og indvandrere i Dagbladet Information [Islam, Muslims and immigrants in the daily *Information*]. In S. Dindler & A. Olsen (Eds.), *Islam og muslimer i de danske medier* [Islam and Muslims in the Danish media] (pp. 120–133). Statens Humanistiske Forskningsråd, Århus: Aarhus Universitetsforlag.

Rabinow, P. (1989). *French modern. Norms and forms of the social environment.* Chicago, IL and London: University of Chicago Press.

Rahbek Pedersen, B., & Skutnabb-Kangas, T. (1983). *God, bedre, dansk? – om indvandrerbørns integration i Danmark* [Good, better, Danish? About integration of immigrant children in Denmark]. Copenhagen: Forlaget Børn & Unge.

Sane, H. Z. (1997). *Børnenes århundrede – Interessen for de fremmede børn i det 20. århundredes Danmark* [The Children's century – The interest in foreign children in 20th-century Denmark]. Studierækken fra Farums Arkiver & Museer. Farum: Farums Arkiver og Museer.

Schwartz, J. M. (1977). Vognmandsmarkens børn. Noter fra midtvejs i et aktionsforskningssprojekt [The children of Vognmandsmarken. Notes on the midway in an action research project]. *Bixen – Tidsskrift om miljøer og medier for børn og unge*, 4(6), 12–23.

Scott, J. W. (2017). *Sex and secularism.* Princeton, NJ: Princeton University Press.

Sheikh, M. K., & Crone, M. (2012). Muslims as a Danish security issue. In J. S. Nielsen (Ed.), *Islam in Denmark. The challenge of diversity* (pp. 173–195). New York, NY: Lexington Books.

Singer, B. B. (1975). Jules Ferry and the Laic revolution in French primary education. *Paedagogica Historica*, 15(2), 406–425.

Skey, M., & Antonsich, M. (Eds.). (2017). *Everyday nationhood. Theorising culture, identity and belonging after Banal nationalism.* London: Palgrave Macmillan.

Stark, R. (1999). Secularization, R.I.P. *Sociology of Religion*, 60(3), 249–273.

Suszycki, A. M. (2011). Welfare nationalism: Conceptual and theoretical considerations. *NordWel Studies in Historical Welfare State Research*, 2(2011), 51–77.

Taylor, C. (2007). *A secular age.* Cambridge, MA and London: The Belknap Press of Harvard University Press.

Trige Andersen, N. (2013). *Profession: Filippiner. Kvinder på arbejde i Danmark gennem fire årtier* [Profession: Philippine. Women at work in Denmark through four decades]. Copenhagen: Tiderne Skifter.

Trige Andersen, N., & Myong, L. (2015). From Immigration Stop to Intimizations of Migration: Cross-Reading the Histories of Domestic(ated) Labor Migration and Transnational Adoption in Denmark 1973–2015. *Retfærd*, *3*(38), special issue on Nordic Biopolitics, 62–79.

Tröhler, D. (2016). Educationalization of social problems and the educationalization of the modern world. In M. A. Peters (Ed.), *Encyclopedia of educational philosophy and theory*. Singapore: Springer (online version accessible, printed version forthcoming).

Tröhler, D. (2020). National literacies, or modern education and the art of fabricating national minds. *Journal of Curriculum Studies*, *52*(5), 620–635.

Weir, T. H. (2015). Germany and the new global history of secularism: Questioning the postcolonial genealogy. *The Germanic Review: Literature, Culture, Theory*, *90*(1), 6–20.

Wright, S. (2017). *Morality and citizenship in English schools: Secular approaches, 1897–1944*. London: Palgrave Macmillan.

Würtz Sørensen, J. (1988). Fjendebilleder. De muslimske fremmedarbejdere i de danske medier i slutningen af 1960'erne [Images of Enmity. The Muslim foreign workers in the Danish media in the late 1960s]. In S. Dindler & A. Olsen (Eds.), *Islam og muslimer i de danske medier* [Islam and Muslims in the Danish Media] (pp. 76–93). Aarhus: Aarhus Universitetsforlag.

16 Nations in the world

Interpreting the *World Yearbooks*

Robert Cowen

The (World) Yearbooks probably deserve to have a serious history written about them because – historically – they gradually became part of the development of 'comparative education' as an academic field of study. Here a much narrower task will be attempted: what were and are the ways in which the WYBs reflect back to us and interpret the theme of the 'nation,' within a world marked by the decline and fall of empires, World War II, post-war reconstruction and other 'posts' (such as post-socialism and post-colonialism) as well as new meanings for the words *East* and *South*?

Even this smaller task promises complications. It is difficult to interpret the WYBs. Certainly the volumes are in a sequence, but only in the simple sense that they are time-linear. They are 'a collection,' but only in the simple sense that they can typically be found close to each other in university libraries. The title *World Yearbooks* (of Education) is not a synonym for continuities: metaphorically, the WYBs are more like slothful chameleons whose moods change in complex environments. Less metaphorically, compressed into the *World Yearbooks* are editorial visions, conceptions of comparative education and 'hot topics.' The WYBs are also influenced by the politics of action which shape some fields of study, the politics of knowledge in universities, the politics of publishing and the growth of academic societies and specialist journals whose reach is at least regional and occasionally worldwide. In addition, the time period which the post-war WYBs covers is about 70 years, and the Yearbooks as a whole date back to the early 1930s – overall, a time period of about 90 years. Not even Superman comics lasted that long! What then can be said about the WYBs and the themes of 'the nation,' nationalism and the nation-state, without the oversimplification of vision necessary to find a needle in a haystack?

The analytical approach used here traces three motifs which change at different speeds: what is identified by the WYBs as 'the world' and significant change within it; the assumptions about action-on-the-world and what 'comparative' knowledge about education is for; and the perceptions of nations as a cultural thesis, nation-states as actors and nationalism, within the WYBs. These three motifs change. Here they will be called 'compressions' into the texts of the WYBs: of the world as such; of assumptions about action-on-the world and what comparative knowledge about education is for; and of 'the nation.' Such compressions permit a way to

DOI: 10.4324/9781003137801-21

begin an interpretation of the WYBs from 1932 until now: a complex time period in which, in their pre-war and post-war entirety, the *World Yearbooks* offer very varied 'readings of the global' (Cowen, 2000, 2009) and offer different interpretations of how the changing political and economic world and the professional world of education, in their interrelationships, should be understood.

Nevertheless, the impact of almost continual change should not be exaggerated. In practice, the texts of many of the WYBs are steady and stolid. They narrate. They offer a competent description of a specific topic without getting themselves too tangled up in major interpretations of what to emphasize about the inter-national world or how to re-think nations as cultures, nationalism, or the nation-state as a political actor. This is particularly the case for policy topics: for example, the economic and social status of teachers (Hall, Hans, & Lauwerys, 1953); the education and training of teachers (Bereday & Lauwerys, 1963); teacher education (Thomas, 2002); the gifted child (Bereday & Lauwerys, 1962); education within industry (Lauwerys & Scanlon, 1968); examinations (Lauwerys & Scanlon, 1969); rural development (Foster & Sheffield, 1974); health education (James, Balding, & Harris, 1989); assessment and evaluation (Harris & Bell, 1990); urban education (Lauwerys & Scanlon, 1970; Coulby, Jones, & Harris, 1992); special needs education (Mittler, Brouillette, & Harris, 1993); inclusive education (Daniels & Garner, 1999); and language education (Bourne & Reid, 2003). This is also often true of 'hot topics' which *ipso facto* tend to be or to become policy topics: for example, what counts as excellence in education (Bereday & Lauwerys, 1961); the gender gap in higher education (Lie, Malik, & Harris, 1994); youth, education and work (Bash & Green, 1995); the evaluation of higher education systems (Cowen, 1996); new technologies (Hall, Hans, & Lauwerys, 1954; Bereday & Lauwerys, 1960; Harris, 1988) including computers (Megarry, Walker, Nisbet, & Hoyle, 1983) and the digitalization of education (Brown & Davis, 2004).

Indeed, at first glance, it seems that the *World Yearbooks* repeat themselves, coming back again and again to the same topics; but they do not. The topics are not the same because the way topics are thought about shape-shifts when the politics and economics of the world change. For example, there are several volumes on higher education (Bereday & Lauwerys, 1959; Holmes & Scanlon, 1971; Niblett & Freeman Butts, 1972; Cowen, 1996), but the framing of the theme of higher education keeps altering: by the time we are in 2008 the volume on higher education includes the concepts of 'geographies of knowledge' and 'geometries of power' (Epstein, Boden, Deem, Rizvi, & Wright, 2008).

Strategically, the chapter proceeds by discussing the three 'compressions' identified earlier: the WYBs as interpretations of the world as such; action on it through comparative education; and examples of the different ways in which the WYBs have construed nations as cultures, the nation-state as political actor and nationalisms. Initially all three compressions are sketched in a section called 'Which world (and whose world)?' and then in a separate section called 'Re-thinking the world,' the theme of 'the nation' is re-visited in more detail.

1 Which world (and whose world)?

The crucial point is a simple one: the political and economic and educational world which the (world) Yearbooks are doing their best to analyze has intermittently needed new intellectual mappings and more complex interpretative perspectives. The political events which have overlapped with the post-1947 WYBs are familiar. They include the rise of socialist states in central Europe after 1945, the ending of empire, the Cold War, the theme of 'development' (of what used to be called The Third World), shifts in the nature of the State in former colonies and in Europe and the relationships between what began to be crudely labelled the local, the regional and 'globalization.'

Certainly, the world discussed and analyzed by the WYBs was and is a world of economic and political power-shifts which sometimes occurred unexpectedly and rapidly, a world with terrifying displays of military power, and often a world marred by 'small wars,' massacre and death. In the early post-war years of the WYB, the 'world' that was first discussed was the world of displaced persons, refugees, a world of destroyed educational systems. The world was and remains – despite the confidence of believers in State socialism, or forms of fascism, or neo-liberalism, or belief in particular theorizations in economics or the benefits of deducing political action from big data – a world that refuses to be easily predictable. The point, in a year that could loosely be called the year of COVID-19, requires no exaggeration.

There is an overlapping irony. The political world after the late 1940s was marked by de-colonization, the reconstruction of Europe and an embracement of the word *democracy* (in state-socialist, state-capitalist and post-colonial meanings). The world, in 2020, is marked by the emergence of new forms of empire (such as the soft power of OECD and the World Bank and the onward-march of PISA), by tensions which tease at the deconstruction of the European Union and by new populist crises about whose is the authentic voice of '*demos*.' We are also seeing the return of religion as a major identity marker (e.g. in the USA and Iran). There is a strong resurgence of the demand, in the name of democracy, that minority identities (such as those of the Catalans or the Scots or indigenous inhabitants in Australia or New Zealand or the USA) be recognized. At the same time, a new 'reading of the global' emphasizes the increasingly visible inter-national governance of educational systems and the emergence of what is normally assumed to be the world economy of the future (competing knowledge economies) – often with the lazy label 'globalization' used without qualifying adjectives to cover, and implicitly explain, everything.

The analytical point, however, is not merely that 'the world' changes in the complex ways just sketched – but how 'the world' is interpreted by the WYBs. The relationship between these changing 'worlds' and the WYB is fascinating – and falls into patterns. If the metaphor 'snapshots from history' can be used instead of the more formal language of the historian ('periodization'), the first patterning of the world is the pre-war world. And for the Yearbooks, that world began in 1932.

What follows is startling – it is the construction of three different worlds (by the Yearbooks) in rapid succession: 1) the world when the Yearbooks begin; 2) a rapid shift, pre-war, into a particular definition of the inter-national; and then 3) in the immediate post-war period, a sharper sense of the European continent. In all of these snapshots of history, however, the assumption of 'action on the world' (through what were later termed the WYBs) continues, though how to think about that world is marked by a range of epistemic refinements by the end of the 1960s.

Seeing the world – and action on it – from an English perspective

In the beginning, the initial question (the puzzle to be solved by the Yearbooks) was how to improve education in the English nation-state by looking elsewhere. The answer gradually became complex, but the initial idea had been well captured years earlier in the famous question of Sir Michael Sadler in 1900: "How far may we learn anything of practical value from the study of foreign systems of educa-tion?" (Sadler, 1900). The politics of the initial position of the Yearbook were clear. The theme of 'the nation' was there, at the very beginning, but it was there in a very particular form. The focus of attention, in the inter-war period, was England.

The initial focus of action was also England. The Yearbooks would report what had happened educationally in various places during that year. The Yearbooks were practical and, in an odd way, very parochial. Brian Holmes (1974), the first of the assistant editors to the post-war Yearbooks, points out in a Postscript to the 1974 WYB (p. 387):

> When the Year Book of Education was founded in 1932 by the Chairman of Evans Brothers, Sir Robert Evans, its Editor in Chief for the first four years (1932–35) was Lord Eustace Percy, formerly President of the Board of Education. Both of these men of vision wanted the Year Book to be more than a volume of academic interest. They hoped it would be of value to politicians, administra-tors and educationists. Articles should help governments to formulate policy and inform a wide lay audience about contemporary educational issue.

Thus, in this 'snapshot from history,' all three compressions are visible: first, there is a definition of the part of the world that matters and, second, in their origins, the Yearbooks were not aimed universities and academics or at 'comparative education': the knowledge in the Yearbooks is for policy makers and is aimed at action. Third, English ethnocentrism, the ethnocentrism of 'a nation,' is sharp and is quickly magnified by a concept of space which, 90 or so years later, still gives a slight sense of shock. The shock is not merely that, in 1932, the concern is par-ticularly with England and the English nation which is taken to be the core of the United Kingdom of Great Britain and Northern Ireland.

The shock is that this formal category of 'space' is almost immediately broad-ened. In 1933, Eustace Percy noted the absorption of the London Day Training College into the University of London. Percy's thinking was that a (London) Uni-versity Institute of Education might "legitimately aspire to be a centre of research and a focus for the . . . Commonwealth" (quoted in Holmes, 1974, p. 393). Percy also noted with approval a chapter in the same 1933 Yearbook by Fred Clarke, which made a plea for an Imperial Institute of Education in London. And that is how 'history' unfolded: Fred Clarke later became Sir Fred Clarke and Director of the University of London Institute of Education (i.e. the former London Day Training College) – and it was Clarke who promoted Joseph Lauwerys, a future editor of the WYBs, to be Professor of Comparative Education in 1947.

Thus, the concept of political space which was first stressed in the Yearbooks was not 'the nations' of the United Kingdom but England in particular, and then the Commonwealth in the legal definition it had after 1931: the UK and the Dominions of Australia, Canada, Newfoundland, New Zealand, South Africa and (at that time) the Irish Free State. Certainly, later, in the world of 'inter-national' politics, notions of separate national identities became strong – for example in 'the Irish Free State;' the concept of Canada was re-thought by Canadians to include Newfoundland; and South Africa continued to have a long period of redefining itself as a nation which went on until and after the end of *apartheid*. In other words, definitions of nation and national identity became increasingly important, politically, within that 'Commonwealth,' but the pre-war political vision of the Yearbooks did not emphasize nations as cultural identities and did not emphasize nationalism.

The Yearbooks emphasized a world centred round the labels 'England' and 'English-speaking.' The pre-war Yearbooks emphasized the educational policy concerns of the English and then – still before the Second World War – emphasized a looser and broader sense of British imperial-nationalism, which saw a world constructed, organized and maintained – acted upon – by an imperial reach. Ironically, these increasingly sharp and urgent imperial educational concerns (which included, among other things, 'development') had to deal with nationalism – for example, in India – well over a decade before the outbreak of the European part of World War II.

Interpreting the world – and action upon it – from 1947

Post-war, there was a shift in sensibility about relevant political space – an increased sense of Europe and of other continents whose educational reform was important within post-imperial and Cold War political agendas. The increased alertness to Europe – in *Realpolitk* obviously affected by the struggles of WW2 – was much influenced for the WYBs by the new editors: two academic specialists in comparative education who were themselves born outside of the UK. Joseph Lauwerys (born in Belgium) had during the Second World War worked in London as Secretary for the Allied Ministers of Education in Exile who were concerned to think through the practicalities of post-war educational visions for their nation-states within Europe. Nicholas Hans, from Odessa and with a distinguished academic and professional career in Russia, had become a refugee after the 1917 revolution.[1] It was the Institute of Education and these two academics in the University of London who re-established the Yearbooks of Education, after 1945 – the Yearbooks had ceased publication during the War.[2]

From 1947, the world was redefined. The initial concern was Europe and war damage and (educational) reconstruction, and Lauwerys immediately asked Hans to find authors who could cover the Soviet Union and Yugoslavia (Cowen, 2020a, 2020b). These countries (not nations) had been Allies during WW2 but also were important because they were examples of state-socialist politics and concepts of education. However the new post-war politics which were the politics of a new War – the Cold War – were already being made visible. They had been signalled as early as March 1946 in Winston Churchill's Fulton, Missouri, speech with phrases such as the 'Sinews of Peace' and the expression the 'Iron Curtain.'

Nevertheless, the WYBs did not move into a Cold War stance. Hans himself was from what was (now being called) the USSR, and Hans had been one of the first consultants to UNESCO. Lauwerys' own reformist commitments were to UNESCO and its programmes, to science and scientists as a force for the good, to what at one point he called 'scientific humanism' and to the idea that comparative education was, ideally, 'educational statesmanship' (Cowen, 2020a). Thus, the world was to be reformed, and the guiding politics were those of reconstruction and mutual understanding to stop wars 'beginning in the minds of men' – a crucial concept drawn from UNESCO. The knowledge provided by the WYBs would be academic and comparative, and the writers would be very senior academics or policy persons, whose responsibility was to think and act as 'educational statesmen'[sic].

This vision continued to inform the Yearbooks until the retirement of Lauwerys from the editorship in 1970, but two of the compressions – the definitions of 'the world' and the kinds of knowledge to be produced by the Yearbooks – sharpened with American involvement.

Interpreting the world – and action upon it – from 1953

The first American involvement in the Yearbooks had initially been signalled by Isaac Kandel from Columbia University (Epstein, 2020) coming onto the Editorial Board in the very late 1930s. However, Kandel's education in Britain and his academic training with Sadler in Manchester, his teaching in Northern Ireland, and his visits to Germany followed finally by his decision to study with Paul Monroe in New York, meant that a distinctive voice of America (the pun is deliberate) had to wait for Robert King Hall, who in 1953 preceded the more famous George Bereday as an editor of the Yearbooks. King Hall was something of a polymath with degrees in physics and administration, and with overseas experience of educational systems in Argentina, Brazil and Chile – and especially Japan in the immediate post-war period of reconstruction. One of his special interests was *shushin* (the Japanese pre-war version of moral education), abolished by the American Occupation authorities. The political implications for which places and nation-states and nationalisms – Africa, Latin America and Japan – should be of interest were immediate and obvious.

Furthermore, in terms of the second 'compression' – action on the world and what comparative knowledge is for – Holmes is generous enough to attribute to

King Hall the concept of 'the problem approach' (a very generous attribution as that approach became Holmes' own lifework after 1964). The Robert King Hall version of the problem approach meant that "wherever possible, an attempt was made (1) to analyse the constituents of a major problem, (2) illustrate them in specific contexts, (3) describe proposed solutions and agencies of implementation; and (4) anticipate some of the outcomes of the policy" (Holmes, 1974, p. 400). King Hall might have added (as he did in a meeting in 1955) that the problem approach offers "a social interpretation leading to a policy" (UNESCO, 1955, p. 25).

Certainly this discourse becomes more complex, with a specialist set of vocabularies and ontological positions ('critical points of decision,' 'educational statesmanship,' 'the problem-solving approach,' 'comparative studies and educational decision,' 'comparative method in education,' 'towards a science of comparative education'), but the basic point is clear: it is this conception of comparative education as action-on-the-world which frames the WYBs up to and beyond the confusion and ambiguities which developed after Lauwerys left the editorship to be the Director of the Atlantic Institute in Canada. In other words, the WYBs stay close to the famous question – identified earlier – asked by Sir Michael Sadler: How far can we learn anything of practical value from the study of foreign systems of education? Overall and for several decades, the optimistic motif of 'reform' is in place for the WYBs, even as they become more and more academic and are increasingly read by students who are doing courses in comparative education in universities.

But what of the third 'compression' – the nation as a cultural thesis about belonging and identity, about nationalism and about the nation-state as powerful political institutionalization of the nation (Tröhler, 2020)?

2   Re-thinking the world – and nations, nationalisms and nation-states

It was suggested earlier that 'the texts of many of the WYBs are steady and stolid. They narrate. They offer a competent description of a specific topic without getting themselves too tangled up in major interpretations of what to emphasize about the inter-national world or how to re-think nations as cultures, nationalism, or the nation-state as a political actor [and] that this is particularly the case for policy topics.' However, this does not mean that ideas about nations as a culture of identity, nationalism and nation-states are routinized and given more or less consistent treatment in the various Yearbooks. These concepts also oscillate, and their sudden invisibilities and varying visibilities are worth analytical comment. The concepts are treated in four main ways – and examples can be given of each though (as already hinted) relative indifference is one of them: WYBs see and narrate educational policies and practices. Nations can disappear.

There are three other modes of treatment, and examples of those can be found also. However, the striking point is that a direct treatment of these concepts, especially of nations as cultures of identity – a crucial theme in the general comparative education literature – and of nationalism (which is clearly a major feature of the post-war world and an explosive force in former colonial and state-socialist territories) is hard to find in the Yearbooks.

Now you see it, now you don't

The first and extreme treatment of the nation and nationalism and even the nation-state in the WYBs is to make them disappear. The disappearance of the nation is well illustrated in Brown and Davis (2004). The first part of the volume captures 'digital transformations' with an excellent theoretical piece by Gunther Kress on the semiotics of learning in the context of digital technologies, and further chapters are on theories of networking and collective intelligence, child-centred concepts of ICT and how to rethink literature and language teaching. The second motif of the volume is the options for innovation and flexibility and rethinking the transmission of basic skills (including to adults). The third part of the volume emphasizes interculturalities, including indigenous cultures and refugee children, and how local instructors made global e-learning culturally and pedagogically relevant in such complex situations. It is only with the last section of the book that geographic areas – for example, the 'new Europe' (chapter 19) and three countries – are mentioned in chapter titles: Canada (chapter 17), Hungary (chapter 18) and Chile (chapter 20).

The Series Editors' Introduction gives a good hint about why the theme of the nation is disappearing and what is taking its place. Coulby and Jones argue that "the volume is appropriate to the Yearbook series not only because its contributions cover a wide range of states, but also because the editors recognize that digital technology and its impact on education are major aspects of the wider process of globalization" (Brown & Davis, 2004, p. 14). The series editors use the concept 'State,' not 'nation' and not 'nation-state.' The editors of the 2004 WYB capture even more precisely why 'the nation' has been made to disappear. Invoking Castells and his concept of 'network society,' they stress the virtual 'space of flows' and try to avoid running their analysis through the concept of the 'space of places' (p. 17). They work with the notion of community (but not national-communities) including communities dispersed in space:

> The notion of community is key to the chapters in this Yearbook. Digital technologies have provided a means for the creation of new virtual communities, for instance around particular social or cultural interests, and for the reproduction, reassertion or reinvention of identity of spatially displaced communities, such as refugee groups. It has also enabled groups and individuals to interact with each other through new media and highlighted the need to address issues of intercultural communication and understanding.
>
> (Brown & Davis, 2004, pp. 16–17)

What is fascinating here is *how* 'the nation' is made to disappear: it is a consequence of a technology of communication which not only has inter-national reach but which constructs learning communities scattered in a range of social spaces:

space-places scattered geographically, religious spaces, gendered spaces, refugee places and space; but their central characteristic is that they are virtual electronic spaces celebrating and clustered around pedagogic need.

The separation of nationalism and the nation

The second construction within the Yearbooks is to strip nationalism from the nation and to narrow the nation to a locus of educational administration: the actor is the nation-state. One of the most ruthless examples of this is the *World Yearbook of 1996* (Cowen) on the evaluation of higher education systems. The list of chapters not only emphasizes nation-states but names them more or less in alphabetical order: Algeria, Australia, Brazil, Canada, The Peoples Republic of China, France, Hong Kong, Japan, the Republic of Korea, the United States of America and the United Kingdom. There is no fuss made about the UK being made up of (at least) four nations, and there is no fuss made about nationalities and the two Koreas. Latin America, a *region*, is offered as the last narrative chapter.

Overall, then, the concept of 'nation' seems to be the bedrock of the volume, but it is not. Although individual authors do indeed bring their nation as a culture and as a politics to life with some brilliance (for example, Cheriet on Algeria, and Sheehan on Australia), the social, economic and political actor is the nation-state. The book offers narratives about spaces and places and the introduction into places of policies for evaluation systems. The vacuous expression 'national context' is used. The individual chapters are strong, and the emphasis on the politics of the introduction of particular forms of more centralized and systematic control and definition of the productivity of academics is clear. However, the comparative vision offered at the front of the text permits the politics and cultures of nation-states to be secondary to the description of the techniques of surveillance (of academics) being introduced in the mid-1990s. The book, de facto, can be read as a survey of 'solutions' (though this was certainly not the intention of the editor):

> Authors were invited to identify what was, say 20 or 30 years ago, the evaluation system for higher education – however informal or unsystematic – and to indicate what had become the major ways of evaluating the higher education system by the 1990s. Authors were asked to discuss what they took to be the forces of change which had produced, in their specific national context or geographic area, these new more systematic ways of evaluating higher education systems. Finally, authors were invited, against a specification of how the new evaluation system is working, to identify the emerging short-term and long-term effects of the new evaluation systems.
>
> (Cowen, 1996, pp. vii–viii)

Overall the book's Preface does not encourage authors of the chapters to concentrate on the political tensions and cultural contradictions within their own nations of old and new, ideal and emergent, systems of evaluation based on the universalization of selected techniques of transparency. Overall, the nation-as-politics and the nation-as-culture do not occupy the centre of the 1996 WYB, which permits the nation to become the State. What was analyzed in the 1996 *World Yearbook* was the nation reduced to the State-nation busily constructing administrative solutions to educational problems, with those solutions being identified and delivered by a state apparatus.

Fortunately, there is also an example within the WYB of the opposite: nations and nationalisms as crises and in crisis.

Identities within the nation and nationalism as identity

There is one relatively recent volume – that edited by Coulby and Zambeta (2005) – which takes the theme of the nation and nationalism very seriously – as both a danger and as being in danger. Full control over the interpretation of the theme is ensured by having half of the chapters within this volume plus the Editorial Introduction written by the editors themselves as individual authors. The volume itself – in the eyes of the editors – clearly is of major importance, an effort at an interpretation of a new 'world.'

The transition is captured in the title: *Globalization and Nationalism in Education*. The volume emphasizes the tension between globalization (with the institutions and technologies of the knowledge economy); the survival of nationalism and national identity; and regional tensions in identity (e.g. within Europe and within specific nations in Europe). Part Four has the subtitle, "Globalization and nationalisms: post-colonial perspectives" and contains chapters by Jagdish Gundara, Zane Ma Rhea and Terri Seddon, as well as Zambeta and Coulby. Coulby himself writes the first chapter in Part Four ("Globalization and the narrative of civilization: classical Greece as curricular construct") as well as the last chapter in Part Four on "Cultural relativism and cultural imperialism in a globalized economy and monopolar polity." The volume is one of the most intellectually complex of the WYBs, and it offers a discordant voice – making fresh claims about what should be 'seen.' What should be seen – here what is 'seen' – is not merely contemporary educational policy (normally the raw material of the WYBs) but also Japanese religion and Japanese identity, classical Greece and contemporary 'Europeanization' as well as 'globalization.' Why the epistemic crisis?

The sudden discord and this shift in focus – an alertness to the themes of 'the nation' and 'nationalism' – overlap with the end of the period in which the WYB had been edited by Coulby and Jones. This discord was not so much a voice from the outside, but a different voice from inside the field of study. Neither Coulby nor Jones self-identified as specialists in comparative education. Although based in the Department of Comparative Education in the Institute of Education, they were both specialists in urban education and, along with colleagues such as Leslie Bash, both had a strong commitment to the study of multicultural education and strong links to the Centre for Multicultural Education headed by the remarkable Jagdish Gundara.

It was this pattern of appointments and academic conversations which released the WYBs to discuss the themes of nations and nationalism and multiculturalism

(Coulby, Gundara, & Jones, 1998) and to offer an early hint that the Sadler question and the Sadler version of comparative education – emphasizing educational policy and action on the world – would not always dominate the WYBs. The Coulby and Zambeta volume was a hint about a transition point in the history of the WYBs.

Another new world?

This altered focus – the fourth shift on the theme of 'the nation' by the WYBs – is a reading of a 'new world.' It was the international sociology and the political economy of that new world, along with a great deal of borrowing of new ideas from a range of the social sciences, which created new theorizations. These were new theorizations from outside of the conventional theoretical positions used in comparative education, and such theory work was (in my judgment) much needed for the revitalization of comparative education as a field of study (McLeod, Sobe, & Seddon, 2018; Seddon & Levin, 2013). The new theories did not stress the application of new ideas in educational policy, but rather emphasized critique of existing policies (Epstein et al., 2008; Ozga, Seddon, & Popkewitz, 2006). The WYBs finally had become serious academic texts. Certainly they began revitalising comparative education from the outside, but it is very much open to question whether the new theorization was aimed at recovering 'comparative education.' It can be suggested that what was on offer was a new 'reading of the global' – created by a flurry of perspectives from a range of social sciences. The new 'readings' did not have the complexity of the muddled Coulby and Zambeta volume, nervously struggling to define a new epistemic territory. They did have the confident voice of an avant-garde (Zanten, Ball, & Darchy-Koechlin, 2015). The core topic for an understanding of this 'new world' was obvious: many of the volumes were concerned with shifts in the nature of the State – i.e. the growth of regional or international forms of governance of educational systems and new definitions of quality in education at the international level (Verger, Lubienski, & Steiner-Khamsi, 2016). Thus few of these new volumes managed to keep 'the national' and 'nationalism' in strong focus – the reverse perhaps: there was a retreat from 'the nation' (with some exceptions such as the volume edited by Seddon & Levin, 2013).

3 Concluding comments

The first point to be made perhaps is not about the huge changes in international political and economic relations from 1930 to 2020, but something much more 'domestic' – and therefore (as with most domestic things) of serious political importance. The WYBs mark a shift in the politics of knowledge in the university *and* in the politics of editing. At the beginning of the life of the Yearbooks in the 1930s, the links between the publisher and the Editorial Board and the writing produced by the WYBs were politically framed by cultural assumptions which hint at the magic arts of a governing elite, a canny, almost devious, approach to criticism of official voices, and an Editorial Board of the great and the good. By the time we were some way into the 21st century, the links between the publisher and the Editorial Board and the writing produced by the WYBs were politically framed by a sense of an international market, and a sense that the academic voice should be used to critique political power. Yes, the writing produced by the WYBs is still to be politically and academically framed by an Editorial Board of the great and the good, but it was a different 'great and the good.' The differences included geography: a shift away from London and the Institute of Education to new worldwide visions and a fresh range of universities; gender – a major shift from an Editorial Board that was manned to an Editorial Board with a majority of female members; and from an epistemic gaze which was narrowing down to become comparative education in the period, say, 1950 to 1970, to an epistemic gaze which has been broadening each year within the last, say, 15 years.

Against a background that includes these changes in the politics of university knowledge and the politics of editing, the main interpretative device of the chapter was the 'compressions' that were sketched earlier. It was suggested that the compressions were three: what was emphasized among the changes in the political and economic world itself – the WYBs' 'reading of the global;' assumptions about action-on-the-world and the knowledge which would be called 'comparative education;' and notions of the nation.

In both versions of the Yearbook, before and after WW2, the intent to change the world is clear. After 1945, the changes in the world were major and massive,[3] and comparative education began to develop new suggestions about the forms of knowledge which should be called 'comparative.' A classic mantra of comparative education was revitalized in complex ways. The mantra was the aspiration of Sir Michael Sadler in 1900: the hope of learning things of practical value from the study of foreign educational systems. The efforts of some of the world's best-known comparative educationists for much of a decade in the 1960s and 1970s were, rather noisily, put into working out how to do this. Most of them (cf. Nicholas Hans) were trying to find alternative ways to think about comparative education that did not emphasize 'history.'

However, none of them (not even Hans) place nationalism at the heart of their thinking, though all of them defined different ways to think about 'the nation.' Thus, year by year – including during this period of an over-emphasized devotion to 'the methodology' of comparative education – the *World Yearbooks* carried on with their annual 'compressions.' The first compression-into-print was what had been seen, had been chosen to be, 'the world' and its politics and its significant educational patterns. The second compression was of action-into-print or – to put the point more precisely – the reverse: text that recommended policy action. Recommendations about 'solutions' to educational problems were offered by the individual chapters or occasionally by the conclusions reached in a specific WYB.

The third compression – the theme captured in the first words of the title of this chapter – was assumptions about the nation. And that compression was a very strange one. 'Everyone knows' that comparative education compares nations (or nation-states or nationalisms). And, obviously, the WYBs in their post-1947 orm are one expression of comparative education. Therefore they must compare nations or nationalisms or – at the very least – nation-states.

However, they do not. The WYBs compare (for most of their history) policy agendas, including contemporary ones such as the reform of higher education systems; efficient schools; teacher education; agendas for the construction of multicultural identities; and – in the last couple of decades – the new inter-national politics of the governance of education; the educational adjustments needed to meet the economic demands of a globalized world economy; the education of local and global elites; new theories of time and space (in international and comparative education); new forms of professionalism; and the pressures, problems and promises of datafication as a form of management and as a policy-shaping apparatus.

Somehow, with a couple of exceptions, the nation (as more than a label for a place) disappears and nationalism is never moved to the centre of the agenda of the WYBs. So comparative education disappeared or died? Not quite.

Historically, comparative education has had five forms: 1) *its pedagogic form*, which involves getting students to know something of another country – a foreign country – and then contrasting the patterns of the educational systems, trying to understand the way they are shaped by their own societies, noting similarities and differences between the domestic and the foreign – and understanding the foreign differences well enough to empathize with those differences; 2) *consultancy comparative education* which is mainly giving advice to others for a fee, with your own ethnocentrism and political agenda under control or your own ethnocentrism and political agenda taking charge and dominating the advice given; 3) *routinized and ritualized comparative education* – which is the conventional comparative article on small topics in the journals (where an aspect of education in two or more countries is compared with a strong emphasis on understanding the ways in which those educational patterns are shaped by social forces); 4) *inherited comparative education*: that is, comparative education which follows the epistemic agendas and areas of academic alertness that clustered around major teachers such as (in one generation) Bereday, Kandel, King, Holmes, Noah-and-Eckstein or contemporaneously around theoreticians such as Bauman, Bourdieu, Foucault, Luhmann and Meyer and Ramirez; and 5) comparative education as *the study of imperium*: in which the international transfer, translation and transformation of educational ideas, institutions and practices is understood, at the intersection of domestic and international politics, as compressions of *imperium* into educational forms. Examples would include critiques of PISA, understanding the mobility of models of the university or primary school education, and efforts to sketch the 'codes' of educational systems through which educated identities are transmitted.

The WYBs typically have been construed within mode three: 'ritualized comparative education' done in most WYBs by loose juxtaposition of narratives about countries. However, this juxtaposition of narratives and their educational systems has been done without emphasising the concept of 'nation.' Australia, France, Japan: the label is both the name of a country and almost of a nation but the label has traditionally meant 'nation-state' – taken as the nation-which-acts, the reform agent, the policy actor. The nation as culture is taken for granted: educational patterns and practices are Australian; French; Japanese. This is comparative education labelling 'the nation' – and leaving it and nationalism as banal.

More recently (in the last 15 years or so), the WYBs have been construed with a far greater emphasis on theory and theorization, but that theorization, drawing on a range of social sciences which have developed (or which can be used to develop) their own analytical categories and agendas, has emphasized the global. These very necessary new theorizations – a major step forward for comparative education which brings it into the 21st century – have traced a new world and its realities: new patterns of global power, new modes of educational governance, new global ways of measuring excellence in education and how this has implications for 'the local' – but not necessarily then drawing sophisticated distinctions about 'a local' marked by nations as a culture of identity, and nationalisms, as well as nation-states.

Of course there are exceptions, but it is a long time since the nation and nationalism were put at the centre of the perspective of a WYB. The point is not that someone could (incautiously but) gleefully sneer at comparative education as an example of the newly discovered sociological disease of methodological nationalism. The point is the irony: studying the nation and nationalism and education is crucial to the continued improvement of comparative education itself. Studying the nation and nationalism is crucial in rescuing comparative education, which has gradually made the nation 'banal' in a quite improper sense. Comparative education has routinized that which is vibrant and sometimes dangerous but vital in understanding the nature of 'educated identities' (Cowen, 2016, 2021). The charm in the irony? The charm in the irony is that it has needed this *World Yearbook* to offer that reminder.

Notes

1 Pre-war, Hans was loosely linked with the Yearbook, but it was only in the post-war period that Hans was offered a permanent academic position at King's College London and became a well-known author in comparative education and one of the first editors of the WYB. In contrast, George Winthrop Young, Marlborough and Cambridge educated, famous as a friend of Kurt Hahn, even more famous as an Alpinist and a mountain climber (who had a wooden leg), was a member of the Editorial Board of the pre-war Yearbook. Winthrop Young gave up his job as a Reader in Comparative Education in King's College London in 1941.
2 Post-war, the Director of the Institute of Education, Jeffrey, pushed the idea with Evans Brothers, the publishers, of restarting the (World) Yearbook of Education and in early 1946, Lauwerys was approached by Jeffrey to sketch an outline of the 1947 volume, and Hans was invited by Jeffrey and Lauwerys to be a co-editor.
3 The *Zeitgeist* was clear: the shock of the war and the huge damage which had occurred on a world scale (and also within Occupied Europe) created the will and, in a sense, a necessity to act. This was the time of the creation of the United Nations and the Marshall Plan, of the Occupation and reform of 'the two Germanies' and Japan. It was a time for recovery of the material and moral order of the world. It was clear that most societies would aspire to be more egalitarian, and it was obvious even to many British politicians when they looked at India (which became independent in 1947) that independence

would and should be a goal for countries within the various empires of the European powers. The USSR was now a world power, and China was finally free of invasion and about to reconstruct itself.

References

Bash, L., & Green, A. (Eds.). (1995). *World yearbook of education 1995: Youth, education and work*. London: Kogan Page.

Bereday, G. Z. F., & Lauwerys, J. A. (Eds.). (1959). *The year book of education 1959: Higher education*. London: Evans.

Bereday, G. Z. F., & Lauwerys, J. A. (Eds.). (1960). *The year book of education 1960: Communication media and the school*. London: Evans.

Bereday, G. Z. F., & Lauwerys, J. A. (Eds.). (1961). *The year book of education 1961: Concepts of excellence in education*. London: Evans.

Bereday, G. Z. F., & Lauwerys, J. A. (Eds.). (1962). *The year book of education. 1962: The gifted child*. London: Evans.

Bereday, G. Z. F., & Lauwerys, J. A. (Eds.). (1963). *The year book of education 1963: The education and training of teachers*. London: Evans

Bourne, J., & Reid, E. (Eds.). (2003). *World yearbook of education 2003: Language education*. London: Routledge Falmer.

Brown, A., & Davis, N. (Eds.). (2004). *World yearbook of education 2004: Digital technology, communities and education*. London: Routledge Falmer.

Coulby, D., Gundara, J., & Jones, C. (Eds.). (1998). *World yearbook of education 1998: Intercultural education*. London: Routledge.

Coulby, D., Jones, C., & Harris, D. (Eds.). (1992). *Urban education. World yearbook of education 1992*. London: Kogan Page.

Coulby, D., & Zambeta, E. (Eds.). (2005). *World yearbook of education 2005: Globalization and nationalism in education*. London: Routledge.

Cowen, R. (Ed.). (1996). *World yearbook of education 1996: The evaluation of higher education systems*. London: Kogan Page.

Cowen, R. (2000). Comparing futures or comparing pasts? *Comparative Education, 36*(3), 333–342.

Cowen, R. (2009). Then and now: Unit ideas and comparative education. In R. Cowen & A. M. Kazamias (Eds.), *International handbook of comparative education* (pp. 1277–1294). Dordrecht: Springer.

Cowen, R. (2016). Comparative Education and Intercultural Education: What are the questions? In L. Bash & D. Coulby (Eds.), *Establishing a culture of intercultural education: Essays and papers in honour of Jagdish Gundara* (pp. 41–60). Cambridge: Cambridge Scholars.

Cowen, R. (2020a). Joseph Lauwerys (1902–1981). In D. Phillips (Ed.), *British scholars of comparative education: Examining the work and influence of notable 19th and 20th century comparativists* (pp. 53–70). London: Routledge.

Cowen, R. (2020b). Nicholas Hans (1888–1969). In D. Phillips (Ed.), *British scholars of comparative education: Examining the work and influence of notable 19th and 20th century comparativists* (pp. 34–52). London: Routledge.

Cowen, R. (2021). Educated identity, concepts, mobilities and *imperium*. In S. Carney & E. Klerides (Eds.), *Identities and education: Comparative perspectives in times of crisis* (pp. 27–46). London: Bloomsbury Academic.

Daniels, H., & Garner, P. (Eds.). (1999). *Inclusive education. World yearbook of education*. London: Kogan Page.

Epstein, D., Boden, R., Deem, R., Rizvi, F., & Wright, S. (Eds.). (2008). *World yearbook of education 2008: Geographies of knowledge, geometries of power: Framing the future of higher education*. London: Routledge.

Epstein, E. H. (Ed.). (2020). *North American scholars of comparative education: Examining the work and influence of notable 20th century comparativists*. London and New York, NY: Routledge.

Foster, P., & Sheffield, J. R. (Eds). (1974). *World year book of education 1974*. London: Evans.

Hall, R. K., Hans, N., & Lauwerys, J. A. (Eds.). (1953). *The year book of education*. London: Evans Bros.

Hall, R. K., Hans, N., & Lauwerys, J. A. (Eds.). (1954). *The year book of education 1954*. London: Evans Bros.

Harris, D. (Ed.). (1988). *Education for the new technologies. World yearbook of education 1988*. London: Kogan Page.

Harris, D., & Bell, C. (1990). *Evaluating and assessing for learning. World Yearbook of education 1990*. London: Kogan Page.

Holmes, B. (1974). The world yearbook of education: A postscript. In P. Foster & J. R. Sheffield (Eds.), *World yearbook of education 1974: Education and rural development* (pp. 387–411). London: Evans Bros.

Holmes, B. H., & Scanlon, D. G. (Eds.). (1971). *The world year book of education. 1971/72. Higher education in a changing world*. London: Evans.

Holmes, B. H., & Scanlon, D. G. (Eds.). (1972). *The world year book of education. 1972/73. Higher education in a changing world*. London: Evans.

James, C., Balding. J., & Harris, D. (Eds.). (1989). *Health education. World yearbook of education 1989*. London: Kogan Page.

Lauwerys, J. A., & Scanlon, D. G. (Eds.). (1968). *Education within industry. World yearbook of education 1968*. London: Evans.

Lauwerys, J. A., & Scanlon, D. G. (Eds.). (1969). *Examinations. World yearbook of education 1969*. London: Evans.

Lauwerys, J. A., & Scanlon, D. G. (Eds.). (1970). *World yearbook of education 1970. Education in cities*. London: Evans.

Lie, S. S., Malik, L., & Harris, D. (Eds.). (1994). *The gender gap in higher education. World yearbook of education 1994*. London: Kogan Page.

McLeod, J., Sobe, N. W., & Seddon, T. (Eds.). (2018). *World yearbook of education 2018: Uneven space-times of education: Historical sociologies of concepts, methods and practices*. London: Routledge.

Megarry, J., Walker, D. R. F., Nisbet, S., & Hoyle, E. (Eds.). (1983). *World yearbook of education 1982/1983: Computers and education*. London: Routledge.

Mittler, P., Brouillette, R., & Harris, D. (1993). *Special needs education. World yearbook of education 1993*. London: Kogan Page.

Niblett, R. W., & Freeman Butts, R. (Eds.). (1972). *The world year book of education. 1972/73. Universities facing the future*. London: Evans

Ozga, J., Seddon, T., & Popkewitz, T. (Eds.). (2006). *World yearbook of education 2006: Education, research and policy: Steering the knowledge-based economy*. London: Routledge.

Sadler, M. (1900 [reprinted February1964]). How far can we learn anything of practical value from the study of foreign systems of education? *Comparative Education Review*, 7(3), 307–314.

Seddon, T., & Levin, J. (Eds.). (2013). *World yearbook of education 2013: Educators, professionalism and politics: Global transitions, national spaces and professional projects*. London: Routledge.

Thomas, E. (Ed.) (2002). *Teacher education: Dilemmas and prospects. World yearbook of education 2002*. London: Kogan Page.

Tröhler, D. (2020). National literacies, or modern education and the art of fabricating national minds. *Journal of Curriculum Studies, 52*(5), 620–635.

UNESCO. (1955). *Comparative education: An international meeting held from 12–16 April, 1955, at the UNESCO Institute for Education, Hamburg*. Hamburg: UNESCO Institute for Education.

Verger, A., Lubienski, C., & Steiner-Khamsi, G. (Eds.). (2016). *World yearbook of education 2016: The global education industry*. London: Routledge.

Zanten, A. v., Ball, S. J., & Darchy-Koechlin (Eds.). (2015). *World yearbook of education 2015: Elites, privilege and excellence: The national and global redefinition of educational advantage*. London: Routledge.

Index

Note: Page numbers in *italic* indicate a figure and page numbers in **bold** indicate a table on the corresponding page.